Philosophy and Schooling

Philosophy and Schooling

Charles Dennis Marler
University of Delaware

Allyn and Bacon, Inc.
Boston

Library of Congress Cataloging in Publication Data

Marler, Charles Dennis, 1932–
    Philosophy and schooling.

    Includes bibliographies.
    1. Marler, Charles Dennis, 1932– 2. Education–
Philosophy. 3. Education–United States–History.
I. Title.
LB885.M2476   370.1   74–17186

To

Lois and Michael
and to Larry Thomas,
each in his or her own way
a teacher, a philosopher,
and a valued companion
in the adventure of becoming.

Contents

PART III
EPISTEMOLOGY AND AMERICAN EDUCATION

PART IV
AXIOLOGY AND AMERICAN EDUCATION

PART V
SOCIAL PHILOSOPHY, IDEOLOGIES, AND AMERICAN EDUCATION

Preface

America, our land, is a land of contrasts: rocky coasts and endless plains . . . icy blasts and searing heat . . . citizens red and citizens yellow . . . roaring cities and quiet farms . . . ideas old and ideas new. The American school, touching as it does the lives of all our people, mirrors these contrasts. Furthermore, they are reflected in each American who grows up in the most pluralistic culture of modern times.

Philosophy and Schooling will introduce you to but one set of these contrasts, namely, alternative philosophical approaches to problems of human and nonhuman reality, knowledge and truth, value and morality, and the individual and society. This strategy has three goals: 1) to help you better understand different viewpoints current in our culture and thus increase opportunities for meaningful communication with neighbor and colleague; 2) to provide raw materials appropriate to making conscious decisions on issues vital to you as an individual, your nation and your schools; and 3) to motivate you to consider what differences your personal philosophical commitments could possibly make to educational policy and practice.

Many of you will come to these concerns with little background in academic philosophy; others, with little field experience in education; most, with no intention of studying for a doctorate in the philosophy of education. You are interested in what philosophy has to do with your own lives and what resources it can provide for making educational decisions. This book is written for you.

Several features may be of especial interest. First, following an introductory chapter and several relatively theoretical chapters, you will find a section explicitly geared to professional problem-solving and personal philosophy-building (Part VI). Hopefully, you will find the treatment of "finding reasons" and "generating possibilities"—and the practical situations and case studies provided for developing these skills—interesting and relevant to your needs. Hopefully, you will also find the suggestions for building and using your own personal philosophy of education just as practical.

Secondly, a serious and somewhat atypical effort has been made to avoid extensive criticism of alternative positions. These positions *are* viable in our culture; facts and/or beliefs can be assembled to defend them. Furthermore, there is no good reason to believe that general acceptance of any one belief system is either possible or even desirable in a pluralistic culture. Then, too, extensive author criticism can encourage the reader to avoid a direct personal encounter with alternative possibilities, especially those initially seen as "different" or "common-sense." At the introductory level, personal struggle and soul-searching should probably precede secondary criticism. In sum, it appears best to describe each alternative as fairly as is humanly possible (optimally, as a knowledgeable advocate might describe it) and then let *you* decide where *you* stand. Serious criticism can and will come, but only with growth in understanding and sensitivity to the full intent of others. Naturally, the author does have his own preferred point of view, namely, that of the pragmatic liberal. And with every sincere attempt at evenhandedness, with every conscious desire to help you develop and use *your* position, this bias will occasionally show. Beware . . . .

Finally, this is not a text in the tradition of language analysis (though there is much attention to the meaning and use of terms important to education). Nor is it one emphasizing philosophical "systems" or "schools" (though such terms as *Existentialism, Realism,* or *Conservatism* are certainly used when they help the introductory reader to organize his thoughts or "get into" the material). Rather, the stress is on philosophical assumptions concerning concepts such as human nature, values, and justice that are deeply engrained in American culture, on how they function in a personal philosophy of education, and on how they interact with nonphilosophical factors to influence schooling.

CdM

PART *I*

Introduction

1

Philosophy and Education: Questions of Meaning and Relevance

Though written well over half a century ago, the words of Thomas Shields provide an appropriate introduction both to this text and to questions which we shall be considering. He wrote:

> *A man's philosophy, by imperceptible degrees, colors the whole of his life and affects his attitude towards all things in heaven and on earth. In like measure, the prevalent philosophy of a people gradually transforms all their social institutions.*[1]

If Shields's position is correct, you and I—as well as the school, surely a most vital social institution—ignore philosophy at our peril. But philosophy is *commonly* ignored. We hear that philosophical inquiry has been superseded by that of science, that its literature contains vocabulary ranging from the abstract to the impenetrable, that it seems to be concerned only with the broadest generalization on the one hand or tedious nit-picking on the other. Of what possible concern could such a discipline be to the preservice or inservice educator who has at his disposal the resources of common sense as well as scientifically-based studies in curriculum, learning and instruction?

If, on the other hand, Shields's analysis still stands, philosophical studies are properly the concern of, and may offer considerable assis-

[1] Thomas Shields, *Philosophy of Education* (Washington, D.C.: Catholic Education Press, 1917), pp. 22–23.

3

tance to, the individual both as human being and as professional educator. In any case, we need to clear up several prior questions before any meaningful decision can be made. For instance, just what do we mean by terms such as "philosophy" and "education"? In like measure, what meaning can be given to "philosophy of education"? Given this base, we may then profitably inquire into the possible relevancy of philosophy to pedagogical[2] concerns. Hopefully, these inquiries will at least suggest the outline of the tasks which face us if we would attempt to philosophize about education.[3]

A. The Nature of Philosophy

1. The General Sense of "Philosophy"

The term "philosophy" appears to be used in both a general and a technical sense. It may, for instance, refer to "one's general view of life, of men, of ideals, and of values."[4] Also in the general sense, we may note that:

> Philosophically unsophisticated persons often speak about the need to have "a philosophy" of life, of education, of child-rearing, or . . . of cooking, sewing, or farming, ad nauseam. "Philosophy" comes to mean anything and hence nothing, although it may be equated vaguely with "theory" or "reasons" or "general objectives."[5]

In truth, this general usage appears to be as unfortunate as it is common and understandable. In the first place, that which is labeled "philosophy" (in the general sense) is usually so vapid as to be meaningless. One does not have to read many documents entitled "Philosophy of . . . School" or "Philosophy of Grade 6 Arithmetic" before concluding that these statements rarely offer any assistance to those responsible for meeting common professional demands. Sec-

[2] Simply treat the terms "pedagogy" or "pedagogical" as rough synonyms of "education" or "educational," terms more common in contemporary literature.

[3] Every effort will be made to define new and sometimes technical terms as we go along. Nevertheless, this is more an age of experimental science than of philosophy. Unless you have a fair background in academic philosophy, your unfamiliarity with its vocabulary may suggest the purchase of a good "dictionary of philosophy." Several will commonly be found in college bookstores.

[4] Stella Henderson, Introduction to Philosophy of Education (Chicago: The University of Chicago Press, 1947), p. 16.

[5] Christopher J. Lucas, ed., What Is Philosophy of Education? (New York: The Macmillan Company, 1969), p. 10.

ondly, the general usage encourages superficial thinking about topics of importance to pedagogy, such as "commitment," "needs," "progress" or "values." (Most educators would probably agree that we do not need added encouragement.) Finally, and perhaps more importantly, the general usage obscures a more accurate understanding of the nature of philosophy and, therefore, the possibility of working out its appropriate and meaningful contributions to education.

2. The Technical Sense of "Philosophy"

A more accurate, technically valid and fruitful meaning can be constructed by viewing philosophy as an interrelated set of activities, content and attitudes. In passing, it might be noted that commentators have tended to define philosophy as primarily activity *or* attitude *or* content.[6] According to the author's view, this will not do. There *must* be the concept of specific and interrelated activities, content and attitudes.

A. PHILOSOPHY AS ACTIVITY. The activity dimension of the term may be discerned by asking what philosophers *do*.[7] Historically, it seems, philosophers have been interested in at least four kinds of endeavor; that is, synthesizing, speculating, prescribing and analyzing. *Synthesis* in philosophy rests firmly on a basic human desire and a basic human need. The history of man suggests he has always desired a complete and consistent view of life to unify his thoughts, his hopes and his experience. At the same time, man has felt—and rightly, we may suspect—that the guidance of human action *demands* such a view. It is difficult enough to be rational about action in any case. It is even more difficult when one's world view includes inconsistent, "compartmentalized" views. Imagine the case of the teacher who honestly believes that children must "learn through doing," that merely reading about a phenomenon will rarely result in learning. At the same time, this teacher believes that mankind, if not *by nature* evil, is at least *predisposed* to do the wrong thing. Students come to her as their advisor and propose that the Student Council be empowered to draw up a "Student Bill of Rights." Perhaps the point is clear. Inconsistencies in one's view of life—however understandable in terms of our development in a pluralistic culture—can cause difficulties in planning a rational course of action. It must be admitted, nonetheless, that

[6] Some even go so far as to restrict the definition to *one kind* of activity, i.e., analyzing. See below.
[7] Hence, this dimension is often referred to as *"doing* philosophy" or "philosophizing."

man's desire and need for synthesis do cause problems in that not all elements to be synthesized are of the same order. For example, we may point on the one hand to scientifically-verified "facts" and on the other to "beliefs" which, however much they may be based on them, clearly go beyond facts.[8] We may also point to the difficulty of synthesizing so vast a body of data, a point today made more intense by the accelerating production of scientific fact. Given these and other problems, some philosophers have demanded that philosophy surrender the synthesizing function and concentrate on quality work within a more limited scope. Others, due to the intensity of both need and desire, feel that synthesis must continue as one aspect of what we mean when we refer to philosophy. The unification of living demands that philosophy continue to fulfill its "double task":

> that of criticising existing aims with respect to the existing state of science, pointing out values which have become obsolete with the command of new resources, showing what values are merely sentimental because there are no means for their realization; and also that of interpreting the results of specialized science in their bearing on future social endeavor.[9]

Speculation in philosophy rests on the fact that were man restricted to acting on the basis of "fact" alone, he would be paralyzed. His thinking

---

[8] The term "fact" refers to an assertion based on an interpretation of sensory data whose truth has been determined at an acceptable level of reliability by empirical processes. Facts are neither the events which give rise to sensory data nor the sensory data themselves; rather, they are assertions which interpret the data according to some conceptual scheme possessed by the interpreter. Facts, then, are well-established hypotheses generalized from knowledge gained in various contexts of time, place and people. *Cf.* George R. Geiger, *Philosophy and the Social Order: An Introductory Approach* (Boston: Houghton Mifflin Company, 1947), p. 168; L. O. Kattsoff, "Observation and Interpretation in Science," *Philosophical Review*, LVI (1947), pp. 683–684; and Gwynn Nettler, *Explanations* (New York: McGraw-Hill Book Company, 1970), pp. 92–95.

The term "belief," on the other hand, refers to a proposition which the individual accepts as true on the grounds that it is justified by what he (explicitly or implicitly) considers to be adequate evidence. This evidence may or may not include facts; it may or may not be adequate to justify the belief; it may or may not support the proposition—indeed, in the case of "wildly dogmatic" or "superstitious" beliefs, it may contradict the proposition. A "rational belief" is defined as one which is justified by adequate evidence, although the factual component of evidence is not sufficient to qualify it as a "fact" per se. Finally, we may note that the belief-structure of an individual is highly intertwined, one belief influencing another and all in interaction with one's aims and attitudes. *Cf.* Anthony Quinton, "Knowledge and Belief," in *The Encyclopedia of Philosophy*, ed. Paul Edwards, IV (1967), pp. 346 and 352; and Israel Scheffler, *Conditions of Knowledge: An Introduction to Epistemology and Education*, Keystones of Education Series (Chicago: Scott, Foresman and Company, 1965), p. 86.

[9] John Dewey, *Democracy and Education: An Introduction to the Philosophy of Education* (New York: The Macmillan Company, 1916); paperback edition (New York: The Free Press, 1966), p. 329.

processes and his technology simply have not as yet produced a core of scientifically-verified data sufficient to provide such a base for action. As a result, the necessity of action and the desire for rational action force man to go beyond what he can prove empirically. As man is able to bring additional facets of experience under scientific investigation, we may hope that the need for speculation will diminish, though it is doubtful that it will ever disappear. For the present, there is clearly a need to make our speculation as systematic, as rational as possible. Therefore, our investigations of "human nature," of the "free will 'versus' determinism" controversy, of "intuition" as a way of knowing or of "moral standards" should surely take all available "facts" into consideration. True, the maximal result of speculation in these, as in so many other concerns, will be the construction of nonempirically-verifiable "beliefs." Nevertheless, as Russell notes,

> . . . *however slight may be the hope of discovering an answer, it is part of the business of philosophy to continue the consideration of such questions, to make us aware of their importance, to examine all the approaches to them, and to keep alive that speculative interest in the universe which is apt to be killed by confining ourselves to definitely ascertainable knowledge.*[10]

Prescription in philosophy involves systematically, imaginatively constructing (and reconstructing) general standards or norms based on our syntheses of fact and belief which we feel may be of future assistance in deciding behavior. Though usually expressed in rather absolutistic "ought" or "should" terms, our prescriptions based on these norms actually function as hypotheses in deciding how we might act in situations, e.g., how we might judge a particular painting or how we might conduct ourselves in a situation involving moral alternatives. For instance, we might construct the following behavioral standard for disciplinary situations: Children should be taught that "when [they] do nice things, nice things happen to [them]. When they do bad things, bad things happen to [them]."[11] Problems with the words "nice" and "bad" aside (at least for the moment), our purpose in constructing such a norm is clearly to give us some help when we face a specific disciplinary problem. And when we face that problem, our norm will serve as an important resource for decision-making—

[10] Bertrand Russell, "Philosophy: Its Nature and Value," *Philosophic Problems and Education,* eds. Young Pai and Joseph T. Myers (Philadelphia: J. B. Lippincott Company, 1967), p. 9.

[11] Charles H. Madsen, Jr., and Clifford K. Madsen, *Teaching/Discipline: Behavioral Principles toward a Positive Approach* (Boston: Allyn and Bacon, Inc., 1970), p. 6.

even though before action we must consider other variables yet to be discussed. The alternative to norm-considering behavior, it should be added, is to face every decision-making situation as if it were entirely unique. And this does not seem to be a particularly viable or rational course of action.

Analysis in philosophy involves a detailed examination of our language and our use of it in an attempt to clarify our understanding of actual problems and possible ways to solve them. Given what seems to be a pedagogical difficulty, for instance, we may find that the *real* (and prior) difficulty lies in our lack of understanding, or our confused understanding, of words such as "nice," "bad," "democracy," "growth," "intelligence," "essentials" or "conservative." We may find that a given word is itself ambiguous and must be carefully defined according to our usage. Analytic activity may suggest that implicit assumptions in our argument need explication, or that our difficulty is rooted in inconsistencies between the facts and/or beliefs upon which our argument is based. We may even find that we have confused fact and belief. Analysis may demonstrate that we have violated established rules of deductive or inductive reasoning, that we have pointed to the wrong data to justify an assertion. Historically speaking, it is clear that analysis is a most important (though not the only) facet of philosophy. If analytic activity does not dissolve what was earlier seen as the real problem, it may often clarify exactly what we do face, as well as the resources at our command, and thus facilitate a solution.

B. PHILOSOPHY AS CONTENT. It would indeed be strange if several millennia of philosophical *activity* had not produced some philosophical products in terms of *content*. True, as science has expanded the realm of facts, areas once relegated to philosophy have tended to be separated from it. Today, for example, psychology and education stand as separate entities; as late as the beginning of this century they were still commonly considered parts of philosophy. In fact, the expansion of experimental science seems to have increased the need for philosophical activity, which in turn has produced distinctive content through synthesis, speculation, prescription and analysis.

Let us take a time-honored path and note that man historically has long asked several fundamental questions around which philosophical content has been organized. For example, he has asked: "What is the nature of reality—both human and nonhuman?" Man's answers to these questions—encompassing both fact and belief alike—have given rise to the branch of philosophy referred to as *metaphysics*. Subsidiary questions have resulted in several subdivisions of metaphysics. Cosmology has resulted from inquiry into the nature, origin and development of the cosmos or universe. Ontology has resulted from answers to the question of what it means to be, to exist.   Other meta-physical concerns have focussed on the nature of God and the nature of man, including his moral status (i.e., good, evil or neutral) and his freedom.[12]

Man has also asked: "What is the nature of knowledge?"   His answers, encompassed in the branch of philosophy known as *Episte-mology,* have spoken to several related concerns, including the possi-bility, kinds and sources of knowledge, and the limitations of human knowledge.   *Axiology,* to take the next step, is the philosophical division organized around answers to the basic question: "What is the nature of value?"   Man has long asked: What is value?   Where is it found?   What types are there?   How is a value claim justified?   How are values ordered?   How may values be improved?   Answers to questions dealing with the nature of the good life (organized under Ethics) and the nature of beauty (organized under Aesthetics) are also included in Axiology.

In terms of content, several additional points need to be made. *Logic,* sometimes subsumed under Epistemology, is properly the study of the nature and techniques of clear and exact thinking.   Hence it seems best to view logic as a *tool* of philosophy, necessary in dealing with metaphysical and axiological concerns as well as with things epistemological.   Philosophy has also been applied to what are today separate disciplines in an attempt to clarify their basic structure, assumptions and problems, and thus facilitate understanding and problem-solving.   Illustrations include studies titled *philosophy of* art, education, history, religion and science.   Social philosophy is of the same order.

Finally, some note must be taken of the various " 'schools' of philos-ophy."   This locution is best taken to refer to a grouping of individuals who have relatively consistent views on the basic questions outlined above.   Philosophical literature includes frequent reference to schools such as Experimentalism, Idealism, Neo-Thomism, Pragmatism and Realism.[13]   As we shall later see, there are serious problems in depending on such labels.   Many schools themselves are subdivided; in a good many others any suggested consistency of views seems more a matter of hope than of fact.   Nevertheless, the notion of "schools"

[12] A more detailed treatment of philosophical content will be found in Chapters 2, 4, 6 and 8.   At this point, the desire is but to sketch the range of questions, answers to which have been organized into content.

[13] Such schools are nearly endless in number.   Those so inclined might consult Vergilius Ferm, ed., *A History of Philosophical Systems,* New Students Outline Series (Patterson, N.J.: Littlefield, Adams & Co., 1961) and Dagobert D. Runes, ed., *Living Schools of Philosophy: Twentieth Century Philosophy,* New Students Outline Series (Patterson, N.J.: Littlefield, Adams & Co., 1962) for additional ex-amples.

does have some value, reference to which will be made in discussing the "relevancy" of philosophy to education and in delimiting the questions to which this text will address itself.

C. PHILOSOPHY AS ATTITUDE. A common definition of "attitude" is "an enduring, learned predisposition to behave in a consistent way toward a given class of objects . . . as they are conceived to be."[14] The question, then, is what behavioral predispositions does the philosopher characteristically bring to his activities and to the substantive products (content) of these activities. In sum, it is suggested that he is strongly and positively predisposed toward comprehensiveness, self-awareness, penetration and openness.[15]

Comprehensiveness refers to an inclination toward assembling all data possibly relevant to understanding a given phenomenon rather than being satisfied with any isolated segment of that data, especially that which is supportive of one's own views. This attitude also involves a deep-seated desire to seek the relatedness of life rather than receiving basic satisfaction from focussing on its parts.

Self-awareness, the second element in philosophy understood as attitude, involves a commitment to being brutally honest with oneself as to one's own assumptions, biases or prejudices. In contemporary jargon, a person has to know "where he himself is coming from" before he can communicate or construct shared meanings with others.

The term *penetration* refers to a tendency to go as deeply into a problem as skill and energy allow. The superficial, the partial and the "quick and easy" are resisted in a thorough, systematic critical search for the basic principles and issues involved and the solution which would best satisfy these factors.

Finally, *openness* involves a sensitivity to new perceptions and to new possibilities for viewing old problems. Openness rests on a learned readiness to undertake the often difficult and painful task of reconstructing comfortable habits of long standing when they are no longer appropriate, to changing life conditions. As Smith points out, however, such "flexibility" does not entail spinelessness.[16] After careful study, one may well decide that a given position—perhaps having to do with leadership, human nature or moral standards—is by and away the most reasonable one available and then act vigorously in

---

[14] W. W. Charters, Jr., and N. L. Gage, eds., *Readings in the Social Psychology of Education* (Boston: Allyn and Bacon, Inc., 1963), p. 334.

[15] *Cf.* John Dewey, *Democracy and Education*, p. 325; Philip H. Phenix, *Philosophy of Education* (New York: Holt, Rinehart and Winston, 1958), pp. 6–10; and Philip G. Smith, *Philosophy of Education* (New York: Harper & Row, 1965), pp. 8–14.

[16] Smith, *Philosophy of Education*, p. 14.

accord with it.   The point at issue lies in one's willingness—even readiness—to change that position given sufficient reason.

In summary, it is suggested that the distinctive character of philosophy both as a discipline and in an individual sense (i.e., a personal philosophy) lies not in any one element—be it activity, content or attitude—but, rather, in the interrelated set of activities, content and attitudes sketched above.   Many other orderings of, and approaches to, experience share *elements* of this set, e.g., science, theology and politics, to name but three.   Science in general is deeply concerned with cosmological and epistemological concerns; the social sciences have given increasing attention to questions of value.   Who would claim that the scientist is less interested in the rules of drawing inferences or less predisposed toward openness than the philosopher?   Was St. Thomas Aquinas as a theologian any less dedicated than the philosopher to understanding the possibility, kinds and sources of knowledge, or the limitations of human knowledge?   Was he less interested in synthesis or less committed to self-awareness?   In each case we probably do best to answer in the negative.   But we may also observe that science does not match philosophy's valuation of synthesis or speculation, or its historic appreciation of the many paths to knowledge,[17] or its predilection for comprehensiveness.   To a degree supported by few philosophers, orthodox Western theology focusses on the relationship between the natural and the supernatural.   And to the same degree it tends to stress the "givenness" of traditional interpretations of religious experience and the indispensability to knowledge of an acceptance of revelation based on faith.

B.   The Nature of Education

Harry Broudy, philosopher of education, defines education as "the process or product of a deliberate attempt to fashion experience by the direction and control of learning [italics removed].   Formal education refers to the process as it is carried on in schools."[18]   Professor Philip Phenix offers the following: "Education is the process whereby persons intentionally guide the development of persons" [italics removed].[19]

[17] True, some philosophers do share the scientist's dependence on the experimental mode of knowing in verifying truth claims, a point which will be developed in Chapter 4.
[18] *Building a Philosophy of Education.*   2nd ed.   (Englewood Cliffs, N.J.: Prentice-Hall, Inc., 1961), p. 8.   Quoted by permission of the publisher.
[19] Smith, *Philosophy of Education,* p. 13.

Perhaps the most adequate general definition to be found in the literature of education, however, is that developed by William K. Frankena, who writes, "The term 'education' may mean any of the following things":

1. What parents, teachers, and schools do, or in other words, the activity of educating the young.
2. What goes on in the child, or the process of being educated.
3. The result or what the child acquires or has in the end, namely, "an education," or
4. The discipline of education, that is, the discipline that studies (1), (2), and (3).[20]

Adding Broudy and Phenix's notion of "intentionality" and taking "education" to include some notion of what we *desire* in terms of child responses and product, we may understand "education" as a term referring to certain intentional activities, to certain goals in the form of student responses, and to the result or product of those activities and responses.   Note that "intentional activities" may be grouped under curricular, instructional, organizational, administrative and professional headings.   Note also that activity and response and product goals are highly interrelated.   Finally, "education" also refers to a discipline which attempts to develop a systematic body of theory adequate to 1) explain the nature and relationships of education as activity and response and product goals, and 2) guide the development of policies[21] which in a specified sociocultural context link desired goals with appropriate activities.   Obviously, this conceptual scheme must indicate how scientific knowledge and rational belief "may be applied to educational problems and how conflicting proposals for education may be subjected to orderly inquiry and adjudication."[22]

At present, education as a discipline is in a rather sad state of

---

[20] William K. Frankena, *Philosophy of Education* (New York: The Macmillan Company, 1965), p. 2.

[21] Philip Smith notes that an educational policy statement reflects "an agreement or compromise reached in light of the exigencies of a particular situation, in contrast to an agreement based entirely on abstract principles. A policy is thus the means for giving contextually operational meaning to statements formulated on a theoretical base" (*Philosophy of Education,* p. 66). "In contrast to both theory and policy, statements about educational practice [activity] should, ideally, be restricted to scientifically controlled descriptions and judgments about the various behaviors and experiences involved in the educational enterprise (*Ibid.*, p. 67).

[22] *Cf.* Smith, *Philosophy of Education,* pp. 65–66. The expression "rational belief" has been added to Smith's formulation.   As indicated above, we simply do not "know" enough to depend on "scientific knowledge" alone. Rational belief, therefore, must also be applied to educational problems.

disarray. There is no carefully formulated educational theory—not primarily because resources or a sense of need are lacking, but, rather, because 1) there is so little agreement as to what an educational theory *is,* and 2) those who necessarily must develop such a theory either have little perspective as to their function or are not working cooperatively with others whose contributions are also vital. To make matters worse, as Smith points out,

> *Without a carefully formulated educational theory, discussions of practice tend to be either a series of uncontrolled, nonsystematic (and hence doubtful and even confusing) empirical generalizations, or a series of exhortations and suggestions offered without empirical evidence. Many such suggestions develop wide popular support and therefore become one more complicating factor that must be considered as educational policies are formulated.*[23]

The task facing those responsible for developing educational theory[24] is as immense as it is pressing. No one group is sufficient to the task; needed is much more cooperative work and many fewer expressions of a "holier than thou" attitude or attempts to dictate.

C.   The Nature of Philosophy of Education

"Philosophy of Education" is not an autonomous discipline. Its contributions to educational theory, policy and practice are based firmly on philosophy's time-tested experience in having systematically explored different outlooks on life, "analyzed the underlying concepts, refined the underlying problems, posed fundamental criticisms and developed alternative answers or at least paths of solution."[25] Its task, in brief, is to bring philosophy—understood as activity, content and attitude—to bear upon the problems of education. Its goal—both separately and cooperatively with others involved in developing educational theory— is through teaching and research to contribute to the resolution of these problems by developing hypotheses for thought and experimentation. Our survey of the nature of philosophy and of education suggests several possibilities for effective contributions.

[23] *Ibid.,* p. 67.

[24] This group surely includes *all* professional educators, including inservice educators, as well as philosophers of education, educational anthropologists, historians, psychologists, and sociologists, curricular specialists and specialists in comparative education, educational administration, educational guidance and special education.

[25] Abraham Edel, "What Should Be the Aims and Content of a Philosophy of Education?" *What Is Philosophy of Education?,* ed. Lucas, p. 141.

There is obviously a wide range of opportunity, as well as great need, for systematic *analytic activity* in education. At this stage of development, even the basic terms of educational theory development need further clarification: "educational theory" itself, "intentional activity," "student response," "educational product," "educational goal" and "educational policy." The same may be said for terms commonly employed in discussing theory such as "desirable," "relate," "guide," "consistency," "fact," "rational belief," "assumption" and "concept." A third group, frequently appearing in professional discourse and giving no end of trouble, includes terms such as "democracy," "intelligence," "ability" and "growth." Note that the scope of analytic clarification extends considerably beyond mere dictionary definition: "When a philosopher asks 'What does *x* mean?', he is not asking for a definition of *x*—at least not in the dictionary sense of 'definition.' He wants to know what are the criteria for the use of the term *x*."[26] In short, the philosopher wants to decide if we can properly use a term given its possible meanings and the context in which it would be used. He is necessarily concerned with the rules or criteria governing such decisions.

This expression of philosophy also has potential for establishing how phenomena of educational import are related. To illustrate, we need to analyze how scientific knowledge and rational belief can be used in developing educational theory, how educational theory can guide policy-making, how intentional activities and response and product goals are related, and how one moves from a statement of educational policy to a decision about an appropriate intentional activity.

Educators need to know just what elements *do* constitute an activity-practice (curricular, instructional, organizational, administrative or personnel) alternative. In a given practice are the elements identified consistent one with another? Are they compatible with scientifically-determined facts and/or related beliefs? All things considered, are they adequate? The same general questions need to be asked about the criteria which in fact guide *choices* of activity-practice alternatives. We need much more information concerning the criteria which do guide these choices, how they are developed and all the rest. Analyses of the consistency, compatibility and adequacy of our entire activity-practice repertoire are also needed.

Finally, philosophical analysis may also help us to explicate the various contributions which philosophers of education can make to resolving educational problems.[27] Effective contributions surely de-

[26] James Gribble, *Introduction to Philosophy of Education* (Boston: Allyn and Bacon, Inc., 1969), p. 4.
[27] Admittedly at an introductory level, the first chapter has involved us in just this task. This is part of what is meant by "doing philosophy."

pend on establishing 1) clarity of meaning and 2) their consistency both in themselves and in relation to the contributions of nonphilosophical theorists. To some extent—if undertaken with humility and an attitude of helpfulness without dictation—philosophical analysis may also assist other theory contributors to deal with similar concerns.

Our brief consideration of analytic possibilities for philosophy of education suggested that the question of "adequacy" should be raised in treating what is actually the case. Where the answer clearly lies in the negative, there are important possibilities for *speculative philosophical activity*. With this background in the exploration, analysis and criticism of fundamental human problems (metaphysical, epistemological and axiological), the philosopher of education brings rich resources to the imaginative construction of alternatives to pedagogical inadequacies. Of course, there is no guarantee that these alternatives will work. Only science can establish that. But there is a case for contending that the educational philosopher's training provides a sufficient rationale for seriously considering his hypotheses.

In addition to the contribution of alternatives, there is a place for systematic speculation concerning the educational activities-practices which might be consistent with "philosophical 'assumptions' "[28] common to a given culture. As noted by Millard and Bertocci,

> There is a legitimate place for developing the educational [possibilities suggested by] major philosophic positions. This is particularly desirable insofar as the philosophic positions themselves form part of the cultural context in which and for which education occurs.[29]

For example, what possibilities are suggested in terms of curricular, instructional, organizational, administrative or personnel practices by

[28] A "philosophical 'assumption' " is the conceptual outcome of tentatively taking a position with regard to alternative meanings of a given philosophical concept such as "human nature." (Thus we might "assume" that human nature is inherently evil or at least predisposed to evil. Or, we might assume that human nature is always either superior or inferior—superiority and inferiority being defined in terms of sex and/or race and/or intelligence.) *Assumptions are usually generated out of a combination of facts and beliefs.* Like beliefs, they tend to assume a distinctive cluster within the individual's belief-knowledge system or frame of reference, supporting and interacting with one another. Assumptions provide a base from which to draw inferences. Inasmuch as 1) they themselves are generally taken for granted (i.e., not questioned) in the inference-drawing, and 2) combining facts and beliefs seems necessary to decision-making, it is necessary that our assumptions be as sound as possible. The philosopher, then, is interested in identifying the assumptions which people do hold, constructing criteria by which these assumptions may be judged as to their adequacy and (in the case of conflicting assumptions) evaluating alternative claims according to these criteria.

[29] Richard M. Millard, Jr., and Peter A. Bertocci, "Philosophy and Philosophy of Education," *What Is Philosophy of Education?*, ed. Lucas, pp. 197–198.

the assumption that "justice" demands that "every man be free to do the work for which he is best suited, and that he receives the rewards which that work deserves, and that no one meddle with him"?[30] What, however, if one assumes that "justice" is a term referring to the quality of an act, idea or process which increases the power of human beings to create a society which makes individuality possible? Of a somewhat different order is the task of suggesting the philosophical assumptions which might be underlying observed educational activities or expressions of policy. It should be noted that there are several (severe) difficulties in directly establishing meaningful connections between theory and practice. Nevertheless, the nature and even the *possibility* of these "connections" appear to be absolutely central to questions of the "relevancy" of philosophy to the interests and tasks of professional educators. Therefore, before turning to examples of such speculative activity in Chapters 3, 5, 7 and 9, and actively involving the reader in speculative philosophizing in Chapter 10, we shall consider these problems in the next section of the present chapter.

The frightening task of developing an adequate educational theory provides many appropriate occasions for engaging in *synthetic activity*, i.e., synthesizing. The establishment of consistency[31] between the various facts and beliefs that go into the formation of educational activity, response and product goal, and policy alternatives is of prime importance. Educational *decisions* can only be the richer and the more rational if, for example, we place every scientifically-verified fact we can assemble about a given phenomenon side by side with relevant philosophical assumptions. There is also a need to develop consistency among the contributions made to the development of educational theory by several disciplines. No one is well served when the insights and skills of the behavioral scientist, the historian, the philosopher and other concerned educators are allowed to remain compartmentalized and, in the worst sense of the word, "competitive."

The difficulties facing synthesis in education are great and must not be minimized. As is the case with philosophy, a vast range of human knowledge and belief is potentially relevant to education. As noted earlier, many philosophers have suggested we surrender this synthetic activity as a central philosophical function. Some philosophers have done so, and the earth has not stopped rotating. It is suggested, however, that the cost of its surrender by education would be somewhat greater: continuing chaos—more years of not really knowing

---

[30] Russell Kirk, *A Program for Conservatives*. Rev. ed. (Chicago: Henry Regnery Company, 1962), p. 168.

[31] Here, the "establishment" of consistency is being contrasted with the *identification* of its presence or absence in a given phenomenon—the latter being more the responsibility of analytic philosophy.

what we are doing, or why, or even that we do not know—more years of a mythological approach to defining and attempting to solve serious educational problems. In truth, the potential of successful synthesis is as inviting as its surrender is repelling.

Prescriptive activity should occur when the philosopher of education concludes that appropriate standards of judgment warrant viewing an hypothesis as reasonable and, therefore, ready for the consideration and testing of others. The development of the criteria of "reasonableness," hypothesis-development itself and the judgment of the hypothesis may be undertaken either in cooperation with other professional educators or on the basis of the philosopher's own background in philosophy and in education. Consideration and testing, however, must involve other educators, including those with skills in experimental research which the philosopher seldom possesses. It is no less reasonable for a philosopher of education to hypothesize that we *should* adopt a given disciplinary strategy (if we want the student to respond in certain desired ways) than it is for a scientist to hypothesize that we *should* use certain new materials in reading in certain specified ways (if we want the student to respond in certain desired ways). Prior to experimental verification in the field, however, it would be equally unreasonable for either philosopher or scientist to hold that the prescription had anything greater than *hypothetical* power.

Given this introductory treatment of the nature and possible functions of the philosophy of education, let us focus even more directly and explicitly on the question of the "relevancy" of the interrelated activities, content and attitudes of philosophy to the common interests and tasks of professional educators.

D.   How Relevant *Is* Philosophy to Education?

Let us begin with an admission: There are many respectable academicians who sincerely believe that our constant "quest for 'usefulness' or 'relevancy'" rests on a deeply anti-intellectual strain in American culture. They feel that the oftheard cry of "So what?" typically expresses an underlying disdain of theory, that answers to this cry generally call for shortsighted, impulsive reactions to the pressures of the moment. They suggest that this phenomenon is one of the important causes of cultural mediocrity. We may respect these men— and even hold our own reservations about the sometimes superficiality and "gadgetry" of our culture—and yet reject their analysis. Indeed, we may agree with Dewey, who wrote:

The problem of the relation of theory and practice is not a problem of theory alone; it is that, but it is also the most practical problem of life. For it is the question of how intelligence may inform action, and how action may bear the fruit of increased insight into meaning: a clear view of the values that are worthwhile and of the means by which they are to be made secure in experienced objects.[32]

The common sense of professional philosophers and laymen alike suggests that philosophy *should* influence educational perspectives and activity. Shields's position, for instance, was noted at the beginning of this chapter. Dewey writes, "Whenever philosophy has been taken seriously, it has always been assumed that it signified achieving a wisdom which would influence the conduct of life . . . If a theory makes no difference in educational endeavors, it must be artificial."[33] Reid, a British philosopher of education, maintains that "it is legitimate and right in that, if anyone holds fundamental beliefs of whatever kind, which are in any way relevant to education, integrity demands that his beliefs should enter in an important way into his educational thinking."[34] Ernest Nagel goes so far as to argue that "only if one abandons all normal canons of evidence and ignores well-established empirical findings, can one deny that the beliefs men hold, or the reasons men advance for what they do and profess, often are crucial determining factors. . . ."[35]

Careful analysis, however, has established that the task of specifying exactly *how* philosophy influences education presents a most difficult problem indeed—common sense or no common sense. Furthermore, in the author's view, this problem is of crucial import to the educator. Where is the logic in requiring (or, perhaps, even recommending) the study of philosophy if you, an educator, cannot be shown how to use it in your professional activities? As a first step in attempting an answer to this problem, let us see exactly where the difficulty lies.

If philosophy were merely activity and/or attitude, there might be less of an issue. The teacher in things professional would be trained to synthesize, speculate, prescribe and analyze in the most comprehensive, self-aware, penetrating and open-minded manner possible.

[32] John Dewey, *The Quest for Certainty: A Study of the Relation of Knowledge and Action* (New York: Minton, Balch & Co., 1929); paperback edition (New York: Capricorn Books-G. P. Putnam's Sons, 1960), p. 281.

[33] *Democracy and Education*, pp. 324 and 328.

[34] L. Arnaud Reid, "Philosophy and the Theory and Practice of Education," *Philosophical Analysis and Education*, ed. Reginald Archambault (New York: The Humanities Press, 1965), p. 29.

[35] *Liberalism and Intelligence*, Fourth John Dewey Memorial Lecture (Bennington, Vt.: Bennington College, 1957), p. 1; cited by Hobert W. Burns, "The Logic of the 'Educational Implication,'" *Educational Theory*, XII, No. 1 (January 1962), 59.

The distorting effect of unexamined prejudices and philosophical assumptions thus minimized, application of these activities and attitudes to education would be a more straightforward and less controversial affair in that it would not necessitate applying the content of one discipline to another.[36]   The difficulty is introduced when we define "philosophy" as *also* including certain *content* in the form of answers to, or assumptions about, basic human metaphysical, epistemological and axiological questions.   The difficulty is heightened when we suggest that our analytic activity—or what have you—is to be carried on with reference *not only* to the educational problem at hand *but also* with reference to that content.   In other words, although the *philosophical* analysis of a term of professional interest, e.g., "democracy," is undertaken with one eye on clarifying a pedagogical problem, the other eye is focussed on the various meanings of "democracy" which are recorded in the annals of philosophy.   It is this context, then, which provides resources for analysis and justifies the use of the adjective "philosophical."[37]

Unfortunately, philosophers skilled in analysis have rather firmly established the functional uselessness of attempting to deduce specific pedagogical practices from philosophical assumptions (the content dimension of philosophy).   To cite an example, they have demonstrated that one cannot deduce a specific disciplinary role for the classroom teacher from philosophical assumptions alone.   Such a deductive leap is useless (if not impossible), they suggest, because it ignores the fact that an educator's decisions must be made in a context wider than that provided by his personal philosophical assumptions alone.[38]   In deciding on a disciplinary role, for instance, he must take into consideration not only his philosophical assumptions but also relevant scientific facts, psychological assumptions about how children

[36] There are some philosophers who claim that it is neither desirable nor even functionally possible, in philosophizing, completely to overcome one's frame of reference (which includes implicit and explicit philosophical assumptions).   See the assumption of "frame of reference as self-in-becoming" in Chapter 4.

[37] This is not to say, of course, that a philosopher of education could never prescribe a certain pedagogical strategy strictly on the basis of a combination of psychological assumptions and scientific facts alone—with no conscious reference to related philosophical assumptions.   Reserving comment for the moment on the reasonableness of such a move, it *is* to say, however, that in so doing he is acting within his general role as educated human being rather than his more restricted, technical role as professional philosopher.

[38] *Cf.* Harry S. Broudy, "How Philosophical Can Philosophy of Education Be?", *The Journal of Philosophy*, LII, No. 22 (October 27, 1955), 617; Paul Hirst, "Philosophy and Educational Theory," *Philosophy and Education: Modern Readings,* ed. Israel Scheffler. 2nd ed. (Boston: Allyn and Bacon, Inc., 1966), pp. 78–84; Reid, "Philosophy and the Theory and Practice of Education," pp. 29–34; and Reid, *Philosophy and Education: An Introduction* (New York: Random House, 1962), pp. 86–96.

might best learn to minimize impulses and overcome limited view-points, sociological factors such as the socioeconomic make-up of his class and hypotheses concerning the ways it affects attitude and learn-ing, historical factors such as the community's long-term views of appropriate teacher-student conduct, and "reality" factors such as the stated school policy on discipline, the preferences of his immediate superiors and his influence vis-à-vis that of significant community figures, including parents. As Reid points out,

> Belief (sometimes grounded in philosophy) enters in an im-portant way into the whole complexity of educational thought and experience, and it gives some general maxims. But what comes out at the other end in a particular practical policy is not just a logical deduction (though it may contain some passages of deduction) but an educational judgment, a principled deci-sion, made in the light of the fullest possible consideration of all the relevant factors in the individual educational situation.[39]

In fact, if any general guidance for decisions in problem areas such as discipline is to be had from theory, it is probably not to be found in *philosophical* theory alone, but, as noted earlier, in an *educational* theory built on the joint contributions of all those interested in educa-tion, including philosophers.

A second group of difficulties is sketched by Brown, who discusses the common assumption that there is a causal connection between philosophical positions and pedagogical practices.[40] Brown notes the difficulties in proving that an educator's beliefs are *the* cause of a professional practice. In his view this difficulty is intensified by a still not uncommon practice in the philosophy of education. Assumptions are grouped under "schools" or "systems" of philosophy. So many assumptions—sometimes not all that consistent one with another—are included under a label such as "Idealism" that even the basic generali-zations to which the label was designed to refer become blurred. Furthermore, given the pluralistic nature of culture, it is difficult to identify *two* philosophers whose belief systems are identical. When it is required that they be grouped with others of "somewhat" similar views, the resultant school or systems study sometimes does violence to the facts, often confuses the student as he attempts to find some-thing of pedagogical significance in philosophy and build his own philosophy of education, and thoroughly muddies just what it is that is supposed to be the "cause" of the given professional behavior.

---

[39] Reid, "Philosophy and the Theory and Practice of Education," *Philosophical Analysis and Education,* ed. Archambault, p. 29.

[40] L. M. Brown, *General Philosophy in Education* (New York: McGraw-Hill Book Company, 1966), pp. 82–83.

If one cannot decide matters of educational policy or practice on the basis of his philosophical assumptions, if it is nearly impossible to establish that one's philosophical assumptions are the cause of one's professional behavior, where does this leave us in our search for the relevancy of philosophy to education? Let us begin by admitting the worst and then going on from there.[41] Let us agree that our educational practices cannot be logically derived directly from our philosophical assumptions. We must admit that individuals professing the same philosophical beliefs *do* sometimes differ as to how those beliefs should be implemented. Does this commit us also to agreeing that our assumptions have no relationship whatsoever to our practices? Far from it—although we must admit a more indirect and modest relationship. Rather than our philosophical assumptions alone, it is the *entire body* of scientific knowledge, historical, psychological, sociological and "reality" factors—as well as our philosophical assumptions—in a given context of time, place and people, which provides the reasons for action decisions. The development of more rational practices and more adequate policy guidelines depends on the construction of an *educational* theory rather than a comprehensive *philosophical* position alone. Nevertheless, it would be folly to minimize the contributions that philosophy may make to such a theory. Philosophy has immense potential value based on its experience in dealing with syntheses of scientific fact and the most deep-seated beliefs of man about himself and his world, in analyzing thinking processes and products, and in working through open inquiry. As a matter of fact, given the continuing limitations of scientific method and technology in producing and synthesizing empirically-verified fact, the contributions of philosophy appear to be quite necessary (though surely not sufficient) to the task.

In summary, you will find nothing in your study of the philosophy of education which will tell you exactly what to do in the classroom, the committee room, the office or on the playing field. What you *will* find, however, is potentially of considerable value and relevancy to your interests and tasks: 1) explications and critical evaluations of philosophical assumptions commonly held in American culture which are of special import to the American school; 2) hypotheses concerning the

[41] Clues to and/or facets of the argument which follows are treated in John S. Brubacher, *Modern Philosophies of Education.* 4th ed. (New York: McGraw-Hill Book Company, 1969), pp. 324–325; Robert S. Guttchen, "The Quest for Necessity," *Educational Theory,* XVI, No. 2 (April 1966), 128–134; Hirst, "Philosophy and Educational Theory," pp. 82–95; and Elizabeth S. Maccia, "The Separation of Philosophy from Theory of Education," *Studies in Philosophy and Education,* II (Spring 1962), pp. 158–169.

possible contributions of philosophy to increasing the rationality of your educational practices, and opportunities for you to become involved in testing them; 3) speculative opportunities to analyze the philosophical reasons underlying observed professional practices and to synthesize these reasons with nonphilosophical factors which also contributed to the practices; 4) opportunities to explicate your own assumptions as to the basic problems of man and his world, thus taking one more step in relating your beliefs, your knowledge of facts and your habitual practices; and 5) opportunity to become involved in a most systematic, comprehensive, penetrating and open-minded inquiry into the present state and future possibilities of American education which, it is suggested, is one important function of any truly "professional" educator.

E. Philosophizing About American Education: The Task Ahead

In bringing philosophical activities, content and attitudes (that is, *philosophy*) to bear upon the problems of education and thus attempting to contribute to their solution, the philosopher of education rather obviously brings rich resources to a great many complex tasks. Our introduction to the "Nature of Philosophy" and our consideration of the relevancy of philosophy to education in Sections C and D above only begin to outline the possibilities.

Not all of these possibilities can possibly be dealt with in any one "introductory" text. Delimitations must be specified on the basis of both the specific student population to which the text is addressed and the author's expertise—not to mention his conception of the nature and function of philosophy of education. The general goal of *Philosophy and Schooling* is reasonably straightforward: Its purpose is 1) to introduce you to the pedagogically relevant resources of philosophy, 2) to help you develop some elementary skill in using these resources to clarify and suggest possibilities for your professional activities, 3) to help you to explicate your personal philosophy of education, and 4) to increase your commitment to making professional decisions based on appropriate facts and rational beliefs rather than upon impulse or expediency.

Following the introductory questions and definitions presented in this chapter, we shall move directly in Chapter 2 through 9 to an explication of assumptions concerning basic metaphysical, epistemological, axiological and social-philosophical concepts of importance to American education. Each group of concepts and related assumptions will be followed by speculation concerning educational policies and practices which appear to be consistent with the assumptions. These exercises are not to be understood as logical deductions from the assumptions. Rather, they represent an attempt to help you better understand the philosophical points involved and to suggest some *possibilities* for your consideration as you try to understand the motivation of others, clarify and resolve professional problems, and build your own philosophy of education. We shall discuss the necessity of considering the explicit and implicit philosophical assumptions of the teacher, the student, the administrator, the parent and the wider community, the school as a social institution (local, district and state) and curricular materials. Efforts will be made to present these assumptions as themselves interrelated, as well as interacting with historical, psychological, sociological and reality factors to influence educational phenomena.

Where it furthers the understanding of relationships, passing reference will be made to four schools of philosophy and to two social ideologies, including Existentialism, Idealism, Realism,[42] Pragmatism,[43] Conservatism and Liberalism. Notes on the history of these systems, as well as a rationale for their inclusion in our studies, will be found in the Appendixes.

Chapter 10 provides an analysis of the techniques for finding, and the criteria for evaluating, philosophical assumptions. Several professional situations will be provided for practice in 1) identifying philosophical assumptions which may be contributing to the practices described, and 2) synthesizing philosophical with the nonphilosophical factors also involved. Finally, a case-study approach will be employed to afford some realistic experience in using philosophy speculatively to suggest possibilities for a variety of decision-making situations.

Chapter 11, the final chapter, moves from the somewhat more impersonal and more technical earlier discussions and exercises to a supremely individual task, the articulation of a reasonably consistent and harmonious *personal* philosophy of education. A variety of considerations and exercises will be followed by suggestions as to how the concerned educator might continue to develop skill in applying philosophy to his particular personal and professional interests.

Rather obviously, this text stresses the possible contributions of philosophy to increasing rational decision-making on the part of pro-

---

[42] Realism and Idealism, parenthetically, are sometimes *jointly* referred to as "classical" or "traditional" schools of philosophy. Both schools were founded during the Classical Age, and early traditions have continued to influence the development of their assumptions.

[43] Pragmatism is also referred to as "Experimentalism" and "Instrumentalism."

fessional educators—people who are not professional philosophers. Hopefully, however, those who are interested in the latter pursuit will find numerous suggestions (however unstressed or implicit) as to ways of applying philosophy to the clarification of immensely complex problems in educational theory-building. You—as well as classroom teachers, administrators and other school personnel—are welcomed as colleagues in meeting the demands confronting all who would teach and all who would learn.

Suggestions for Further Reading

"The Aim and Content of Philosophy of Education" (Symposium). *Harvard Educational Review*, XXVI, No. 2 (Spring 1956). Twenty-three authors develop a variety of approaches to the philosophy of education.

ARCHANBAULT, REGINALD D., ed., *Philosophical Analysis and Education.* New York: The Humanities Press, 1965. See especially L. Arnaud Reid, "Philosophy and the Theory and Practice of Education," pp. 17–37, and Edward Best, "Common Confusions in Educational Theory," pp. 39–56.

BROWN, L. M., *General Philosophy of Education.* New York: McGraw-Hill Book Company, 1966. Chapter IV ("Implications in Educational Philosophy").

BRUBACHER, JOHN S., *Modern Philosophies of Education.* 4th ed. New York: McGraw-Hill Book Company, 1969. Chapters XIV (educational philosophy) and XVI (schools of philosophy).

BURNETT, JOE R., "Observations on the Logical Implications of Philosophic Theory for Educational Theory and Practice," *Educational Theory*, XI, No. 2 (April 1961), pp. 65–70. Relates philosophy and educational theory and practice; reprinted in Pai and Myers, below.

BURNS, HOBERT W., "The Logic of the 'Educational Implication'," *Educational Theory*, XII, No. 1 (January 1962), pp. 53–63. Relates philosophy and educational theory and practice; reprinted in Pai and Myers, below.

BUTLER, J. DONALD, *Four Philosophies and Their Practice in Education and Religion.* 3rd ed. New York: Harper & Row, Publishers, 1968. Pages 4–10 (philosophy contrasted with other disciplines) and 13–33 (problems of philosophy).

GUTTCHEN, ROBERT S., "The Quest for Necessity," *Educational Theory*, XVI, No. 2 (April 1966), pp. 128–134. Relates philosophy and educational theory and practice.

HOOK, SIDNEY, "The Scope of Philosophy of Education," *Harvard Educational Review*, XXVI, No. 2 (Spring 1956), pp. 145–148. Relates philosophy and educational theory and practice; reprinted in Pai and Myers, below.

KATTSOFF, L. O., "Observation and Interpretation in Science," *Philosophical Review*, LVI (1947), pp. 682–689. Discusses the nature of scientific facts.

LUCAS, CHRISTOPHER J., ed., *What Is Philosophy of Education?* New York: The Macmillan Company, 1969. The latest anthology of articles dealing with the nature of philosophy and the philosophy of education; a solid list of suggestions for further reading.

PAI, YOUNG, and JOSEPH T. MYERS, eds., *Philosophic Problems and Education*. Philadelphia: J. B. Lippincott Company, 1967. Part I (philosophy and education; see especially the Burnett, Burns and Hook articles).

PHENIX, PHILIP H., *Philosophy of Education*. New York: Holt, Rinehart and Winston, 1958. Chapter I (philosophy, education, and philosophy of education; philosophy as a way of looking at knowledge which we already have).

QUINTON, ANTHONY, "Knowledge and Belief," *The Encyclopedia of Philosophy* (1967), IV, pp. 345–352.

REID, L. ARNAUD, *Philosophy and Education: An Introduction*. New York: Random House, 1962. Chapters I (philosophy), IV (philosophy and educational assumptions) and VI (relating philosophy and educational theory and practice).

SCHEFFLER, ISRAEL, *Conditions of Knowledge: An Introduction to Epistemology and Education*. Keystones of Education Series. Chicago: Scott, Foresman and Company, 1965. Chapter IV (knowledge and belief).

———, ed., *Philosophy and Education: Modern Readings*. Boston: Allyn and Bacon, Inc., 1966. 2nd ed. Parts I and II (education; see especially Paul Hirst, "Philosophy and Educational Theory," pp. 78–95).

SMITH, PHILIP G., *Philosophy of Education: Introductory Studies*. New York: Harper & Row, 1965. Chapters I (philosophy), II (education) and III (philosophy of education).

PART *II*

Metaphysics and
American Education

2

Metaphysics: Its Nature, Function, Concepts and Assumptions

For the moment let us assume that you are a class counsellor. You are firmly convinced on both religious and historical grounds that man's nature is basically corrupt—that given half a chance he is far more likely to err than to choose the right. The student president comes to you and requests permission for a class party at a state park some fifteen miles from the school. If you approve the request, are there any regulations that you would impose?

You are still the counsellor, but this time you really cannot believe that children are born evil—or good—or any other way for that matter. They are simply *born*—that is the given. Each individual must then build his nature—what he *is*—through the choices he makes and for which he takes responsibility. In the last analysis, whether these choices are good or evil can be determined only by the individual himself. Only in case of the greatest societal pressure will you interfere—and then as little as possible. Respond to the student president under these conditions.

This time you are a student judge serving on your school's judiciary board. A fellow student stands before you accused for the third time of having cursed his science teacher. Sheepishly, he admits that he knows such behavior is wrong and even explains why he reacts so negatively to this particular teacher. You believe in the notion of "free will," i.e., an individual really is free to choose how he will act in spite of background events predisposing him to certain behaviors. True, he must consider the problem, understand why he is drawn to the undesirable behavior and know which behavior is morally preferable. Furthermore, under these conditions he is *responsible* for exercising his free will—to put it another way, he is responsible for being truly human. Indicate how you will rule on this case.

In the second segment of this set, the facts of the case remain constant. The differences lie in your own assumptions. You are convinced that all behavior is determined by causal factors in the individual's background. Merely punishing a person for having acted in ways consistent with these determiners is just a little ridiculous. Rather, *we* are responsible for selecting strategies which are best calculated to modify his present undesirable behavior. Rehabilitation is the keynote. Indicate how you will rule under these conditions.

This is not the time to consider answers to the questions posed above. No doubt the possibilities will be much clearer upon the completion of your studies in "metaphysics and American education." It *is* time, however, to underline what you have probably already surmised: metaphysical assumptions will influence—though not determine —the answers. But what is metaphysics?[1]

A. Metaphysics: Nature and Function

Metaphysics is that branch of philosophy which studies the very nature of reality—both human and nonhuman. It is important to realize that there is no necessary conflict between Metaphysics and science. Even when the various branches of science have accumulated their facts, there still remains the necessary task of synthesis and interpretation. To these problems philosophy has long directed its attention. Historically, Metaphysics has included several divisions of study.

Ontological questions are central to Metaphysics. What do we mean when we say that something *is*, that it exists? Is basic reality found in matter or physical energy—the world we can sense—or is it found in that spirit or spiritual energy which both underlies and gives meaning to that which we can sense? It is composed of but one element (e.g., matter or spirit), or two (e.g., spirit and matter), or

[1] The following categorization of metaphysical topics is clearly indebted to J. Donald Butler's treatment in his *Four Philosophies and Their Practice in Education and Religion*. 3rd ed. (New York: Harper & Row, Publishers, Inc., 1968). The serious student is directed to this text which contains a wealth of philosophical and historical material which lies beyond the scope of the present introduction.

many? Or, must an answer to the question of basic reality ultimately remain closed to man who is unable to penetrate beyond his own human experience? Is this reality purposeful or does man impose his own purpose on it? Is it orderly and lawful—or is it merely orderable by man? Is it fixed and stable—or is change its keynote? And is this reality friendly to man—or unfriendly—or is it merely neutral in terms of affecting human activity?

Cosmology is that branch of Metaphysics which studies the nature of the cosmos, including explanations of its origin and development. Questions of time, space and causality are central to cosmological inquiry.

Metaphysical study necessarily gives considerable attention to the human being. What do we mean by the self? How are man's mind and body related? What is man's moral status? Is he born good, evil, superior or inferior, or is he born morally neutral later to work out his essence? To what extent is he free? Does he have "free will" or are his actions determined by his attitudinal, experiential and physiological background?

Finally, Metaphysics is interested in what we mean by "God" and the implications for human action of the various meanings which have been attributed to this concept.

Philosophy and Schooling will not attempt to include a presentation of all these metaphysical concerns. Indeed, as you will see, our treatment will be sharply delimited. A consideration of assumptions concerning the concept "mind" will be deferred until our study of Epistemology. With regard to the remaining concerns, we shall stress those concepts and related assumptions of common concern to those in this culture who are unskilled in general philosophy. Many points more directly related to the history of ideas than to the specification of contemporary assumptions will be relegated to a series of historical appendices. The purpose of these delimitations is to allow you, an introductory student, time to gain some understanding of basic metaphysical assumptions which you will encounter in contemporary American culture (especially the culture of the school), to consider ways in which these assumptions can influence professional policies and practices, and to begin to explicate your own assumptions and synthesize them into a consciously-held philosophy of education. This approach is seen proper for the beginning student. No doubt some of you will be motivated to go considerably further. In this case, suggestions for additional reading will be offered at the end of Chapter 3. You will also need to consider other approaches and other courses both in general philosophy and in the philosophy of education.

Let us now turn to a consideration of common assumptions concerning the metaphysical concepts of basic reality, human nature, free will and determinism, and God and faith.

B. Metaphysical Concepts and Assumptions

1. Basic Reality

A. BASIC REALITY: THE ORDERLY, KNOWABLE, SENSIBLE WORLD. With regard to that which is ultimately real, the introductory student will probably find the basic assumptions of philosophical Realism to be quite understandable. Indeed, these assumptions so permeate the modern scientific temper that they are more likely to be taken as "common sense" than to be understood as *assumptions*.

For the realist, basic reality is to be found in the familiar, orderly, sensible world of space and time which includes our perceptions of and experiences with this world. It is a world which existed long before our coming and will probably exist long after our bodies have returned to dust. We do not construct this world in the process of coming to know it. Indeed, our task lies in discovering it, along with the physical and moral laws which express its harmonious operations, and then acting within the bounds of given reality. Let no one think, however, that even the task of discovery—let alone of action—is an easy one. A multitude of perceptual and evaluative errors may be made by even the most sophisticated of observers. In principle, however, the world and its laws are capable of being known through systematic objective observation, reporting and generalization. We shall consider the details of this knowing process when we turn to the realist's epistemological assumptions.

Developing over the millennia, realistic assumptions have—not surprisingly—been expressed in different ways. Although suggestive notes will be found in the appropriate appendix to this text, a full development of these emphases is probably best left to studies in the history of ideas and more advanced work in the philosophy of education. Suffice it to say, for present purposes, that realists have differed as to what makes up the familiar world to which reference has been made. Some realists have felt that matter and associated processes lie alone at the heart of reality. Others, such as Aristotle, the father of Realism, have felt that both matter and ideas are real. Still others have suggested a pluralistic reality, finding reality in matter, ideas, processes, mind—and even a personal spiritual god. Realists have also differed epistemologically, some feeling that we directly know that which exists and others suggesting that we directly know only our experiences and the ideas which existing things cause us to have.   In all, however, the assumption that basic reality consists of an orderly, knowable, sensible world, a world existing quite independently of our efforts to know it, stands as the foundation of a realistic Ontology.

B. BASIC REALITY: CREATIVE, PURPOSEFUL, SPIRITUAL ENERGY. The philosophical idealist is quite unimpressed with suggestions that basic reality can be found in the world of sensible things.   Indeed, even the most cursory observation tells us that this is a world of change, disorder, uncertainty—even of decay. Furthermore, how could there possibly be objects without a creator of these objects?   Do we not, then, have to go beyond the senses to find the ultimate?

At first glance, this notion—so out of keeping with the modern scientific spirit—seems rather odd.   But let's see if it really is all that strange.   In your mind's eye, picture your first class of the day and then attempt the following exercise.   Four individuals are asked to come to the front of the room and face their fellow students.   The first, a female, has a yellowish-bronze complexion, straight black hair, dark eyes and is about 5'10" in height.   The second, a male, has a blackish-brown complexion, tightly curled black hair, brown eyes and is around six feet in height.   The third, a female, has a rather pinkish-white complexion, wavy light-brown hair, blue eyes and is about 5'7".   The last student, a male, has a reddish-bronze complexion, long dark hair, dark eyes and is all of 6'3".   You are asked to contemplate these four classmates and suggest what they have in common—what unites them. *Student:* "You've got to be kidding!" *Teacher:* "No, observe—think." Finally, after many false starts and much discussion, one girl gets the idea: "Well, the unifying factor is surely not found in the things we can observe—but I think there's more.   Aren't they really the same in that they share 'humanness'?" *Teacher:* "Of course, that's it!"

This little incident does get us thinking about the idealist's assumptions concerning basic reality.   We must penetrate the level of physical and even sociocultural "accidents," for beyond these phenomena lie the ideas (or forms) which give every existent (existing) thing its meaning, its being.   Every human being finds its deepest reality in the idea of humanness which is "objectified"[2] in a specific being whom we can describe.   Every dog, from Spot to Ch. Natasha Tchumi of Lagunita, finds its meaning in the idea of—dogginess (?).   These ideas, then, are the archetypes of existents.   Without them, we cannot

---

[2] Horne writes of the painting as it "objectifies the thought, feeling, and purpose of the artist" in "An Idealist Philosophy of Education," *Philosophies of Education,* The Forty-First Yearbook of the National Society for the Study of Education, Part I, ed. Nelson B. Henry (Bloomington, Ill.: Public School Publishing Company, 1942), p. 143.

really understand the meaning of any existent. No important knowledge is possible. We are "put off" by surface accidents, phenomena which modern man delights in sensing and quantifying.

The idealist goes beyond these immaterial ideas and holds that they as well as their objectifications in the natural world are creations or "thoughts" of a purposeful, spiritual energy. Here, both immanent and transcendent, is found the basic reality we have been seeking. In holding that this reality must be of the nature of mind, the idealist argues that matter is inanimate and object; only in living mind as subject can we find the creative principle. In attempting to communicate about this creative, spiritual reality, the idealist has used several expressions. For example, he has also referred to "absolute Self" which encompasses individual human selves. The human self is the essence of a person, his center of consciousness and personality, and the "cause" of his material body in the natural order. Finally, he has spoken of a personal Ultimate Being. In all he has referred to the realm of permanence, order, certainty—eternal life.

Note that most idealists do not claim that the things of this world are *without* reality, but only that their deepest reality, the source of their creation and the key to their ultimate meaning and purpose, is to be found only in the realm of spirit. Nor is there complete agreement among idealists as to the nature of the spiritual. Many hew to the notion that Absolute Mind as the All includes human minds which are at one and the same time both individual and united with the All. Others suggest that Absolute Mind is an expression which refers to the sum total of individual minds. Absolute Mind is, as it were, a community of minds. And, finally, there are those who see the notion of Absolute Mind as so basic that individual minds have little reality other than as a momentary, transitory expression of the Absolute. In harmony with the Hindu tradition, at death that energy which is the human mind-soul simply returns to the source of all being (in Hindu terms, the "brahman"[3]).

C. BASIC REALITY: THE EXPERIENCE OF INDIVIDUALS-IN-SOCIETY.

The key to understanding the pragmatist's assumptions concerning basic reality is to be found in his doctrine of "experience." Conceived as a thoroughly naturalistic phenomenon, experience includes both those accidental and planned encounters between all objects in the environment through which each is defined, ordered and given meaning. It includes the relationships created in these encounters, as well as the processes by which they develop. Antecedent to the

[3] For comments on the "brahman principle" see Frederic Spiegelberg, *Living Religions of the World* (Englewood Cliffs, N.J.: Prentice-Hall, Inc., 1956), pp. 13, 29, 30, 35, 50, 147–148 and 153.

definition of both physical and mental phenomena—to the very definition of both self (that with which the organism identifies) and nonself (or the other)—experience stands as the flowing, dynamic totality
of all events and reference points upon which man would impose
order and meaning as he feels, thinks and acts. The pragmatist does
not deny that a more ultimate reality—be it material or immaterial,
personal or mechanistic—*may* lie behind human experience. He does
assert, however, that the human being can know things only through
their relationships with other things and as filtered through or colored by his assumptions. In this regard, Lawrence G. Thomas writes,

> *Any inquiry into the nature of an object requires explicit refer-*
> *ence to surrounding conditions, including the perceiving ob-*
> *server. The nature of the object consists of the relationships*
> *which both connect it to, and distinguish it from, the perceiving*
> *subject and other perceived objects in the environment. Simi-*
> *larly, any inquiry into the nature of the subject's self requires*
> *explicit reference to surrounding conditions. His selfhood con-*
> *sists of relationships with environments of the past, present, and*
> *anticipated future. In short, when the ultimate nature of one's*
> *self and one's environment is sought, the experimentalist finds*
> *that they dissolve into relationships within the flow of experi-*
> *ence.*[4]

Change is clearly the keynote of the pragmatic conception of reality.
As we define ourselves and the other, we must be aware that an
object is never just what our senses suggest it is; rather, even in the
making, it is the sum total of the meanings attributed to it by man in
specified contexts of time and place. The pragmatist advises us to
approach terms such as "truth," "value"—or "man"—as useful, but
limited, generalizations of our experience. He advises us to consider
human progress as possible but not guaranteed, and existence, determined largely by human purposes, as orderable but not already
ordered.

The traditional metaphysician is generally troubled by this conception of basic reality. We hear him murmuring, "But what of the
lawful reality lying behind our changing experience? What of the
Maker of the object to which the pragmatist secondarily attributes
meaning? What of that spiritual energy which is the essence of all
existents? What, in short, is *ultimate* reality?" For at least two
reasons, the pragmatist must admit his inability to deal with these
questions.[5] In the first place, the undifferentiated state referred to as

[4] Lawrence G. Thomas, "The Ontology of Experimentalism," *Educational Theory,*
VI (July 1956), p. 180.
[5] See Thomas's "The Ontology of Experimentalism" upon which this point, indeed
this entire section, is based.

"experience" is held to be prior to the emergence of both self-conscious subjects and objects of knowledge. How then, the pragmatist asks, can one possibly inquire into its nature when one cannot have access to the reports of a conscious observer, including specifications of his time, place and assumptions? Secondly, the empirical method deals only with *perceived* reality. We may well speculate about the nature of a reality beyond empirically explorable events. We may well inquire into the consistency or inconsistency of an hypothesis drawn from such speculation with similar hypotheses or that which we know through empirical investigation. Such speculation and inquiry, moreover, are scarcely meaningless in man's quest for meaning. Nevertheless, no hypothesis concerning a possible unperceived reality can be asserted as empirically true or false. And the pragmatist contends that most knowledge claims must rest on the proper employment of the experimental mode of knowing.

An adequate development of the ways in which man may gain that knowledge of reality open to him must necessarily await an extended discussion of the pragmatist's epistemological assumptions. Nevertheless, it should be pointed out that his metaphysical assumptions fail to reduce him to despair. The transactional relating of objects in experience provides a rich source of knowledge, however relative to the context (or situation of people, place and time) in which it is constructed. Regulated human experience itself, rather than obedience to *a priori* laws or a supernatural lawgiver, is our authority for assertions about reality. While eschewing overconfidence, the pragmatist holds considerable hope for an authority which is open and checkable rather than one restricted to a golden elite or to the solitary individual.

D. BASIC REALITY: THE EXPERIENCE OF THE SOLITARY INDIVIDUAL. In order to bring into some focus existentialistic assumptions concerning basic reality, let us imagine the following incident. Suddenly, with no warning, you find yourself in an utterly unfamiliar setting. Every aspect of this experience is utterly without meaning. It is just "there"—as you are "there." How are you to relate to this "is"? How are you even to begin? But that *is* the beginning! *YOU ARE!* You *exist;* that, if only that, is certain. And in a basic sense the decisions, the choices you make will create the meaning and, hence, for all practical purposes the "reality" of existents in that situation.

Is it surprising that waves of fear and trembling sweep over the solitary individual now realizing the extent of his responsibility? He cannot *refuse* to choose, for that itself would be a choice, a choice engendering increasing guilt and meaninglessness. And yet *to choose* is fraught with risks, danger, insecurity. Creating meaning, the self-operating-in-the-cosmos-of-choice will necessarily limit his own possibilities. The "created" will press in upon him; their demands and his necessary responses in a communal world will make it ever more difficult for him to continue to build and express himself. Given no prior assurances of a friendly cosmic scheme, no assurances that it values and needs him, filled with anxiety, increasingly aware of his imperfections and the certainty of death, he may retreat into despair. He may, on the other hand, summon that kind of courage born of facing things-as-they-are and accept the dangerous challenges of becoming.

2. Human Nature

A. HUMAN NATURE: INHERENTLY EVIL OR PREDISPOSED TO EVIL. Deeply engrained in occidental thinking is the notion that man is by nature either evil or at least predisposed to do evil. For example, even Plato could not always avoid the suspicion that evil is deeply rooted in the natural order, that "evils . . . can never be done away with, for the good must always have its contrary; nor have they any place in the divine world, but they must needs haunt this region of our mortal nature."[6]

The Judaeo-Christian tradition has added much to this living assumption concerning human nature. Original Man was created in the image of God, in that he was given the spiritual powers of thought, communication and self-transcendence. Turning away from his filial obedience to God, however, he committed Original Sin. Bowie writes, "The image of God in him was blurred and broken and could only be restored by a long process of redemption."[7] Two traditions concerning this experience are of import to our account. One, generally found in Aquinas and the later Catholic tradition, suggests that man's choice of pride-based disobedience did not result in God's simply destroying the nature which he had infused into man. Rather, He but removed certain special gifts which man had been given in light of his relationship to God. No longer could man depend upon an inborn immortality, a natural submission of his body to his soul's reason and will, or automatic faith and prudence. Nevertheless, however predisposed to continue his disobedience, to do evil, he still retained his original human nature and with it the potential power to cooperate with God in the process of redemption. The second tradition suggests that man's very nature was so corrupted by Original Sin as to leave

[6] Plato, *Theaetetus*, p. 176.
[7] Walter Russell Bowie, "Exposition," Book of Genesis, *The Interpreter's Bible*, Vol. I (Nashville: Abingdon Press, 1952), p. 485.

him with but an empty outline of God's image. Man, so conceived, is terribly weakened. Sin and passive acceptance of God's judgment are his usual lot.

St. Augustine and Calvin seem to have sided with the second or more extreme tradition. Few would argue that their thought has had anything but a massive impact on the American culture. Wolfe adds that this tradition is also deeply rooted in the thought of the nonreligious West, being reflected, for example, in the writings of Machiavelli, Thomas Hobbes, Darwin and Freud.[8] We see this position expressed, however extremely, by Cardinal Lothario de' Conti who was later to become Pope Innocent III (the Great) in A.D. 1198. Cardinal de' Conti writes:

> *Man is made of dust, of mud, of ashes; worse yet, of the foulest seed; conceived in the itch of the flesh, in the heat of passion, in the stench of lust; and worse, in the depths of sin; born to labor, to dolor, to horror; more miserable still, to death. He acts wickedly, offending God, offending his neighbor, offending himself; he acts infamously, polluting fame, polluting conscience, polluting character; he acts vainly, neglecting the serious, neglecting the useful, neglecting the necessary. He is food for fire ever blazing and burning unquenched; food for worms, ever gnawing and eating without end; a mass of putrescence, ever noisome and horribly foul.*[9]

Given either alternative tradition, however, natural man is in trouble. The contemporary idealist, J. Donald Butler, states the case succinctly:

> *Idealists are not romantically blind to the fact that in actuality men are guilty of all kinds of evils, great and small. Left to themselves without some higher guidance men are pretty sure to produce and involve themselves in all kinds of moral difficulties. While man is intended for goodness and godliness, he more easily gives himself to activities which fall far short of these high ends, if they are not outright contradictions of them. It is apparent that he needs to be allied to a sustaining power not in himself alone in order for him to fulfill his true purpose.*[10]

In fact, orthodox Christian thought—whether idealistic, realistic, neo-Thomistic or even existentialistic in its philosophical expression—has often been drawn to this assumption. Its effect on American education throughout the centuries has been incalculable.

[8] See Don M. Wolfe, *The Image of Man in America.* 2nd ed. (New York: Thomas Y. Crowell Company, 1970), pp. 7–8.

[9] Cardinal Lothario de' Conti, *De Contemptu Mundi, sive De Miseria Conditionis Humanae Libri Tres,* Migne *Patrologia Latina,* **CCXVII,** Paris, 1889, Columns 701–46, I:1; quoted in Radoslav A. Tsanoff, *The Nature of Evil* (New York: The Macmillan Company, 1931), pp. 48–49.

[10] Butler, *Four Philosophies,* pp. 234–235.

B. HUMAN NATURE: INHERENTLY GOOD. A second assumption holds that by nature man is good—that his original instincts predispose him to do the good, the right, the noble. For many thinkers, exposed to the Christian tradition, it was inconceivable that man created in the image of God could be otherwise. "Morality, compassion, generosity," wrote Thomas Jefferson to Dupont de Nemours, "are innate elements of the human constitution."[11] Evil does exist in the world, but it is explainable on natural grounds. Man's given nature must be protected and nurtured if it is not to be corrupted by environmental pressures.

Although not foreign to the thought of earlier writers such as Cicero and Plutarch, Arminius and Milton, this assumption reached our shores during the time of the American Enlightenment. Not only Jefferson, but Emerson, Whitman, Channing and Alcott were drawn to this more gentle view of man's natural endowment. And their thought was of great importance to the cultural milieu out of which rose the reformist "Common School Movement."

As nineteenth century American educators began traveling and studying in Europe, they observed the outworking of this assumption in the schools of pedagogues such as Pestalozzi and Froebel both of whom had been highly influenced by the earlier Rousseau. Froebel, for instance, likened the child to a seed whose natural destiny is to germinate, grow and flower according to Divine plan.[12] Much can interfere with this natural course of events; hence, the teacher must assume the role of the "good gardener" who cultivates, waters and protects the organism against the elements. One such American educator was Colonel Francis Wayland Parker (1837–1902) whom Dewey referred to as "more than any other person . . . the father of the progressive educational movement."[13] Parker's position on human nature was quite directly expressed at the 1889 meeting of the National Education Association: "Tell me, tell me not," he writes, "that the Divine is not in every child. God made the child and put his sweetness and light and love in its heart, and it is our duty, the most important of all duties, to discover, direct, and develop it."[14] In spite of the opposition of Dewey whose thought was much more influenced by the New (experimental) Science, this assumption entered the

[11] Letter of 1816 from Thomas Jefferson to Dupont de Nemours; quoted in Edward Boykin, ed., *The Wisdom of Thomas Jefferson* (Garden City, N.Y.: Garden City Publishing Co., Inc., 1943), p. 40.

[12] See Robert Rusk, *Doctrines of the Great Educators.* 4th ed. (New York: St. Martin's Press, 1969), pp. 270ff.

[13] John Dewey, "How Much Freedom in New Schools?" *New Republic,* **LXIII,** No. 814 (July 9, 1930), p. 204.

[14] Francis W. Parker, "The Child," *N.E.A. Journal of Proceedings and Addresses,* Session of the Year 1889 (Nashville, Tenn.), p. 480.

Progressive Education Movement to find the strongest expression in the writings of leaders such as William Kilpatrick and Harold Rugg. Shaken by three-quarters of a century of near-constant war, it still is echoed in the liberal faith that a people freed from the crushing social pressures of poverty and alienation will grow as naturally themselves as they will contribute to the growth of the society as a whole.

C. HUMAN NATURE: INHERENTLY SUPERIOR OR INFERIOR. According to S. Samuel Shermis, a third assumption concerning human nature is to be found on the American Scene. Sometimes described as the assumption of "two essences,"[15] it, like the two preceding, is classical or traditional in that human nature is a given which provides the boundaries within which the details of human existence are to be worked out. The human minority is fitted with one (a superior) nature and the majority with another (an inferior) nature. Shermis points out that Plato and Aristotle offered this theme to Western thought. Plato, for example, points out that people are born with innate capacities which fit them for different occupations. Philosopher-kings are born with the virtue of wisdom; the guardians, with courage; the farmers and artisans with temperance. All three groups with their associated virtues are necessary to the well-being of the state.[16] Aristotle follows Plato's preference for wisdom, suggesting,

> *The rule of the soul over the body, and of the mind and the rational element over the passionate, is natural and expedient; whereas the equality of the two or of the inferior is always hurtful. . . . [In like measure] for that some should rule and others be ruled is a thing not only necessary but expedient; from the hour of their birth, some are marked out for subjection, others for rule.*[17]

In the American experience, superiority and inferiority have found several definitions. One such definition assuredly rests on the fact of sex.[18] We read of gross economic discrimination against women. A woman college graduate, for instance, earns about the same as a man with an eighth grade education. In 1968, women (who held forty-two percent of all jobs) constituted approximately nine percent of all full

[15] See S. Samuel Shermis, *Philosophic Foundations of Education* (New York: American Book Company, 1967), pp. 206–207. Shermis provides an excellent treatment of this assumption. Additional examples may be given, but his basic outline must be taken as a model.

[16] Plato, *Republic*, ii, 367E–327A and iv, 427C–434D.

[17] Aristotle, *Politics*, i., p. 5.

[18] The statistics which follow are gleaned from Senator George McGovern's remarks concerning "Equal Rights for Women," as included in the U.S. *Congressional Record*, 92nd Cong., 1st Sess., 1971, Vol. 117, No. 109.

professors, seven percent of all physicians, three percent of all lawyers, one percent of Federal judges, and one percent of the U.S. Senate. Most Americans are well aware of the prejudice facing a woman who chooses not to marry or to combine marriage with a career. At best pregnancy is equated with "illness." Worse, we are increasingly conscious of how very difficult it is for a woman in our culture even to become aware that there *are* viable alternatives to traditional patterns.

With regard to the intelligence factor, we may turn to the late eighteenth century writings of Samuel Williams, Hollis Professor of Mathematics and Natural Philosophy at Harvard. Williams writes, "To some the Author of Nature has assigned superior powers of mind, a strength of reason and discernment, a capacity for judging, and a genius of invention not given to others."[19]   G. Max Wingo also comments on our tendency to define inferiority or superiority as the basis of intelligence. Noting the difficulties traditionalists face in speaking to problems caused by our national commitment to mass education, he attempts to hypothesize a possible classical answer, writing:

> *Why do we not admit that a substantial part of the population is simply uneducable in any real sense of the word* educate *and shape our plans accordingly? This would mean giving up the peculiarly American sentiment of equalitarianism and all the havoc it has created in American education. As Mr. Albert J. Nock observed a generation ago, our educational system rests on three false premises: equality, democracy, and the belief that the literate society is the good society. It follows that any theory of education derived from these false ideas is itself bound by logical necessity to be false.*
>
> *Conservatives who follow this line of thought are apparently convinced that humanity is composed of three groups: a relatively small group of the talented, a larger middle stratum of moderately intelligent people who are able and willing to accept the leadership and authority of the elite, and at the lowest level a great mass of people who may with great effort be capable of simple literacy but very little beyond that. The great error of egalitarian educational ideals lies in failing to take account of these ineradicable differences.*[20]

Americans are no less familiar with the argument which assigns superiority or inferiority on the basis of race. Red man, black man, yellow man—all have had their day. Race is the factor which basically determines behavior; here are the determined limits for human

[19] Samuel Williams, *The Natural and Civil History of Vermont* (Walpole, N.H., 1794), I, ixff *et passim;* quoted in Merle Curti, *Human Nature in American Historical Thought* (Columbia, Mo.: University of Missouri Press, 1968), p. 57.

[20] G. Max Wingo, *The Philosophy of American Education* (Boston: D. C. Heath and Co., 1965), p. 109.

action. Such arguments have forceful precedent in American thought. Although both called for equality of rights, it was Lincoln who guardedly conceded the inferiority of the black,[21] and it was Jefferson—reluctantly and desirous of finding contradicting evidence—who suggested that the black was "innately deficient in the powers of abstract reasoning."[22]

Given our contemporary difficulties with desegregating education, it is interesting to note that Jefferson associates inferiority by race with inferiority by reasoning. As the most superficial observer of the American scene will note, this tradition still lives. In a recent journal article, for instance, a black educator rails against the common assumptions that ability to learn is relatively fixed, unchangeable, predetermined by heredity and—with reasonable accuracy—measurable by current intelligence tests.[23] He writes:

> These pervasive and outmoded assumptions have led to unfortunate practices in our schools. Ethnic minority youths are often placed in low academic tracks, classified as mentally retarded, and exposed to unstimulating educational environments because they perform poorly on I.Q. and other tests which were standardized on a white middle-class population. These practices result in the self-fulfilling prophecy: Teachers assume that these pupils cannot learn, and they do not learn because teachers do not create the kinds of experiences which will enable them to master essential understandings and skills.[24]

D. HUMAN NATURE: CONSTRUCTED AND EVALUATED TRANSACTIONALLY. For the pragmatist, as for other philosophical and scientific relativists,[25] man's human nature does not exist as a "given" or an "essence" within which he can only work out the secondary details of his existence. The "normal" organism, born with but a handful of brute constitutional needs (e.g., his need for sustenance) and "plastic" genetic limitations, is itself the given. His nature—i.e., the habitual ways in which he meets the possibilities presented by his constitutional needs and genetic limitations, his acquired desires and the impact of others—is constructed through transactions between the organism and

---

21 Wolfe, *The Image of Man in America*, p. 105.

22 Curti, *Human Nature in American Historical Thought*, p. 45.

23 James A. Banks, "Imperatives in Ethnic Minority Education," *Phi Delta Kappan*, LII, No. 5 (January 1972), p. 269; quotes arguments summarized in Wilbur B. Brookover and Edsel L. Erickson, *Society, Schools, and Learning* (Boston: Allyn and Bacon, Inc., 1969), p. 3.

24 Banks, "Imperatives in Ethnic Minority Education," p. 269.

25 See Curti, *Human Nature in American Historical Thought*, Ch. III ("The Commitment to Scientific Explanation"); also Wolfe, *The Image of Man in America*, pp. 9–11 *et passim* (the "plastic" theories of human nature).

other objects within experience. In turn, the specific behavioral habits which constitute his nature—in themselves morally neutral—are evaluated as good or evil by men in social groupings.

In all, we must remember that man's nature at a given point in time is a product of ever-changing experience. He has developed-learned certain habits in order to solve certain problems. As experience continues to ebb and flow, many new problems will call for varying degrees of modification-adjustment in his behavioral patterns. To the extent that man courageously and intelligently faces up to these new demands, we must expect to see both continuities and change in his nature. At this point the pragmatist refuses to be either pessimistic or optimistic. The force of learned habits must not be underestimated. Indeed, as Dewey points out, many of the arguments for fixed human nature are based on the observable resistance of ingrained habits to change.[26] It *is* possible to reconstruct experience, and such reconstruction is really the only alternative to increasing individual and societal impotence. Nevertheless, men demonstrably often fail to meet the changing demands of experience. To the extent that the pragmatist holds a general assumption about "evil," one important facet must involve a conscious unwillingness to face the challenge of modifying one's habits when intelligence deems change to be necessary.

Finally, it must be emphasized that one's nature is developed in a social setting, in the setting of experiential transactions. We are as influenced by the impact of the other as the other is by us. If in a communal setting we are to minimize expected pressures toward "other-directedness,"[27] man has no choice but to stress interpersonal inquiry into both the desirability of given habit changes and the means necessary to bringing them about. To suggest that the solitary individual is capable of resisting these pressures is utterly out of keeping with twentieth century realities.

E. HUMAN NATURE: CONSTRUCTED AND EVALUATED INDIVID-UALISTICALLY. One is tempted to treat existentialistic assumptions concerning the nature of human nature in much the same vein as the position labeled "constructed and evaluated transactionally" has been treated. There are, after all, strong and inescapably transactional elements in both the "I-It" and "I-Thou" relationships dis-

---

[26] John Dewey, "Does Human Nature Change?" *Problems of Men* (New York: Philosophical Library, Inc., 1946), p. 190.

[27] A term used by the social scientist David Reisman in *The Lonely Crowd: A Study of the Changing American Character* (New Haven: Yale University Press, 1950); refers to the increasing tendency among the middle class to look to the peer group (rather than parental and other traditional sources) for behavioral norms.

cussed in the literature of Existentialism. Nevertheless, there is also an inescapably individualistic emphasis in this same literature which suggests that a separate development of this assumption is not without justification.

In agreement with the assumption that human nature is "constructed and evaluated transactionally," the existentialist sees one's human nature, one's essence, to be ever in the making. The individual is not born with a given essence common to all men and then expected to work out his existence within these bounds. Rather, one is simply *born*—that is the given. The fact that there may be brute constitutional needs or genetic limitations is of far less importance than is the meaning given to these factors by the individual. The prime human task lies in *creating* our full human reality—our nature, if you will—through choice and action. The task, needless to say, is somewhat more difficult than the saying.

As indicated in treating existentialistic assumptions concerning basic reality, the individual is free to create an "authentic"[28] or meaningful essence, though he must do so in the face of difficulties not completely of his own making. A growing realization of his own finitude, his full responsibility for choice, the lack of inherent meaning in brute experience and his sense of alienation in such a world, cause no little anguish. As choices are in fact made, other existents, personal relationships, social institutions and his own evolving essence are given meaning and objective status. To employ the common existential terminology, "facticities" of living press in upon him from every side and make increasingly more difficult the generation and choosing of "possibilities" opened through experience. And yet it is the very nausea born of this tension between possibility and facticity which may spur the individual to overcome his anxiety and determine to give direction and meaning to his life.

Determination in itself, however, is scarcely enough. The individual still faces the excruciatingly difficult task of working out his individual selfhood in a world now including the inescapable and limiting Other (i.e., all that is not self). To make matters even more difficult, working out a meaningful relationship with the Other looms as a necessary (though not sufficient) step in building one's own

[28] "Authenticity" is a key concept in existentialistic thinking. The primary attributes of the authentic man include: 1) a positive acceptance of the fact of constant change in himself and the Other; 2) an awareness of his freedom and capacity to mold facticity; 3) a commitment to self-knowledge and full self-actualization; 4) constant involvement in constructing and reconstructing his own being in the light of facticity and possibility; and 5) acceptance of personal responsibility for his actions. *Cf.* Mitchell Bedford, *Existentialism and Creativity* (New York: Philosophical Library, 1972), pp. 313–314.

essence. The issue centers on whether the Other will be a stumbling block or a partner in this process. Existentialistic literature tends to emphasize the Other-as-limitation. In fear or out of a convulsive spasm of self-affirmation, we tend to turn the Other into an object or thing. We keep him at arm's length; we use him for our purposes and, as Edgar Z. Friedenberg suggests, once having used him we discard him as we would a soiled Kleenex.[29] The possibilities opened through these relationships often go unrealized, for such contact strikes but to the periphery and not to the heart of being. Then, too, like tends to beget like; defenses raised by being used may take the form of using others. An alternative to this position *is* found in existentialistic literature. For example, the Jewish existentialist Martin Buber affirms that authentic living demands that man take the risk inherent in human contact and open his innermost being to the Other. He must see the Other as itself a free subjectivity, encountering it as it is itself rather than looking down on it as if it were an object for conquest and possession. In such an interactive, nonparasitic, inter-subjective relationship, each organism may find richer possibilities for, and fewer limitations to, self-development.

Interaction or no, however, the quest for meaning is still essentially the responsibility of the solitary human being. The products of either the "I-It" or former relationship with the Other or the "I-Thou" or latter relationship must still be freely rejected by the individual or freely accepted and used to fire the lifelong quest for self-development.

3. Free Will and Determinism

A. FREE WILL AND DETERMINISM: THE FREE SELF. Well-grounded in American culture is the assumption that a human being can never be simply a cog in a thoroughly machinelike universe, that his dignity as a human being rests on his possessing the freedom to transcend the determinisms of the ordinary world.[30] Those who so accent the freedom of the self, however, are *not* arguing for a complete absence of determinism in the natural world. Indeed, the world —be its ultimate essence physical or spiritual or whatever—is generally characterized by order. Causal factors do generally result in predictable effects. Most human action is simply unconscious and follows

[29] Edgar Z. Friedenberg, *Coming of Age in America* (A Vintage Book; New York: Random House, 1963), p. 240.

[30] B. F. Skinner's *Beyond Freedom and Dignity* (New York: Alfred A. Knopf, 1971) provides a thorough treatment of, and argument against, this assumption.

the dictates of instinct or acquired habit. In this realm there is little human control and, hence, little moral responsibility.

The assumption of the free self involves several positive facets. In the first place, man possesses the freedom of "inner assent." He is free to refuse to certify an action as moral—to inwardly, consciously refuse to accept it (to take responsibility for it as his own). True, he may be externally compelled to take the action—but under such conditions he is not morally responsible for it nor is his freedom violated. Man's experience with torture, concentration camps and "brainwashing" testify to the possibility of his being "in this world but not of it." Secondly, and perhaps more important to this assumption, man possesses the freedom at crucial turning points in the development of his self or personality to stand against natural determiners and assert what he will be. Man *as man* intuitively knows that he possesses this freedom; the feeling of exercising it is so intense and unforgettable as to prove its reality.

For a free choice to be made, man must consciously become as aware as possible of the causal factors predisposing him to certain courses of action, the moral quality of these actions and his own intentions in terms of what he desires to be. Equipped with such awareness, he is capable of choosing either to act contrary to the causal factors or to identify alternative behaviors each of which would "satisfy" the causal determiners and then choose the alternative which he judges best.

If the former, more extreme course is chosen, this assumption holds that our willful interference with the cause-effect chain does not cause chaos in the natural order. "Statistical generalizations will still give us rules that can be used to bring about social regulation."[31] In one sense, the human being has injected his own will as a causal determiner in the natural order. Here the self is far more than a mere mediator of causes external to himself. Then, too, we must remember that the very concept of "determination" is of human making. H. H. Horne writes:

> *Man may seek to convince himself by scientific ratiocination that he is not a free moral agent, but his sense of being such remains with him nevertheless. Man denies his own freedom through some concept of his own, like determinism, mechanism, causation, and the like. But these concepts were devised by man to assist him in understanding and in controlling for his own purposes the course of nature. They are themselves the evidence of man's mental creative freedom. Man shows his freedom in applying his own concept of determination to his own*

[31] John L. Mothershead, Jr., *Ethics; Modern Conceptions of the Principles of Right* (New York: Holt, Rinehart and Winston, Inc., 1955), p. 61.

behavior; he does not have to do so; he does so because he wills to do so.[32]

In any case, this assumption holds that were *all* human behavior predictable on environmental, physiological or psychological bases, man could not possibly be held morally responsible for his actions. Reason and experience, let alone authority and revelation, tell us that this state of affairs would be impossible.

Idealists commonly accept this assumption; indeed, their beliefs in the primacy of spirit and the human self as both an expression of Absolute Mind-Self and the prime reality of the self in the natural order would seem to require it. Many theistic realists also accept it. And finally, with some variation from the account presented above, it stands as a central assumption of Existentialism.

Each individual, suggests the existentialist, has absolute freedom. Not that this extreme statement is taken lightly: the existentialist is well aware of the many pitfalls open to the individual who would exercise his freedom. As we have seen, limiting factors may arise out of the realities of man's alienation from the world into which he has been thrust or out of the meanings he has assigned both to himself and the Other. If man so chooses, despair and facticity can paralyze his choosing and hence his freedom. How many test scores, how many parents or administrators, how many "moral standards" have been blamed for personal failure when in fact the failure was really occasioned by the individual's choosing to accept the determiner as absolute? The man who would strive for a meaningful life, an authentic life, must take a quite different course, choosing courage rather than despair, *himself* rather than the pallid image of himself reflected in the eyes of the world. In retrospect, failure will often be seen to have been but one of several possibilities. The very choosing of a goal will be seen to have illuminated new means by which the possibility of success was first glimpsed and then actualized. For the existentialist, then, it is in a conscious choosing which transcends despair and facticity alike that man becomes aware of and exercises his freedom, gains a measure of dignity and joy, and fashions a life of meaning out of the raw materials of meaninglessness.

B. FREE WILL AND DETERMINISM: BASIC DETERMINISM. For those who assume that man's actions are basically determined (e.g., most pragmatists and many realists), the notion of the "free self" appears prescientific, understandable—and unfortunate. For millennia,

---

[32] H. H. Horne, "An Idealist Philosophy of Education," *Philosophies of Education,* ed. Nelson B. Henry, p. 148.

we in the Occident have assumed that *man to be man* must possess the freedom to stand apart from and above the world of nature. If not, he is just so much more matter—an animal—surely not "human." We have said this and written this so often that it has become indigenous to Western thought. But is it true?

The assumption of basic determinism holds that views of man as having the power to make choices unrelated to antecedent factors in his background are clearly mistaken. This position is buttressed with evidence from many studies, particularly in the behavioral, life, natural and social sciences. Skinner sketches the nature of the assumption with clarity and precision, writing:

> *The hypothesis that man is not free is essential to the application of the scientific method to the study of human behavior. The free inner man who is held responsible for the behavior of the external biological organism is only a prescientific substitute for the kinds of causes which are discoverable in the course of a scientific analysis. All these alternative causes lie outside the individual. The biological substratum itself is determined by prior events in a genetic process. Other important events are found in the nonsocial environment and in the culture of the individual in the broadest possible sense. For them he is not responsible, and for them it is useless to praise or blame him. It does not matter that the individual may take it upon himself to control the variables of which his own behavior is a function or, in a broader sense, to engage in the design of his own culture. He does this only because he is the product of a culture which generates self-control or cultural design as a mode of behavior. The environment determines the individual even when he alters the environment.*[33]

The commentary which follows will deal with several points raised by Professor Skinner's summary.

The assumption of basic determinism admits that instances of human choosing—as in the case with *all* human behavior—are caused, i.e., they are determined by the combined effect of all factors associated with a given choice. In turn, however, many determinists point out that human choices are themselves one of the important causal factors which determine resultant behavior. Indeed, as Thomas notes, they can be especially powerful factors

> *when the external compulsions to two or more possible courses of action are approximately balanced. Then, by his ability to think, anticipate the range of probable consequences of each course, and estimate how he will feel in regard to the conse-*

[33] B. F. Skinner, *Science and Human Behavior* (New York: The Free Press, 1953), pp. 447–448.

quences of each, a person develops his own "internal determin-
ism" to a course of action—i.e., he desires one outcome over
another and acts accordingly to the best of his ability.[34]

Consistent with Skinner's terminology, we may hold that the locution
"internal determinism" is somewhat misleading inasmuch as man
engages in thinking, anticipating, estimating, desiring and acting "only
because he is the product of a culture which generates [these activ-
ities]." On the other hand, it seems only reasonable to suggest that
the notion of "balanced compulsions" (a not infrequent occurrence)
does seem to allow for a *certain*—but very important—*kind* of freedom. Here, true, the word "freedom" is used *within* the context of
determinism; it is a "freedom in and among actual events, not apart
from them."[35]   Surely, Thomas's person who can generate more
alternative hypotheses (or plans of action), who can foresee more
consequences of acting on various possibilities and who can estimate
which goals are of longer-term significance to him is more free in this
sense that the student who has not mastered these activities. Skinner
himself suggests that there is a certain kind of freedom in avoiding or
minimizing the effect of aversive stimuli and in arranging "positive
contingencies which have no objectionable by-products," and that "the
student who can do things for himself is independent of others, and
the larger and more effective his repertoire, the freer he is."[36]   Dewey
states this case as follows:

> *It is assumed sometimes that if it can be shown that deliberation*
> *determines choice and deliberation is determined by character*
> *and conditions, there is no freedom. This is like saying that be-*
> *cause a flower comes from root and stem it cannot bear fruit.*
> *The question is not what are the antecedents of deliberation and*
> *choice, but what are their consequences. What do they do that*
> *is distinctive? The answer is that they give us all the control of*
> *future possibilities which is open to us. And this control is the*
> *crux of our freedom. Without it, we are pushed from behind.*
> *With it we walk in the sunlight.*[37]

This line of reasoning also suggests that determinists can give considerable meaning to the notion of "responsibility." Basically, man is
responsible for creating an environment which will generate those

[34] Lawrence G. Thomas, "What Metaphysics for Modern Education?," *The Educational Forum*, VI, No. 2 (January 1942), p. 120.

[35] John Dewey, *Human Nature and Conduct* (New York: Henry Holt and Company, 1922), p. 303.

[36] See B. F. Skinner, *The Technology of Teaching* (New York: Appleton-Century-
Crofts, pp. 172–174.

[37] Dewey, *Human Nature and Conduct*, p. 311.

behaviors which define "freedom"—an environment which in turn will influence him. That he does this by manipulating forces of which his choosing is but a part does not seem any less "dignified" than the intervention of the free self in a natural order of which it is only an "associate member." Dewey outlines this conception of responsibility, writing,

> *Hence responsibility in relation to control of our reactions to the conduct of others is twofold. The persons who employ praise and blame, reward and punishment, are responsible for the selection of those methods which will, with the greatest probability, modify in a desirable way the future attitude and conduct of others. There is no inherent principle of retributive justice that commands and justifies the use of reward and punishment independently of their consequences in each specific case. To appeal to such a principle when punishment breeds callousness, rebellion, ingenuity in evasion, etc., is but a method of refusing to acknowledge responsibility. Now the consequence which is most important is that which occurs in personal attitude: confirmation of a good habit, change in a bad tendency.*
>
> *The point at which theories of responsibility go wrong is the attempt to base it upon a state of things which precedes holding a person liable, instead of upon what ensues in consequence of it. One is held responsible in order that he may become responsible, that is, responsive to the needs and claims of others, to the obligations implicit in his position.*[38]

The determinist suggests that the high status our culture gives to more orthodox conceptions of freedom and responsibility provides part of the answer as to why the science of shaping human behavior remains in its infancy. The determinist prefers a notion of responsibility which rewards the assignment of resources to rehabilitation, to finding ways of permanently modifying behavior rather than merely punishing man for that which he cannot help.

Many contemporary determinists hold that our goal must be to subject human behavior to prediction and control. Contrary to those who confuse "control" with "regimentation," however, they feel in principle that we can define the behaviors which we now only label freedom, individuality or creativity, and then "begin to search for the conditions of which [these behaviors are] a function and design effective instruction."[39] It is true that our knowledge of cause-effect relationships is limited in various ways. For instance, the scientific principle of indeterminancy suggests that:

[38] John Dewey and James H. Tufts, *Ethics*. Rev. ed. (New York: Henry Holt and Company, Inc., 1932), p. 338.
[39] Skinner, *The Technology of Teaching*, p. 184.

> *The very act of observation—made within the dynamic concept of the universe as a whole—changes both the observer and the observed. As Skinner put it in* Science and Human Behavior *(p. 17), if the scientist "chooses to observe one event, he must relinquish the opportunity of observing another." So we are at sea in a shifting, elusive universe, fated to live with the knowable —some indeterminate residue of reality forever beyond our ken.*
>
> *This condition of indeterminancy—paradoxically not incompatible with the postulate of absolute determinism in physical nature—obliges us to accept uncertainty and give up our cherished hope of absolute, certain knowledge. We are consequently obliged to resort to probabilistic reasoning and to deal with observable events in terms of their relative probabilities and of the relative accuracy with which we can predict and control their occurrence.*[40]

It is important not to allow these limitations to paralyze our efforts to shape outcomes in terms of human purposes. In the main, most natural events are probably unpredictable only when regularities in nature go unperceived, when the "novel" first appears in experience in distinguishable form, or when our technology is insufficient to the task of specializing the complex, interacting matrix of involved factors.

Finally, it is important not to allow the preceding discussion to obscure differences between determinists, particularly between individuals such as Dewey and Skinner who have exerted so powerful an influence upon American education. It must be noted, for instance, that as a contemporary figure Skinner is more fearful than the earlier Dewey for the very survival of our culture. He stands ready to place great power in the hands of "scientific managers" who will directly condition those behaviors necessary—in Skinner's view—to ensure that survival. His utopian novel *Walden Two* suggests that doing what is necessary to create individuals who are "automatically good," i.e., who will do the "right" thing without even thinking about it, is a small price to pay for survival.

Dewey, by contrast, reflects the confidence that it is possible to develop habitual behaviors referred to as "rationality" or "reflective intelligence" in most if not all of the citizenry. Admittedly, this position, characteristic of American thought in the earlier decades of this century, is losing some ground in the more tension-ridden America of the 1970s. In Chapter 4 we shall consider these rational habits which collectively are referred to as "mind" in the assumption of mind as purposeful, problem-solving behaviors. For now, it is probably suffi-

---

[40] Mary Jane McCue Aschner, "The Planned Man: Skinner," *The Educated Man: Studies in the History of Educational Thought,* eds. Paul Nash, Andreas M. Kazamias and Henry J. Perkinson (New York: John Wiley & Sons, Inc., 1965), pp. 407–408.

cient to note that Dewey felt it was their development which afforded the only possible hope that man would not only survive, but—more important—that he would survive *well*. After all, procedures involving a weighing of both human purposes and other variables in the specific decision-making situation can be corrected by rational men when ever-changing experience presents new and unfamiliar problems. One wonders whether this possibility is truly open to the man conditioned to react (however effectively) to the survival needs of one particular context of people, place and time.

4. God and Faith

A. GOD AND FAITH: THE ORTHODOX GOD.   It is interesting to note that philosophical Idealism, however unsympathetic to the modern scientific temper, retains a quiet, somewhat "subliminal" vigor in American thought.   Various commentators have suggested that one factor in its continuing cultural influence is to be found in its close affinity with traditional conceptions of God.[41]   An examination of metaphysical assumptions thus far considered lends support to this view.   It is not difficult to find theological parallels in metaphysical assumptions which hold that basic reality is to be found in creative, purposeful, spiritual energy; that in the reality, referred to as Absolute Mind-Self, we find the creative explanation of natural existents; that man shares in this reality (which is both in the natural world and yet transcends it) through his immortal mind-self-soul, although he is distinguishable from it, in part through being temporarily "objectified" in matter; that his natural destiny is to realize a harmony with the Ultimate; or that free will is an appropriate mark of a creature holding such power, position and potential.   On the basis of intuition—buttressed by reputable authority, logical reasoning, observation and revelation—philosophical idealists have generally drawn these parallels and declared their faith in what we may call the "Orthodox God." (It will be noted that the full range of contact between the natural and the supernatural is studied in "theology," a discipline which goes far beyond the metaphysical matters appropriate to this text.)

Given Idealism's natural affinity with the "Orthodox God," one might instinctively posit a natural enmity on the part of Realism.   This would be a serious error.   In fact, the realist's metaphysical assumptions suggest that there is no *necessary* antagonism between the two. For many realists, the notion of natural physical and moral law naturally raises the question of a lawgiver.   Furthermore, it is surely

[41] See Wingo, *The Philosophy of American Education*, pp. 140–141.

demonstrable that man has engaged in religious experiencing over the centuries. The content of that experience has understandably whetted the investigatory interest of many realists. At the very least, the duration, intensity and inclusiveness of this reality suggests that far more is operating than myth alone—however encrusted it may be with myth. Realists from the time of Aristotle to the present have responded to this direct encounter with "something beyond ourselves" with an acceptance of the "Orthodox God." Other realists, it is true, have responded by denying the necessity of such an explanatory principle. Still others have held positions regarding the nature of God (e.g., pantheism, polytheism) which need not concern us at this point, given the delimitation of this text to assumptions more commonly encountered in contemporary American culture. Some have developed humanistic assumptions which will be treated in the next section.

Theistic existentialists such as Kierkegaard, Jaspers, Buber and Tillich have been no less concerned than realists with their direct encounters with the source of being. Generally they have refused to intellectualize the encounter, feeling that in so doing one destroys its essence. Nevertheless, they have suggested that the very possibility of God's existence, pointed to if not proved by man's age-old religious experiencing, justifies the individual's acting "as if" God lives, "as if" God provides the explanatory principle of his being, "as if" God alone can fill the abyss of nothingness. Such a faith reminds man of his responsibility to choose life rather than passivity. The contact of the I and the Eternal Thou, opened by faith, may illuminate possibilities heretofore unperceived. And, finally, this belief guards against the solipsism possible in an extreme Existentialism which sees the very existence of all phenomena as resting on human perception. Be this as it may, the achievement of a true, meaningful humanness is still the supremely religious task of the individual in the present, a task which suggests that historically-based questions about immortality must remain open.

B. GOD AND FAITH: THE HUMANISTIC GOD. In the course of mediating (regulating, giving meaning to) experience, we have seen that pragmatists and other naturalists develop generalizations about themselves and other objects in their life space. If verified in experience, these generalizations serve as resources for later decision-making. As we shall later see, knowledge claims are generally made *only* on the basis of experiential verification. There are several problems in such a position, problems which confront any philosophy which would confine its energies to the natural order. If knowledge claims must generally rest on experiential verification, just how much can we really say we "know"—even in an age of science? Given such limitations, do we really know enough to permit rational action? What of man's age-old attempts to go beyond the limits of such knowledge? Are they irrational—or even immoral?

The pragmatist does in fact appreciate the distinction between "fact" and "belief" (*supra,* Part I, footnote 8). Moreover, in his speculative-synthetic activities, he attempts to relate the two so as to promote a qualitatively richer, more human existence. In so doing, philosophical Pragmatism has necessarily developed several assumptions about the nature of God and faith.

Man, admits the pragmatist, clearly cannot live-act by what he knows alone. His knowledge is far too limited. Man must and does make commitments or acts of faith which go beyond known facts, however much they should be based upon them. Entering the realm of belief, however, we are quickly met by questions concerning the criteria appropriate to rational commitment-making. The pragmatist answers that we must surely assemble those facts which we hypothesize are relevant to the particular decision-making situation. Moreover, we must turn to our ideals. The term "ideal" is associated with an act, object or idea which has been experientially proved to be "valuable" (i.e., worthy of choice and perpetuation) and then assigned even greater and more pervasive importance. This wider import is based on the demonstrated capacity of ideals to make more sensitive our efforts to build meaning in the midst of continual change and to motivate us to better both self and other.[42] Additional import is found in the occasional capacity of an idea (not unlike that of a scientific hypothesis) to illuminate sensory data in ways which afford us perspectives before unexperienced. Ofttimes it is such a vision which facilitates our construction of hypotheses which can be subjected to experimentation and evaluation.

The pragmatist refers to the structure of our ideals very differently: this is what is meant by "God." Here are found man's assembled goods and his efforts to expand them; here, his deepest commitment to the method of free intelligence; here, the security and harmony possible in a world of change. Lawrence G. Thomas presents the pragmatic case in words of near-poetic power:

> *The God-Idea incorporates man's highest ideals. It came out of nature and thus is omnipresent if man will but see. It is omniscient because it symbolizes the ever-evolving ideal of knowledge that man constantly seeks to possess. And a few have learned that it is omnipotent, for once they have pursued this God-Idea, they know with sublime fervor that they need no*

[42] *Cf.* Dewey's discussion of the nature of an ideal in *Ethics,* p. 301.

other goal for their lives. It is man's Purpose of purposes. It is worth defending as any great purpose is worth defending. It is worth criticizing in order that it may truly represent what can be out of what is.[43]

A rational faith built on man's unity with nature, suggests the pragmatist, is "one which most harmoniously embraces his ideals of living in a context which permits his subsequent experience to validate, refine, and reconstruct his present ideals."[44]   That effort is religious which is directed at refining the quality of life in the present, as well as constructing ideals which motivate us to overcome failure and face the reality of insecurity with courage and dignity.   How can such a faith be any less inspiring, any less demanding of reverent effort or any less open to aesthetic celebration than one which places Creation in the past, removes ultimate power from human hands, posits God as an unimprovable Fact and defers man's happiness until his entrance into the *Civitate Dei?* And if at death we rejoin the elements out of which we sprang—if our immortality lies but in the memories of those whom we have touched, helped toward a more abundant life—may we still not cry with Paul, "O death, where is thy victory?   O death, where is thy sting?"[45]

C. GOD AND FAITH: THE DENIAL OF GOD.   As noted in discussing the assumption of the "Orthodox God," there are those realists who feel that matter and associated physical processes offer a quite sufficient explanation of the reality we experience.   Theirs is the world of cosmic and biological evolution, a world explained in terms of natural laws rather than by any form of the God-Idea.   They evidence little willingness to waste time in idle *meta*physical speculation when so many secrets of *physical* nature demand the energy involved in empirical investigation.

The "atheistic" existentialists, including Sartre, Nietzsche and Heidegger, tend to see the God-Idea as being (at the very best) quite dangerous to the human being.   Even to act "as if" there were a God can vitiate the individual's already shaky resolve to choose, hence his freedom, and thus his humanness.   Man must choose to stand up under his own power, build his reality in the face of the world-as-it-is and achieve his justification or worth in his own eyes and through his own efforts.   Too often the God-Idea has but provided man with easy

[43] Lawrence G. Thomas, "The Faith of an Experimentalist," *Harvard Educational Review,* XVIII, No. 3 (Summer 1948), p. 156.

[44] Thomas, "The Faith of an Experimentalist," p. 152.

[45] I Cor. 15:55 (RSV).

reasons, thus excusing him from that personal effort necessary to transcending facticity. In like measure, speculation about future immortality is of far less worth than a unified human response to the present and immediate future.

Let us now turn to a consideration of the role these assumptions can play in shaping educational policies and practices.

3

Metaphysical Assumptions and Educational Possibilities

You will remember from our discussion of the difficulties inherent in inferring practice from theory and the factors which must be considered in arriving at a professional decision (*supra,* pp. 17–21) that there is no *direct* connection between theory and practice. This means that although the educator's philosophical assumptions provide him with one (important) resource for making professional decisions, they cannot in themselves logically or in any other way *determine* what he *should* do in a specific situation. Only the educator can make such a determination. In addition to his own assumptions, he must also consider those of his students, their parents and the wider community, his administrators, and his school and district—as well as those assumptions inherent in the teaching materials with which he must work. Furthermore, he must consider that which we have discussed under the headings of historical, psychological, sociological and "reality" factors.

The commentary which follows, then, is not by way of saying, "If you hold assumption *x,* then you should *y.*" Rather, it is supplied for two more defensible reasons: 1) Out of these studies should come a more conscious, more considered realization of the nature of your *own* philosophical assumptions. Some consideration of how assumptions *might* be operationalized in educational settings may help you to explicate where you yourself stand. On considering what an assumption might look like in practice, for instance, your experience may parallel that of the elementary education major. The story goes that she "just loved" both children and the piano—but when they were put together in student teaching she reacted with a nausea which put Sartre to shame! 2) Once your own philosophical assumptions become more clear, you too will feel the urge to express them in professional practice. You too will face the problem of developing plans of action for specific situations which are as consistent with your assumptions as is possible given other necessary considerations. Hopefully, some imaginative commentary on "assumption-practice consistency" will provide you with possibilities worthy of being considered in your own decision-making.

Let us proceed initially by moving from the several assumptions concerning each metaphysical concept to a development of seemingly consistent educational practices. Be reminded, however, that this is but a starting point. Rarely—if ever—can a professional behavior be explained by reference to a single philosophical assumption. Even in those situations where philosophical assumptions can be inferred to have influenced behavior, this influence seems to be exerted by the interaction of several assumptions and/or by the interaction of assumptions and nonphilosophical factors. In this and other parallel sections of the text, therefore, we must necessarily consider the details of such interaction.

A. Basic Reality

1. Basic Reality: An Orderly, Knowable, Sensible World

In thinking about educational policies and practices consistent with the details of this assumption, the notion of "ordered structure" must surely be of central concern. Does it not seem reasonable, for instance, that we need a curriculum structured to provide for an orderly development of knowledge about the natural reality which we inhabit and which in principle is capable of being known? Does it not seem reasonable to call upon academic specialists to inform us concerning the inherent structure of their disciplines and the order of study which can lead us to understanding their discovered truths? After all, who knows more about the structure or study of mathematics than the mathematician? In like measure, must we not also depend on specialists to inform us of the stages in human maturation and the times at which desired content and skills can be taught most efficiently? These facts appear to be necessary (if not sufficient) to curriculum development by specialists in professional education. The successful curriculum will maximize learning about the natural world by ensuring that its content is both appropriate to the maturational level of the student and consistent with the order in which the content must be studied to produce understanding. It must also provide for the development of those skills prerequisite to continuing the discovery of nature's laws. Finally, it should also lead to greater *joy* in learning. In the last analysis, "joy"—indicated by pleasure and interest—can only be found where effort meets with success and when teacher and student alike are enabled to adjust to reality in a positive and productive manner.

The notion of "ordered structure" also seems to have some application to the strategies and technology available to the educator. If basic reality is orderly, knowable and sensible, we must create educational environments wherein this order can be perceived and generalized. Such perceiving and generalizing would seem to demand emphasis upon an objective study of what *is*, rather than upon subjective reaction. Such concentration would seem to demand an orderly classroom. The tasks of careful perceiving, generalizing and behavioral adjustment to discovered laws appear sufficiently difficult in themselves without adding to their difficulty by allowing constant classroom disruption. In terms of instructional strategies and techniques (i.e., general plans of action and specific ways of implementing them), this assumption would appear to permit *any* approach which aids the student to come to grips with the real world which he inhabits.[46] Lecturing, reading, discussing, experimenting, writing and the use of field trips, programmed materials, audiovisual aids and computer-assisted instruction are *all* possibilities. The more quantifiable the relationship between instructional technique and learning, however, the more it should be encouraged. If, as Thorndike suggested, "whatever exists at all exists in some amount,"[47] hard empirical data but strengthens the reliability of our generalizations of perceived data and inhibits the pollution of what *is* by that which someone wishes *would be*. Thus we see this assumption lending the strongest support to a "science of education," a situation in which teaching and learning variables are controlled so as to maximize learning and allow us to transmit our knowledge of reality to those who would teach. Such a cry is also found in professional situations other than the classroom. For instance, we hear Bobbitt calling for a science of

---

[46] Societal living normally demands that an approach be "legal"; other assumptions often lead educators to demand that the approach also be "morally good." See the assumption of "growth toward an ultimate goal" in Chapter 6.

[47] Edward L. Thorndike, "The Nature, Purposes, and General Methods of Measurements of Educational Products," *The Measurement of Educational Products*, Seventeenth Yearbook of the National Society for the Study of Education, Part II (Bloomington, Ill.: Public School Publishing Company, 1918), p. 16.

educational administration which would allow the administrator to provide the teacher with "detailed instructions as to the work to be done, the standards to be reached, the methods to be employed, and the appliances to be used."[48]

This assumption also suggests possibilities for personal roles, human interrelationships and groupings in the school. Obviously, the teacher bears heavy responsibility for creating the environment discussed immediately above. Just as directly, this assumption suggests something about the arrangement of personnel relationships. The old adage that administrators are in the school to administer, teachers to teach and students to learn reflects one arrangement which has been posited as consistent with the notion of ordered structure. As is the case with any smoothly-running mechanism, e.g., a watch, each part has its (vital) role to play but no part is allowed to interfere with the operation of the others. Finally, it will be remembered that this assumption is often accompanied by demands that a claim to have discovered the natural order of things must be submitted to the empirical test. Indeed, this assumption has provided the school testing movement, especially related to grouping students, with no little philosophical support. Perhaps the flavor of this point can be captured in Lawson's comment that as a human being the student

> requires recognition, success, acceptance, and a certain kind of security. These satisfactions he can find only when confronted with a learning situation that allows him to achieve comparably with his immediate associates and in line with his own peculiar aptitudes and interests. And these latter elements are measurable within ranges of significant statistical validity by use of standardized testing devices, whose results provide the basis for effective planning and guidance as steps toward intelligent grouping.[49]

2. Basic Reality: Creative, Purposeful, Spiritual Energy

Educators who have accepted this view of basic reality have generally supported the notion of a given orderly reality to which the individual must adjust, but have rejected curricula based strictly on the sensible

[48] F. Bobbitt, "Some General Principles of Management Applied to the Problems of City-School Systems," *Supervision of City Schools,* Twelfth Yearbook of the National Society for the Study of Education, Part I (Chicago: University of Chicago Press, 1913), pp. 7–8.

[49] Douglas E. Lawson, "Analysis of Historic and Philosophic Considerations for Homogeneous Grouping," *Change and Innovation in Elementary School Organization,* ed. Maurie Hillson (New York: Holt, Rinehart and Winston, Inc., 1965), p. 58.

world.   In place of such a focus they have maintained that the curriculum must help the student to understand the sensible in terms of the underlying spiritual reality which provides both its cause and its meaning.   The development of such curricula poses no easy task, especially in a materialistic culture set in an age of experimental science.   At first glance it is far easier to deal with the natural order than with a reality which can be glimpsed only in part and then but fleetingly.   Believing that the student must be motivated to discover the spiritual realm in spite of such difficulties, this tradition has laid heavy stress on introducing students to human beings who *have* glimpsed ultimate reality and throughout the ages have served as beacons, guiding their fellow men toward unchanging truth.   Let us walk hand in hand with Plato, they have said—as with other saints and seers—and in the walking catch a glimpse of both the richness of human potential and of the Ultimate.   Let us have a curriculum that stresses the certainties of both man's place in the natural order and his dependence on the supernatural order. Let us sensitize man to the fact that his mind-soul-self is superior to the natural order and capable of influencing it.

Though predicated on a given order, this is necessarily not as "exact," as "quantity-conscious" a curriculum as that proposed by those who see basic reality in the knowable sensible world.   Rather, it is a curriculum that gropes for ultimate meanings behind physical and socioeconomic "accidents" and insists that statistical manipulation can never illuminate the depths or significance of being.   Science *will* be taught, for man *is* a creature of the natural as well as of the supernatural order.   Nevertheless, "scientism" (the belief that science can provide us with an ultimate explanation of our existence) will be resisted.   To de-emphasize literature, the arts, history or man's religious experience is to neglect studies of vital import to man's quest for meaning.

Man's religious experience has, of course, posed difficulties for adherents of this position who are also dedicated to the public school. Factors such as our nation's historic separation of church and state and reality factors such as Supreme Court decisions concerning the place of religion in the public schools have led to positions which can only be described as inconsistent with an assumption of the supremacy of the spiritual.   It is difficult to understand how "teaching 'about' religion"[50] could ever satisfy this assumption—which, of course, only provides one more example of our contention that philosophical assumptions (in themselves) rarely explain professional behaviors.

---

[50] This locution refers to the position that the public school can and should familiarize students with the variety of man's religious experiencing, although it may not directly teach a specific religious creed.

More consistent is the stance taken by church-related schools which often frankly state:

> *No subject can be taught in the totality of its truth if the Creator is ignored or denied. Knowledge is purified by the recognition of God's place in it. . . . All curriculum [at this school] is Christ-oriented. We are aware that merely adding the Bible class to a school does not cause that school to be a Christian School. It is only when each subject is taught from the standpoint of that subject as it relates to the Christian life, that the student can gain a total, well-rounded and useful education.*[51]

The present assumption concerning basic reality suggests possibilities with regard to instructional strategies and the use of technology as it does for the curriculum. Objective tests, for example, may allow quick checks on whether the student is able to recall (not unimportant) facts. Rarely, however, do they encourage the student in his studies to search for the meanings of those facts. Even given our culture's general commitment to mass universal education, it is necessary, therefore, to find *some* place for essay tests and for more intensely personal student-teacher dialogue. Quite possibly, American education can allow these techniques only at crucial points in a course of study when synthesis and significance-seeking are absolutely vital. At the same time, we must not neglect those occasional classroom situations where student insights into the human significance of "facts" simply happen and can be reinforced by the knowledgeable teacher. Everyday lessons in the humanities, science and mathematics, and the arts also provide many opportunities for the teacher to pose significance-seeking questions. They also provide opportunity for the teacher to aid the child vicariously to see a phenomenon through the eyes of human exemplars. The fifth grader, for instance, may be able to understand much more about the meaning of the Civil War by trying to view problems of the time through the eyes of Robert E. Lee and Lincoln than by merely assembling facts about the South's economic investment in slavery or the North's superiority in railroad mileage. To the extent, then, that any instructional strategy, technique or technological device allows us to involve the child in a quest for such meanings, it is surely appropriate. To the extent that it encourages the child to conclude that learning is more a matter of assembling quantifiable facts about the natural world than of seeking the qualitative meanings behind those facts, it is open to question.

Surely, opportunities for meaning-seeking demand order in the classroom. Reaching beyond sensory data is difficult and it is subject to innumerable distractions. Herein the teacher plays a central role.

[51] From the 1971–1972 "Student Handbook" of a Mid-Atlantic church-related school, p. 21.

Perhaps, however, it is not quite the role exemplified by the stereotype of the cool, detached scientific researcher. Rather, there is the flavor of the warmer personal relationship, of subjective encounter, of a less structured "mutual groping toward." Although it is difficult to find words which will capture such a mood, intuition does suggest a difference between it and the former role. The educator must create such a mood in the classroom, the office and the playing field. In part the educator does this by serving as a model of all that is best in humankind. For this if for no other reason, those charged with the education, certification and hiring of educators bear a heavy responsibility. Though couched in the language of a more romantic period, Horace Mann, the leader of public school reform in nineteenth century Massachusetts, expressed this responsibility quite directly:

> The school committee are sentinels stationed at the door of every schoolhouse in the State, to see that no teacher ever crosses its threshold, who is not clothed, from the crown of his head to the sole of his foot, in garments of virtue; and they are the enemies of the human race,—not of contemporaries only, but of posterity,—who, from any private or sinister motive, strive to put these sentinels to sleep, in order that one, who is profane, or intemperate, or addicted to low associations, or branded with the stigma of any vice, may elude the vigilance of the watchmen, and be installed over the pure minds of the young, as their guide and exemplar.[52]

Even more explicit, in terms of the spiritual emphasis of this assumption, are questions appearing in the 1971–1972 application for a faculty position at a Mid-Atlantic religious school. The candidate is required, for example, to respond to problems such as the following:

> Give a concise but adequate statement of your personal relationship with God. Would you take an active part in church work? Have you had any courses in Christian philosophy of education dealing with academic school subjects? Have you had other courses giving specific training for Christian Day Schools? State what you consider to be the important functions of the Christian School and the distinctive characteristics of its educational practice. State how your handling of the subject matter itself in a Christian School would differ from your handling of it in a public school. As a teacher in a Christian School, on what basis would you require obedience of your pupils? Do you subscribe without reservation to our Statement of Faith? Please share your personal convictions as a Christian toward liquor, tobacco, and matters of recreation and entertainment.

[52] Horace Mann, "Fourth Annual Report" (1840); quoted in *The Republic and the School: Horace Mann on the Education of Free Men*, ed. Lawrence A. Cremin, Classics in Education, No. 1 (New York: Bureau of Publications, Teachers College, Columbia University, 1957), p. 52.

Man, then, is more than animal, as reality is more than material. The task of all truly professional educators—administrators, teachers, coaches and counsellors alike—is to motivate the student to gain a personal knowledge of that basic reality which is found in the realm of creative, purposeful spirit.

3. Basic Reality: The Experience of Individuals-in-Society

However dissimilar the details of the first two assumptions concerning basic reality, their agreement that reality *is* a "given"—a sure "something" which man must discover and to which he must adjust—has given rise to suggested policies and practices which in themselves bear a noteworthy similarity. The very notion of a given reality—be it material or spiritual—suggests relative stability in the curriculum; instructional strategies, techniques and technology devised to bring the student to a knowledge of and harmonious relationship with that reality; the teacher acting as an authoritative guide toward reality; and the arrangement of people and institutional components so as to establish harmony with an order where change occurs slowly and then according to pre-established patterns. If, however, we assume that the only knowable reality is man's experience and that change is the keynote of that reality, consistency may well demand a somewhat different set of suggested policies and practices.

In the first place, curricula are likely to be rather short-lived—if we examine the content and skills which carry traditional labels such as "history," "language," "mathematics" and the like. The changing needs of people will continually place new demands upon the school as well as offer new opportunities for service. We are likely to demand an important place for emergent knowledge in the curriculum. History, for instance—even in the elementary school—will be expanded to include the fruits of man's explorations in anthropology, economics, political science, psychology and sociology. A greater place will also be demanded for issues where answers are honestly in doubt—as well as for an explicit examination of the exploratory procedures by which answers can be developed. It does not seem inaccurate to suggest that this assumption demands that problems encountered in the here and now by human beings—most assuredly including school children—must provide the focal point of the curriculum. Neither subject matter nor skill development will be neglected, but the rationale for including specifics in the curriculum will lie in their demonstrated power to provide resources for solving present problems. Their status as part of the "heritage of the race" or the *possibil-*

ity that they will provide a "foundation for later adult responsibilities" are secondary inclusion criteria. Of course, this is not to say that present problems are not found in the aesthetic and religious domains as well as in areas of more narrowly utilitarian concern. In any case, the school's curriculum has a much wider role than merely transmitting knowledge, for it must fit the individual to construct reality within a social milieu.

In terms of strategies and techniques, this assumption seems to suggest a greater accent on problem-solving than it does on fact-discovery and generalization or on significance-seeking per se. Experience is the given, a given which in its ebb and flow continually throws the individual off balance. The task is to help the maturing organism find ways of effectively working through such difficulties, of restoring equilibrium if only momentarily. Given the social "contexts" (situations which can be specified in terms of time, place and people) in which man normally exists from conception to death, this "working through" or restoration necessarily involves others. Indeed, the fact that the problems are both real and the student's lessens the need for an emphasis on external discipline suggested by the first two assumptions. *Involvement* in meeting the problems posed by experience creates a different environment in classroom, office and gymnasium than one where the *imposition* of a pre-existent reality is deemed necessary. Imposition does not appear to be consistent with the assumption under consideration. Rather, the *meaning* of experience in a given situation (or context) must be worked out by those involved.

The leader, having had greater experience in such activity, may properly aid those less experienced in problem definition, assembling resources relevant to the problem at hand, hypothesis development, action, evaluation of action results and generalization of gained knowledge. Nevertheless, the leader is also a member of the group; as such, his status carries no gifts of omniscience, omnipotence or omnipresence.[53] He is in no position to give answers, for the *specific* problem setting is as new to him as it is to the students. (This is to say that the experience he has had in past contexts has given him *resources* for solving problems which appear to be similar to those previously encountered, but offers no *guarantee* that these resources are appropriate or sufficient to solving a problem in a new context.) His task is to assist the child in assigning meanings to present experience which are both satisfying in themselves and yet provide him with resources, skills and motivation prerequisite to meeting the new problems occasioned by solving old ones.

[53] See summary notes on "democratic leadership" in Ralph K. White and Ronald O. Lippitt, *Autocracy and Democracy: An Experimental Inquiry* (New York: Harper & Row, Publishers, Inc., 1960), pp. 26–27.

There is another facet to this task of giving meaning to experience. The goal is neither individual meaning nor societal meaning as such. Once again, basic reality is to be found in the experience of the individual-in-society. As such, its meaning must be true to both the experience of the individual and the group. Let us take the example of a fourth grade class involved in democratically working out behavioral guidelines for its coming field trip. The class will be visiting a nearby Indian mound in order to observe the uncovering of new artifacts. The guidelines developed should be perceived as being as reasonable as possible by each student. Where group decisions must be made which limit individual action, two points must be remembered. In the first place, societal living does often demand group decisions to which the individual's *action* must conform. This does not mean that the individual's view of what is meaningful was necessarily incorrect, nor should he be made to feel that it was. In fact—to carry the point one step further—he should be helped to develop positive ways of influencing group reconsideration. Secondly, inasmuch as "societal living" is not an absolute external standard for judging the correctness of meanings assigned to experience (being, rather, man-made and accepted as necessary on occasion), and inasmuch as experience does change, the majority must learn to appreciate and defend dissent. Small wonder that this assumption supports an open and checkable authority. Small wonder that it cautions against using strategies, techniques or technology merely for the purpose of efficiently ensuring the learning of authority-sanctioned facts or seeking pre-established meanings. In the last analysis, however, specific instructional strategies, techniques and devices are not really in question. The basic concern is that the *results* of any such activity must be viewed as but a first step: a development of resources for cooperative meaning-giving by individuals-in-society. This process is the key to teaching, learning, discipline and even evaluation. It must not be impeded by artificial status hierarchies—all educators and educands must be involved as coparticipants. It must not be hindered by constantly separating individuals into artificial groupings, e.g., those based on "tested intellectual aptitude." Society is demonstrably a heterogeneous thing and needs the open participation of all sorts of people for its health and growth.

4. Basic Reality: The Experience of the Solitary Individual

With its belief that basic reality lies in human experience—albeit the experience of the solitary individual rather than that of an individual much more interrelated with society—we might expect that policy and practice possibilities would bear greater similarity to those just discussed than to those suggested by a given reality to which man must adjust. As we shall see, this does in fact appear to be the case. Where differences occur, they seem to be related to the more individualistic emphasis of Existentialism, which is the school of philosophy most given to this assumption.

The existentialist is generally unimpressed with the value of generalizations, e.g., those concerning the curriculum, for individuals other than those who developed them. Of course, this is not to say that a student could not freely accept a curriculum pattern worked out by someone else; however, if it is imposed on him it will severely limit his possibilities for self-development. When coupled with the notion that human experience is ever-changing, a disdain of fixed curricula reaches monumental proportions. At the very least, this assumption suggests that schools should break up every required course sequence over which they have any control and facilitate the provision of a host of short-term student-developed electives.[54] In the so-called "free schools," of course, one may go even further in blurring the line between traditional subjects. Here the student's choice to engage in activities cutting across several "disciplines" receives its most consistent support. If the high school student, for example, sees a project as properly involving art, history, language and wood shop, this *is* his curriculum for the duration of the project. The school stands ready to help him "do his own thing." If, on the other hand, he chooses to ignore a traditional subject—or to do nothing whatsoever—the educator might first remember that hatred rooted in imposition is not ventilated overnight and then defend his right to choose with vigor even if with personal regret. Only when the student approaches externally imposed (e.g., college entrance) requirements, must the free school make possible more traditional preparation. Even then, as at A. S. Neill's Summerhill, the student is free to choose not to play another's game.

We may also note a curricular emphasis on presenting man as he is. There is no desire, given this assumption, to minimize the difficulties facing man, to idealize his accomplishments or to rationalize his failures. Rather, there is an emphasis on providing a series of direct encounters with himself as well as with the Other, a series of opportunities to find out subjectively what he is instead of what others have made him out to be. This is perhaps another way of saying that the

---

[54] See L. Craig Wilson, *The Open Access Curriculum* (Boston: Allyn and Bacon, Inc., 1971) for a rich variety of curricular suggestions which are generally consistent with this and related assumptions, as well as being appropriate for the public school. The student may also be interested in his telling criticisms of more traditional curricula.

opportunities for the student to give personal meaning to experiences encountered in the curriculum is of greater importance than the content and skills included in the curriculum per se. Finally, there is a curricular emphasis on encouraging the student to make choices for himself—to grasp possibility rather than passively to give way to facticity—choices which are the key to creativity and a growing sense of the meaning of one's own humanness.

In light of contemporary pressures to mold the student to a preexistent reality or even to a man-constructed "System," the educator, especially the classroom teacher, has a central role to play in creating an environment conducive to the growth of the free individual. Wilson feels that

> *the liberation of the teacher from a production-like job description is the ultimate requisite for an open access curriculum; such emancipation cannot be documented in advance by research—its initiation must be an act of administrative faith backed by an environmental design so fully committed that it can survive only by responsible individual and voluntary group initiative. (A play-it-safe management model with built-in suspicions of individual initiative can only fail.)* [55]

Unfortunately, teachers are rarely so "liberated." An administrative "management model" coupled with an assumption that teachers—no less than students—will err given half a chance is more the rule than the exception. In terms of strategies and techniques, therefore, the real question concerns what the *teacher* can do to provide the rudiments of such an environment for the student—a situation over which he has *some* control, at least when the "captains and the kings depart," i.e., when administrators have left his classroom and the door closes behind them. (To understand this as implying that we need not also strive for a better teacher environment would be as incorrect as it would be logically unjustified.) In this regard, books such as Herbert R. Kohl's *The Open Classroom* (a New York Review Book distributed by Vantage Books; New York: The New York Review, 1969) and Wilson's *The Open Access Curriculum* suggest many possibilities.

Why *must* "cume folders" be read and predispositions toward certain children be developed before each child has had opportunity to determine what he will be in your classroom? Why *must* we fear different learning (and teaching) styles? What is so sacred about seating charts? (If you have a poor memory, why not try large-print name tags which could also be made available to the substitute

---

[55] *Ibid.*, p. 65.

teacher?) Why not allow children to arrange classroom furniture in ways *they* see appropriate to *their* work? Does the teacher *really* have no influence over such phenomena—or has she *chosen* to exert no influence? The direction of these questions, of course, is to suggest that the teacher does have more influence than she ever suspects— even in fairly traditional schools. It *is* possible to create choice- making opportunities in such settings, and this is as true for the high school as it is for the middle and lower schools. Teachers choose to make schedules more important than people. Teachers choose to make meanings assigned to phenomena in the past more important than those which might be developed in the present. Teachers choose to act as if they were above anger—or joy. Teachers choose to treat students as if they were things rather than free subjectivities. Today's schools only make it easier to make the standard choices. It is, in short, quite possible to use a *can opener* on the "System"—if you choose to do so.

Our culture has been under increasing internal and external pres- sures since the 1930s. It is not surprising that we fear free and open relationships with others. At times the pressure of numbers alone makes intolerable the very thought of intense personal interrelation- ships. And yet a person to whom this assumption makes sense would probably be best advised not to enter professional education unless he will fight these pressures and feelings. Without interpersonal open- ness, without an environment characterized by intensely emotional encounters, without encouraging and allowing choices sometimes un- comfortable to the teacher, without a willingness to expend energy in protecting the maturing organism against the "System," there is little hope indeed for an authentic existence—for anyone.

B. Human Nature

1. Human Nature: Inherently Evil or Predisposed to Evil

Suggesting professional policies and practices consistent with the first assumption concerning human nature presents no problems if we turn to accounts of seventeenth and eighteenth century American educa- tion. Such accounts are replete with descriptions of attempts to control corrupted student nature by appeals to supernatural sanctions, restrictive regulations laid upon students and teachers alike, curricula so tightly prescribed as to minimize opportunity for (instinctively sinful) student expression and other evidences of suspicion.[56]   Interesting as these are, they somehow tend to miss the mark in terms of our present study.   Remember that we are concerned with assumptions viable in contemporary American culture.   Hence, our discussion must suggest consistent policies and practices possible (and, when possible, observable) in today's schools.   Otherwise, we are likely to underestimate the continuing force of the assumption by suggesting implicitly that its days of power lie in the past.

With some hesitation—for the public school educator may find it too easy to minimize such evidence as being appropriate only to private schools—let us first turn to the 1971–1972 "teacher's handbook" of a large K-12 Mid-Atlantic church-related school.   Under the heading of the "teacher-pupil relationship," we find nineteen categories of regulations and exhortations, ranging from "winning the pupil's confidence and respect" to "outside play."   We read that the teacher must "be careful about too much joking" with her students; she should "not attempt to be 'one of them.'"   Each class should know specifically what the teacher expects of them before class, during class and after class; furthermore these expectations must be submitted to the Director in writing.   "Teachers *must* be in the hall when classes change. Stations will be assigned. . . . All teachers must be at the doors or in the halls at entrance and dismissal time."   "Do not be afraid to use the paddle!   Other forms of physical punishment are to be used only in extreme cases—wisely and sparingly."   "Classes taking exams must be monitored at *all* times. . . .   Arrange the seats in your room to discourage copying on an examination."   (In the 1971–1972 "student handbook," students are told that they "should consider it a sin to tolerate wrongdoing.   Known offenders should be reported to the Administration or the Director for the sake of the testimony of the School and the Lord.")   Concerning library privileges, "Be careful! Send only trustworthy students."   Finally, if the teacher "should wish, on occasion, to take [her] class outside, [she must] consult with the principal before doing so."   In speaking about faculty meetings, the teacher is told to "remember that this is a professional meeting. Give it your full attention and refrain from personal conversations, joking, etc."   Teachers must also "be *very* careful to observe the dress standards . . . as set down in the student handbook."

The "student handbook" is no less consistent with this assumption.

---

[56] See, for example, E. E. Bayles and B. L. Hood, *Growth of American Educational Thought and Practice* (New York: Harper & Row, Publishers, Inc., 1966), Ch. I; R. F. Butts and L. A. Cremin, *A History of Education in American Culture* (New York: Holt, Rinehart and Winston, Inc., 1953), Chs. I–IV; and C. H. Gross and C. C. Chandler, *The History of American Education through Readings* (Boston: D. C. Heath and Company, 1964), Part I, especially pp. 25–31.

"Running, shoving, yelling, and undue boisterousness or 'horse-play' shall be considered out of order at all times." "Students reading, writing, or passing notes will be subject to disciplinary action." Furthermore, although the school recognizes that it has "no direct control of the student when away from [school], any violations of accepted behavior . . . will be considered serious. Smoking, drinking, gambling, dancing, playing cards, etc., should have no place in the life of the Christian." Concerning "Boy-Girl Friendships," the handbook reads (in part) as follows:

> It is our belief that the pattern of "going steady" at a young age is unfair to the individual, as well as being dangerous morally. For this reason, boy-girl friendships will not be pursued . . . so that "going steady" becomes the general pattern of life. To avoid unbecoming behavior and life-long regrets, students shall not come to school and leave after school in mixed groups unless accompanied by an adult approved by the Administration. Outward shows of affection in public, such as holding hands, having arms around one another, and the like, is unbecoming to a Christian young man or woman, and therefore will be prohibited in the [school] or on the school grounds. A genuine Christian behavior toward the opposite sex is manifested in a discreet manner, and will shun the practices of the world.

The section entitled "Girls' Dress Rules" includes the following notations:

> The dress or skirt length of girls must be of the length that the skirt will touch the floor when the girl is kneeling. Skirts must be long enough so as not to rise more than one inch above the knees when the girl is seated. . . . Parents will pay particular attention to growing girls, so that dresses will not become too short or tight during the school year, and go unnoticed. Sheer blouses will not be permitted in the [school]. Slips are to be worn under any thin blouse or dress. If a turtleneck is worn with a blouse, the blouse is to be buttoned as it would be without the turtleneck. All blouses and shirts must be tucked in, with the exception being square-hemmed blouses. Blouses, sweaters, and dresses must have a modest neckline, fit modestly, and not be too tight.

Boys are told that "ALL trousers must be neat and fit modestly. Extreme fashions, colors, or designs are not to be worn; this includes bell bottoms or flares." (Though somewhat apprehensive about Church opinion, the Director indicated that moderately-flared pants would be allowed during the academic year 1972–1973.)

It is suggested that these educational policies and practices are quite consistent with an assumption that human nature is inherently evil or at least predisposed to evil. They offer explicit suggestions for control by appeals to supernatural sanctions and regulations designed to inhibit the inherent sinfulness of both student and teacher. Suggestions for an appropriate curriculum have been and will be offered in other sections of this text. If we couple this assumption with that which holds that basic reality is found in the realm of the spirit, which at very least is superior to the natural order (a very common association in American culture), the degree of consistency even increases.

And what of the *public* schools? Is this assumption restricted to the halls of a few more fundamentalistic church-related institutions? We think not, and maintain that it is a viable assumption in an American culture whose expressions can commonly be observed in both secular and sectarian schools. True, an explicit appeal to supernatural sanctions in the public schools of late twentieth century America is rare—at least in writing. But the spirit of keeping people in line lest all hell break loose is more than common. Curricula are so tightly prescribed that it is difficult indeed for the student (actively) to stray from the straight and narrow.[57] Regulations are piled on top of regulations, differing little from those noted above other than in the lesser awareness they demonstrate of the assumptions which justify them. Suspicion of the child's natural instincts is the rule and not the exception.

An August (1971) letter directed to parents of students attending a large Mid-Atlantic public high school reads:

> Students are encouraged *NOT* to drive to school. We have observed over the years that a student who drives to school, or rides with another student who drives, is more likely to be tardy, truant, and earn low grades than is the student who does not drive to school.

Is "observation" the *only* ground for justifying this regulation—or do you sense a concealed and quite familiar assumption at work? In the same letter, the following statement is found:

> We will not release the student from school without the written permission from the parent. Especially, the youth will not be dismissed solely on the basis of a telephone call. We plan to verify each request for an early dismissal. Please include in your written request a telephone number where you can be reached by our staff, or the name and the number of the doctor with whom we can confirm the appointment. If the student

---

[57] The author is reminded of a well-known teacher education program which until just one year ago required 131 units for the baccalaureate degree. The program prescribed 105 credit hours course-by-course; an additional 15 were required in a "field of concentration" which had to be approved by the student's advisor; and all of 11 were given to the student as "free electives."

*does not bring your written request for early dismissal with him,
then it will be necessary for the parent to come to the school and
sign the student out.*

Personal contact with the school confirmed that this regulation was *not*
required as such by state law, although to some extent it had grown
out of state compulsory attendance laws.   Since many if not most of
the school's students were sixteen years of age or older, it was candidly
admitted that the regulation was in fact based on the school's desire to
cooperate with parents in preventing hooky and similar misconduct.

A final example is found in a regulation from a second public high
school.   The section of its 1968–1969 "Student Handbook" dealing
with "corridor passes" reads as follows:

> *Discretion must be used in issuing Corridor Passes.   Teachers
> should not permit more than one student to leave the room at
> any given time.   Special attention must be given to eliminate
> hall roamers.*
>
> *A Corridor Pass must be filled out and signed by a teacher
> before it is issued to the student.   This pass permits the student
> to be excused from the teacher's assigned class or study area.
> No student is permitted in corridors without a pass except dur-
> ing lunch periods when traveling from cafeteria to the lounge.*
>
> *Passes issued for a student to see another teacher must be
> signed by the recipient teacher before the student returns to the
> room again.   The issuing teacher will collect the pass.*
>
> *Students are to show hall passes to any teacher they meet in
> the halls, rest rooms, or other destinations when requested.*

Admittedly, it is difficult at all times to separate expressions of this
assumption from behaviors influenced by reality or psychological
factors, e.g., the need to provide reasonable working conditions for one
to two thousand students in a relatively limited space, or the school's
natural desire to control expressions of the student's aversion to its
constant manipulation (made somewhat more difficult by his having a
car!).   Nevertheless, it does seem clear that contemporary American
educators who really believe that human nature is inherently evil or
predisposed to evil have access to many models when they desire to
operationalize their belief.   A closer examination of many seemingly
"common sense" regulations in our schools may suggest other interesting expressions of this assumption.

2. Human Nature: Inherently Good

Initially one might hypothesize that a far more open and permissive set
of educational policies and practices should flow from this assumption

than from one which posits human nature as inherently evil. Indeed, learned commentators on education have taken such a position, railing against pedagogues who accept the assumption but disavow an "open classroom." In one of the most provocative and useful texts dealing with the history of ideas in education, for example, we read:

> . . . It is obvious that Froebel was in no sense an educational permissivist. But it seems equally obvious that the doctrine of education as unfoldment does logically entail educational permissivism. Therefore, to invoke unfoldment in theory and deny it in practice is to be guilty of gross self-contradiction . . .[58]

Beyond noting earlier arguments that professional behavior can rarely be explained by appeal to any one causal variable and that the whole notion of "logical entailment" is faulty, it appears that the charge of "gross self-contradiction" is itself open to serious question.

The "doctrine of education as unfoldment" rests squarely on the assumption that man's original nature is good and suggests that the facilitation of its expression is the basic task of education. The key words here are "original nature." In fact, man's *original* nature is constantly being distorted by contacts with a manipulative oppressive society, contacts that give rise to habits which are inconsistent with that nature. A generally permissive attitude in the classroom would do little but allow these distorted habits to gain expression and reinforcement. Based on Froebel's *The Education of Man,* Bayles and Hood themselves quote Froebel as writing:

> Hence the only and infallible remedy for counteracting any shortcoming and even wickedness is to find the originally good side of the human being that has been repressed, disturbed, or misled into the shortcoming, and then to foster, build up, and properly guide this good side. Thus the shortcoming will at last disappear, although it may involve a hard struggle against habit, but not against original depravity in man . . .[59]

It will also be noted that this assumption ususally finds the genesis of the "originally good side of the human being" in the purposeful involvement of the Divine with His creation. Although true of many earlier seers, this was especially true of American advocates of the position, e.g., Jefferson, Emerson, Channing and Francis W. Parker. Goodness, then, is a pre-existent reality defined by a Supreme Reality. Its details are transmitted to man; they are not constructed by natural

[58] Bayles and Hood, *Growth of American Educational Thought and Practice,* p. 177.
[59] *Ibid.,* p. 173.

man existing apart from the supernatural. Helping the child to express his original nature, then, involves protecting him against perverting forces to which he is susceptible at the various stages of his development; providing positive guidance toward the good as defined in religious creeds and other experiences with the Divine; reinforcing human reason; and carefully, systematically constructing right habits. The task for the teacher is to accomplish all of this in a way which *restores* the child's essential liberty through exercising necessary restraints. Surely he must secure the child's cooperation. As Ulich suggests, he must also do

> *his best to harmonize his secret educational strategy with the natural conditions of a child's growth. He encourages his pupils to imitate good example. He creates scenes and experiences favorable to the right conditioning of the pupil's behavior and to his preparation for life. And as the child senses this care without feeling thwarted by it, he develops for his tutor a higher and more intimate sense of respect than could ever be created by any external authority.*[60]

In short, it is *educational permissivism* which is ultimately inconsistent with the doctrine of education as unfoldment. Rousseau realized, as did Froebel and many American progressivists after him, that "liberty and constraint are compatible."[61] Much tradition to the contrary, those in this culture who advocate a classroom wherein the child is maximally free to "do his own thing"—as he defines it—would do better to embrace the assumption that human nature is "constructed and evaluated individualistically" than a view which sees human nature as "inherently good."

3. *Human Nature Inherently Superior or Inferior*

Educators given to the assumption of two essences have faced no easy task in implementing their position in American culture. Their very belief that intellectual power is the mark of a superior nature and in its full power is restricted to a relatively small elite, has received strong and continuing opposition from the egalitarian tradition in America. For egalitarians, "democracy" means (at least in part) removing essentially man-made inequalities between men. As an historical factor, faith in the ability of the "common man" to surmount almost any problem has challenged the two essences position at every turn.

[60] Robert Ulich, *History of Educational Thought.* Rev. ed. (New York: American Book Company, 1968), p. 219.
[61] Rusk, *Doctrines of the Great Educators,* p. 168.

A psychological aversion to being labeled "inferior" is related to and strengthens this challenge.

In addition to opposition, however, there also exists a basic confusion among the assumption's adherents.   Some, including Arnold Bestor, have suggested that the maximization of intellectual power is so vital that every schoolchild, whatever his ability-level, must be exposed to the most rigorous mental diet. Some students *will* fail, but the number who will profit may be far higher than we might suspect. Success depends on convincing each student that school is a serious undertaking and then providing well-trained teachers to present essential academic studies in the most thorough and stimulating manner possible. Other advocates of this assumption, however, have pointed out that ineradicable differences between those born with superior and inferior natures suggest somewhat different curricula for those with different endowments.   They avow, for example, that there is something fundamentally wrong in distinguishing between English-Honors, English-College Preparatory, English-General, and English-Basic Skills courses upon the basis of intellectual rigors alone.   English-Basic Skills should not simply be the most "watered down" version of the ultimate, English-Honors.   Rather, quite different approaches and materials should be devised for children of different stations in life who are destined for quite different vocations.   That each child's intellectual powers should be developed as far as possible goes without saying. The latter position is reflected in a section of a Mid-Atlantic public high school's 1971–1972 "Course Selection Handbook" which reads,

> The English 10 Honors course is designed for students whose maturity and verbal aptitude qualify them for a class involving more enrichment activities and a less structured approach than in College Preparatory English 10. Though the course content is the same as that outlined in English 10 C.P., it goes beyond it both in the nature of the work and particularly, in the approach to it. The English Honors 10 class should be viewed as a prerequisite for English Honors 11. To be eligible for English 10 Honors, the student should have proficiency in the mechanics of language and should have demonstrated an above-average performance in Grade 9 English. The course provides the qualified student with opportunities for varied and extensive reading experiences, for a certain amount of independent study, and for experiences in a variety of writing assignments. Under no circumstances should the course be viewed as an elective or a course in creative writing.
>
> Using American literature as its focal point, the college preparatory [course] prepares the academic student in the language skills and background expected of those entering higher education. Most assigned readings (novels, stories, essays, poems) are major works of American literature, which are often demanding

> *and/or adult in nature. The treatment of literature is usually chronological, emphasizing the literary, cultural and social history of America. In the area of writing skills, complete mastery of mechanics is expected. Emphasis is on organization, especially the expository paragraph and essay, and maturity of expression. Grammar and usage are reviewed and related directly to the writing; vocabulary study is geared to more difficult reading; and the proficiency in oral and listening skills is stressed. Sometimes the college preparatory classes are taught by a team of two teachers. Learning activities involve the entire group, separated groups or several smaller groups, depending on the nature of the material covered.*
>
> *The [English 10 General course] is designed to prepare students for the future by teaching them to master the fundamentals of the English language in reading, writing, speaking and listening. Considerable work is done with the common mechanics of spoken and written language. Writing assignments are planned to be as close to reality as possible: character analysis, reactions to readings, explanations and descriptions. Reading selections emphasize the contemporary, with the goal of fostering reading pleasure and insights into life.*
>
> *The Basic Skills 10 program stresses the fundamental skills of reading, writing, speaking and listening as they apply to the job-centered student. Contemporary readings from novels, magazines and newspapers, records and films are frequently used to improve communications skills. Writing assignments are closely related to life and work.*

Given this assumption, then, intragrade homogeneous grouping and intergrade tracking appear to follow. The disagreements in practice concern the treatment of students so grouped. These disagreements are as much influenced by historical and psychological factors as they are by those philosophical in nature.

Based on this reasoning, students of different natures should be identified as early as possible and treated accordingly. We should either provide for their differences in comprehensive schools, or, if necessary, provide separate institutions and "counsel" students into the appropriate institution. James Conant notwithstanding, there is something to be said for the German model providing *both* excellent technical schools (e.g., those designed to prepare brewers) and excellent *gymnasia* (academic secondary schools which prepare students for the university). To the extent that race and intelligence are related, fight integration by every legal means possible. If the maintenance of *de facto* segregation demands resistance to school busing, be prepared to fight for "neighborhood schools." Through such strategems, it may be possible to minimize the influence of egalitarian sentiment in American culture and thus provide for the best education for both those of superior and inferior natures.

4. Human Nature: Constructed and Evalulated Transactionally

To assume that "human nature" refers to the ways in which we learn habitually to respond to constitutional needs, genetic limitations, acquired desires and the impact of others—and, further, to assume that these habitual behaviors are learned and evaluated in social settings—is to place the heaviest of burdens on our entire educational system. If we are to build and evaluate the adequacy of these habits and when necessary (due to their inadequacy or to changing experience) reconstruct habits, we must know in fact what the child is learning in the American school. Empirical research is slowly building a factual basis for answers. In addition, the last decade has seen the emergence of an important body of "protest literature."[62] With a remarkably united voice, this literature has cried that the American student is learning much which is fundamentally destructive both to individual and societal development. We hear, for instance, that students are learning that unquestioning obedience to regulations however trivial is demanded. We hear that public authority, e.g., the school administration, in its concern for producing pliant consumers impersonally imposes norms strictly on the basis of precedents and convenience rather than on any ethical or moral basis. The schools are very successful indeed, this literature suggests, in teaching that power is a much more important criterion in settling disputes than is the legitimacy of a grievance. Given this interaction pattern, the student (and, in terms of the administration, the teacher) does well to learn how to make a good impression as well as other manipulative techniques. Subservience may result in at least a few scraps being thrown down from the table—which is more than can be said for the expression of honest feelings, loyalties and reasoned arguments. Small wonder that the student reacts with generalized fear, with a weary surrender of privacy and autonomy, and with doubt or even rejection of self. Over time, of course, this reaction pattern may make him even more critical of divergent behavior than the power structure itself. Small wonder that he is more easily pressed into an answer-centered curriculum which rewards him not for pointing out intellectual and/or ethical problems but for collecting and recalling facts. With some reason the student learns to check his increasing anger over such treatment.

[62] A minimal listing might include Charles E. Silberman, *Crisis in the Classroom* (A Vintage Book; New York: Random House, 1971); Neil Postman and Charles Weingartner, *Teaching as a Subversive Activity* (New York: Delacorte Press, 1969); John Holt, *How Children Fail* (New York: Pitman Publishing Corp., 1964); Edgar Z. Freidenberg, *Coming of Age in America;* and Jerry Farber, *The Student as Nigger* (No. Hollywood, Calif.: Contact Books, 1969).

Often this anger is turned in upon itself, thus transforming it into obsequiousness. Occasionally his feelings break out in brief flashes of fury and despair. Unfortunately they are often so generalized as to obscure the real issues, which adds little to the student's case and gives the system but one more chance to reinforce its authority. More often students simply drop out of the system—physically and/or mentally— and we are confronted by the absurd spectacle of administrators wringing their hands over dropouts and faculty turnover.

To the extent that the arguments of this protest literature are accurate, those who see human nature as constructed and evaluated transactionally are indeed faced with a need to transform the school. Every academic meeting place—classroom, gymnasium, office and auditorium—must be transformed into an environment so open and supportive that an examination of what *in fact* is being learned can take place. Given the increasing external and internal pressures upon this culture, the sense of malaise and general anxiety which has developed, and the resulting reinforcement of more authoritarian assumptions quite vigorous in this pluralistic society, we may rightly fear whether such an environment can be created. In the 1970s there does seem to be a somewhat bittersweet flavor to the historic progressive emphasis on rationality—on reasoning, cooperation, compromise—in a society where faith in human reason may well be the ultimately *irrational* faith.

How do you create such an environment and hence the possibility of a better human nature? In spite of the difficulties sketched above, the following points are offered for thought and discussion. The first concerns a definitional problem. Individuals need to accept the notion that a definition of leadership which involves "contributing" to the growth of others is just as possible a *definition* as the one which contains a more familiar emphasis on "controlling" the growth of others. Secondly, we need more adequately to define and test the hypothesis that the input of different perceptions can result in a more workable problem resolution than one developed basically by a leader and his "court." Constructing human nature is, after all, not quite as simple a task as making trains run on time. Furthermore, the claim that "time flies" is not an adequate defense for pressured decisions. Professional history offers considerable support for the contention that the constant deadlines thrown at educators are usually more a matter of convenience and/or control than a matter of necessity. Testing this hypothesis calls for at least some heterogeneous grouping in order to facilitate the widest mix of perceptions. A constant checking process follows. There must be checking with ourselves wherein we evaluate what we are really teaching and its consistency with our own philosophy of education and the other factors which influence professional outcomes. Teacher behavior consistent with the "inherently evil" assumption of human nature, for example, may do a good deal more to teach children to be defensive than we can undo with all our words. There must be a constant checking with others. Even a group of third graders may know more about what they are learning than we do—inasmuch as we ourselves have been out of third grade for some time and have developed different learning modes. Every educational problem—be it a fourth grade science curriculum problem or a problem involving the demands of high school students for a stronger student council—must be cooperatively examined to see if the habits of those involved are adequate to resolving the problem. If they are not, then there must be a common consideration of the desirability of possible alternative solutions, prerequisite habits and the ways in which they might be developed. Finally, there must be a common and explicit consideration of the criteria and the decision-making processes by which we evaluate learned behaviors as "good" or "bad."[63]

The basic behavioral pattern consistent with the assumption of human nature as "constructed and evaluated transactionally" is fairly clear: It involves examination *with people,* decision-making *with people,* action *with people* and evaluation *with people.* In these transactions we create the only possible environment adequate to constructing the richest human nature for both the individual and the species.

5. Human Nature: Constructed and Evaluated Individualistically

Given this assumption we must necessarily consider those educational policies and practices which might aid the individual to resist pressures to see facticity as determined and to free those creative powers necessary to adding meaning to the brute fact of his existence. The starting point of this consideration probably lies in a faith that human beings are potentially *capable* of building their own natures or essences in a mass society. This is surely not to say that faith in itself is sufficient. Indeed, the physical and mental cost of implementing this commitment, especially in the public schools of a pluralistic culture, is high and must not be underestimated.

The initial commitment to implementation may well be the most trying. We shall have to live through the "recovery period" described

---

[63] Given its consistency with this assumption, you may wish to look at the assumption of "values as the product of contextual inquiry" in Chapter 6.

by A. S. Neill.[64]   Hatreds built up in both teachers and students as a result of having long been manipulated must be "ventilated" before an individual can devote his energies to more positive learning.   Expect expressions of anger against the "System."   Expect fear of punishment—and self-protective behavior.   Expect expressed disinterest and/or passivity concerning anything having to do with "school."   If the teacher and administrator refuse to despair and offer proof upon proof that they will not manipulate—or be manipulated—this reaction pattern will gradually wane.   Neill writes,

> Children who come to Summerhill as kindergartners attend lessons from the beginning of their stay; but pupils from other schools vow that they will never attend any beastly lessons again at any time.   They play and cycle and get in people's way, but they fight shy of lessons. . . . The recovery time is proportionate to the hatred their last school gave them.   Our record case was a girl from a convent.   She loafed for three years.   The average period of recovery from lesson aversion is three months.[65]

As the individual "recovers" we must consider more positive curricular strategies.   Here we run into difficulties.   The literature of Existentialism offers us few guidelines, partially due to its rarely dealing specifically with educational questions as such.   Learned commentators who have studied this literature in depth and posed policies and practices seemingly consistent with it demonstrably differ.   Their prescriptions, however, do appear to fall into three general groupings: a) Retain the traditional curriculum, but markedly alter our treatment of it; b) Modify both the traditional curriculum and its treatment; and c) Establish basic student control over content, the methods by which it is to be taught and the rate at which it is to be learned.   Due to the importance of curricular strategies to the building of a human nature, we must now turn to a more adequate consideration of these three alternatives, giving some attention to the strengths and weaknesses of each.

Those who stress retaining the traditional curriculum offer several reasoned arguments.   After all, the individual does need the skills which are normally taught through basic subjects to *exist* in the modern world.   Furthermore, essence-building cannot take place in a vacuum.   Raw materials must be at hand when the individual reaches that "existential moment" when he is aware of self and ready to define the personal meaning of his *is*-ness.   Before that moment, which

[64] A. S. Neill, *Summerhill: A Radical Approach to Child Rearing* (New York: Hart Publishing Company, 1960), p. 5.
[65] *Ibid.*

is closely allied with the coming of puberty, the development of raw materials must proceed systematically. Following that moment, the objective content of the curriculum is probably less important than the student's *attitudes toward* that content—the opportunities various subjects afford the student for grasping personal meaning from the curriculum and thus building his own nature.[66] Malik is quite specific, writing that both facticity and possibility demand that the student

> *master the body of traditional subject matter and the basic skills of language and logic. Learning fundamentals and universals is not against the spirit of existentialism and the existentialist student studies almost the same curriculum as every other student of his age. To gain freedom for uninhibited creative effort, the student needs to know the basic facts and master the basic skills. . . . But the existential student is not just learning the factual content of the curriculum, he is appropriating it to enhance his freedom and to be aware of new modes of human consciousness.*[67]

As far as this line of thought goes, it seems reasonable. Surely any resource provides opportunities for open and subjective encounters between individuals and for personal meaning-building, choosing, appropriation—call it what you will. It is also true that the traditional curriculum contains resources rich in such possibilities. It may even be admitted that the individual does need many basic skills and knowings to exist in a complex society. The danger of this position lies in the historical fact that American educational tradition weighs so heavily on the side of presenting such content and skills to be learned objectively rather than emphasizing their subjective appropriation. This tradition is reinforced by the ever-increasing flood of facts which demands inclusion in the curriculum and makes it easier year by year to ignore the personal element. It is further reinforced by the commonly-held assumption that leadership involves exerting power over people rather than sharing it with them as a prerequisite to solving common tasks. Such difficulties have led to the posing of major alternatives.

One such alternative is found in the pages of *The Open Access Curriculum*, one of the more provocative texts to appear in the literature of professional education over the past two decades. Craig

---

[66] *Cf.* Van Cleve Morris, *Existentialism in Education* (New York: Harper & Row, Publishers, Inc., 1966), pp. 111ff., 120–122 and 123.

[67] Anand Malik, "Existentialism in Education," *Current Themes in Philosophy of Education*, Publication No. 198 (Saskatoon, Saskatchewan: Extension Division, University of Saskatchewan, n.d.), pp. 43–44.

Wilson clearly indicates his preference for "authentic environments." "But," he writes, "authentic environments can be created only when curriculum designs first admit the possibility that existing structures and processes can, in fact, betray teachers or students under certain conditions."[68]   For instance, "whoever controls teacher role definitions *directly* controls something else even more stable and critical—the curriculum proper."[69]   In order, therefore, to facilitate the student's access to knowledge of himself and his surroundings, we must necessarily alter school relationships so as to ensure for both teacher and student a more important voice in curricular decisions.

Teachers must be given time to theorize about their disciplines and curricular design.   Such time may be provided by ensuring that no more than fifty percent of their time is spent in more formal "information giving."   Furthermore, their personal interests and their life styles must be given just as much weight in setting responsibilities as their academic specializations.   Given more explicit knowledge of the optimum learning modes of individual students, we may properly create situations in which students can be brought into contact with teachers most supportive of their learning styles and, hence, most open to "I-Thou" relationships.   This may, of course, happen in the regular core courses, although Wilson emphasizes restricting these to no more than one-fourth of the program.   More likely, it will happen in the one-half of the day when students should have direct control over their curriculum, perhaps in the many short-term elective courses to be designed by students and teachers alike.   The possibilities for encouraging student choices—within modified school structures and processes—are nearly endless.   They do, however, demand that we cease to deny college preparatory students

> *work experience while in school; laboratory experience with technical and scientific equipment; in-depth study in the cultural and expressive arts; intensive seminar-type learning . . . ; independent research and study . . . ; leadership experience with heterogeneous student groups; exploration of the newer dimensions of the classical disciplines, for example, genetics . . . ; alternate "entry points" to any body of knowledge; also, alternative methods of scholarship based upon "natural" life styles and maturation levels; "saturation" learning in any field—that is, large concentrated blocks of time for study in a single area; personal reflection, private curiosity, unstructured opportunity to pursue individual interests and purposes; [and] interdisciplinary study. [Italics removed.]*[70]

[68] Wilson, *The Open Access Curriculum*, p. 74.
[69] *Ibid.*, pp. 153–154.
[70] *Ibid.*, pp. 24–26.

In like measure, it will necessitate our ceasing to deny nonacademic students

> *the creative aspects of any discipline or area of study—for ex-*
> *ample, laboratory science as opposed to general science . . . ;*
> *opportunity for personal responsibility and self-direction; contact*
> *with the best teachers; school sanction and genuine respect for*
> *the technical and vocational curricula to which nonacademic*
> *students are often assigned . . . ; [and] opportunity to work in*
> *areas of personal strength (as opposed to remediation of weak-*
> *nesses). [Italics removed.]*[71]

In all, the strategy is to give the student much greater powers than is presently the case. The student is not to be fitted to a pre-existent curriculum, nor are we to suppose that an actively interventionist teacher can long resist controlling choice. To the extent that non-graded, team-teaching, interest grouping, individualization and flexible scheduling strategies facilitate this procedure, they should be considered. To the extent that they provide little more than new terminology for more familiar System-controlled programming, they must be resisted. Palliatives only distract our attention from the pedagogical revolution suggested by the assumption that the individual can and must construct and evaluate his own human nature.

We see in the Wilson position a thoroughgoing modification of more traditional educational relationships and structures. We might expect a professor of educational administration to focus on structural and procedural possibilities designed to free the student's (and the teacher's) choice-making, nature-building powers. Wilson does not fail us. Even agreeing that these factors are necessary to freedom-gaining, however, we may still wonder if the steps he suggests are really sufficient to shake the structure of American education in the late twentieth century—if in fact we conclude that it *should* be shaken. In a thoroughly pluralistic culture much influenced by more traditional views of man and the world, can this revolution really be effected by expecting teachers and administrators who hold *markedly* different assumptions to implement "open access" curricula? Does it seem reasonable to expect that students and teachers long trained in more passive responses to authority will suddenly "sprout and flower" when external conditions are altered? The suspicion that something far more radical than tinkering with the System's structure is needed to free the individual has led others who share this assumption to pose a third major pedagogical alternative.

[71] *Ibid.*, pp. 26–27.

A. S. Neill probably stands as the prime example of those who—in despair of gaining their objectives within the school as we know it—would reverse traditional educational trends by granting the student control over major pedagogical variables. True, he does voice an allegiance to the assumption of "inherent goodness,"[72] but there is nothing of the "restrictiveness," the necessary "guidance in terms of the known good," in Neill's writing that suggests this assumption—at least as expressed in American culture. Rather, Neill renounces all externally imposed discipline, direction, suggestion, moral training and religious instruction.[73] The result of even the most well-meant "guidance" is the molded, conditioned, disciplined, repressed individual. As long as it does not adversely affect others, the human being must be given the freedom himself to define what he is and will become. Restrictions will be imposed only upon interference with the rights of others; the mutual acceptance of equals will characterize the educational climate. The near-absolute "freedom to be" seems central to the assumption that one's human nature is both "constructed and evaluated by the individual." It is in the very exercise of such freedom—in deciding what and when to learn, when to attend classes, when and whether to take tests, what to wear, how to relate to others—that one defines what he is.

Neill seems to believe that in today's education such freedom is possible only in small experimental schools which are able and willing to remain independent of the emotional and financial support of the general community. Herbert Kohl, as we have seen, believes that far more than the linguistic flavor of Neill's proposals can be maintained in the public school classroom. After the parameters of the transitional period through which American education is presently suffering have become more clear, we may find that much of the reform energy remaining to this century will be spent in deciding who is correct.

C.   Free Will and Determinism

1. Free Will and Determinism: The Free Self

For those to whom human freedom is an inescapable reality, there exist important pedagogical questions. The classicist, for example, must ask how the individual's will can best be trained to exercise its power. The existentialist must ask what environmental conditions will

---

[72] Neill, *Summerhill*, p. 4.
[73] *Ibid.*

best facilitate that conscious choosing which, grasping possibility, alone can transcend both despair and facticity.

We have already seen that the training of the will must involve the classically-oriented educator in helping the student become aware of the determiners in his—and the species'—background. Instruction must be given concerning the relative morality of common human acts and the standards which are so vital to guiding action in less common decision situations. Finally, the student must come to a deeper and more abiding realization of what he chooses as his long-term and ultimate goals. Although these three concerns are surely not the sole responsibility of the school, it is also true that the knowledgeable educator can make a substantial contribution toward their achievement.

There is scarcely a course in the school's curriculum—or for that matter, any educational setting—which does not provide possibilities for making the child aware of the importance of regularities in the natural order. With reservations we may refer to the "law" of cause and effect. The physical and life sciences, literature, the social sciences and incidents from the classroom to the playground to the counsellor's office, are especially rich in opportunities for object lessons and evaluative discussions. Of course, they also provide opportunities for pointing out instances in which man—a creature of both the natural and supernatural orders—has risen and can rise above natural determiners.

Direct instruction in moral standards and guided exercises in moral decision-making probably must be left to the private school, especially the church-related school. The public school educator may make some contribution through "teaching about" the moral codes of religions and encouraging moral instruction where there is support in the home. For the rest, he must clearly depend upon the home and the church. This is part of the price we pay for our society's separation of church and state; it is also suggestive of the motivations which have led to the development of private church-related schools.

The thin line which public school educators must walk on questions related to church and state also affects what they can do by way of helping the child develop commitments to long-term and ultimate goals. Again, the possibility of direct involvement within educational settings seems to be restricted to the private school. Depending chiefly on home and church, the public school teacher must walk with a very light tread indeed. On the one hand, he will not want to neglect his concern and thus lead the student to conclude that it is unimportant. On the other, even suggestion in such an area can quickly result in outraged screams of protest directed at everyone from the principal to the district superintendent. Although the classicist will no doubt reject much of the assumptive base upon which it rests, Louis Raths's "value clarifying method" offers some interesting possibilities. Without fail the interested educator should read his *Values and Teaching*, which fully develops the stragegy and offers many worthwhile examples. In brief, Raths suggests that

> the responding strategy is a way of responding to a student that results in his considering what he has chosen, what he prizes, and/or what he is doing. It stimulates him to clarify his thinking and behavior and thus to clarify his values. . . .[74]

For the existentialist, freedom refers not so much to a human "faculty" or power, i.e., free will, as to a necessary condition of human existence. The awakening of the human being to the reality of his freedom (and his responsibility for choice-making) is of prime concern in existentialistic pedagogy. This awakening cannot be forced by the educator. On the other hand, he can create an environment where such awareness can more easily come about and in which it is nourished rather than starved. We see an optimal environment suggested in A. S. Neill's Summerhill. Freedom is not identified with license, i.e., violating the personal rights of others. For instance, the student should be free to go to class or not to go, but once having arrived he is not free to disrupt the activities of the other students. Given this distinction, however, the child is allowed to live his own life. There is none of the training of the individual will which characterizes the approach of classicists who also accept the assumption of "the free self." Rather, living one's own life means having the power to control dress, speech, length of hair, class attendance—and many of the other matters concerning which educators take delight in detailing regulations. The existentialist asks how important it is to education that they be controlled. Moreover (keeping in mind the results of using a crutch when no longer medically necessary), he asks what effect their control has on self-development. He concludes that external control is not only unimportant but is actually dangerous to an education which would cultivate free subjectivities. This goal is well expressed by Van Cleve Morris:

> When [the] individual stands apart and alone, awake to his existing, aware of his freedom, responsible and in charge of his own life, he will see for himself why he may, for the first time, be called authentic.[75]

[74] Louis E. Raths, Merrill Harmin and Sidney B. Simon, *Values and Teaching; Working with Values in the Classroom* (Columbus, Ohio: Charles E. Merrill Publishing Co., 1966), p. 51.

[75] Morris, *Existentialism in Education*, p. 154.

2. Free Will and Determinism: Basic Determinism

The educator drawn to the assumption of basic determinism is quite unimpressed with the notion that human dignity necessitates an ability to stand outside natural processes—to exercise "free will." Convinced that educational outcomes are caused by natural determiners, he prefers to devote his energy to attempting to "shape" these outcomes systematically and rationally rather than allowing them to "happen" haphazardly. Furthermore, he feels that our ability to shape professional outcomes is fast developing through scientific investigation. For example, a recent text suggests:

> *We do know some very important things about human behavior and we can do something about predicting and changing it.*
>
> . . .
>
> *Changing significant pupil behavior is not an impossible, improbable or even difficult task. . . . Behavior can be significantly altered in the school* even if parents do not cooperate.[76]

Given a world in trouble, man must design a desirable society which is capable of surviving. Through scientific exploration we can gradually gain more precise knowledge of the causes of human behavior—as complex as these causes may be—and then put this knowledge to work in developing the cognitive, attitudinal and psychomotor habits necessary to optimal individual and group behavior in such a society.

The literature of "operant conditioning" offers a wealth of suggestions for designing and implementing both a classroom and a school society consistent with the assumption of "basic determinism." Works by B. F. Skinner suggest an extension of this literature to questions of the design and implementation of the wider human community.[77] Becker summarizes the essentials of operant conditioning:

> *In its simplest form, operant conditioning involves the systematic use of consequences to strengthen and weaken behaviors under specified stimulus conditions. Operant behavior is strengthened by some consequences called reinforcers, and weakened by other consequences called punishers. Withdrawal of reinforcing consequences will also weaken behavior. This procedure is called extinction.*

[76] John T. Neisworth, Stanley L. Deno and Joseph R. Jenkins, *Student Motivation and Classroom Management: A Behavioristic Approach* (Lemont, Pa.: Behavior Techniques, Inc., 1969), pp. 1–2.

[77] For a series of readings drawn from such literature see Wesley C. Becker, *An Empirical Basis for Change in Education; Selections on Behavioral Psychology for Teachers* (Chicago: Science Research Associates, Inc., 1971). Relevant works by B. F. Skinner include *Beyond Freedom and Dignity, Science and Human Behavior, The Technology of Teaching* and *Walden Two* (New York: The Macmillan Company, 1948).

> *The laws of operant behavior are generalizations drawn from the experimental analysis of behavior. They summarize which events influence behavior in what ways. Many persons seem shocked when first exposed to the idea that there are systematic ways of influencing the behavior of others (or one's own). They find it a difficult idea to accept; it smacks of* Brave New World. *Actually, the law of reinforcement is no more revolutionary today than the law of gravity. . . . The teacher does not have a choice in the question of whether or not her children will be influenced by reinforcing and punishing events. The only choices the teacher has are 1) to use reinforcement principles systematically to optimally help her children develop, 2) to blindly and haphazardly approach the training of her children, or 3) to leave the training to less competent sources of reinforcement and punishment, such as other children.*[78]

Quoting B. F. Skinner, Becker admits that the teaching technology he espouses could conceivably be used to stifle creativity and initiative, to "robotize" mankind. These outcomes, however, are not entailed by the technology itself, for it could also be used to develop individual competence and diversity, to heighten man's contribution to the development and survival of his culture.[79] Much depends on the behaviors which knowledgeable educators choose to reinforce. With regard to these behaviors, a quotation from John Dewey seems especially pertinent:

> *With respect to freedom, then, the task of the educator is threefold. First, to keep alive plasticity, initiative, capacity to vary; to prevent induration and fixation in fossilized automatic habits. Even a thoroughly good habit needs to be kept flexible, so that it may be adapted, when the need arises, to circumstances not previously experienced even by way of anticipation. Secondly, to confirm preference; to build up and strengthen positive and constructive interests in specific directions. Nothing is more fatal practically than the growth of a spirit of indifference, of boredom, or of miscellaneous and easily diverted responsiveness. Thirdly, to make preference reasonable; that is to say, to develop in individuals the habit of forecasting the consequences of acting upon a given preferential tendency, of comparing one set of results with another, and by these means enlightening preference as to its own deeper and more abiding nature. Capacity transforms habit when required. Steady and specific interests, foresight, and deliberation—given these factors of character, and purely speculative difficulties in the concept of freedom may be left serenely alone.*[80]

[78] Becker, *An Empirical Basis for Change in Education*, pp. 131–132.

[79] *Ibid.*, p. 18.

[80] John Dewey in *Cyclopedia of Education*, ed. Paul Monroe (New York: The Macmillan Company, 1911), II, p. 706.

Many of the criticisms of operant conditioning appear to stem from its growing use with 1) children having special learning disabilities, e.g., mental retardation or social and emotional disturbance, and 2) children in the earlier elementary grades who need to master gross academic and social behaviors, e.g., placing x's at correct points on a map or developing the habit of placing one's name on a paper. Here the behaviors to be shaped are quite basic. The handicapped children are less able or ready to engage in more complex behavior labeled foresight, initiative or creativity than are their healthy peers. Gross academic and social behaviors must be mastered by the healthy child at the same time as a foundation is being laid for learning more complex behaviors. Admittedly, we must remember that operant conditioning provides a very powerful tool. In dealing with gross behaviors, it can sound thoroughly mechanistic. There are instances of teachers emphasizing its potential for student control rather than for fostering independence. However, to leap from these instances of focussing on gross behaviors or overcontrol to the conclusion that operant conditioning per se is appropriate only to shaping gross behaviors and/or that it is at heart an authoritarian and/or mechanistic approach to education is clearly fallacious. True, identifying the behaviors which mark initiative, foresight, deliberation and creativity, and then designing educational strategies which will maximize their learning will not be easy. At least the nature of the task is more clear than it is under a position which really sees these traits as instinctive and not open to systematic development.

D. God and Faith

1. God and Faith: The Orthodox God

Several references have already been made to educational policies and practices consistent with the assumption that basic reality is found in creative, purposeful, spiritual energy. These references are also appropriate to the present discussion.

We may reiterate that the public school teacher who holds to "the orthodox God" faces many problems in today's school. America's historic separation of church and state expressed in both law and tradition, the very pluralism of American culture and a powerful trend toward naturalism not unexpected in an age of science, do make it difficult to act with utter consistency. With preparation, care and attention to nonphilosophical factors, however, he can teach "about" religion. He can deal factually with religious experience when discussing, for instance, Dante's *Divine Comedy*, Greek institutions or the intuitive dimension of the scientific method. It was the very need for preparation to meet these needs that led the American Association of Colleges for Teacher Education (AACTE) to sponsor the "Teacher Education and Religion Project" between 1953 and 1958. In a volume filled with practical suggestions for classroom use, the report concluded:

> The education of a teacher is incomplete if it avoids or ignores the materials drawn from the field of religion that are implicit in the academic subject matter field and intrinsic to it. The teacher, as purveyor of culture, must be prepared to convey more than a partial view.[81]

When dealing with phenomena which inescapably involve a religious dimension, it would also seem consistent that the public school teacher would encourage the child to add resources from his home and religious institution—even if the addition of these resources is not graded on tests. Consistency might also lead the public school educator to allow released time for religious instruction and observances and even to support—at least in principle—the existence of sectarian schools.

In spite of strong religious sentiment, historical factors do at times weigh more heavily than metaphysical assumptions in deciding one's position on questions dealing with God and faith in the public schools. The Bill of Rights translated concepts such as freedom of worship into legal principles to be applied by the courts rather than decided by political majorities. For example, the Dirksen (prayer) Amendment of 1966, which through a constitutional amendment attempted to overturn the Supreme Court decisions in *Engel* and *Abington,* was opposed by most American religious leaders.[82] This tradition of church-state separation also seems strengthened by the sociological factor of religious pluralism in the United States. Under these conditions, many individuals who hold to the orthodox God feel that the religious rights of all are best protected by refusing to allow governmental or popular majorities to decide questions of faith or its public expression in religious ceremonies.

As mentioned earlier, policies and practices consistent with the assumption of the "orthodox God" seem more directly achievable in the church-related school. Freed from the restraints of public school

[81] A. L. Sebaly, ed., *Teacher Education and Religion* (Oneonta, N.Y.: The American Association of Colleges for Teacher Education, 1959), p. 228.
[82] Herbert M. Kliebard, ed., *Religion and Education in America: A Documentary History* (Scranton, Pa.: International Textbook Company, 1969), pp. 20–22.

pluralism, a Roman Catholic teacher, for instance, can advocate a school in which the child:

> *1. . . . learns systematically and thoroughly about his religion. . . .*
> *2. . . . enjoys regular opportunities, direct and indirect, for the deepening of his sense of religious dedication. . . .*
> *3. . . . learns an ordering of knowledge in an atmosphere in which the spiritual and the supernatural hold the primacy in the hierarchy of temporal and eternal values. He learns that his faith is not something apart but is related to the whole texture of life.*
> *4. . . . acquires a "Catholic" attitude or outlook on life based upon the firm knowledge of his duties and privileges as a follower of Christ; he gains pride and love in—and loyalty to—his Catholic heritage.*[83]

2. God and Faith: The Humanistic God

Suggestions concerning the pedagogical outworking of a faith in the humanistic God must begin with the realization that the humanist does not see religious experience as different in kind from other experiences. Kuebler captures this realization, writing:

> *Religious experiencing need not be different from other experiences; any experience has a religious quality if[:] it touches the inner core of the individual personality, strengthens it, and encourages it to go on; . . . it gives the person deeper insight into his own motives for action—his good actions or his mixed up, "bad" actions; . . . because of it, a person is able to relate himself to other people in ways that are mutually satisfying; . . . it leads a person into intimate relationships with nature . . . ; . . . it awakens a child to wondering, questioning, searching; . . . [or if it provides] the thread that binds together their own wonderings with those of men and women of long ago who walked fearfully, but wonderingly, upon the earth.*[84]

In moral terms, as Dewey points out, "all the rest is mint, anise, and cummin. . . . The teacher who operates in this faith will find every subject, every method of instruction, every incident of school life pregnant with moral possibility."[85]

[83] Neil G. McCluskey, S.J., *Catholic Viewpoint in Education.* Rev. ed. (Garden City, N.Y.: Image Books, 1962), p. 73.
[84] Ernest W. Kuebler, "Religious Education for Today," *A Pocket Guide to Unitarianism,* ed. Harry B. Schlofield (Boston: The Beacon Press, 1954), p. 15.
[85] John Dewey, *Moral Principles in Education* (Boston: Houghton Mifflin Company, 1909), p. 58.

The school provides "religious" experiences by supporting experiences and ideas which give the human being room to grow. It eschews a passive role for the student in favor of a participatory role in an open school community wherein both individual and social betterment are of fundamental concern. Day after day, it confronts the individual—teacher, student and administrator—with decision-demanding situations wherein he must analyze the nature of the problem, analyze forces pressing upon him, construct alternative plans of action, act upon a chosen plan and evaluate the consequences in terms of actual human relations. In all it heightens his awareness of and responsiveness to both himself and the social whole of which he is a part. These experiences can be built into every school experience, permeating the activities of the science laboratory, the student government association, the metal shop, the football field, the faculty room—and even the assistant principal's office. In time their benefits will extend far beyond the walls of the formal school.

For some humanists there will also be a place for the church school. Kuebler writes:

> *We think of a church school as a place where we can emphasize consciously the religious qualities that can permeate all experience, provide supplementary experiences, make available specifically religious and theological material that public schools cannot legally handle, make explicit felt meanings, and celebrate with like-minded persons life's high moments.*[86]

3. God and Faith: The Denial of God

Although "militant" (as contrasted with "unreflective") atheists have not played a vital role in American education, there have been instances of their activity. There have, for example, been strong contemporary reactions to rules such as the 1905 decision of the Board of School Commissioners of Baltimore City (Maryland) which provided for the "holding of opening exercises in the schools of the city, consisting primarily of the 'reading, without comment, of a chapter in the Holy Bible and/or the use of the Lord's Prayer.' "[87] Margaret Murray, an atheist, and her son, a student in the Baltimore schools, appealed to the Maryland courts, maintaining that the rule violated their rights

> *in that it threatens their religious liberty by placing a premium on belief as against nonbelief and subjects their freedom of con-*

[86] Kuebler, "Religious Education for Today," pp. 16–17.
[87] Kliebard, *Religion and Education in America*, p. 213.

science to the rule of the majority; it pronounces belief in God
as the source of all moral and spiritual values, equating these
values with religious values, and thereby renders sinister, alien
and suspect the beliefs and ideals of your Petitioners, promoting
doubt and question of their morality, good citizenship and good
faith.[88]

The trial court refused to admit the petition, a decision which was upheld by the Maryland Court of Appeals but struck down by the Supreme Court, which granted *certiorari*. The facts presented in this case were considered in the highly controversial *Abington v. Schempp* Supreme Court decision of 1963, which declared that the State must be neutral in all matters religious. The battle for reinstating religious ceremonies in the public schools, however, has intensified in the years since *Abington v. Schempp*.

The position of atheists need not, of course, be purely negative. Positively, we may expect atheists to call for many of the activities sponsored by fellow humanists and discussed in the section immediately preceding.[89]

It is still somewhat early in our study of philosophy and education to reach any firm conclusions concerning trends or similarities between positions or to decide what meaning such trends or similarities might have. In passing, we might note several interesting developments. Those who hold to a view of basic reality as a *given* which is independent of the subject (however much they may differ on what is given), tend to agree that human nature also represents given boundaries within which we work out our existence, tend to agree that man has free will, tend to accept the orthodox God and tend to emphasize the need for greater teacher guidance of the student. This "group" includes, as we have seen, most idealists and many more traditional realists. On the other hand, those who for all intents and purposes believe that reality must be *constructed* (be it transactionally or individualistically), tend to agree that one's human nature must also be constructed, either are drawn to religious humanism or deny God altogether, and tend to promote a much higher level of student voice in school affairs. This "group" includes the pragmatists, many scientific realists and existentialists. It will be noted that this "group" does disagree on questions concerning freedom and determinism, the prag-

---

[88] *Ibid.*, p. 214, quoting the Murray petition.
[89] Note the positive actions of Mrs. Murray as reported in Jane Howard, "The Most Hated Woman in America: Margaret Murray," *Life*, LVI (June 19, 1964), pp. 91–92.

matists and the scientific realists being generally in the determinist camp while existentialists argue strongly for freedom. It will also be noted that the theistic existentialists accept a relatively orthodox view of God. Let us keep these very preliminary comparisons in mind as our study continues.

Suggestions for Further Reading

The Nature and Basic Problems of Metaphysics

Brubacher, John S., *Modern Philosophies of Education.* New York: McGraw-Hill Book Co., Inc., 1950. Chapter II.

Butler, J. Donald, *Four Philosophies and Their Practice in Education and Religion.* 3rd ed. New York: Harper & Row, Publishers, Inc., 1968. Pages 15–22.

Morris, Van Cleve, *Philosophy and the American School: An Introduction to the Philosophy of Education.* Boston: Houghton Mifflin Company, 1961. Chapter II.

Taylor, A. E., *Elements of Metaphysics.* 12th ed. London: Methuen & Co., Ltd., 1946. Book 1.

Metaphysical Assumptions and Their Expression in Educational Policies and Practices

Bayles, Ernest E., *Pragmatism in Education.* New York: Harper & Row, Publishers, Inc., 1966. Chapter I (relativism), Chapter II (the nature of man), pp. 53–55 (reality, order in nature), and Chapters V and VI (expression in education).

Breed, Frederick, *Education and the New Realism.* New York: The Macmillan Company, 1939. Chapter III (the realist's argument for absolute reality and a rational world).

Broudy, Harry S., *Building a Philosophy of Education.* 2nd ed. Englewood Cliffs, N.J.: Prentice-Hall, Inc., 1961. Pages 108–112 (science and Metaphysics), and Chapters X and XI (a classical realist on moral and religious values and their expression in education).

Brown, L. M., *General Philosophy in Education.* New York: McGraw-Hill Book Company, Inc., 1966. Chapter VII (freedom and determinism).

Brubacher, John S., ed., *Eclectic Philosophy of Education; A Book of Readings.* Englewood Cliffs, N.J.: Prentice-Hall, Inc., 1951. Chapters III (reality), IV (human nature), XXIV (freedom as method), XXIX (moral education) and XXX (religious education).

Burns, Hobart W., and Charles J. Brauner, *Philosophy of Education; Essays and Commentaries.* New York: The Ronald Press Company,

1962. Pages 74–134 (helpful summaries of viewpoints on the nature of reality, with related readings).

BUTLER, J. DONALD, *Four Philosophies and Their Practice in Education and Religion.* 3rd ed. New York: Harper & Row, Publishers, Inc., 1968. Pages 147–162 (Idealism), Chapter IX (Idealism in education), Chapter X (Idealism in religion), pp. 273–283 (metaphysics of Realism), Chapter XIV (Realism in education), Chapter XV (Realism in religion) and Chapter XXIII (Existentialism and education).

DEWEY, JOHN, *A Common Faith.* New Haven: Yale University Press, 1934.

———, *Experience and Nature.* 2nd ed. New York: W. W. Norton & Co., 1929. Chapter II (qualities of existence).

———, *Human Nature and Conduct.* New York: Henry Holt and Company, 1922.

———, *Moral Principles in Education.* Boston: Houghton Mifflin Co., 1909.

———, *The Quest for Certainty.* New York: Minton, Balch & Co., 1929. Chapter II (the effect of a demand for certainty upon Metaphysics).

DIAMOND, MALCOLM L., *Martin Buber, Jewish Existentialist.* Harper Torchbooks ed. New York: Harper & Row, Publishers, Inc., 1968.

GEIGER, GEORGE R., *John Dewey in Perspective.* New York: Oxford University Press, 1958. Chapters I (experience), IX (education) and X (scientific humanism as a religion).

GREENE, MAXINE, *Teacher as Stranger: Educational Philosophy for the Modern Age.* Belmont, Calif.: Wadsworth Publishing Company, Inc., 1973. Chapters III and IV.

HENDERSON, STELLA, *Introduction to Philosophy of Education.* Chicago: The University of Chicago Press, 1947.

HOCKING, WILLIAM E., *Types of Philosophy.* New York: Charles Scribner's Sons, 1929. Chapters XIX, XXIV and XXIX (metaphysics of Idealism and Realism).

KILPATRICK, WILLIAM H., *Philosophy of Education.* New York: The Macmillan Company, 1951. Pages 184–196 (freedom and determinism) and Chapter V (change).

KNELLER, GEORGE F., *Existentialism and Education.* New York: John Wiley & Sons, Inc., 1958.

MORRIS, VAN CLEVE, *Existentialism in Education.* New York: Harper & Row, Publishers, Inc., 1966.

———, *Philosophy and the American School.* Boston: Houghton Mifflin Co., 1961. Chapters III (metaphysical assumptions) and IV (Metaphysics and education).

MOTHERSHEAD, JOHN L., JR., *Ethics; Modern Conceptions of the Principles of Right.* New York: Holt, Rinehart & Winston, Inc., 1955. Chapter IV (freedom).

NAUMAN, ST. ELMO, JR., *The New Dictionary of Existentialism.* New York: Philosophical Library, Inc., 1971. Extensive definitions based on and including primary source materials.

PLATO, *Republic.* The idealist classic on Metaphysics and consistent educational practices.

REINHARDT, KURT F., *The Existentialist Revolt.* 2nd ed. New York: Frederick Ungar Publishing Co., 1960.

SHERMIS, S. SAMUEL, *Philosophic Foundations of Education.* New York: American Book Company, 1967. Chapters III, IV and XIX.

TAYLOR, A. E., *Elements of Metaphysics.* 12th ed. London: Methuen & Co. Ltd., 1946.

THOMAS, LAWRENCE G., "The Faith of an Experimentalist," *Harvard Educational Review,* XVIII, No. 3 (Summer 1948), pp. 151–157.

———, "The Ontology of Experimentalism," *Educational Theory,* VI (July 1956), pp. 177–183.

———, "Three Orientations to Life," *School and Society,* LXVI, No. 1710 (October 4, 1947), pp. 266–267.

———, "What Metaphysics for Modern Education?," *Educational Forum,* VI, No. 2 (January 1942), pp. 113–131. Comparison of classical and pragmatic traditions on change, reality, experience and freedom.

ULICH, ROBERT, *Philosophy of Education.* New York: American Book Company, 1961. Chapter VI (an idealist view of "cosmic reverence").

WINGO, G. MAX, *The Philosophy of American Education.* New York: D. C. Heath and Company, 1965. Pages 49–50 (conflicts over cosmology and human nature), 136–145 (Idealism), 164–181 (Realism) and 297–300 (Pragmatism).

For an excellent working bibliography of other readings on Metaphysics and the relationship between Metaphysics and the nature and aims of education, curriculum, school organization and policy, and teaching-learning, see Harry S. Broudy *et al.,* eds., *Philosophy of Education: An Organization of Topics and Selected Sources.* Urbana: University of Illinois Press, 1967. This bibliography was supplemented in 1969 (Christiana M. Smith and Harry S. Broudy, eds.) and 1971 (Ronald P. Jeffrey, ed.).

PART *III*

Epistemology and American Education

4

Epistemology: Its Nature, Function, Concepts and Assumptions

We find ourselves in the gymnasium office of a large urban lower school. You are having a heated debate with a colleague as to the basis on which students will be graded in physical education. On your part, you are firmly convinced that there are definite skills which fifth graders should master. Furthermore, various levels of each skill can be identified and defined behaviorally. Much of this material is set forth in the district's curriculum guide. As for the rest—well, you *are* certified in physical education! Grading, therefore, cannot be based on the student's "preference" for certain activities—or his "effort"—and most certainly not on the basis of your personal, *subjective* response to the student's "personality." Explain to your colleague the details of how you would go about establishing an *objective* grading scheme in physical education. Just how would you assign A's, B's, C's, D's and F's? What factors would you take into account—and why?

We are still in the gymnasium office, and you are still the teacher. This time, however, you are just as firmly convinced that there is just no way that anything can be defined once and for all—things such as skills and grades, for instance. As a matter of fact, the way we perceive ourselves and other things develops over time and through mutual contact. If you really want to be "objective" under these conditions, you are going to have to share your perceptions of what is possible and what is important with others also involved in that situation at a given time and in a certain place (e.g., students, administrators, parents). Factual data and "reality factors" (such as the curriculum guide) have to be added to this mix. Reasonable discussion will then shake out the most "objective" view possible. Your colleague is aghast! How are you *ever* going to come up with p.e. grades? Explain how you would go about it.

It is now about eight o'clock on the second Tuesday night of the new term. Suddenly your roommate slams a textbook down on the desk, turns to you and explodes: "That Professor Simes is just too much! I think she believes we're a bunch of robots. She's got us programmed in that course—'September 20: Read pages 23–57 of the text and complete Chapter III in the workbook . . . October 3: Deadline for making appointments for school observations . . . December 18: Submit term project by 10:00 A.M. (Note detailed guidelines on pp. 4–7 of the syllabus.) . . . Lecture—reading—test— paper!' No doubt about it: We're going to do it her way or flunk! And it's a course in the philosophy of education! Doesn't she think I have something to say? Are *my* assumptions completely meaningless? Shouldn't I have a voice in determining the project? Is *this* 'teacher education'?" Try—calmly—to explain to your roommate why Dr. Simes may feel that optimal learning can take place only if she controls the important classroom variables.

Same night, same place, a similar explosion: "Why in the world won't that Professor Simes tell us what to do? I'm not the only one in the class who is completely confused! We've spent an entire week planning and scheduling class discussion topics. Now she's scheduled extra *group* meetings to work out guidelines for different kinds of projects. As if I didn't have four other courses! Today she said that we should also decide on five or six topics for student reports or debates—I wonder when *she'll* start doing some teaching! Is *this* 'teacher education'?" Try to explain to your roommate why Dr. Simes may feel that optimal learning can take place only if she shares control over important classroom variables with the students.

At this point in our studies, you already know that these vignettes are intended as little more than introductions to professional problems which involve philosophical variables. In this case we have two such sketches: one involving different assumptions as to the meaning of "objectivity," the other dealing with the degree to which the limitations of student "frames of reference" can and/or should be overcome by the more experienced teacher. These are, of course, *epistemological* problems. But what is "Epistemology," and what are the functions of epistemological study?

A. Epistemology: Nature and Function

As noted in Chapter 1, Epistemology is that branch of philosophy which has developed around answers to perennial human questions concerning "knowledge." Age after age, man has inquired: "Is knowledge possible?" "If so, are there limits to human knowledge?" "What are the principal kinds of knowledge?" "How do we come to know?" "How do we know that a knowledge-claim is true?" Epistemology, then, is properly taken to involve the study of the possibility, the limits, the development and the validation of knowledge-claims. In addition to these concerns, philosophers of education are also normally interested in how different answers to these epistemological questions may affect educational policy and practice. Finally, it may also be helpful to distinguish between the related but separate foci of "Epistemology," "Logic" and "Psychology":

> Logic *is concerned with the specific and formal problem of correct reasoning, whereas* Epistemology *deals with the nature of reasoning, with truth and with the processes of knowing.*
>   Psychology *is concerned primarily with a* descriptive *study of behavior[al] phenomena, and the like, whereas* Epistemology *deals with our claims to knowledge, and what we mean by "knowing."*[1]

In the pages which follow we shall be interested in the details of claims that knowledge of the reality we inhabit is—and is not—possible. Obviously, the metaphysical studies just concluded will be of no little concern. After all, differences do exist in American culture as to the nature of that "basic reality"! We shall observe conflicting claims with regard to the degree of knowledge which can be achieved even among those who agree there is a knowable reality beyond the self. And conflicts as to what can be known will also be found among those who feel that our reality is functionally restricted to human experience.

There will be those who accept *a priori* knowledge, knowledge based on "principles which, when once understood, are recognized to be true and do not require proof through observation, experience, or experiment."[2] We shall also find those who to various degrees accent *a posteriori* knowledge, knowledge based on sensory data as received and systematically recorded, ordered, evaluated and generalized.

[1] Milton D. Hunnex, *Philosophies and Philosophers*. Rev. and enlarged ed. (San Francisco: Chandler Publishing Company, An Intext Publisher, 1971), p. 3.
[2] J. Donald Butler, *Four Philosophies and Their Practice in Education and Religion*. 3rd ed. (New York: Harper & Row, Publishers, 1968), p. 44.

Depending on related metaphysical and epistemological assumptions, we shall be able to identify an extensive number of suggested "modes of knowing," that is, ways in which we may come to gain knowledge. Accented will be *deductive reasoning* based on a priori postulates, *disciplined intuition* in which the truth of a statement is immediately evident to the subject, and the *acceptance of reputable authority* (e.g., the Pope when speaking *ex cathedra*) or the *acceptance of revelation.* There will be those who will argue for *common sense.* And there will be those who will demand *experimentation,* involving both inductive and deductive reasoning on the basis of sensory observation, reference to related variables, hypothesis construction, regulated action, evaluation of action consequences and generalization. Basic to our study of the various modes of knowing will be a consideration of different assumptions as to the nature and function of the "mind," "ideas," "objectivity" and "frame of reference."

Finally, leaving an extended treatment of Epistemology and education to the next chapter, we shall inquire into the verification of knowledge-claims. Is truth based on the *consistency* (or coherence) of these claims one with another—especially with those already accepted as true? Or is it a matter of the degree to which they *correspond* with an objective, discernible, external reality? Could truth be a function of the *consequences of transactional relationships* established in successfully mediating experience? Not unexpectedly, we shall find adherents of all three positions, as well as of a fourth, namely, that truth refers to those knowledge-claims which an individual chooses to *appropriate*—accept as his own—and express in his actions.

As in our study of Metaphysics—and in our studies yet to come—the accent will be upon those philosophical variables common to contemporary American culture, especially to the contemporary American school. Not all of the concerns sketched above will receive full development, for this is an introductory text. Also, rather than follow the question format thus far employed, common answers will be considered in relation to the treatment of specific epistomological concepts and assumptions which follows.

B. Epistemological Concepts and Assumptions

1. Mind

A. MIND OR SOUL AS AN IMMATERIAL ENTITY. Though probably rooted deeply in prehistory, the classical understanding of the mind as being above the laws of physics, as having a nonphysical and supernatural quality, as being an entity—a "something"—which performs certain functions retains a considerable hold on popular thought. Identical with the soul, the mind in Plato's view is of the same stuff as that creative, purposeful, spiritual energy referred to as Absolute Mind. In this assumption, therefore, we find both the explanatory principle of man's immortality and the basis for the familiar notion that the body must be subjected to the control of the mind. One idealist tradition holds that the mind at birth contains all of the archetypal ideas "thought" by Absolute Mind and, hence, theoretically the keys prerequisite to man's unlocking and retaining knowledge. At the same time, however, in the human being the mind is "married" to flesh-matter, a phenomenon which introduces grave epistemological difficulties and, when coupled with environmental factors, results in differences between men as to their ability to grasp and use ideas, that is, to gain knowledge.[3]

In the knowledge-gaining process, man's mind functions in two somewhat different ways. It may, as it were, attempt to avoid the distortions of the sensory world, focussing directly, contemplatively, on the archetypal ideas within mind which are the source of reliable knowledge and Truth. Nevertheless, this world when understood as a particular objectification of Absolute Mind does serve as a reality factor for man; his mind, therefore, must also deal with sensory data. In terms of the earlier discussion of the essential unity of four classmates, ideas are brought to the conscious level and allowed to "illuminate" our perceptions of sensory data. In so doing, the distortions introduced by physical and sociocultural "accidents" are minimized, our perceptions are made more intelligible and we may more systematically organize and generalize our ideas in the search for Truth.

It must be noted that the mind's powers—however much they can be refined and strengthened—are exercised under certain limitations. Man is a creature of the natural world as well as of the supernatural. Matter functions as an anchor. It constantly creates "static" and "fog" which interfere with the mind's efforts to communicate with Absolute Mind in perceiving and conceptualizing Truth. Our considerations of the "consistency theory of knowledge and truth" will deal further with the ways in which these factors affect the epistemological quest.

B. MIND AS A FUNCTION OF BODILY PROCESSES. Let us now turn to a position which, like the one just discussed, is deeply rooted in the

---

[3] In this, of course, we are referring to the normal, "average" individual. In the case of brain damage, severe social and emotional disturbance, and other anomalies studied in "special education," *additional* epistemological problems are introduced.

classical tradition; namely, the assumption that "mind" is but a term referring to certain bodily processes, particularly to functions of the brain. It will be noted that this tradition essentially denies that mind is an entity (material or immaterial) and leaves open the question of mind's relation to the soul and, hence, man's relation to the super-natural realm.[4] There are, nonetheless, similarities between these two positions within the classical tradition, some more substantial than others. The metaphorical language sometimes used to express the present realistically-oriented assumption does at times lead one to suspect that mind is still being viewed as a distinct entity. We read, for example, that "mind is a blank tablet upon which is written a person's perceptual experience and out of which emerges his conceptual possessions—his stock of ideas."[5] More telling, perhaps, is the similarity also noted by Brauner and Burns, who write:

> In this tradition, whether the mind is seen as an independent nonmaterial entity causally linked to the dependent, material brain, or merely the brain as it functions in certain ways, it is said to act as exterocepter and interocepter. That is, it acts externally (by analogy to the eye of a mirror) to serve as a lens that reflects or transmits perceptions of the physical world to the intellect; and it acts internally (by analogy to a computer) as a receiver, classifier, and codifier to translate perceptions into conceptions, or ideas, by which a person comes to have knowledge.[6]

Over time and with an increasing disposition to view man as a strictly naturalistic organism, the assumption of "mind as a function of bodily processes" which receive, sort, classify and connect data emanating from an external reality has been expressed with growing clarity. Under the influence of philosophers such as Hume and Kant (and the earlier Locke), the notion of mind as a powerful and independent entity controlling the body was gradually weakened. Their "mental-states" theory came to be associated with the notion of mental "faculties," powers or functions by which knowledge was obtained. In Rousseau, Pestalozzi, Froebel and Herbart, we see mind increasingly anchored within man. We see the strongest emphasis on the notion

---

[4] *Cf.* Charles J. Brauner and Hobert W. Burns, *Problems in Education and Philosophy* (Englewood Cliffs, N.J.: Prentice-Hall, Inc., 1965), p. 33. In fact, proponents of the assumption have included both theists and naturalists. (The term "theists" refers—at minimum—to those who hold the assumption of the "Orthodox God." The term "naturalist" refers to those who prefer to base their explanations of phenomena upon the world of nature, ignoring or denying the possibility of a higher, controlling supernatural realm. In passing, it might be noted that a naturalist *could* hold the assumption of the "Humanistic God"—or deny God altogether.)

[5] *Ibid.*, p. 32.

[6] *Ibid.*, pp. 32–33.

that ideas and impressions must be transmited *by* the teacher *to* the student and that the child's experiences are of vital import to his ability to receive these impressions.[7]

With the maturing of the "New (Experimental) Science," the psychological investigations of individuals such as J. B. Watson, Pavlov, Edward Thorndike and B. F. Skinner have supported the strongest expression of this assumption. "Mind" is the result of purely naturalistic processes, basically chemical-physical processes of the body. A neurological response or reaction to environmental stimuli gives rise to reflex action which we term "human behavior." Our habitual responses to specific stimuli provide the conditions under which learning takes place; in fact, all learning

> *is a process of building up new reflexes. This is done by coupling up stimuli with new responses so as to make new [S-R] pairs. A reflex action which is thus built up in the course of experience by joining a stimulus to a new response is called a "conditioned reflex," in contrast with reflexes which are inborn.*[8]

Skinner has extended this position by pointing out that there are many observed behaviors whose learning we wish to reinforce but whose stimuli are unknown. His investigations have contributed much to establishing the specifics by which these (operant) behavioral responses can be conditioned or reinforced. By way of illustrating how far this assumption has deviated from its classical sister, it may be noted that this conditioning tends to disregard the behavioral relevancy of human purposes, wishes or attitudes. The focus is strictly on the environmental conditions which will effectively reinforce and hence maintain the desired behavior, not upon the "inner states" of the learner. The brain is thus "programmed" as we might program a computer, a process which—as Skinner points out—can lead to greater instructional effectiveness, although it need not necessarily lead to greater regimentation.[9]

C. MIND AS PURPOSEFUL, PROBLEM-SOLVING BEHAVIOR. For the pragmatist, "mind" is not an immaterial entity often identified with the

---

[7] *Cf.* Douglas E. Lawson, "Changing Concepts of the Mind," *Phi Delta Kappan,* **XX** (1937), pp. 44–46; also John S. Brubacher, ed., *Eclectic Philosophy of Education: A Book of Readings* (Englewood Cliffs, N.J.: Prentice-Hall, Inc., 1951), Selections 61, 62, 63, 65b and 66.

[8] Boyd H. Bode, *How We Learn* (Boston: D. C. Heath and Company, 1940), p. 177.

[9] B. F. Skinner, "Man," *Models of Man; Explorations in the Western Educational Tradition,* ed. Paul Nash (New York: John Wiley & Sons, Inc., 1968), p. 433. Also see Skinner, *Science and Human Behavior* (New York: The Macmillan Company, 1953; Free Press paperback ed., 1965, pp. 87–90.

"soul," nor is it to be identified strictly with the brain-guided physio-logical functions of the organism. Rather, it is a word which refers to the behaviors involved in establishing a certain relationship between self and that identified as nonself in a specified experiential context or field. We have already noted that the pragmatist takes experience to be our basic human reality and that change or flux is a prime charac-teristic of that reality. We have seen that both self and nonself are differentiated by the organism out of experience, that both constructs are shaped by their mutual influence upon each other and that the nature of self and nonself alike must constantly be reconstructed as the flow of experience continues. For this reason, it may be noted, the pragmatist sees "minding behaviors"[10] as being as much a function of the physical and social environment as of the biological organism per se.

As long as organism and environment are in balance, in a state of relative equilibrium, reflective thinking (as contrasted with other activ-ities sometimes referred to as thinking, e.g., aimless fantasizing, the imaginative invention of mental images or believing)[11] is simply not necessary. Demonstrably, this is rarely the case. Events arising in experience constantly push the organism off balance. Such disequilib-rium, however, still may not call for minding behaviors. Learned habit patterns may quickly be brought into play: There is discom-fort—you reach for your sweater. There is discomfort—my pipe is packed and lit. A physiological sense of well-being is restored with but minimal cognition. On occasion, however, one's repertoire of habit patterns is inadequate to restoring equilibrium. Perhaps the complexity of the situation does not allow the brain (working essen-tially at subconscious or unconscious levels) to select an appropriate habituated response. Then discomfort intrudes upon consciousness and minding behaviors may be called into action. Dewey writes:

> *Thinking begins in what may fairly enough be called a* forked-road *situation, a situation that is ambiguous, that presents a dilemma, that proposes alternatives. As long as our activity glides smoothly along from one thing to another, or as long as we permit our imagination to entertain fancies at pleasure, there is no call for reflection. Difficulty or obstruction in the way of*

---

[10] Philosophical language has been heavily influenced by the foundational contri-bution of classical—especially Greek—philosophers. Not surprisingly, to this day "mind" generally carries with it the connotation of a thing—an object. Consider such familiar expressions as "It came to mind," or "That just stuck in my mind." As a result, pragmatists often prefer to speak of "minding behaviors," a somewhat clumsy locution which attempts to capture the *process* rather than the "static" quality of mind.

[11] *Cf.* John Dewey, *How We Think.* Rev. ed. (Boston: D. C. Heath and Com-pany, 1933), pp. 3–7.

*reaching a belief brings us, however, to a pause. In the suspense
of uncertainty, we metaphorically climb a tree; we try to find
some standpoint from which we may survey additional facts,
and getting a more commanding view of the situation, decide
how the facts stand related one to another.*[12]

The first stage in "tree climbing"—or, if you will, the first of those
behaviors pointed to by the word "mind"—consists of *defining the
problem.* Thus far, you just feel uncomfortable—uneasy—disturbed.
Now you must define just *what is wrong.* Perhaps you are cold—but
your students are complaining about the heat. Perhaps you have
paused in front of a painting expressed in a style which heretofore you
have found displeasing—and yet in *this* case there is something about
it. Perhaps it is the first day of school and one of your new students
has just referred to you with a string of Anglo-Saxon words mostly of
one syllable and all unprintable. On the one hand, you know enough
about psychology to hypothesize that he is not reacting to *you* at all.
On the other, you have an instinctive desire to really "let him have it."
Furthermore, you know that your relationship with that child—
indeed, with all the children in that class—will be much affected by
your response. You want to act "professionally," and yet. . . . Here
is the quandary—and the problem.

The next stage involves the *imaginative construction of some plans
of action* which seem likely to "solve" the problem or at least "reduce"
it to a level which allows the restoration of equilibrium.[13] Actually,
this behavior includes at least three (often overlapping) dimensions:
1) the *consideration of antecedent variables,* i.e., factors which must
be considered prior to acting; 2) the *examination of possible plans of
action in light of evaluative criteria* which will later be applied to the
actual consequences of acting on your idea in order to determine if it
really "worked"; and 3) the *selection of the most promising hypothesis*
for implementation.

Antecedent variables include factors such as the force of the problem. For instance, we may ask: "How pressing is it?" "How much
has it thrown you off balance?" One's habitual ways of meeting
similar problems present another factor. After all, it is possible to
change one's *modus operandi,* but the cost in energy is great and such
an expenditure may not be justified if one's present habits are deemed
adequate to the task at hand. A third factor is contained in a careful
evaluation of the needs and rights of others who are involved in the
problematic situation. Closely allied is the careful evaluation of one's

[12] *Ibid.,* p. 14.

[13] Although in science such "plans of action" are normally referred to as "hypotheses," in philosophical Pragmatism the technical term is "ideas." For our
purposes, these three terms may conveniently be treated as rough synonyms.

self-interests. Whether we term them moral standards, theories or axioms, it also seems necessary to consider generalizations of human experience which we see as potentially relevant to the situation. These include both the facts and beliefs supplied by disciplines such as history, philosophy, psychology and sociology. Finally, we do well to look at any external constraints within which we will be forced to seek a problem solution. Prior administrative decisions, the nature and adequacy of physical facilities and available finances provide examples of such "reality factors."

As noted above, hypothesis-construction also involves looking ahead to three evaluative criteria which will be applied to the consequences of our eventual action. Surely, the idea must either solve or markedly reduce the problem and thus restore equilibrium. Furthermore, it is difficult to see how equilibrium could be restored unless the idea were "reasonably consistent" with antecedent variables.[14] Finally, the plan of action which truly works will evoke no unforeseen consequences with which we cannot at least coexist. By way of an example, let us take another look at the student who cursed us on that (memorable) first day of school. It is surely *possible* that we might give way to sarcastic invective and verbally tear that youngster to shreds before the class. Momentarily, we might even feel better—given the shock occasioned by his behavior. But how will we feel when we later consider the needs of a youngster who turns out to be (marginally) socially and emotionally disturbed?—when we compare our action with our personal and professional standards?—when we consider the attitudinal costs in terms of classroom climate? What if our behavior results in such trauma that the child has to be institutionalized and the incident placed before the District Superintendent? We simply didn't foresee that consequence. Is it something with which we could easily live?

As we consider antecedent variables and evaluative criteria, we slowly start to construct possible plans of action. In this there is surely nothing mechanical. After all, human judgment is surely the central element in the process—no matter how many resources have been assembled as aids. Finally, a judgment is made as to the most likely hypothesis and we move on to the next dimension of mind, *action consistent with the chosen idea.* This step is surely no more mechanical than the one which preceded it.

---

[14] To say "reasonably consistent" is surely not to say that antecedent variables, including moral standards, can in and of themselves *determine* plans of action. It is simply to point out that ideas too inconsistent with the individual's frame of reference may introduce dissonance so great that the restoration of equilibrium is highly unlikely. The line beween "too inconsistent" and "reasonably consistent" involves the most sensitive exercise of human judgment in a given context.

Having acted, we are now faced with the task of *evaluating actual consequences*. To the extent that these consequences match up with the prediction of what would happen (contained in the plan of action), we now have "knowledge," albeit "contextual" knowledge. We know that under the specified situational conditions—including antecedent variables, time, place and people—a specific idea did in fact result in specific consequences, that in this sense the idea is "true." (These points and those which follow will be developed more adequately under the "transactional theory of knowledge and truth.")

Finally, the word "mind" refers to the *generalization of our contextual knowledge*. In some cases we merely refine existing generalizations, e.g., about learning, discipline or teacher-student roles. In others, we may begin to develop new generalizations. In all, these generalizations—whether they take the form of theories, moral standards or axioms—serve as antecedent variables for future decision-making in seemingly related problematic situations. Obviously, they cannot be applied mechanically; they cannot tell us exactly what to do. After all, they were formed out of only a *sample* of *past* human experiencing. The new problem lies in the here and now, not in the past. One must also consider the possibility that the past sample was biased. Nevertheless, as noted earlier, they do provide a vital resource for problem-solving. Given the amount of evaluated human experiencing upon which generalizations are based, they cannot be lightly dismissed.

These, then, are the behaviors pointed to by the word "mind": defining the problem, imaginatively constructing plans of action, acting consistently with the chosen plan, evaluating actual consequences of action and generalizing contextual knowledge. This is the process—interrupted only momentarily by instances of transitory equilibrium—by which is created a transactional relationship between the organism and its experiential field. This is the process by which the human being "mediates" or "processes" experience to bend it to his purposes, realizing full well that the agent, its purposes and the product alike will be shaped-modified-defined in that process. And to the extent that one learns to perform the acts making up this integrated process with increasing accuracy, efficiency, flexibility, sensitivity and speed, we say that he is behaving "intelligently."[15] True, everyone learns them to some extent, although we must never minimize the social milieu in which they are learned nor the importance of structuring that milieu so as to allow them to be learned more effectively, more enjoyably and with greater profit to all concerned.

[15] Lawrence G. Thomas, "Implications of Transaction Theory," *Educational Forum*, XXXII, No. 1 (January 1968), p. 151. By permission of Kappa Delta Pi, An Honor Society in Education, owners of the Copyright.

2. Ideas

A. IDEAS AS ARCHETYPES OF EXISTENTS. "Primarily," writes Antz,

> *an idea is an object of knowledge—something knowable or known. Taken as a guide for action, an idea becomes an ideal. The perfect or ideal squares and circles of geometry are psychologically suggested by the imperfectly square or circular objects of the sense world, but they themselves are of a very different order of being. They are intelligible objects, visible only to the eye of the mind [one's powers of reason]. They can never, being immaterial, be exactly copied in the material world, but they are the patterns which we follow—roughly or carefully according to the needs of the situation—whenever we make a square or circular object. The same condition holds for man in relation to the most fundamental of Platonic Ideas, the* Good, *with its special forms, the* True *and the* Beautiful, *and their species, temperance, harmony, spiritedness, wisdom, justice, and the like. Through a good education, and through the long effort of reason and wise living, man can come to comprehend them; but again, since they are immaterial, he can embody them only to a degree in his natural life and institutions. But, knowing and loving them, he can through his aspiration toward them avoid the life of mental sloth, of bestial and unreasoning pleasure, and of soul-destroying false ambitions . . .*[16]

When encountered in experience—albeit for the moment and but dimly—the mind intuitively grants the claim of Ideas to truth, perhaps on the basis of a previous, more direct encounter with them prior itself to being objectified in this world.[17] As perfect and as permanent as the objects of our senses are defective and transitory, the Ideas are the key to that reason which would discern the outlines of reality and guide men toward Truth.

B. IDEAS AS REFLECTIONS OF A NATURAL, EXTERNAL REALITY.
In the realist tradition, albeit expressed in different accents, "ideas" exist neither as supernaturally-created archetypes of existents nor as elements of the mind's supernatural endowment. Rather, ideas are cognitive phenomena naturally developed as the organism's brain-guided sensing interacts with a reality which is independent of, and external to, itself. Their function lies in reflecting or mirroring that external reality and allowing us to recall and compare our experi-

[16] Louise Antz, "Idealism as a Philosophy of Education," *Philosophy of Education; Essays and Commentaries,* eds. Hobert W. Burns and Charles J. Brauner (New York: The Ronald Press Company, 1962), pp. 238–239.
[17] *Cf.* J. Donald Butler, *Four Philosophies and Their Practice in Education and Religion,* p. 113; also W. E. Hocking, *Types of Philosophy* (New York: Charles Scribner's Sons, 1929), p. 220.

ences and systematically to organize, criticize and generalize our knowledge in search for Truth.

Aristotle saw ideas as mind-developed abstractions of an object's form or essence resulting from the interaction of our sense organs with the external world. Locke understood them to be objects of understanding developed in the thinking process. For him, they arose either upon stimulation of the sense organs or upon reflection on our own conscious mental activity. Also in this tradition, Hume viewed ideas as "faint images" or "memory copies" of sense impressions.

A prime epistemological problem for Realism, of course, has been the degree to which our ideas do in fact correspond to the reality which they signify. Admittedly, over the centuries the answers have varied widely. Some realists have held that we can know objects as they are apart from our ideas about them. Others have tended to see man as relatively trapped in an internal, ideational world of his own making (however much his ideas are caused by, and point to, an external world of matter and natural process). Most realists, on the other hand, would probably agree that statements of our ideas can be corrected and refined (especially through science) until a relatively high level of correspondence with things-as-they-are is achieved. We shall return to this point in discussing the "correspondence theory of knowledge and truth."

C. IDEAS AS MAN-CREATED PLANS OF ACTION. As discussed under the assumption of "mind as purposeful, problem-solving behavior," thought involves devising means of solving problems defined in human experience in ways that further the well-being of both individual and society. True, there are moments of simple aesthetic appreciation of experience-as-it-is. There are also cases where equilibrium is restored quickly, predominately on the basis of reflective and/or habituated organism response. Brauner and Burns, for instance, note that

> A brain can function without at the same time engaging in "mental" (as differentiated from physiological) activity. Mental activity, or mind ("mind-ing" activity) is present only when a person deliberately employs his biologically given, environmentally developed, and brain-centered intelligence to design or plan a specific course of action.[18]

And to these specific designs or plans for action Dewey and other pragmatists assign the term "ideas."

Consciously constructed by man, ideas link the perceived self with the perceived nonself; they link what is perceived to be with that

[18] *Problems in Education and Philosophy*, p. 48.

which (hopefully) might be. As is the case with scientific hypotheses, they lead us to look at our present structurings of experience from new vantage points. In so doing, at times they suggest new meanings, new paths to solving the problems constantly besetting us. Thereby, they fire our resolve to overcome old habits and engage in less familiar behaviors necessary to translating the desired into the possessed.

Guiding and clarifying, ideas so defined contain an implicit prediction of what will happen if we act upon them. Thus they are instrumental to the constant reconstruction of experience which is the task of intelligence. And it is to the consequences of acting on them in a given context to which we must turn if we would determine their truth.

3. Experience

A. EXPERIENCE AS CONTACT WITH A GIVEN REALITY. In the classical tradition, experience is "the process of bringing together two independent, antecedent entities into a knowing relationship. . . . Experience, if it is accurate, discloses to the subject the objects which actually exist independently of his experience. The purpose of experiencing is to gain knowledge of what is."[19] It is not that the child's solving of problems which he sees as relevant to his interests and his gaining of satisfactions in so doing are unimportant—far from it. Nevertheless, experience must be focussed on gaining knowledge of an antecedent reality to which one must adjust for physical and moral survival. Clearly, other products of experiencing are secondary to this primary purpose.

Given this assumption, however, the classicist is quick to point out that the learner is not, and must not be, restricted to direct sensory experience—however varied such experience might be. Indeed, "raw experience" restricts the learner to the very limitations of space and time which must be transcended in the search for knowledge.[20] It is in education that the child's raw sensory experience can be corrected and expanded by the disciplining of the senses, the "honing" of the mind's rational powers and a growing, inspirational acquaintance with the finest products of man's spirit and hands. In education as discipline we must also remember that both direct and vicarious experiences have their place. It is simply not profitable (if indeed possible)

[19] Lawrence G. Thomas, "The Ontology of Experimentalism," *Educational Theory,* VI (July 1956), p. 178.
[20] William C. Bagley, "Education as a Unique Kind of Experience," *Eclectic Philosophy of Education,* ed. John S. Brubacher (Englewood Cliffs, N.J.: Prentice-Hall, Inc., 1951), p. 134.

to present all knowledge via direct experiences. The past experiences of man not only allow him to evaluate his present experience but also allow him to profit from the time-effort expended by the species' exemplars in searching for and refining their understanding of Truth. If every experience arranged for the student were unique—if he were cut off from knowledge already gained—continued human progress would be questionable indeed.

B. EXPERIENCE AS TRANSACTIONAL DOING AND UNDERGOING. Reflecting the pragmatic position as set forth in *Democracy and Education* and introducing the epistemological significance of the assumption that basic reality is found in the "experience of individuals-in-society," Saunders writes:

> *Experience, according to Dewey, is an active-passive affair in which something is done and something is undergone in consequence of what has been done; experience becomes reflective when the relation between what is done and what is undergone is perceived.*[21]

Lawrence Thomas refers to experience as the "given," "the flowing totality of all events and reference points,"[22] which is to be regarded "not as a personal possession, not as a link of awareness which develops between me and objects in the environment, but as an engulfing flow of events."[23]

Out of this undifferentiated, dynamic, natural reality, the organism over time and in different contexts defines both self and other. Here are to be found both the sources of disequilibrium and the stimuli which call for "minding behaviors" to mediate or give meaning to experience. Experience, then, cannot be understood simply as the process of bringing a given subject and a given object into a knowing relationship. Rather, in itself it *is* the given—the moving, raw *is-ness* out of which is constructed both what I am and what I am not.

Self and other are ever-in-the-making. As such they are best regarded as dynamic generalizations of human experiencing. Both are *products* of countless actions and reactions. Each transaction modifies the meanings ascribed to both self and other and, thus, the experiential base which will color future perceptions. Over time, of course, we do construct a sturdier, more reliable self-concept. We do achieve

[21] William J. Saunders, "Thomism, Instrumentalism, and Education," *Harvard Educational Review*, X, No. 1 (January 1940), p. 102. *Cf.* John Dewey, *Democracy and Education* (New York: The Macmillan Company, 1916); (paperback ed.; New York: The Free Press, 1966), p. 163.
[22] "The Ontology of Experimentalism," p. 179.
[23] "Implications of Transaction Theory," p. 145. Quoted by permission.

greater constancy in our view of the "nature" of significant others, things, ideas and processes in our experiential field. We err, however, when we fail to remember that all such constructs are generalized from transactional relationships which occurred in given contexts. We also err when we fail to realize that attributes "(e.g., big, hard, green, warm, brief, nourishing, beautiful, dangerous, loving, useful, saintly) become qualities of the transactions between the emerging Subject and Object rather than inherent characteristics of either one."[24]

Finally, we should note that experiential transactions occur at different levels. Naturally, there is a difference between John's absent-mindedly petting Rover and the laboratory scientist's meticulously checking out the results of mixing two compounds. Some experiences are simply aesthetically enjoyed in and for themselves. They do not give rise to problem-solving behaviors. Insights or hunches usually find their source in those transactions which occur at the unconscious or subconscious levels. More reliable knowledge is normally developed through "inquiry," "reflective or critical thinking," or "science." By these terms we simply refer to various levels of conscious, systematized, regulated experiencing. We do in certain ways; we observe our doing; we observe the consequences of (or responses to) our doing. We synthesize our knowledge of the relationships between our doing and undergoing and develop generalizations variously referred to as laws, theories or moral standards. We compare our knowledge with that developed by others, thus achieving a certain kind of "objectivity" based on intersubjective corroboration. And we grow in intelligence as we gain skill in developing hypotheses which really predict what will happen when we and others under similar conditions act upon them.

C. EXPERIENCE AS BEING IN THE WORLD. Classicists, it will be remembered, view "experience" as the process involved in a given subject's coming into knowing contact with a given object; pragmatists, as that basic reality within which both self and nonself emerge as definitional products of countless social transactions. Denying that the self is either a given or a transactional product, the existentialist, by comparison, emphasizes the inescapably personal nature of experience in which our choices define and reveal the self. To illustrate, Jourard writes:

> *Everyone experiences the world in a way that is unique to him. My experience of the world is different from yours. Experience refers to our perceptions, feelings, meaning, fantasies, or more generally, to our being in the world. This being changes con-*

[24] *Ibid.*, pp. 147–148. Quoted by permission.

> *tinuously from instant to instant. What we refer to as our Self (actually, our idea of our self, or our self-concept) is an inseparable part of our being in the world. Our concepts of things and of other people, and our perception of these phenomena are also part of our being in the world as are our thinking, reasoning, remembering, and fantasy. We exist in the world; we are in the world. We experience the world. Nobody but me can ever have a direct glimpse of my being, that is, my experience. I am the only one to whom my experiencing happens. I cannot dictate my experience to myself. Experience happens to me. It goes on from birth to death, in waking and in sleep. It is private and personal, but I can disclose it to other people if I choose, just as they can choose to disclose their experience to me, thus enriching my experience in my world.*[25]

Not surprisingly, the existentialist rejects authority-controlled, and would minimize authority-involved, experiences in favor of an accent on the personal experiencing of the subject. The accent is placed on "interaction *within* the subject, not between the subject and the agent. The agent serves not as a partner or active cooperator, but as a catalyst. He interacts as does a mirror."[26]   The agent's task is to provide an environment wherein the subject can experience opportunities for making choices, choices which sharpen his perception of both self and Other. Harold Rugg, commonly counted an exponent of "Progressive Education" (though not of Pragmatism), anticipates the existentialistic outlook:

> *The Man-as-Artist maintains that whereas science builds on the principle of the adjustment to the external environment, art builds on the adjustment of the individual to his inner environment, his own personal norms. Science aims at producing a "true" interpretation of the external environment—one possible of confirmation or refutation; art aims at a unique individualized interpretation. The scientist succeeds only if he finds uniformity, states "law"; the artist succeeds only by producing variation. As an individual he is unique; hence his art, if valid, must be just that.*[27]

[25] Sidney M. Jourard, "Counseling for Authenticity," *Philosophical Guidelines for Counseling*, ed. Carlton E. Beck.   2nd ed. (Dubuque, Iowa: Wm. C. Brown Company Publishers, 1971), pp. 185–186.   Quoted by permission of the publisher.

[26] Richard W. Dettering, "Philosophical Idealism in Rogerian Psychology," *Educational Theory*, V, No. 4 (October 1955), p. 208.   (Dettering's argument that Rogerian thought has "treaded into idealistic ground" is interesting, although not entirely convincing.   Given the earlier-discussed problems with "labeling" according to "schools" or "systems," it seems best not to take strong issue with Dettering at this point. It is hypothesized, however, that many of Carl Rogers's positions are far more consistent with existentialistic assumptions than with those of Idealism.

[27] Harold Rugg, *Culture and Education in America* (New York: Harcourt, Brace and Company, 1931), p. 235.

As we create environments wherein human beings feel free to *be* themselves, they will involve themselves vigorously in the adventure of becoming. No longer will they feel a need to deny their own experience and play a role dictated by the Other or by some fantasy. Indeed, they will not fear the Other. Rather, they will more freely reveal their own being, their experience, and thus enjoy the added possibilities opened only in I-Thou relationships.

4. Objectivity

A. OBJECTIVITY AS ALIGNMENT WITH A GIVEN REALITY. The classicist's assumption as to the nature of objectivity appears to resemble that common sense position which views "objectivity" and "subjectivity" as antonyms. One is closest to being objective when one is furthest from being subjective, and vice versa. Objectivity, then, consists of knowing and aligning oneself with a given reality, with the way "things really are independently, not only of human wishes and preferences, but also of any distortion from perceptions and [raw, undisciplined] experiences."[28]

In all fairness to the classical position, however, it must be emphasized that this assumption does not denigrate subjectivity. Indeed, a personal knowledge of where one stands at a given point in time seems prerequisite to being able to move efficiently toward a more objective position. "Know thyself" has long been a classical maxim. Furthermore, it must be realized that our present store of established truths has its limitations. Not all Truth is known; nor is the full Truth of every phenomenon known. Once one develops an objective view of such a phenomenon—to the extent that present knowledge permits— examining it subjectively may suggest new and creative ways of furthering knowledge. Here, untutored subjectivity is not interfering with objectivity. Rather, a subjectivity which realizes its supportive function can extend knowledge and hence facilitate greater objectivity.

B. OBJECTIVITY AS INTERSUBJECTIVITY. In considering the pragmatically-oriented assumptions of "basic reality as the experience of individuals-in-society," "mind as purposeful, problem-solving behavior" and "experience as transactional doing and undergoing," we have seen that both self and nonself are differentiated over time out of ongoing experience. Both constructs are social products of transactions between the organism and other perceived elements in its life space. Lawrence Thomas writes:

[28] Thomas, "Implications of Transaction Theory," p. 148. Quoted by permission.

> *The natures of both the Subject and the Object are significantly conditioned by each other. The nature of the Subject (the observer, the knower) is a product of past experiencings, past differentiatings, now built into habits, dispositions, and expectancies which give a distinctive set toward the stimuli he is likely to see in the present situation. The nature of the Object (the focus of attention, the thing known) is a product of what's there that the Subject is expecting, is ready for, can respond to, can assimilate. The Subject responds, not to a given environment, but to what he takes to be the environment. . . . Part of the subject is projected into the nature of every object; part of the observer is present in every object observed.[29]*

Although time does bring a gradual "hardening" of the meanings we assign to self and to the more significant nonself phenomena in our life space (e.g., brother, sand, automobile, wife), even the firmest of definitions are subject to modification on the basis of a continuing mediation of experience.

Given the pragmatist's denial of the possibility of any knowledge of a reality beyond our human experience and a related rejection of the classicist's separation of "subjectivity" and "objectivity," we face some problems in assigning meaning to "objectivity" within this frame of reference. The following definition, then, is offered only as a reasonable hypothesis: Objectivity is the product of sharing and, when possible, reconciling subjective perceptions of a given phenomenon in a specified context.

Operationally, the achievement of objectivity first calls for involved individuals frankly and openly to express how they perceive the phenomenon, e.g., how well Mr. Bolte is performing in his first year as a faculty member at Jefferson High. Informal discussion involving administrators, department faculty and students ready for such a sensitive task could then be supplemented by other data such as returns from student and supervisory evaluation measures, other information from the instructor's dossier and observations of other competent observers—including, to be sure, Mr. Bolte himself. Out of this open consideration of all available data by those concerned will hopefully come some consensus. In some cases, to be sure, full agreement will be impossible; the " 'more' objective" view may have to reflect compromise and even the willingness of individuals to co-exist with their fellows with regard to some issues. Nevertheless, a contextually objective view will have been achieved through sharing subjective perceptions—if you will, on the basis of "intersubjectivity."

C. OBJECTIVITY AS INTRASUBJECTIVITY. In discussing the therapeutic and pedagogical position of Carl Rogers, Dettering notes the

[29] *Ibid.* Quoted by permission.

Rogerian emphasis on understanding the individual's behavior from within his *own* frame of reference. Rogers, he maintains, "stands opposed to *any* external imposition of norms, whether based on authority, custom, logic, or consequences. It is contrary to Rogers' morality to assess the person from without; [the] intersubjective must yield to [the] intrasubjective verdict."[30]   Perls, the originator and developer of the existentialistically-oriented "Gestalt Therapy," writes:

> *I personally believe that objectivity does not exist. The objectivity of science is also just a matter of mutual agreement. A certain number of persons observe the same phenomena and they speak about an objective criterion. Yet it was from the scientific side where the first proof of subjectivity came. This was from Einstein. Einstein realized that all the phenomena in the universe cannot possibly be objective, because the observer and the speed within its nervous system have to be included in the calculation of that phenomenon outside. If you have perspective, and can see a larger outlook, you seem to be more fair, objective, balanced. But even there, it's you as the subject who sees it [roman added].*[31]

Although it will be noted that Perls commits the common error of assuming that a concept, e.g., "objectivity," *must* be treated in terms of the assumption of "objectivity as alignment with a given reality," his accent on the perspective of the subject, the individual—the "intrasubjective verdict"—is clear.

Once again, however, a basic existentialistic problem reappears: the Other just will not go away, disappear. Are Rogers and Perls and so many others of this persuasion really telling us that the Other is simply irrelevant to the subject's achieving a certain kind of "objectivity"? Surely this does not seem to be the case.

In discussing the assumption of "experience as being in the world," the possibility was introduced of creating environments in which fear of the Other was reduced—where self and Other could meet as free subjectivities and thus enjoy the added possibilities opened only through I-Thou relationships. Earlier considerations noted that working out a meaningful relationship with the Other stands as a necessary if not sufficient step in building one's own human nature or essence. With regard to these themes, Sartre actually uses the term *"intersubjectivity,"* writing:

> *Contrary to the philosophy of Descartes, contrary to that of Kant, when we say 'I think,' we are attaining to ourselves in*

---

[30] "Philosophical Idealism in Rogerian Psychology," p. 209.

[31] Frederick S. Perls, M.D., Ph.D., *Gestalt Therapy Verbatim*, compiled and edited by John O. Stevens (Moab, Utah: Real People Press, 1969), pp. 12–13.

> *the presence of the other, and we are just as concerned with the other as we are of ourselves. . . . I cannot obtain any truth whatsoever about myself, except through the mediation of another. . . . Under these conditions the intimate discovery of myself is at the same time the revelation of the other as a freedom which confronts mine, and which cannot think or will without doing so either for or against me. Thus, at once, we find ourselves in a world which is, let us say, that of "intersubjectivity." It is in this world that man has to decide what he is and what others are.*[32]

Marcel provides a key to understanding Sartre's use of this term in his treatment of the impact of another person as it has potential to add to one's own self-concept. Providing the strongest of cautions, he observes:

> *Even the term "intersubjectivity" might give rise to misunderstandings, for one might conceive of a content—still an objective content—that could be, as it were, transmitted from subject to subject. But the very notion of transmission must be excluded at this level of discourse; the communion in which presences become manifest to each other, and the transmission of purely objective messages, do not belong to the same realm of being. . . .*[33]

It does appear, if we are to follow Sartre and Marcel, that "objectivity" may have to be achieved in situations involving other people—although some existentialists would certainly take sharp issue with such a conclusion. Of the utmost importance, however, is the notion that the exposure of subjectivities possible in such a situation is *not*, as pragmatists might maintain, for the purpose of building a "contextually objective" view of a phenomenon. Such "sharing" does not, to sharpen the contrast by paraphrasing Marcel, exist for the cooperative building-transmission of more common content. Rather, individuals are brought into contact in a facilitating environment for *communion* —for that contact which illuminates richer possibilities for each *individual* involved. The responsibility for deciding what is to be appropriated to the self out of these possibilities still rests squarely upon each individual. Therefore, the meaning given to "objectivity" by the existentialist still retains the full flavor of *intra*subjectivity—whatever the locus in which it may be developed.

[32] Jean Paul Sartre, "Existentialism is a Humanism," in *Existentialism from Dostoevsky to Sartre*, ed. Walter Kaufmann (Cleveland: Meridian Books, The World Publishing Company, 1956), p. 303.
[33] Gabriel Marcel, "The Mystery of Being, II"; cited in Maxine Greene, ed., *Existential Encounters for Teachers* (New York: Random House, 1967), p. 63.

5. Frame of Reference

A. FRAME OF REFERENCE AS LIMITATION-TO-BE-TRANSCENDED.
Two assumptions concerning the concept "frame of reference"[34] will be
considered in this section. Both have certain similarities which are
probably best considered at this point in our study. For instance,
one's frame of reference is generally taken to refer to the sum total of
our assumptions—or, if you will, what we take for granted.[35] Rarely
questioned (unless subjected to conscious scrutiny), they subtly affect
both one's perceptions and one's interpretation of that which is perceived. In this sense, they color or refract that which is seen; they
serve as does the prism in our eye-glasses or the filter on a camera lens
through which sensory data must pass.

From the standpoint of the classical tradition, the individual's frame
of reference is necessarily limited and must be transcended in the
interests of apprehending Truth. Thomas writes:

> If objectivity means the way things actually are independent of
> the way they become known, as the classical position maintains,
> then any frame of reference that conditions its objects of knowl-
> edge is a limitation, a restriction, a liability to be overcome.
> Variety in frames of reference should be progressively elimi-
> nated. The push is toward some ultimate, all-inclusive frame of
> reference, perhaps God's frame of reference. In it resides the
> true knowledge that all men should seek.[36]

The nature of the transcending process depends, as one might suspect,
upon various assumptions of the particular classical tradition in question. Historically, for example, philosophical realists have emphasized
the most meticulous, systematic observation, reporting and generalization possible. Errors in both perception and reasoning are extremely
difficult to avoid and even more difficult to correct, as may be seen in
the literature on hallucinations, mirages and the like. Philosophical
realists and idealists have jointly stressed the nature of, and ways to

[34] The author is indebted to Professor Lawrence G. Thomas of Stanford University
for the notion of "frame of reference" as a philosophical concept or idea, as well
as for many details of the treatment which follow.

[35] There appears to be a valid distinction between the locutions "frame of reference" and "(personal) philosophy of education." The former refers to the assumptions which one does in fact hold—however limited in scope these may be.
Furthermore, the content of one's frame of reference includes assumptions properly
labeled historical, psychological, sociological and the like—as well as philosophical.
The latter locution, on the other hand, not only focusses strictly on philosophical
assumptions but also demands that assumptions be held concerning the great bulk
of concepts treated in philosophy, at least those of particular importance to professional education. Hence, even the most adequate philosophy of education would
only comprise part of one's frame of reference.

[36] Thomas, "Implications of Transaction Theory," p. 149. Quoted by permission.

avoid, fallacies in reasoning.   In addition, idealists have also emphasized overcoming the limitations of one's frame of reference through
trying to see things as they might be seen by those human beings
whose visions of Truth have received mankind's general acclaim.
How would Plato have viewed this problem?   What would Jesus have
done?   Such are questions representative of this tradition.   In all, the
search is for Truth.   In principle, much Truth is open to our discovery—however difficult and sensitive the task.

B. FRAME OF REFERENCE AS SELF-IN-BECOMING.   As noted in
the preceding discussion, the expression "frame of reference" refers to
the sum total of our assumptions—what we take for granted—and,
hence, represents that "filter" which subtly influences both our perceptions and our interpretation of them.   We have seen that the classicist,
with his view of an exterior reality at least partially knowable, logically
views the individual's frame of reference as an impediment in search
for Truth, as a limitation-to-be-transcended.   Just as logically, pragmatists and most existentialists tend to take a more benign view of this
concept.   In these traditions, that which we assume is so inextricably
intertwined with the self-concept as to be virtually indistinguishable
from it.   In a real sense, we *are* what we *assume* we are.   Hence, any
external interference with the student's frame of reference can only be
viewed as a flagrantly immoral act.

For most purposes, especially those relatively individual in nature, it
is probably sufficient that we simply be aware of 1) the assumptions
which make up our own frame of reference, and 2) the assumptions
which are commonly included in the frames of reference of others in
our life space.   In the first case, the individual will himself make those
modifications which he deems necessary on the basis of fact and belief
development.   In the second, we establish one element of that foundation necessary in a pluralistic culture for better understanding and
enjoying those who for us are "significant others."   Examples include
professional colleagues and members of one's own family.   The insights of others may, of course, suggest modification of our own frame
of reference but, once again, control remains in our hands.

A quite different situation confronts both pragmatist and existentialist when a problem-solution seemingly demands the active, understanding cooperation of several individuals.   At the very least, each
individual must attempt to understand the problem from within the
others' frames of reference.   In this vein, Professor Greene maintains:

> The teacher . . . must attempt to distinguish each individual
> student in his uniqueness, to avoid stereotyping or objectifying

> *him, and—when possible—to take the "other's" vantage point to-*
> *ward a situation engaging them both.*[37]

The weaknesses of this first suggestion *are* apparent: Shifting frames of reference—perhaps through engaging in "as if" dialogues—involves terribly difficult work. Furthermore, the differences do remain and a common base for problem-solving may be as absent after the process as before. We may wonder, to illustrate, how much agreement might be generated by asking a dedicated Skinnerian and a dedicated Freudian to view—from each other's perspective—the problem of developing a program for treating emotionally disturbed children. This, admittedly, is not to say that many relatively simple and less emotionally-charged problems might not be alleviated by more insightful behavior.

Pragmatically-oriented literature suggests that an additional problem-solving step may often be necessary, especially given the violent contrasts between frames of reference which characterize a culture as radically pluralistic as our own. Namely, the individuals involved will have to work out a more common, *group* frame of reference with regard to the variables of the problem in question. The basic details of this process have been presented under the assumption "objectivity as intersubjectivity." In summary, each individual must have opportunity to express frankly and specifically how he views the problem variables. Open and extended discussion must identify basic differences and similarities—especially in fact-interpretation and the belief component of assumptions. The group must then identify those elements on which there is consensus, those elements where compromise seems possible and those elements where still-divergent views demand that group members simply co-exist until continuing experience provides more "contact points." The desideratum, as Thomas points out, is to construct a new frame of reference which incorporates as many as possible of the facts and beliefs seen important by the members. It is this more common frame of reference which is a "necessary precondition" of:

> 1) *establishing the objectivity of the object, 2) the testability*
> *of claims made about the object, and 3) the clarity and precision*
> *of communication about the object.*[38]

It is suggested that the building of a more common frame of reference in a complex problem-solving situation does not necessitate doing vio-

---

[37] *Existential Encounters for Teachers*, pp. 53–54.

[38] Thomas, "Implications of Transaction Theory," pp. 152–153. Quoted by permission.

lence to the self-concepts of the group members. And this is held true even for an individual whose frame of reference differs markedly from the group product. Two reasons come immediately to mind: In the first place, the dissenting individual need not be placed under any external compulsion to internalize (i.e., accept as his own) unacceptable elements of the group frame of reference. If protected from excessive peer and/or teacher pressure, he can still maintain control over modification of his own position. He might be protected, for example, by being given the choice of continuing to work with the original group, joining another group or electing to attempt an individual approach to solving the problem.[39] Secondly, the need for the group frame of reference disappears once the given problem is solved. At that point, each member is perfectly free to accept or reject any element of the instrument cooperatively devised to reach the desired goal.

If both self and nonself are constructed out of experiential transactions and if human experience does in fact ebb and flow, pluralism in frames of reference is surely not to be feared. Indeed, it may provide a wellspring of richer resources for wiser problem-solving.

6. Knowledge and Truth

A. THE CONSISTENCY THEORY OF KNOWLEDGE AND TRUTH. In accord with the assumption of "mind or soul as an immaterial entity," the consistency theory holds that knowledge is sought in two basic ways. We may attempt, in the first instance, to bypass the senses and contemplatively focus directly on the Ideas contained in our minds. Many of the insights afforded the great "saints" and "seers" of mankind have resulted from just such activity. Truth has been grasped directly or "intuited" distortions introduced by more complex cognitive processes thus being reduced. Perhaps more often, however, due to man's existence in both the natural and supernatural realms, we seek knowledge by bringing Ideas to the conscious level, fitting an appropriate perception of sensory data with its illuminating Idea, forming a human idea of the desired object of knowledge and then systematically organizing and generalizing our human ideas in a search for

---

[39] Did he elect to continue working with the original group, he might well be required to cooperate in constructing a solution consistent with the group frame of reference. Temporarily requiring *action* consistent with a minimal set of democratically-developed assumptions, however, is surely not the same as requiring the *internalization* of those assumptions. He need not be made to feel guilty concerning his disagreement with other group members. He probably should also be instructed in ways of getting the majority to reconsider his objections, include a "minority report," etc.

Truth. In the latter case, epistemological activity may (at different stages) involve disciplined intuition, logical or experimental inquiry, or the acceptance of reputable authority or revelation. It may be noted that experimental inquiry—bound as it is to specific contexts of time, place and people—is usually of limited value in the pursuit of Truth, although it may have some value in lower-order knowing. For example, we do not usually await a revelation in deciding which of several insecticides is more effective against a particularly destructive bug. The point is that such contextual knowledge is not of especial significance in coming to know more important truths such as the proper ends of education or of man.

Epistemologically, severe difficulties are introduced by the marriage of mind and body, the latter interfering with our ability both to focus on Ideas and to bring them to the mind's conscious level. Severe difficulties are introduced by the fact that that which we sense is but a transitory "objectification" of that creative, purposeful, spiritual energy which is basic reality. Furthermore, as we have seen, sensory data may mislead the mind into interpreting as reality that which is but a physical or cultural "accident." Finally, severe difficulties are introduced by the fact that the individual mind does not possess the omniscient (all-knowing) or omnipresent (universally present) qualities of Absolute Mind. Therefore, it must generally form human ideas in attempting to conceptualize a reality far greater and more complex than they can ever represent. For the most part, our human condition does indeed allow us to "see but through a glass darkly."

We may take heart, however, in realizing that basic reality is non-material and that man's mind or soul is an integral part of this ultimate spiritual energy. Hence, all hope is not denied us at the very onset of our epistemological quest. Complete knowledge is closed to the human mind so limited in comparison with Absolute Mind or Pure Spirit. Nevertheless, we may be confident that a reasonably high level of certainty with regard to many questions is open in this life to those who pursue Truth with a disciplined intent.[40] True, the "quest for certainty" is neither easy nor direct. In a memorable passage, Van Cleve Morris captures the complexities of our epistemological mission, writing:

> *Our minds proceed by getting successive "plots" on our position, by taking this and that "reading" of the situation, this and that "sighting" of landmarks; then, by a process of organization and comparison, an assessment is made of "where" we are, i.e., what our existence is all about. It is as if, to use a nautical metaphor,*

[40] Cf. Stella Henderson, *Introduction to Philosophy of Education* (Chicago: The University of Chicago Press, 1947), p. 220.

> *we were "triangulating" our way through the sensory (and there-*
> *fore ontologically inferior) world heading for the ultimate harbor*
> *of the Absolute Mind.*[41]

With regard to a given object of knowledge, the desideratum is clearly for our "plots," our "readings" and our "sightings" to coalesce. As our human ideas begin to fit together into a cohesive and consistent whole wherein each element supports every other element, as our ideas seem to assume a natural order and as we find over time that reputable authorities seem to support the directions in which we are moving ever so slowly and gropingly, we may have increasing confidence that our rough-hewn concepts are in fact leading us toward Truth.

C. THE CORRESPONDENCE THEORY OF KNOWLEDGE AND TRUTH.
The correspondence theory, usually attributed to realists, represents a second approach to knowledge and truth within the classical tradition. It will be remembered that this tradition sees basic reality as existing antecedent to the human being, as providing the boundaries of that stage upon which we act out our lives and, for some theists, as deter-mining our status in a life yet to come. Given an ordered reality, ours is the task of discovering its nature—of coming to know, adjusting to and cooperating with its physical and moral regularities. Within these bounds, we exercise that freedom and realize that promise open to man. Van Cleve Morris, for instance, suggests that "the Realist . . . is epistemologically concerned primarily with the business of discovering—literally *dis-covering*, removing the cover from—a pre-existent and existentially independent reality and thereby gaining knowledge of it."[42] The noted realist Ralph Barton Perry writes:

> *Knowledge I regard as essentially the facing of facts, the con-*
> *forming of belief to that which, relatively to the belief, is ante-*
> *cedent and fixed.*
>   *The greater good is not the mere outcropping of the deeper*
> *natural propensity, but can be attained only by the procrustean*
> *fitting of plastic materials to a mould defined by reason.*[43]

This dual process of discovering and conforming is humanly possible, however difficult and frustrating the practical details.[44] It begins in a

[41] *Philosophy and the American School; An Introduction to the Philosophy of Education* (Boston: Houghton Mifflin Company, 1961), p. 140.

[42] *Ibid.,* p. 144.

[43] Ralph Barton Perry, "Realism in Retrospect," *Contemporary American Philoso-phy* (New York: The Macmillian Company, 1930), II, pp. 201 and 207; quoted in Frederick S. Breed, *Education and the New Realism* (New York: The Macmillan Company, 1939), p. 73.

[44] It must be noted that not all realists agree as to the nature of these "practical details," although few have dismissed the difficulties and frustrations inherent in

sensory-based awareness of the so-called "secondary qualities" of external objects. Professor Broudy writes:

> *The core of all our knowing, then, is sensation, a process that depends on energy emanating from the external object. Out of the changes effected in the sense organ and the nervous system by light waves, sound waves, pressures, heat and cold, chemical solutions, and vapors, the mind abstracts infallibly a particular color, sound, touch sensation, taste, or odor. It separates the particular sense quality from the complex physical process going on in the sense organ and the nervous system.*
>
> *The more complete this separation is, the more objective it is, and the more accurately it represents the quality which the object has sent out. Thus sight and hearing do their jobs of separation more efficiently than touch, smell, and taste, with the result that we see the blueness in the sky, but we taste the fishiness partly in the mouth and partly in the fish.*[45]

Unfortunately, as Broudy also notes, this awareness of sensation can also be stimulated by bodily processes alone. Disease, dreams and drugs do provide such stimulation, thus opening to question the trustworthiness of our senses and the possibility of proving that an external world lies behind our perceptions.[46]

Broudy provides a key to answering such questions in his treatment of how we apprehend the so-called "primary qualities" of an object, i.e., its distance, motion, position, shape, size and weight. No sense organ exists by whose operations we can immediately discern such qualities. We do, however, receive clues from the different senses, and we may turn to the experimental or scientific mode of knowing to check and correct our individual perceptions. In this mode, the clues provided by one sense are used to check those provided by another. Furthermore, different observers are introduced to judge under controlled conditions whether the sensory stimulation is merely internal to the perceiver or appears to be emanating from an external object. To cite a near infamous example, the oar in the water which appears bent to one individual—and even to a camera—is decidedly not bent when *all* sensory data are systematically considered by different observers under controlled conditions.[47] If, then, we grant basic similarities in

---

the knowing process. This introductory account will not attempt to deal with all of the approaches suggested over the centuries by realists. Rather, the emphasis will be upon more contemporary variations.

[45] Harry S. Broudy, *Building a Philosophy of Education*. 2nd ed. (Englewood Cliffs, N.J.: Prentice-Hall, Inc., 1961), p. 113. Quoted by permission of the publisher.

[46] *Ibid.*, pp. 113–114. Paraphrased by permission of the publisher.

[47] *Cf.* Christian O. Weber, *Basic Philosophies of Education* (New York: Holt, Rinehart and Winston, 1960), pp. 205–206.

human perceptual and cognitive processes and if we have confidence in the ability and willingness of trained researchers to seek Truth in spite of potential cost, the cases mount for the argument that the senses aided by rational inquiry can give us some reliable knowledge of an external world, a world not of our own mental creation. As Lawrence Thomas suggests,

> In principle, the subjective factors can be eliminated or controlled by finding out more about individual peculiarities (e.g., differences in reaction time, color sensitivities, prejudices, distorting preferences) and progressively standardizing or correcting for these individual differences in order to get a common or universal perception of what is really out there. Similarly, current limitations on our means of knowing can, in principle, be corrected by getting better and more refined means of knowing.[48]

Through reason we develop generalizations about the nature of things and their relationships. In refining these sense-based generalizations, we develop ideas and statements which attempt to reflect the fundamental regulative principles of the moral and natural orders. To the extent that these ideas and statements correspond with what in fact *is*, they are true. Obviously, this is not a purely mechanical process. Imagination *is* involved in this process, particularly in the construction of hypotheses. Nevertheless, the products of imagination must constantly be compared with cognitively controlled and corrected sensation in order to decide whether imagination has led us toward Truth or toward error.[49] Hypotheses "work" *because* they reflect a reality which lies beyond them. In so doing, they help us to establish a productive relationship with that reality, rather than one of discord and cross-purposes.

C. THE TRANSACTIONAL THEORY OF KNOWLEDGE AND TRUTH.
For the pragmatist we have seen that minding behaviors are directed to transforming an indeterminate, disturbing situation into one where problem-definition and resolution restore equilibrium to an individual's or group's experiential field. For this restoration to take place, transactional relationships are established between that construct defined as self (or subject) and those defined as nonself (or object). In this process *both* constructs are (to some extent) shaped or modified by those actions deemed appropriate in a given context to solving the defined problem. Less technically, the subject does things to objects (i.e., those things defined by the plan of action) and then carefully,

---

[48] "Implications of Transaction Theory," p. 146. Quoted by permission.
[49] Henderson, *Introduction to Philosophy of Education,* pp. 306–307.

systematically observes the consequences of his behavior both in terms of his perceptions of the object and of himself. Out of experience, then, our definitions of both self and nonself are transactionally ever being modified, although, as we have also seen, some continuities are established over time with respect to each.

If the transactions are successful (i.e., if the problem is in fact solved or markedly reduced in terms of the criteria discussed under the assumption of "mind as purposeful, problem-solving behavior"), knowledge is produced. True, such knowledge is limited and contextural. The subject simply knows that under certain specified conditions of time, place and people, a given plan of action *did* result in the consequences predicted for it.

Several related points are now in order. For instance, not all experiencing results in knowledge. One may simply be aware of a color or a sound which is simply "had" or, perhaps, aesthetically enjoyed. No discomfort need be introduced—no problem defined—no knowledge produced.[50] Furthermore, mediated experiencing involving the transactional process may not solve the problem. In this case, as in science, it means "back to the drafting board," back to the task of constructing and/or choosing another hypothesis which may work. Thirdly, achieved contextual knowledge usually serves to create more problems than were originally solved. New goals become clear with the solution of the present problem. The knowledge which attended the solution is transformed into potentially useful means for achieving these new goals. Finally, contextual knowledge must be used to refine existing generalization and/or develop new ones. These, in turn, may serve as antecedent variables in future problem-solving. Yet, even these generalizations must be viewed as limited both by their openness to correction in new contexts and by their formation on the basis of but a *sample* of *past* human experiencing. As Dewey notes,

> The conclusions of prior knowledge are the instruments of new inquiries, not the norm which determines their validity. Objects of previous knowledge supply working hypotheses for new situations; they are the source of suggestion of new operations; they direct inquiry. But they do not enter into reflective thinking by way of providing its premises in a logical sense.
>
> . . .
>
> There is no knowledge self-guaranteed to be infallible, since all knowledge is the product of special acts of inquiry.[51]

[50] *Cf.* John S. Brubacher, *Modern Philosophies of Education.* 4th ed. (New York: McGraw-Hill Book Company, 1969), pp. 230–231.

[51] John Dewey, *The Quest for Certainty: A Study of the Relation of Knowledge and Action* (New York: Minton, Balch & Co., 1929); (Capricorn Books Ed.; New York: G. P. Putnam's Sons, 1960), pp. 186–187 and 193.

This, of course, is not to discourage making our generalizations as reliable as possible. It is just at this point that the pragmatist demands that individual knowledge claims be capable of public confirmation given an honest and skilled recreation of the original problem-solving context. Given the confirmation of others over time, our generalizations about discipline, evaluation or any other phenomena assume greater significance as antecedent variables. The pragmatist does not deny purely private experience; he does deny that it can produce resources of optimal use in human problem-solving.

Truth, according to transactional theory, refers to a property of an idea (hypothesis, plan of action) which did in fact produce the consequences which it predicted would follow upon action consistent with it. In short, the idea "worked" in terms of the criteria of working earlier discussed. Furthermore, it "worked" in terms of the conditions presented by the *problem* rather than by any private, purely personal feeling. Note that only truth claims or hypotheses—not truth itself—can exist prior to a contextually-defined instance of mediating experience. Truth is a function of the transactional relationships established in successfully mediating or reconstructing experience. As ever-changing experience is the "given," truth is the "achieved."

Truth claims, then, are ultimately public and testable. Judgments of truth refer to ideas occupying specific contexts and hence are subject to modification as experience continues to be mediated. The implications of such a position are suggested by Dewey, who wrote:

> To generalize the recognition that the true means the verified and means nothing else places upon men the responsibility for surrendering political and moral dogmas, and subjecting to the test of consequences their most cherished prejudices.[52]

In the transactional theory, we may conclude that truth—like knowledge—must always be accepted with reservations, held open to question and to refinement. The pragmatic attitude toward both concepts may perhaps best be likened to the liquid "eye" of a surveyor's table: never quite still—never quite perfect—at best resting in a state of dynamic tension—always existing with reference to those who are doing the surveying.

D. THE APPROPRIATIONAL THEORY OF KNOWLEDGE AND TRUTH.
In relative consistency with the pragmatic position, most existentialists at least accept the *possibility* that an external reality—a realm of absolute knowledge and truth—lies behind our human experience. In concert

---

[52] John Dewey, *Reconstruction in Philosophy* (New York: Henry Holt & Co., 1920); enlarged paperback ed.; Boston: The Beacon Press, 1957), p. 160.

with pragmatists, they also generally deny that the human being can gain knowledge of such a realm. "The individual is too limited by time and circumstance to be certain of ever knowing that objective truth. Therefore, for him, the only truth is subjective, that is, relative to his own ability to discover it."[53] Kierkegaard, Jaspers and Marcel, for example, join in teaching that "truth can never be known in its totality; it is multidimensional and influenced by mysterious elements which are an abiding characteristic of life."[54]

Unlike other philosophical "schools" or "systems," however, the existentialistic tradition has refused to depend primarily upon sensory-based inductive reasoning and/or formal (or authority- or revelation-based) deductive reasoning for that knowledge which is open to man. Nevertheless, one must also realize that "Existentialism is not a revolt against reason. It is a revolt against mere reason, the absolute primacy and superiority of man's reason. . . . To the existentialist an absolute belief in reason is itself unreasonable."[55] As a vital *supplement* to reason, the existentialist has called for an exploration of man's noncognitive resources: his feelings, his intuition. He has vigorously resisted the depersonalization and disregard of the unique human being which he feels must necessarily follow experimental science's ignoring important human variables and man's basic subjectivity.[56] At times this resistance has led to an unbalanced accent on the illogical; at the very least, it has resulted in the strongest cry for individual autonomy and responsibility in exploring *all* available paths in the search for knowledge.

Sartre draws a distinction between "knowledge of being-in-itself" and "knowledge of being-for-itself" which has received serious and extended attention by existentialists. In brief, the former refers to knowledge of the reality, the world in which we find ourselves; the latter, to the very consciousness of being aware of that world, to pure subjectivity—if you will, to the central core of being which cannot even be described without turning it into an object—an element not of being-for-itself but of being-in-itself.

Knowledge of being-in-itself (also referred to as "Mode I Knowledge" by Morris, as "controlling knowledge" by Paul Tillich and as the potential products of "I-It" relationships by Buber) is surely not

[53] St. Elmo Nauman, Jr., "Subjectivity," *The New Dictionary of Existentialism* (New York: Philosophical Library, 1971), p. 159.

[54] George F. Kneller, *Existentialism and Education* (New York: Philosophical Library, Inc., 1958); (Science Editions paperback ed.; New York: John Wiley & Sons, Inc., 1964), p. 58.

[55] Anand Malik, "Existentialism in Education," *Current Themes in Philosophy of Education.* Publication No. 198. (Saskatoon, Saskatchewan: Extension Division, University of Saskatchewan, n.d.), p. 40.

[56] Kneller, *Existentialism and Education,* p. 58.

without importance. As in the "correspondence theory of knowledge and truth," the subject comes into a knowing relationship with the object. Knowledge of subject and object gives rise when necessary to mutual adaptation. Through experimental science, the possibility is opened for the subject to control the object for its own purposes. Basic is the detachment, the objective stance, which the subject brings to the knowing process.

The products of this process may be viewed on every side, for our ever-expanding control over nature has given rise to a technological age without peer in human history. From knowledge of his sexual patterns to an ability to destroy an entire culture, modern man stands head and shoulders above his forefathers. And yet—something is missing. All of the knowledge about ourselves—contained in countless computer banks and "cume folders"—does not quite seem to get to the *heart* of our being. It is peripheral, tangential. Even after reading a file, the *educator* must still come to know the person as he is. Aware of such data, e.g., of the "track" to which he has been assigned, the *student* may begin to accept the external verdict: He is a "brain"—or a "dummy." With all our knowledge of being-in-itself, we still seem powerless to control wars, alienation or poverty. We still turn people into objects—mere shadows of what they really are. Indeed, our development of external, rational knowledge may actually interfere with our penetrating to the heart of being, for it distracts our attention from the serious choices concerning where we are going and why. It may even convince us that such questions are unanswerable—or unimportant. In Nietzsche's view, according to Reinhardt,

> A *purely encyclopedic knowledge of historical and scientific facts represents . . . a mortal threat to the integrity of human existence and culture because it leads to an attitude of irony and cynicism in regard to everything that has a claim to greatness and nobility.*[57]

Platitudes come to reflect reality; computer punch cards supplant human beings; unauthenticity replaces authenticity.

In knowledge of being-for-itself (also referred to as "Mode II knowledge" by Morris, "receiving knowledge" by Tillich and the potential products of "I-Thou" encounters by Buber) is to be found the corrective for the schizophrenic situation described above. Tillich writes:

> *Existentialism tries to save the freedom of the individual self from the domination of controlling knowledge. . . . Existential-*

[57] Kurt F. Reinhardt, *The Existentialist Revolt: The Main Themes and Phases of Existentialism.* New enlarged ed. with an appendix on existentialist psychotherapy. (New York: Frederick Ungar Publishing Co., 1960), p. 78.

ism is the most desperate attempt to escape the power of control-
ling knowledge and of the objectified world which technical
reason has produced.[58]

The corrective involves taking far less seriously the entire structure
and methodology of "controlling knowledge" and subjectively turning
for significant knowledge of the human being to a direct, conscious
encounter with being.   In this encounter, the entire range of human
emotions must be intensely involved.   Herein, as Nauman indicates,
reason also has its place:

> *One must begin with things as they appear to be.   This means,*
> *with reference to the personality, that the emotions should be*
> *analyzed, not ignored as "accidental."   Thus existentialism has*
> *analyzed such emotions as fear and dread, boredom and passion,*
> *believing that such an analysis is necessary for the correct under-*
> *standing of the nature of existence.*[59]

Nevertheless, Watts reminds us that analysis in itself is not enough:
"To 'know' reality you cannot stand outside it and define it; you must
enter into it, be it, and feel it."[60]

Neither the processes nor the products of a knowing relationship
with being are easily expressed in cognitive terms—nor, being subjective, are they open to datafication.   In some sense, knowledge must
well up from the depths of the self's innermost being.   Approaching a
decision, he must allow his whole being—including every rational and
nonrational element—to engulf the problem, passionately to become
involved in it and to generate a subjective, personal choice.   Approaching another person whom he desires to "know"—with whom he
desires to have an authentic relationship—he must affirm the person
"as existing just as it is, in its own right, independently of our purposes."[61]   Rather than control, the provision of additional, richer
possibilities for *mutual* meaning-making, a process which turns neither
the I nor the Thou into an object for conquest and exploitation, is of
central concern.

Knowledge of human concerns so gained will never be absolute, for
each situation is unique.   Some existentialists do maintain, however,
that such encounters with being can give rise to an *intuitive* knowledge

[58] Paul Tillich, *Systematic Theology* (Chicago: The University of Chicago Press, 1951), I, p. 100.

[59] *The New Dictionary of Existentialism*, p. 159.

[60] Alan W. Watts, *The Wisdom of Insecurity* (New York: Vintage Books, A Division of Random House, 1968), p. 114.

[61] Malcolm L. Diamond, *Martin Buber: Jewish Existentialist* (New York: Oxford
University Press, Inc., 1960); (Harper Torchbooks ed.; New York: Harper & Row,
Publishers, 1968), p. 30.

of truth and values. Such knowledge is sufficiently compelling as to provide a most adequate base for vital human decisions. It may also open to experimentation additional possibilities concerning the world which we inhabit. In any case, strongly denied is the notion that existential knowledge can be held at arm's length—one interesting specimen among many to be examined dispassionately, admired and then put back on the shelf with still other specimens.

Whether concerned with knowledge of being-in-itself or of being-for-itself, the individual alone is responsible for determining the problems he will face, the means he will employ and the solutions he will accept. Absent is that effort to combine the individual and the social dimension of problem-solving which characterizes the pragmatic approach.[62] In like measure, it is the individual who must determine when knowledge has been won, as well as the content of that knowledge. He *and he alone* is the Supreme Court for judging all claims of truth. He may not avoid personal responsibility, for instance, by justifying his actions on the basis of the "dictates" of logic or authority or revelation, the "facts" of scientific experimentation or the "consequences" of intelligent inquiry.

"There is an element of *personal appropriation*," Morris writes, "in all knowing. When all of the data are in, each individual on his own must make a personal choice to believe something, a personal commitment."[63] The individual will appropriate from a life situation what he chooses to appropriate, and no "objective" criteria can guide that appropriation. His choices, in turn, will indicate what knowledge he has taken unto himself—they will determine what he will become. In a most important sense, "truths" refer to our ultimate commitments which are actively *lived* rather than passively *known.*

> *The alternative projects, in reason or in awareness, are tentative explorations of what we are for in the world. Furthermore, they are not being undertaken by some abstract entity called "man." They are being undertaken by each one of us in our own lives. Each life is a project to determine the meaning of man. Each individual must choose what he wants his life to say concerning man's definition in the world. Each individual shapes an answer to this question in terms of what he chooses to devote his life to.*[64]

Having treated the basic epistemological assumptions current in American culture, let us now turn to the possibilities they suggest for educational policy and practice.

[62] *Cf.* Dettering, "Philosophical Idealism in Rogerian Psychology," p. 209.

[63] *Philosophy and the American School,* p. 167.

[64] Van Cleve Morris, *Existentialism in Education: What It Means* (New York: Harper & Row, Publishers, 1966), p. 93.

5

Epistemological Assumptions and Educational Possibilities

Browse through just about any textbook concerned with "education." (Its origin really doesn't matter. Perhaps it is a product of studies in "curriculum and instruction" such as those in physical or science education; perhaps, of studies in the "educational foundations" such as those carried on in educational history or psychology; or perhaps, of studies in the "professional services" such as those of concern to educational administration or guidance.) Observe, or talk about, any activity carried on in the social institution known as the "school." Write any paper for an education course or individual study project. To which common concerns will your reading, observing, discussion or writing be drawn? Or, to put the question another way, what is it that forms the very basis of *educational* inquiry—that which is necessarily considered no matter how specialized your particular interests? Most will probably agree that it is *teaching and learning*—and their support—which provide the focal points of education understood as intentional activities, response and product goals, outcomes and discipline.

What should be taught? What materials, technological devices, instructional strategies, structural arrangements, administrative activities and professional stances will facilitate its transmission? What difficulties may we expect to encounter in teaching that which we have decided should be taught? How do students learn? Given our decisions with regard to what should be taught and the variables connected with how it should be presented, what learning difficulties might students encounter? How do we recognize that students *have* learned what we have set out to teach? Difficult but crucial questions, these! But as we have seen in the first chapter, the development of an educational theory which might afford us more definitive guidance in answering such questions remains in its infancy. In truth, the tasks facing teaching-learning experimentation involving human beings are both enormous and complex. Nevertheless, research in the behavioral sciences, especially in educational psychology, is slowly developing a body of knowledge of significant potential for this needed educational theory.

Unfortunately, contemporary experimentation often seems implicitly to ignore epistemological studies concerning the possibility, the limitations, the development and the validation of knowledge claims—studies indicated in the preceding chapter. Metaphysical studies indicated in the second chapter are even more consciously, more explicitly ignored. And yet, what is more central to teaching-learning questions than the limitations imposed upon what can be learned by the student's human nature—or the degree to which his responses are determined by environmental or genetic factors? In both cases it seems apparent that many scholars interested in educational phenomena suffer from overconfidence as to the availability of *facts* and underestimate the necessity and power of *beliefs*—the two elements comprising assumptions. Once again, a *synthesis* of resources appears necessary to the development of an adequate educational theory.

Following the format and rationale developed in our earlier considerations, the present chapter will attempt to suggest educational possibilities consistent with common epistemological assumptions. Perhaps, although often in an implicit and merely preliminary manner, that which follows will also point to the kinds of syntheses helpful in building theory.

A. Mind

1. Mind or Soul as an Immaterial Entity

When correlated with the assumption of "basic reality as creative, purposeful, spiritual energy," the assumption of "mind or soul as an immaterial entity" suggests that only the (human) mind can come to that knowledge of (Absolute) Mind necessary to guide the activities of the natural-supernatural creature which is man. With appropriate attention to proper procedures and materials, the mind-soul's powers can be strengthened or "disciplined" and thus given increased control over the body. In the tradition of Idealism, furthermore, it is the school which is assigned immense responsibility for this most vital of tasks.

The school's role in "mental discipline" consists of two interrelated activities: It must develop and train the latent but inborn powers of the mind, and it must "stock" the mind with that knowledge basic both to living in this stage of existence and preparing for a higher stage yet to come.[65] The idealist Theodore M. Greene writes: "The goal is, first and foremost, the cultivation of the well-disciplined, highly individualized, and lively mind—of a mind strong in structure, rich in texture, dynamic and creative." For Greene this is the "well equipped," "well trained," "well informed" mind, the mind which has a "cultivated capacity for evaluation," the "mind able to put the disciplines to its own uses—to express correctly and felicitously its own ideas, to gather and interpret facts in its own way, to encounter and judge values on its own matured responsibility." It is also a mind "insatiably curious and critical, imaginative and creative."[66]

What are these latent, inborn mental powers which must be developed and trained? Any list must surely include the ability to recognize those ideas or propositions whose truth is "self-evident," the power of "intuition," and the disciplined willingness to accept the guidance of reputable authority and revelation. Probably the most important truths—the metaphysical truths about ultimate reality, man, his world and his destiny—are gained through these powers alone. Another vital mental power, of course, consists of the ability logically to reason out additional truths from the prior base of accepted "first principles." We may also add the powers involved in systematically regulating, observing, evaluating and generalizing human experience— the experimental or scientific method—in order to produce contextual knowledge. Under the present assumption, however, these mental powers are of somewhat lesser value. The idealist *agrees* with the pragmatist that they merely produce contextual knowledge and insists that the guidance of central human affairs demands absolutely certain knowledge which can be secured only through the exercise of powers mentioned earlier.

Many of the means for disciplining our mental powers—for minimizing the body- or matter-centered "static" or "fog" which so interferes with the mind's proper functioning—depend upon the school's emphasizing a rigorous diet of basic knowledge. "Only those disciplines are basic," writes Greene, "which equip men with *general* skills which are

---

[65] *Cf.* Brauner and Burns, *Problems in Education and Philosophy*, pp. 35–40.
[66] Theodore M. Greene, "Liberal Education Reconsidered"; quoted in *Selected Readings in the Philosophy of Education*, ed. Joe Park. 3rd ed. (New York: The Macmillian Company, 1968), pp. 170 and 167.

adaptable to a variety of situations, in contrast to particularized skills for very specific activities."[67] Greene identifies four disciplines central to a general or liberal education: *linguistic proficiency* (involving studies in English, foreign language and the language of the arts and mathematics), *factual discovery and testing* (involving studies in the natural and social sciences), *normative evaluation* (involving humanistic studies designed to increase man's aesthetic, moral and religious. sensitivity and evaluative standards), and *synoptic interpretation* (involving studies in history and philosophy which help man to relate and harmonize knowledge gained throughout his education).[68]

Obviously, we are not expected simply to memorize the details encountered in the basic studies, although they do contain guidelines as relevant to man's activities today as in the times during which they were written. Rather, we are expected to gain inspiration for developing the powers inherent in mind, stimulation of the flow of inborn Ideas which are the keys to understanding sensory phenomena, and increased capacity to order that knowledge already gained by man as a basis for directing continuing efforts at discovery. True, these are the fruits of mastery; study will not always be easy or intrinsically enjoyable. There will be times when the energy demanded for mastery will prevent extensive application to contemporary "problems," although application cannot be absolutely ignored given the human condition. In any case, through the imitation of the best in man and his works, through the classroom interaction of minds and Mind, and through a school environment characterized by seriousness and sensitivity, the individual mind can be disciplined to realize more of what it means to be truly "human."

2. Mind as a Function of Bodily Processes

As noted in Chapter 4, the assumption of "mind as a function of bodily processes" has had a long history and, over time, has been expressed with a variety of emphases. Not unexpectedly, given its deep roots in the classical tradition, certain of its philosophical and pedagogical expressions bear some resemblance to the nature and outworking of the assumption of "mind or soul as an immaterial entity." To add to the confusion, several of these earlier interpretations (e.g., the "blank slate" theory) still find present-day advocates. The trend in contemporary educational psychology, however, is clearly toward a behaviorism which lends support to the view that "mind" simply refers to

[67] "Liberal Education Reconsidered," *Selected Readings in the Philosophy of Education*, ed. Park, p. 170.
[68] *Ibid.*, pp. 171–172.

functions of the brain. Given this development (and its massive impact on professional education), it seems proper that this latter-day interpretation should serve as the primary base for the speculation as to current educational possibilities which follows.

Education in this tradition comes to be a matter of habit formation: learning, a matter of acquiring new behavior patterns—including verbal behavior—which, when expressed, can be observed, evaluated and modified as necessary. Basic is the notion that even such concepts as "fear," "insight" or "creativity" are in fact simply terms which refer to complex matrices of physical behaviors.[69] Once the elements in a particular matrix have been identified, reinforcement schedules can be devised to develop and maintain desired behavioral responses. Human purposes—or, for that matter, internal neural processes—come to receive less and less attention as the emphasis shifts to the environmental conditions under which the human brain can, like a computer, be "programmed" to respond in ways deemed desirable by external agencies such as the teacher. The only alternative is to allow the individual's responses to be conditioned by chance events or by less desirable agencies such as his peers or the mass media. Teaching and learning, then, are both viewed as strictly natural processes which are open to scientific experimentation and control.

On the basis of their best insights—themselves conditioned, although modifiable if the environment permits—responsible social authorities must determine behaviors. Experimentation must then determine the conditions under which they can be developed given the lawful regularities of nature. Such conditions include, as one might suppose, all of the variables which together give meaning to the term "education." Be its locus a workbook or a machine, the model for such activity is perhaps best suggested by the carefully designed "program." M. Daniel Smith summarizes the nature and problems of the program:

> In programmed instruction one presents a task or question or statement that requires some response of the student, usually a verbal response and usually limited to one or a few words; the student writes his answer in a space provided for it. Then he is given the correct answer, or finds it, and compares with his own. Then another such task or question or statement is presented, and so on. A high level of success in responding or answering is maintained by developing the tasks so that the probability of success is great; . . .
>
> The combination of requirements put on programming, first that it permit the student to respond actively, second that it make possible for him to be successful in responding, and third

---

[69] Over time each of these concepts has become "reified," that is, taken to refer to "a 'something' in itself" rather than to the *behaviors* to which it points.

*that it give him the correct answer or other information to allow
him to judge his own responses, all of these put a great burden
on the programmer.*[70]

Another, somewhat "looser" model, is found in the so-called "criterion-
specific" educational programs which involve the specification of behavioral objectives for relatively small segments (often called modules
or units) of study, pre-assessment of competencies, instructional activities, student-assessment of achieved competencies and instructor-
evaluation of achieved competencies. These programs *do* differ
considerably, usually in the degree to which the formation of student
habits is controlled by the teacher. The present assumption would
seem to support working toward the highest possible degree of control.

Most teaching and learning activities, needless to say, have not
received the specification of the models described above. Nevertheless, extensive ability and achievement testing; test-based homogeneous grouping or strict individualization; an emphasis on sequenced
and guided perceiving, classifying, ordering and generalizing; and an
accent on subject-matter learning to adjust the student to the realities
of his natural world, all seem to represent early-scientific efforts at
controlling the educational environment in order more effectively to
program the computer-like brain.

3. Mind as Purposeful, Problem-Solving Behavior

Every teacher develops a list of books which have had a high degree of
influence on his or her intellectual development. For the author one
of the most influential of these is *Reflective Thinking: The Method of
Education,* written by the late H. Gordon Hullfish and Professor Philip
G. Smith. Their words provide the most appropriate introduction to
this section of our studies:

> *Teachers confront neither bodiless minds nor mindless bodies.
> They do face human entities, individuals, each having a unique
> and distinctive history, and each capable of behaving mindfully.
> We may state this differently by saying that the individual is
> capable of doing one thing in order to achieve something else, of
> planning and organizing his behavior and of deliberately control-
> ling aspects of his environment in order that an end held in view
> may be realized. In short, the individual is capable of acting
> with foresight; he is able to engage in mindful behavior. This
> does not suggest that he always does, or that he inevitably will.*

[70] M. Daniel Smith, *Theoretical Foundations of Learning and Teaching* (Waltham,
Mass.: Xerox College Publishing, 1971), p. 236.

It merely recognizes, first, the existence of the potentiality and, second, that educative experiences of the individual (in school and out) will determine the degree to which mindfulness is characteristic of his actions. What happens in the classroom will be a potent factor in determining whether his actions remain routine and blind or are distinguished by an awareness of what they are about.[71]

Inasmuch as the environment provides important elements with which the individual will enter into transactional relationships, the pragmatically-oriented educator necessarily must turn his attention to the types of environment which will facilitate the learning-expression of minding behaviors. In brief, pragmatists in education have long favored a markedly "liberal" interpretation of the so-called "democratic" environment.[72] For instance, Dewey writes:

An undesirable society . . . is one which internally and externally sets up barriers to free intercourse and communication of experience. A society which makes provision for participation in its good of all its members on equal terms and which secures flexible readjustment of its institutions through interaction of different forms of associated life is in so far democratic. Such a society must have a type of education which gives individuals a personal interest in social relationships and control, and the habits of mind which secure social changes without introducing disorder.[73]

Firmly committed to the pragmatic interpretation of democracy, Lawrence Thomas reminds us that the concern for providing an environment conducive both to developing and refining minding behaviors demands that belief be subjected to fact-developing experimentation. In discussing intelligence testing, for example, he takes exception both to the notion of innate intelligence and even to an exclusive concern for predicting intelligent minding. His argument is cogent and pointed:

But the transactionist may not be as interested in predicting intelligent minding as he is in improving it. In this light, appropriate intelligence tests should be diagnostic. The guiding concerns would then be what kind of environments for what kind of persons at what times of life in what frames of reference are most effective in enhancing intelligent minding.[74]

[71] H. Gordon Hullfish and Philip G. Smith, *Reflective Thinking: The Method of Education* (New York: Dodd, Mead & Company, 1968), pp. 153–154.

[72] The details of the " 'liberal' interpretation of 'democracy' " will be developed in Chapter 8.

[73] *Democracy and Education*, p. 99.

[74] "Implications of Transaction Theory," p. 152. Quoted by permission.

Experimental data encompassing the complex variables proposed by Thomas are not yet available.[75]   Given the pragmatist's overall frame of reference, however, *were* it available it would only increase the reliability of the hypotheses suggested below as educational possibilities.

The school is to be viewed as an environment specifically designed to involve the child in certain kinds of activities which can lead to reconstructions of experience vital to his continuing growth.[76]   Both the metaphysical and epistemological assumptions of the pragmatist suggest that his central goal cannot lie in "disciplining" the child's mind to ingest absolute knowledge (which in many cases is said to transcend human experience) or in "programming" his brain to respond in ways deemed appropriate by external authorities.   Rather, the student must learn how to define and overcome obstacles to his growth as encountered in his experience.   Necessarily, this process will involve other people and both content and skill resources not yet under his command.   Such considerations have led the pragmatist to pose a problem-solving format as a vital instructional-design variable.   Therein, the emphasis shifts from a priori knowledge set out to be learned to the very processes of problem-defining and solving and to the qualitative improvement of these processes.   The transparent reference, of course, is to the teaching and improvement of "minding behaviors."

It is most important to avoid the dual errors of viewing such a pedagogical stance as either "permissive" (that is, "child-dominated") or "teacher-centered."   True, the child must be interested in the problem at hand, a factor which neither the teacher nor the curriculum may ignore.   Be the concern arithmetical, artistic, historical, linguistic or scientific, this variable remains constant.   Nevertheless, the reconstruction of experience involves the child in a hardnosed, transactive encounter between himself and other elements in this experiential field.   The child must learn, therefore, how to deal with others of various ages—especially when so many solutions demand cooperative effort—how to *use* traditional content and skill resources in his problem-solving and how progressively to reorganize his experience so as to encompass new knowledge which comes as a by-product of that problem-solving.

[75] There is, of course, a wealth of literature on the relationship of *selected* elements in the classroom environment and learning.   The interested student is directed to journals referenced in *Education Index,* texts in the social psychology of education and to manuals such as the N. L. Gage edited *Handbook of Research on Teaching* (Chicago: Rand McNally & Company, 1963).   In general, however, the degree of contextual specification desired by Thomas still awaits experimental implementation.

[76] *Cf.* Bode, *How We Learn,* pp. 245–246.

Teaching defined as actively assisting the child to achieve these learnings is scarcely a less important or complex professional activity than when it is defined in more traditional terms. The point is that the accent shifts from child *or* teacher to a cooperative relationship between child *and* teacher. Even if the "solid" subjects are viewed with somewhat less awe—as "only" instrumentally valuable—they are perhaps more highly dignified, the pragmatist maintains, by being put to work in increasing human control over his environment. And if this increase in control is experienced by a second grader, so be it. The denigration of the child's experience in a democracy is but a prelude to the denigration of the adult citizen's experience in favor of that of an elite.

B. Ideas

1. *Ideas as Archetypes of Existents*

The conception of educational aims and activities discussed in connection with the notion of disciplining the mind was seen to rest heavily on the mind-strengthening potential of the basic disciplines. In turn, the power of these disciplines was found in their incorporating man's experience in coming to grips with the central ideas which stand as archetypes or models of all things existing in and beyond our sensory world. Butler stresses the centrality of these ideas to education:

> *One overall characterization of idealist-inspired education is that it is ideal-centered. It is not wholly child-centered, subject-matter-centered, nor society-centered; it is ideal-centered.*
>
> . . .
>
> *Since ultimate reality is ultimate, and since present man and his society are transitory, education must be conformed to the ultimate, which is God, rather than to present man and present society, which are uncertain and changing.*
> *This is what is meant by ideal-centered education. Are they centered in ideals because they are wishful, man-made objectives? No. They are centered in ideals because the Ideal, now poorly realized in man and society, is the ultimately real foundation of all things.*[77]

These, then, are the beacons whose "sighting" by the "mind's eye" allows us to tack toward ultimate reality.

If man is successfully to transverse this transitory existential stage, it is vital that decisions concerning all educational variables focus on Ideas, for they alone can give meaning to the sensory and spiritual

[77] J. Donald Butler, *Idealism in Education* (New York: Harper & Row, Publishers, 1966), p. 97.

phenomena he will encounter along the way. The mind, for example, is itself disciplined for the very purpose of aiding him to recognize and use these life-giving resources. Although it is true that history, literature and art provide rich examples of man's greatest triumphs—and failures—in so doing, it must also be realized that science and mathematics, too, can be studied *not* as collections of dry facts concerning purely natural objects and processes, but as attempts to penetrate to the principles of ultimate meaning. Studied in this way, they, like all other serious efforts, stimulate the flow toward consciousness of Ideas inborn in our human minds. The mind so equipped is ever more capable of true creativity, imagination, integrity, intellectual drive and spiritual refinement—of discerning and realizing a self-concept which conforms to the Ideal (i.e., Absolute Mind, the brahman, God), union with which is its ultimate destiny.

2. *Ideas as Reflections of a Natural, External Reality*

Ideas have been defined as cognitive products of the naturalistic interaction of an organism's brain-guided sensing and an external reality. Their function has been defined as reflecting aspects of that reality. When we imaginatively recreate and compare our interaction experiences, our ideas allow us to discover, organize, criticize and generalize knowledge in the search for Truth. Two questions immediately appear to have pedagogical import: 1) How can we train the mind-brain to form more accurate ideas, that is, ideas which correspond more accurately to the reality they are designed to reflect? 2) How can we train the brain to recall original interaction experiences when needed for more complex epistemological activities?

With regard to training in more accurate idea-formation (assuming that one's sense organs are functioning "normally"), the emphasis should probably be placed on guided experiences in verbally and/or pictorially reflecting a process or a sensed object and then comparing one's own reflections with both the original object and also the illustrations produced by acknowledged authorities. For instance, the lower school science student is requested to observe a flower's sepal and then to draw it. When finished he will compare his drawing with the sepal itself and the textbook illustration.

More accurate idea-formation would also seem to demand gradually developing the student's psychomotor and linguistic skills (i.e., his ability to express what he senses), expanding his familiarity with the knowledge domain to which the object or process in question belongs and training him to minimize his subjective responses to the object prior to perceiving what is there with maximal accuracy. Let us say, for example, that a student is requested to view a microscope slide of an amoeba. He has had very little experience in knowing what to look for in viewing such an object and is maturationally unprepared to draw even a reasonably accurate reproduction. Furthermore, the activity appears to have very little connection with his previous experiences or knowledge. The idea he forms is not likely to be very accurate, nor is the crude picture of the "monster" he will produce likely to further his knowledge of microscopic life. If, on the other hand, the student is "ready" for the task, guided experiences in sensing, perception, expression, comparison and evaluation can contribute to such learning. Eventually the student will be prepared to extend the boundaries of knowledge rather than simply come to terms with that which is already known.

With regard to training the mind-brain to recall an earlier experience, it appears that several behaviors are involved and that they can be taught. For instance, Skinner writes:

> Special kinds of precurrent behavior which encourage the appearance of ideas can be taught.
>
> . . .
>
> A very simple example of precurrent behavior which has the effect of encouraging the emission of a verbal response is familiar. In recalling a name we have forgotten, we probe our behavior with supplemental stimuli. We generate formal probes by reciting the alphabet or by repeating a stress pattern if this has been recalled; we generate thematic probes by reviewing occasions on which we have used the name. We suppress competing responses which "get in the way" and "keep the mind a blank" by refraining so far as possible from incompatible responding. They all can be taught. In operation they are likely to be covert and their effects in evoking responses hard to trace and explain. It is then particularly easy to call them mental and allow them to go unanalyzed, but a direct attack [at analysis and teaching] is worthwhile.[78]

For Skinner, as for many contemporary behavioral scientists who operate within a basically realist frame of reference, neither the nature nor the recall of ideas involves reference to a supernatural or even a uniquely "mental" realm. Involved, rather, are quite natural, physiological responses which can be reinforced by the teacher who will

> recognize the problems to be solved, discover the steps to be taken and ways to get the learner to take them, and decide how and when the learner is to go on to other steps.[79]

[78] B. F. Skinner, *The Technology of Teaching* (New York: Appleton-Century-Crofts, Educational Division, Meredith Corporation, 1968), pp. 139–140.
[79] *Ibid.*, pp. 142–143.

3. Ideas as Man-Created Plans of Action

Building on the earlier discussion of mind as purposeful, problem-solving behavior, your students will have defined the problem(s) which confront them as individuals, small work groups or as a class or school. Having also canvassed the variables which are seen antecedent to solving the problem in any meaningful way, they now face the task of constructing ideas or hypotheses which will function as plans of action as they continue to mediate experience. In the naturalistic tradition, Pragmatism holds that this task subsumes various behaviors which can be taught and learned. At this point in our study, therefore, it seems useful to review both the characteristics of potentially useful ideas and the factors which affect their development, and to suggest possible instructional strategies.

The potentially useful idea appears to have several characteristics. The pragmatic emphasis on the word "potentially" is not to be taken lightly, however, for all knowledge is held to be a posteriori. In no particular order, these characteristics include the following:

1. *It is reasonably compatible with the major facts and beliefs accepted by those involved.*

2. *It is stated in terms consistent with a specified frame of reference.* For instance, the term "discipline" conjures up images of scowling schoolmasters with razor-sharp tongues for some; for others, it refers simply to "intellectual and emotional self-management." If "discipline" occurs in a plan of action, then, the student should at least be aware of the meaning he assigns to the term. If the idea is being considered by a group, a shared frame of reference will probably have to be developed prior to hypothesis construction.

3. *It is designed to solve the defined problem with no "side effects" with which the individuals involved could not at least co-exist.* Rarely, of course, does action result in that intended and *only* that intended. Unanticipated results are more often the rule. Nevertheless, the potential side effects are imaginatively considered in order to *reduce* the occurrence of unanticipated undesirable consequences.

4. *It suggests the most simple plan of action consistent with the given context.* Some differences in problem-solving will exist given the most carefully developed, shared frame of reference; the different skills of the various group members will introduce still other difficulties. Better, then, that the "leading hypothesis" be as simple and direct a plan of action as time, place and people allow. If it fails, more complex ideas may be implemented.

5. *It is stated so clearly that the consequences of acting on it can be readily observed and evaluated.*

6. *It seems capable of solving or markedly reducing the defined problem, all things considered.*

Obviously, ideas do not appear out of the air. In every case their suggestion has a developmental history, however dim and marked by seemingly untraceable gaps in the background of the constructor(s). Certain general factors, however, do appear frequently in these histories. The list which follows—based primarily on Burton, Kimball and Wing's text on teaching thinking[80]—appears to be reasonably accurate:

1. *Differential capacities to discern and discriminate.* At present, the degree to which these capacities rest on genetic factors, as compared with environmental factors, remains unclear. It is clear, however (but for reasons not easily identified), that people do differ in the ease, speed, quantity, variety and quality dimensions of hypothesis development.

2. *Attitudes.* Positive attitudes include curiosity, pleasure in dealing with problem-solving variables and processes, orderliness and the patience to plan before acting. Also needed is the foresight to envision a painstaking evaluative process following action, a psychological and procedural preparation for which must be built into the idea rather than being deferred to a stage when other factors exert major pressures (e.g., the demand that results make power figures "look good," or the necessity of moving on to other problems).

3. *Experiential background.* This includes its depth and breadth, as well as the fund of interests, skills and generalizations of contextual knowledge available to the individual.

4. *Recent activities and interests.*

5. *Pure chance or accident.*

We must now move on to those instructional strategies which are suggested by pragmatic theory. Again, it is most important that these be viewed as *possibilities*—if you will, *hypotheses* about ways in which the educator might facilitate hypothesis-development—and not as deductions from theory presented in Chapter 4. Once again, *Education for Effective Thinking*[81] provides a richly suggestive, though not exclusive, resource.

1. Encourage students to "brainstorm" their experience, their hunches and guesses, and as wide a range of other seemingly relevant resources (e.g., people, books) as contextual demands allow. Accept the quantity and variety of suggestions at this stage, deferring refinement until a later time.

2. When the students appear to be "blocking," warn them of the

[80] William H. Burton, Roland B. Kimball and Richard L. Wing, *Education for Effective Thinking* (New York: Appleton-Century-Crofts, Inc., 1960), p. 65.
[81] *Ibid.*, pp. 65–67.

tendency to be overwhelmed by the complexities of the problem when viewed as a whole. Redirect their attention to the different parts of the problem, that is, the initial indeterminate situation, the problem definition, antecedent variables and the "criteria of 'working.'" Suggest they focus exclusively on one part after another. In this connection, Burton, Kimball and Wing note:

> *Unskilled thinkers often sit and stare at a problem in apparent bafflement. They seem almost to expect the solution or a hint toward a solution to appear magically. Training enables a student to break the problems up, to look first here, then there, and so on. The more aspects that are consciously considered, the more connections are possible; hence, more recall and suggestions are likely.*[82]

3. Suggest related problems with which they have dealt and which may contain resources otherwise overlooked. In addition, they may stimulate additional thinking from another angle.

4. When there is general agreement that a list of reasonable length has been compiled, encourage the students to select the more promising hypotheses and develop them in some detail. Hopefully, this process will suggest a "leading hypothesis," that is, one selected for the first attempt at problem-solution.

5. In some cases you, the teacher, will yourself miscalculate the complexities of the task. The group simply doesn't have sufficient resources to suggest reasonable hypotheses. In these situations, it doesn't hurt to admit your own difficulties and to set about cooperatively developing whatever is needed. Nevertheless, with proper teacher preparation, even younger children can experience success in problem-solving.

6. Occasionally suggest changing the pace and type of activity, temporarily retreating from an especially frustrating problem until another day.

7. Keep your sense of humor and maintain an attitude of tolerance, patience and sympathetic assistance—however frustrated you may become. *Remember:* a) children must learn skills you already possess; b) solving the problem for them will only teach them to wait for an authority to solve their problems on future occasions—and that's not exactly the idea; and c) when especially frustrated, even teachers have been known to complain bitterly about meetings given over to "democratic problem-solving"!

Two additional points should be noted: Direct minding behaviors may occasionally have to be halted at the stage of idea-development

[82] *Ibid.*, p. 66.

(to be followed by vicarious minding, e.g., discussions of what *might* happen *if* a certain plan were acted upon—as in a sex education class). Nevertheless, the development of both minding behaviors and knowledge demands that the child have maximal opportunity "to test his ideas by application, to make their meaning clear and to discover for himself their validity."[83]   Finally, the pragmatist might do well to follow the scientific realist's lead in behaviorally defining terms such as "capacity" and "attitude" and in further specifying the many behaviors subsumed in (and often obscured by) discussions of the various *stages* of hypothesis development.   With regard to those behaviors which democratically promote open and refineable hypothesis-development, he would then be in a better position to identify contingencies which would reinforce appropriate behaviors.   An interesting question, of course, concerns whether one can meaningfully speak of " 'conditioning' 'openness.' "

C. Experience

1. Experience as Contact with a Given Reality

Classically-oriented educators have long given searching attention to experience's function in bringing a given subject into a knowing relationship with the antecedent reality to which he must adjust for moral and/or physical survival.   Realists and idealists alike have inquired into the *facets* of reality with which the student must be brought into contact and the *instructional conditions* under which this can best be accomplished.

Contact with certain facets of reality has been emphasized by both realists and idealists.   This is not to say that *every* individual generally associated with these schools or systems would agree as to each facet or even the importance which a given facet should be assigned.[84] Nevertheless, however different the wording on occasion, considerable agreement has been voiced on such matters as the student's necessary contact with human authority, with the Divine Spirit or object of religious experiencing and with his fellow men individually and in social groupings.   It has also been generally agreed that the student should be brought into contact with aesthetic, intellectual and

[83] Dewey, *Democracy and Education,* p. 163.

[84] This is especially true of many contemporary "scientific realists," e.g., B. F. Skinner, who often tend to side with the pragmatists rather than with more classical realists.

spiritual models of the best in the species. Finally, agreement is noted as to the student's coming to a more intimate, conscious awareness of his own potential as encompassed in his mind-soul or brain, will and body.

Realists have tended to emphasize a necessary contact with the natural world, its processes and regularities or laws. In like measure, idealists have written at length on contact with those universals—Ideas, forms—"thought" by Absolute Mind. In neither case, however, have our studies indicated these facets have received the exclusive attention of the philosophical schools mentioned.

Many of the instructional variables involved in providing experiences designed to facilitate such contacts have been extensively discussed in other sections of this text and will be correlated in Chapter 9. In the present chapter, for instance, the comments under classical assumptions concerning "mind" and "ideas" are especially relevant to the problem at hand. Briefly, appropriate instructional conditions include:

1. A solid mind-disciplining curriculum structured in terms of its logical order as discerned by subject-matter specialists and expressed consistently in classroom materials.

2. Instructional technology which makes the learning of subject-matter more efficient. (Idealists would generally insist that technological devices may have their place in providing extra drill, but they must not supplant that necessary personal contact between minds Absolute and human.)

3. Essentially teacher-controlled approaches to instructional strategies such as discussion, experimentation, lectures and projects. We might also add direct instruction in logical and scientific reasoning and note the more idealistically-oriented penchant for direct instruction in the processes of contemplation, meditation or prayer. Increasing control over teaching-learning processes made possible by behavioral science has led many realists to become much more interested in emphasizing in-school activities—despite their historic preference for a good measure of "direct experiencing." As yet, however, they cannot possibly match the disdain for out-of-school experiences expressed by some idealists such as Horne, who wrote:

> It is also possible that the out-of-school type of experience as a model for in-school learning is somewhat idealized. . . . Only a few of them [pupils] are little Darwins. They usually face concrete situations and are weak in generalizing.[85]

[85] Herman H. Horne, *The Democratic Philosophy of Education: Companion to Dewey's Democracy and Education; Exposition and Comment* (New York: The Macmillan Company, 1932), p. 208.

4. Organizational (school system, individual school, classroom), administrative and professional policies and procedures supportive of the conditions noted above.

2. *Experience as Transactional Doing and Undergoing*

Few assumptions introduced in this text suffer from as long and unfortunate a history of misinterpretation—especially among educators—as does the pragmatic assumption concerning "experience." Not only opponents but many proponents of Pragmatism have suggested that knowledge, interest and discipline (indeed, almost everything else pedagogically bright and beautiful) somehow flow magically from constant, direct child activity or "doing." "Learning by Dewey-ing" is not only a (very) bad pun but represents the depth of misunderstanding with regard to what is suggested for education by the assumption of "experience as transactional doing and undergoing."

Experiences, involving transactions in a social milieu through which the meanings of both subject and object are constructed and reconstructed, are of uneven educational value.[86] Some are surely *maleducative*, an example being a child's unhappy experiences with a particular teacher or subject which colors his whole attitude toward "school." Others are of *neutral* value in that, while they do not result in damaging constructions, they simply do not take the child or the class anywhere. Their connections with other experiences are so unclear as to contribute little to student understanding of the present or the extension of their intelligent control over the future. The filmstrip shown out of sequence (perhaps because the correct one failed to arrive) or the activity "thrown together" by the substitute teacher who was not provided with adequate lesson plans furnish examples of this type of experience. The *valuable* or educative experience, by contrast,

> grows out of the conditions of the experience being had in the present, and . . . is within the range of the capacity of students; and, secondly, . . . it is such that it arouses in the learner an active quest for information and for production of new ideas. The new facts and new ideas thus obtained become the ground for further experiences in which new problems are presented. The process is a continuous spiral.[87]

[86] *Cf.* John Dewey, *Experience and Education* (New York: The Macmillan Company, 1938; New York: Collier Books, 1963), pp. 25–27.
[87] *Ibid.*, p. 79.

Once again, although this point is widely misunderstood, the teacher has a most active role in helping to provide school experiences through which the student's experience will become progressively richer and more organized. In brief, he is responsible for coordinating the establishment of classroom learning situations wherein such growth can take place. In order to fulfill this function, he must obviously take into consideration the whole range of variables involved in learning: facts and beliefs regarding those attitudes conducive to learning; facts and beliefs concerning the background, interests and learning modes of the students with whom he is working; and the total human and nonhuman, physical and social, resources and demands of the environment in which learning must take place. Such a consideration involves coordinating individual factors, subject-matter factors, process (minding) factors and societal factors. Desired is the creation of a situation conducive to integrating and giving meaning to present experience and providing the basis for reconstructing the past in giving meaning to the future.[88]

It would be a serious error were the preceding paragraph interpreted as a call for teacher-centered policies and procedures. As noted earlier, the child's interests and capacities are an integral part of the learning situation. Pragmatists have generally maintained that learning should *originate* in the ordinary, everyday activities-experiences of the child. Dewey illustrates this feeling, writing:

> *Anything which can be called a study, whether arithmetic, history, geography, or one of the natural sciences, must be derived from materials which at the outset fall within the scope of ordinary life-experience.*
>
> . . . .
>
> *But finding the material for learning within experience is only the first step. The next step is the progressive development of what is already experienced into a fuller and richer and also more organized form, a form that gradually approximates that in which subject-matter is presented to the skilled, mature person.*[89]

The demands of this position, especially upon teachers working with the older child or the experientially disadvantaged child, are severe. One cannot start, for instance, with subject-matter as logically organized by the skilled specialist—such organization represents a fairly distant goal and not the starting point. Rather, one must begin with those aspects of the subject with which the student has had experience. If children have not had many experiences with a given unit of

---

[88] *Ibid.*, Chapter III ("Criteria of Experience").
[89] *Ibid.*, pp. 73–74.

study, e.g., the Far North, one may have to *introduce* the unit with bulletin board displays and films and, perhaps, even the classroom visit of a neighbor's Siberian Husky (one of the sled-pulling northern dogs). Furthermore, at every stage of the process when their previous experience readies them—or can be expanded to make them ready— for educative participation, they must be involved in school decision-making, evaluation and generalization.

It is through these cooperative transactions between teacher, student and the other variables in the classroom environment that learning takes place and a sense of involvement and responsibility—the key elements in discipline—is established.[90] Knowledge, interest and discipline (indeed, much else pedagogically wise and wonderful) come, then, not merely through "doing," but through the transactional mediation of experience involving cooperative, evaluated and generalized "doing and undergoing."

3. *Experience as Being in the World*

Perhaps the appealing "human dimension" of Existentialism is no better illustrated than in its concern for the inescapably personal nature of an individual's being or experience. Not the least of reasons for concern on the educator's part, of course, lies in the fact that one's being or experience includes his choice-defined and revealed self-concept. If, as has been suggested, the general end of education lies in the development of the human being into full selfhood,[91] the provision of an environment wherein an individual can freely experience opportunities for self-choosing must provide a means basic to that end. "So where do we find ourselves?" asks Perls. He answers:

> We find ourselves on the one hand as individuals who want to actualize themselves; we find ourselves also embedded in a society . . . which might make demands different from the individual demands. So there is the basic clash.[92]

Given the definition of the "basic clash"—which seems reasonable enough within this frame of reference—the question remains as to how the existentialist's concern for the individual's being may be expressed in education. Actually, there are two general possibilities. The more direct one is presented by Sidney Jourard, who maintains that "mental

[90] *Ibid.*, pp. 56–67.

[91] *Cf.* Karl Jaspers, *Man in the Modern Age,* trans. Eden and Cedar Paul (New York: Doubleday Anchor Books, 1957), p. 116.

[92] *Gestalt Therapy Verbatim,* p. 31.

health is best fostered by seeking to make it safe for a person to acknowledge his experience to himself and to other significant people who confirm him as the one he is."[93]   Here we see the optimal environment for choice-making: the situation where it is safe to be, to experience openly.   Though perhaps more easily established in a therapeutic situation, there does seem to be a good deal that can be done to establish such an environment in the classroom.   Students can be approached as free subjectivities rather than as computer cards or threats to teacher power.   The mutual introspection which results may not completely erase the threat or the occurrence of objectification.   It should, however, slow the process and create a breach in the wall of facticity through which possibilities can first be glimpsed and then grasped.   Curricular alternatives can be devised by both students and educators which are so rich and diverse that they excite *all* children— not just the college-bound—to explore and to choose.   In this regard we remember the exciting suggestions presented in Craig Wilson's *The Open Access Curriculum*.   Many aspects of both problem-defining and problem-solving can be placed in the hands of individual students, thus slowing the drift toward teacher- or group-dominated thinking, choosing and acting.

And what of the teacher's role?   As Maxine Greene puts it, "Classroom situations can be made occasions for strengthening [the student's] will to be authentic and free—that is, if we who teach are willing to open ourselves sufficiently to be *present* there."[94]   *Being* there as a subjectivity and not as just one more object may involve a relationship which "*invites, challenges,* or *permits* the emergence of authentic being"[95] in the student.   We may have to "apply enough skilled frustration so that [the student] is forced to find his own way, discover his own possibilities, his own potential, and discover that *what he expects from the* [*teacher*], *he can do just as well himself.*"[96]   Again, we may take the more passive role of the catalyst.   All of these are possibilities for the teacher—but, after all, *she* will have to choose in the unique situation which confronts *her*.

Considering the conditions under which most teaching and learning go on in America today, the establishment of such an environment may often be difficult if not impossible.   In those cases where a clear possibility of misunderstanding and/or punishment exists, it may be impossible for a teacher—or a student—to develop enough trust to assume

[93] "Counseling for Authenticity," *Philosophical Guidelines for Counseling*, ed. Beck, p. 190.   Quoted by permission.

[94] *Existential Encounters for Teachers*, p. 161.

[95] Jourard, "Counseling for Authenticity," *Philosophical Guidelines for Counseling*, ed. Beck, p. 190.   Quoted by permission.

[96] Perls, *Gestalt Therapy Verbatim*, p. 37.

an I-Thou posture vis-à-vis the other. Jourard goes so far as to suggest that the "basically secure" person may occasionally have to be taught to be "in this world but not of it," that is, to go along with the rules without visible protest, to fake conformity as the lesser of two evils.[97] His suggestion is not without merit. Probably every counsellor, parent or teacher who has developed an open relationship with a child caught in settings inimical to the former's frame of reference has responded in this manner. There are also basic dangers which bear mentioning. For instance, observation suggests that if one *lives* a lie long enough, he may *become* that lie. Furthermore, it is not always easy for the classroom teacher to differentiate between a "basically secure person" and one who for the moment has succeeded in disguising deep personality difficulties. Overall, the direct approach—in which we try to make it safe for an individual to *be*—appears far safer than this strategy, which should probably be used only as a last resort.

D. Objectivity

1. Objectivity as Alignment with a Given Reality

"Education," wrote Horne, "is the eternal process of superior adjustment of the physically and mentally developed, free, conscious, human being to God, as manifested in the intellectual, emotional, and volitional environment of man."[98] Unfortunately, many classicists maintain, freedom has often been considered antithetical to "adjustment" or "alignment." It has, in short, been confused with "license." Actually, such a confusion is both unnecessary and dangerous. How can an individual possibly grow or express his freedom if he is constantly "stubbing his toe" against physical and/or moral realities? With some exceptions, subjectivity simply catches him up in a cycle of frustration and failure. It is when he is objective—working in concert with known reality—that he can best discern the possibilities for growth.

American education has given strong expression to the assumption of "objectivity as alignment with a given reality," teaching students to "line up" in many ways (and in many situations other than the hallway). In discipline, for instance, the student is taught to conform to

97 *Cf.* "Counseling for Authenticity," *Philosophical Guidelines for Counseling*, ed. Beck, p. 190. Paraphrased by permission.
98 Herman H. Horne, *The Philosophy of Education.* Rev. ed. (New York: The Macmillan Company, 1927), p. 285.

regulations which he usually has little voice in establishing. Grades and other reinforcers are generally awarded on the basis of how close he approaches standards set by authorities. The "objective test" actually tries to minimize the possibility of subjective errors on the part of the test-maker, the test-taker and the test-grader. Few students are involved in the writing of "programs" for workbooks, computers and the like. A basic dictum of "performance-based teacher education" consists in holding the student "accountable, not for passing grades, but for attaining a given level of competency in performing the essential tasks of teaching."[99] Many individuals involved in this effort today are insisting that teacher trainers and practicing teachers, not prospective teachers, make the basic decisions as to which competencies should be developed and the methods by which they should be taught.[100]

As noted in the theoretical discussion of the assumption, however, complete objectivity is possible only when absolute knowledge is held with regard to a given phenomenon. Humility is an important human virtue, especially with regard to the unknown and the partially known. If our response to these realms is confused with our obligations to absolute knowledge, learning may suffer. An excessive and unjustified appeal to authority may actually stifle the student's subjective creativity and imagination and thus inhibit their proper function in producing that more certain knowledge prerequisite to objectivity. Although he fails to note that the teacher may be as important a classroom focal point as the group, Crutchfield describes the plight of a child too long subjected to excessive conformity pressures:

> The outer pressure and inner compulsion to conform arouse extrinsic, ego-involved motives in the problem-solver. His main efforts tend to become directed toward the goals of being accepted and rewarded by the group, of avoiding rejection and punishment. The solution of the problem itself becomes of secondary relevance, and his task-involved motivation diminishes. In being concerned with goals extrinsic to the task itself, and particularly as rendered anxious about potential threats in the situation, his cognitive processes become less flexible, his insights less sensitive.[101]

[99] Stanley Elam, *Performance-Based Teacher Education: What Is the State of the Art?*, PBTE Series: No. 1 (Washington, D.C.: American Association of Colleges for Teacher Education, 1971), p. 1.

[100] *Ibid.*, p. 18.

[101] Richard S. Crutchfield, "Conformity and Creative Thinking," *Contemporary Approaches to Creative Thinking; A Symposium Held at the University of Colorado*, ed. Howard E. Gruber *et al.* (New York: Atherton Press, 1964), p. 125.

2. Objectivity as Intersubjectivity

Theoretical considerations in Chapter 4 suggested that "objectivity" was probably best defined as the product of sharing and, when possible, reconciling subjective perceptions of a given phenomenon in a specified context. Achieving objectivity in a manner consistent with this definition and the related assumptions upon which it was based, appeared to involve several factors: 1) keeping subject and object definitions open to reconstruction, 2) creating an environment conducive to involved individuals being willing to "tell it the way they saw it," 3) identifying resources supplementary to the perceptions of directly involved individuals, and 4) employing dissonance-reconciliation techniques.

Much of that suggested throughout this chapter as being pedagogically-consistent with pragmatic epistemological assumptions surely bears upon teaching behaviors involved in the four activities enumerated above. Objectivity is fostered by—and contributes to—the development of a democratic, cooperative classroom environment; the extensive use of the problem-solving format to teach and improve minding behaviors; helping the student become aware both of his own frame of reference and those of others, as well as the skills involved in constructing a shared frame of reference; and the development of certain attitudes toward generalizations of contextual knowledge. As we have seen, our very ability to develop and test knowledge-claims often depends upon our success in developing agreement as to the objective nature of central variables.

Several other considerations should also be noted. In the first place, we must remember that achieving contextually objective views of a phenomenon on the basis of intersubjectivity involves behaviors which can be taught and learned. In light of the dominance in our culture of the assumption of "objectivity as alignment with a given reality," however, we cannot assume that even older students will have learned these behaviors. The assumption that younger children will have learned them is, of course, even more tenuous. Direct teaching will generally be in order.

While one is creating the all-important classroom climate about which we have spoken, it might be helpful to give the students some opportunities to construct contextually objective views. Select a phenomenon with which they have had some experience and which is not too emotionally-loaded. Perhaps, for example, the frustrations you consciously allowed to develop during the first two weeks of class have already taught your fourth graders that *some* rules are necessary with regard to using supplementary materials in their "resource center." In a rather nonchalant manner, suggest that some role-playing might help

them decide what to do.   Have several students take common stereo-
typed roles, e.g., the "I'm going to do my own thing" role, the "student
with a pressing need for a given book" role, the "student irritated by
all the commotion" role, the "student having to complete his project by
the end of the period" role, the "student sick of nit-picking regulations"
role and the "teacher not wanting to play the authoritarian" role.   Let
them "tell it the way they see it"—in terms of their assumed roles.
Perhaps you might also bring in a fifth grader (probably one of your
former students) to serve as an additional-resource person.   (Better
not involve yourself or the principal.   At this stage of the game—role-
playing or not—the chances are that either one of you would only
activate the all too common habit of lining up with external reality!)
The students' experiences in achieving a more objective view of the
necessary rules *in a situation where they do not have to disclose themselves* may provide a most useful introduction to later situations where
objectivity will have to be constructed under more complex and
emotion-laden conditions.   It may also give them some helpful practice in "getting into" frames of reference not their own.

Finally, all that democratic theory suggests for protecting minority
opinion seems applicable to this discussion.   For a variety of purposes,
Pragmatism is dedicated to establishing more conscious and controlled
transactional relationships between the individual and the social elements, not to overcoming one at the expense of the other.   An individual who cannot accept the majority's opinion may be required to
conform to a minimal set of democratically-derived regulations.   But
he is surely *not* required to internalize that opinion as his own, or to
cease to attempt—democratically—to motivate others to side with him.
The educator has an inescapable obligation to this student—and to
the present majority which must also deal with him.

3. Objectivity as Intrasubjectivity

In the final analysis, we have seen that the existentialist places the full
responsibility for determining the nature of the phenomenon—subject
or object—squarely on the individual.   No matter what the contributions of the external environment, this determination of "what is"
basically involves an *intra*subjective process.   True, *inter*subjective
relationships *are* established with the Other.   Their primary purpose
from the standpoint of the subjectivities involved, however, is to open
up new possibilities for each subject's self-actualization, not to produce
shared, communicable knowledge concerning the nature of those
selves.   Such knowledge of being-for-itself is personal, intuitive and
noncommunicable.   Naturally, common understandings on the part of

several individuals as to the nature of given environmental *objects* do develop. These, however, represent knowledge of being-in-itself (not being-for-itself), and individuals are not relieved of their personal responsibility to certify the truth of such knowledge simply because it is supported by experimental data, authority, the majority or what have you.

With regard to determining the objective nature of the nonself, most of the pedagogical strategies suggested in the preceding discussion are applicable. This is not surprising, given the substantial metaphysical agreement between pragmatists and existentialists and their joint acceptance of the experimental method when knowledge of objects (though not of subjects) is desired. Differences will be observed in a somewhat lesser valuation of democratic decision-making process and a somewhat more explicit reinforcement of the obligation of the individual actively to *question* the majority product in certifying the objective nature of the phenomenon. This active, conscious *criticism* serves as a necessary counterbalance to inevitable group pressures for conformity. Nevertheless, the words "question" and "criticism" have been chosen with care, for there are also grave dangers in *automatically rejecting* group insights. Such rejection involves alienating ourselves from the possibilities which others may sight in dealing with common human problems. Furthermore, the energy consumed by such hostility, as well as the rewards given by many segments of society for conspicuous (but superficial) nonconformity, may weaken the creative powers needed for problem-solving and self-actualization.[102] In short, the group represents *both* an "inevitable and real threat to man's becoming authentic" and a reality with which the authentic individual must deal.[103]

Dealing with children each of whom must *also* determine the nature of his own self, however, presents a quite different set of pedagogical problems. Intuition is the keynote, but the child's intuitions may be incorrect. As teachers, the best we can do is to encourage the child to turn to his feelings and make decisions about what he is when he feels the moment is right. This is surely not to say that an evaluation of past experience, an awareness of the present and an anticipation of the future cannot be taken into account. Nor is it to say that the products of I-It relationships or relationships with significant others should be ignored. Indeed, such is not the case. What is being denied is that the child even implicitly should be encouraged to determine what he is and/or will become on the basis of factors such as grades, test scores

---

[102] *Ibid.*, pp. 137–138.
[103] Mitchell Bedford, *Existentialism and Creativity* (New York: Philosophical Library, 1972), p. 277.

or a parent's wishes.   When and if the child feels that he has erred in defining what he is—or when his definition has been outgrown in the process of becoming—we can also encourage him to choose anew, to risk failure anew.   For this is his responsibility and his dignity—and his anguish—as an authentic human being.[104]

E.   Frame of Reference

1. *Frame of Reference as Limitation-to-Be-Transcended*

The following discussion represents a summary of generally accepted ways for assisting the student to overcome the limitations of his individual frame of reference.   Possibilities are suggested for adult personnel, materials, procedures and school structure.   True, some differences do exist between determinists and those who posit free will as a basic power and mark of the human being.   Nevertheless, both sides emphasize the child's reaching that point where *he* recognizes the truth of the wider, more accurate frame of reference, accepts-internalizes it as his own and behaves accordingly.

Teachers, administrators and professional staff are exhorted both to provide personal models worthy of emulation and to temper expression of their proper authority by both humane concern for those under their charge and an awareness of their own human limitations.   At the same time, adult personnel in the school should keep some distance between themselves and the students.   Familiarity does breed contempt; humane concern must not be confused with being "one of the gang."   Finally, professional control must be maintained over basic educational decisions.   The student should not be given powers which he is not yet ready to exercise.   As a related point, nonprofessionals cannot be allowed constantly to interfere with school operations.   The school must, therefore, manage to secure financial support from the community while maintaining as great a measure of independence as is politically possible.

Classicists generally agree that instructional materials should be as intrinsically motivating as possible.[105]   When this is not possible, we

---

[104] *Ibid.*, pp. 269–270 and 272–274.

[105] "Intrinsic" motivation involves the student's feeling drawn to the materials out of interest *in them*.   Rewards are directly related to the skills or pleasures which *accompany* their mastery.   "Extrinsic" motivation, on the other hand, draws the student to the material not for itself but for the supplementary rewards which *are given* for its mastery, e.g., tokens, grades, the use of the family car.   Traditionalists emphasize that a judicious use of extrinsic motivators may often lead to intrinsic motivation.

should at least try to hasten the transition from extrinsic to intrinsic motivation. Programming strategies such as ensuring student success provide a means of meeting this goal. In any case, the child must be exposed to a mind-disciplining curriculum. Such a curriculum focusses on that knowledge of content, skills and attitudes whose mastery will allow the child to adjust to natural and/or moral reality. Of necessity, these materials must be presented in ways appropriate to the developmental level of the children concerned. Although the child cannot be treated as an automaton, a relatively high level of teacher-specialist control over objectives, learning activities and evaluation is desirable in order better to ensure that what is taught will be learned. Where viable alternatives exist, the child must surely become aware of them; where they do not, he must be led toward truth. This is not a mechanical process, and we must not assume that control need eliminate honest and spirited inquiry.

Positive reinforcement is the rule, gradually shaping desired behaviors as the student approaches or approximates externally-set standards. Undesirable behaviors are best ignored, for we may be reasonably confident that the "natural consequences" of acting contrary to reality will soon teach the child to avoid them.[106] On rare occasions, moderate punishment may have to be administered, but the child must understand its rationale and the sincere concern which prompts it. The goal is that the student understand what is desired and be given opportunities to practice desirable behaviors until a habit is established. After the child senses the true freedom and the room for creativity which accompany acting in ways consistent with more accurate frames of reference—more accurate because they better reflect reality—he will be drawn to accept them as his own. Compulsion really doesn't enter into the process. Does the teacher *force* the (sane, knowledgeable) child to refrain from jumping out of an eighteenth-floor window?

The school's physical plant is planned to facilitate the instructional strategies, materials and technology appropriate to a given developmental group. Children will generally be grouped homogeneously, for there are potentially disruptive variations among *normal* children both in general ability and in specialized abilities needed to master different areas of study. Where necessary and possible, special classes will be established for the student having *extreme* learning problems. This is done both to minimize the disruption of regular classes and to provide a more appropriate learning environment for the afflicted child.

---

106 Naturally, we are talking about the relatively "normal" child; others will be treated in part as their special problems dictate. For instance, some authorities suggest that the emotionally disturbed child may have to be given tranquilizers if any learning is to take place.

Contemporary critics of classical assumptions often cry that helping the child to overcome the limitations of his individual frame of reference involves immoral manipulation, conditioning or indoctrination. The traditionalist replies, however, that such help allows the child to act *more* freely, *more* creatively. He argues that acceptance of the most accurate frame of reference is just as necessary to the realization of human potential as are the basement and lower floors to the stability of a skyscraper. To capture the full power of the traditionalist's case, consider the following Scripture:

> *Every one then who hears these words of mine and does them will be like a wise man who built his house upon the rock; and the rain fell, and the floods came, and the winds blew and beat upon that house, but it did not fall, because it had been founded on the rock. And every one who hears these words of mine and does not do them will be like a foolish man who built his house upon the sand; and the rain fell, and the floods came, and the winds blew and beat against the house, and it fell; and great was the fall of it.*[107]

2. Frame of Reference as Self-in-Becoming

For the pragmatist and the existentialist, one's frame of reference was seen to be so inextricably intertwined with the self-concept as to be virtually indistinguishable from it. The view that in a real sense we *are* what we *assume* we are, suggested the immorality of external tampering with the individual's frame of reference. Cases were identified, however, where decision-making might be facilitated if the subject were aware of the assumptions making up his own frame of reference and/or those of others in his life space. In addition, pragmatic theory suggested situations where a group might have to construct a more common (though temporary) frame of reference prior to solving a problem demanding cooperation. The pedagogical questions to which we must now address ourselves seem reasonably clear: 1) How might the teacher help the student become more aware of his own frame of reference? 2) How might the teacher help the student become more aware of other frames of reference viable in our culture? 3) How might the teacher help a group construct a more common frame of reference in order to solve a problem demanding joint effort?

Becoming more aware of our own assumptions is not a particularly

[107] Matt. 7:24–27 (RSV).

easy task.   Several possibilities do seem worthy of consideration, the
first of which is offered by Thomas, who writes:

> *The best clue I know in locating what I take for granted is to
> find out what makes me indignant or outraged.   When I find my
> blood pressure rising because someone breaks into the line ahead
> of me, I soon find out that I am deeply attached to the rule of
> first come, first served.*[108]

A second possibility is suggested by what Louis Raths calls the "clarifying response."   Useful in a variety of school situations where the
educator is trying to help the student clarify his beliefs (rather than
obtain data or lead the student to a predetermined answer), the
clarifying strategy involves responding to student comments or other
behaviors without moralizing or evaluating.   Responsibility is placed
on the individual student to respond or not as he sees fit.   Finally, it
relies on short interactions between student and teacher regarding
small segments of behavior.   The effect of a single interaction will
probably not be earth-shattering, although their cumulative effect
could be quite impressive.[109]   Raths stresses the immediacy and the
creativity necessarily involved in this strategy.   Although he also
emphasizes that its justification will lie in its effect upon student
behavior, rather than the degree to which teacher behavior conforms
to some preconceived criteria, he does provide some thirty examples of
possible teacher responses.   Examples include: "Is this something you
prize?"   "Have you felt that way for a long time?"   "Are you saying
that . . . [repeat the statement]?"   and "Would you do the same
thing again?"[110]
   The technique used in this text suggests a third possibility by which
the teacher might help the student to become aware of the assumptions making up his frame of reference.   Reflect on what is happening
in Chapters 2 through 9.   Assumptions viable in our culture have been
presented both as theory and as they might be expressed in professional situations.   In one sense, they are being held up in front of you
as "mirrors."   At this point, the questions are implicit: "Hey, how does
this fit?"   "Where do you agree? . . . disagree?"   "Why?"   Later on,
as noted in the introductory chapter, you will be asked to take a stand,
to attempt to define your personal assumptions with regard to several
concepts of your choosing.   Finally, you will be asked to relate your

---

[108] Lawrence G. Thomas, "Response to the Presidential Address," *Educational
Theory*, XVII, No. 4 (October 1967), p. 296.

[109] Louis E. Raths, Merrill Harmin and Sidney B. Simon, *Values and Teaching:
Working with Values in the Classroom* (Columbus, Ohio: Charles E. Merrill Publishing Co., 1966), pp. 53–54.

[110] *Ibid.*, pp. 260–261.

philosophical assumptions, to suggest consistencies or inconsistencies between them and with other disciplines, and to note the implications suggested for you as a human being and as a professional educator.

Given the pluralism of our culture, the chances are that neither your classmates nor your professional colleagues will share very many of your assumptions. *Greater* congruity may occasionally be found in a few isolated sections of the country or among relatively isolated and self-sufficient subcultures, e.g., the Amish communities. Even in these cases, however, the mass media and the rapid changes being forced by the intense pressures of this particular era have left few areas untouched. This phenomenon suggests that a deeper understanding of your colleagues' frames of reference will often be necessary for communication—let alone cooperative effort. How can this understanding be brought about?

Direct instruction in the various assumptions concerning basic concepts may help. Yet, this technique is rarely possible at the elementary or secondary levels and is appropriate only to a handful of studies in higher education. Even when it is possible and appropriate, there is another problem in that it is often viewed by students as something of a "cognitive game." There is an empathetic element involved in coming into contact with another human being which is just not touched by this technique alone. It may, however, be made more personal in a variety of ways. As in this course, the student may be asked to assume his acceptance of several assumptions (and his freedom to act upon them) and then to suggest how he might carry out a common task—e.g., setting up rules for the use of the classroom resource center—in a manner consistent with the assumptions. Or, the student can be exposed to a videotaped or verbally described incident and then be asked to suggest the assumptions which *might* have influenced specified behaviors had the subject been free to express his assumptions. In addition to the case study approach used in Chapter 10, another strategy involves the "paired debate" wherein two student teams and two controversial issues such as "student rights" and "busing" are chosen. One team debates the first issue from the standpoint of one frame of reference and then must assume a contrasting frame of reference in debating the second issue. Bedford seems to grasp the central intent of all these strategies:

> *The authentic personality does not demand that others duplicate his type of existence, for each man is confronted by a different combination of circumstances. . . . Yet, because the authentic man is concerned about his fellowman, he does seek to challenge him to penetrate his personal existence a little more thoughtfully.*[111]

[111] *Existentialism and Creativity,* p. 317.

The skills involved in building a more common frame of reference in situations demanding cooperative effort have been discussed generally in Chapters 4 and 5 under the assumption of "objectivity as inter-subjectivity." They also received specific attention under this assumption in Chapter 4. Although they will not be repeated here, the student is encouraged to review the earlier discussions.

F. Knowledge and Truth

1. The Consistency Theory of Knowledge and Truth

Having to deal directly with the "consistency theory of knowledge and truth" may prove to be somewhat ego-shattering for the teacher oriented to another frame of reference. There is something frightening about suddenly realizing that there is absolutely *nothing* you can do to *ensure* that your students will gain knowledge of Truth. Every single pedagogical strategy only "cooperates" with Absolute Mind in preparing the child's mind-soul to fulfill its supernatural potential. It, and it alone, must "see" and examine the relationships of ideas within disciplines and between disciplines. It, and it alone, is capable of judging the degree to which its operations are leading toward Truth. Learning finally comes down to a direct relationship between mind and Mind. At the crucial moment, you—the teacher—are excluded. The experience is akin to that of parents who after years of active involvement see "their" child suddenly realize that he is a separate being, a separate self—and, with regret and pride comingled, must "let go" in order to express their love.

The details of pedagogical cooperation with Absolute Mind—i.e., the ways in which the teacher makes his (necessary) contribution to preparing the child's mind to fulfill its foreordained role—have been presented throughout this chapter. In short, the potential powers of the mind must be disciplined-strengthened in readying it to seek knowledge through meditation, disciplined intuition, logical and ex-perimental reasoning, and the acceptance of revelation and reputable authority. His mind must be habituated to "hard and accurate think-ing" based on standards of lucid, profound, fruitful and careful reasoning.[112] In like measure, it must be well-stocked with genera-tive knowledge. Through discussion, reading, the lecture and proj-ects, the teacher provides the child with experiences capable of

[112] Michael Demiashkevich, *An Introduction to the Philosophy of Education* (New York: American Book Company, 1935), p. 280.

evoking Ideas inborn in mind. These experiences bring him into contact with human authority, the Divine Spirit, his fellow men individually and in society, exemplars of the species and his own potential. He is familiarized with the criteria of coherence and is helped to stay on the right track, to "line up" with known reality, to overcome the limitations of his own frame of reference. In short, the child himself is brought to the threshold of knowing.

The steps by which he crosses this threshold are—fortunately or unfortunately, depending on one's frame of reference—not susceptible to behavioral definition. Having been provided with the parts of the puzzle and familiarized with puzzle-solving skills, the child's mind must now attempt to "see" the whole picture—which, of course, is Reality itself. To some extent its success will be limited by mind's being "set" in a material base. Then, too, the specific operations of learning themselves must remain shrouded in some mystery, for they belong to another realm of being altogether. Sufficient to say, we as teachers are called by that realm to cooperate in helping others to become.

2. The Correspondence Theory of Knowledge and Truth

Our metaphysical and epistemological studies have established that the classical tradition encompasses a second position more confident of man's ability to dis-cover reality than is the position just considered. Although the skills be difficult to identify and teach—let alone learn[113] —man is capable of developing knowledge statements so refined as to correspond to reality as it is apart from his perceptual processes and personal wishes. And he is capable of using this knowledge to adjust to physical and moral regularities or "laws" in ways allowing his activities to be more productive and satisfying. Although much is known, much more remains to be known. Hence, society has given the school basic responsibilities in transmitting achieved knowledge of content, skills and attitudes to students, thus preparing them to expand man's knowledge of a pre-existent reality.

Most educators oriented toward Realism call for the lower, middle and high schools to provide a "general education." According to Harry Broudy, for example, such an education must stress those habits and skills involved in acquiring, using and enjoying truth.[114] Not

---

[113] Skinner agrees that their *identification* presents difficulties. Once identified, however, he feels that their teaching and their learning may be made both more easy and more efficient.

[114] Broudy, *Building a Philosophy of Education*, pp. 314–315. Paraphrased by permission.

only are these the habits and related resources necessary to expand knowledge, they are exactly those fostered by the curriculum and activities of a general education. For Broudy, they include the ability skillfully to use the symbolic tools of learning, thinking and communication; the ability to use knowledge from a variety of disciplines to analyze and structure—though not to solve—pressing human problems; and the ability to analyze personal problems given knowledge of oneself and the surrounding situation. The development of these abilities, however, demands that we come to know about the basic concepts, relations, investigative modes and evaluative criteria of the sciences; about the culture's past achievements which afford perspective on the present and orientation to the future; and about man's outstanding efforts to create ethical systems and their celebration in great works of art.[115] Teaching, guided by the findings of educational psychology, involves increasing the student's capacity to approach the expert's knowledge and his powers to perceive, express, classify and relate.

Contemporary educational psychology is deeply involved in an analysis of the behaviors involved in learning and teaching, as well as the environmental conditions under which they can most effectively be exercised.[116] Analyses of the behaviors involved in "knowing how . . ." as distinguished from "knowing about . . . ,"[117] for instance, promise markedly to increase our ability to ensure that the student will learn what the educator sets out to teach—whether this be facts about the formation of igneous rocks, inquiry skills in history, basic American values or the behaviors to which we refer collectively as "creativity."[118]

3. The Transactional Theory of Knowledge and Truth

Pragmatic epistemological theory maintains that knowledge is a by-product of those problem-solving and related satisfactions which are the direct result of successfully mediating experience. Such knowl-

---

[115] *Ibid.* Paraphrased by permission.

[116] Not all realists, however, are enamoured of the behavioristic bent of much of today's work in this discipline. For the reactions of a "classical realist," see Harry S. Broudy, *A Critique of Performance-Based Teacher Education*, PBTE Series: No. 4 (Washington, D.C.: American Association of Colleges for Teacher Education, 1972).

[117] *Cf.* Skinner, *The Technology of Teaching*, pp. 200ff.

[118] The details of such analyses are generally encountered in educational psychology courses. The student who has not yet entered upon these studies might examine B. F. Skinner's *The Technology of Teaching* and M. Daniel Smith's *Theoretical Foundations of Learning and Teaching*.

edge is limited and contextual, although it is vitally important to suggesting new problems and plans of action and to creating and/or refining knowledge generalizations. Truth refers to the quality of an idea which has proved to produce the predicted consequences of acting upon it. We also found that the criteria of an idea's "working" depended upon the entire problematic situation, only one element of which involved the individual problem-solver's own purposes. Truth claims must be generalized and opened to public confirmation in order to increase their reliability and, hence, their potential usefulness to human concerns.

In this section we shall touch upon the potential pedagogical relevance of pragmatic theory to *using* and *evaluating* contextual knowledge. Attitudes and school personnel policies which seem supportive of these activities will also be examined. Note that school policies and procedures suggested for knowledge *development* have been considered earlier in this chapter and might well be reviewed as an introduction to the discussion which follows.

The theory presented in the preceding chapter is highly suggestive of ways in which we might *use knowledge.* A basic criterion of experience, for example, was that it "take us somewhere." Mere unrelated doing is not enough. Hence, knowledge gained in solving one problem must be examined to see what it suggests for organizing our experience, for suggesting new problems the solution of which may expand our experience and for forming additional ideas for solving both these new problems and other ones at hand. For instance, how can facts about the lessened use of sled dogs be related to our knowledge about advances in transportation? To the changing culture of the Eskimos and Indians of the Far North? Do they suggest any new problems to which we might turn, e.g., the effect of a greater use of modern transportation (and the related need for new fuel sources) upon the Alaskan ecology?

Secondly, explicit attention in the classroom must be given to examining contextual knowledge in terms of its possible use in constructing and/or refining knowledge generalizations. For instance, do class experiences in analyzing a particular series of poems have anything to say about the criteria presently being used to evaluate poetry? Does new contextual knowledge suggest we need to build some generalizations which heretofore have been unnecessary? After all, in the early writing stages, the use of commas may not be of great concern. But sooner or later communication difficulties will create a need for developing some guidelines concerning their use. Will the teacher be sufficiently aware of the educational potential created by the students' growing experience and their incipient perception of this additional need? And will she help them to relate the new generalization to their writing in the social studies or in science? Will the revised poetry evaluation criteria be used in the next poetry unit? Will they be further revised next year? And will the teacher submit herself to the frustrations of involving students in suggesting refinement, construction and application possibilities—or will she inhibit their growth by taking full responsibility unto herself?

Knowledge may also be used for personal development and sheer pleasure. Why must the knowledge of specified content and the development of specified skills so often provide the basic course objectives? Shouldn't the student have opportunity—explicitly structured into every course—to ask: What does this content and these skills mean to me as a human being? As a professional educator? What inconsistencies have they uncovered in my frame of reference to which I want to give some attention? Given my belief in "free will," should I take that advanced course in "behavior modification" which will allow me more adequately to consider the facts developed in Skinnerian research? And what of pure pleasure? The Far North unit may lead the student to becoming a member of the local Siberian Husky Club and eventually taking part in training and racing his dog—especially if the teacher has placed some club pamphlets on the resource table. And what is so wrong with providing opportunities for learnings developed in a unit on Africa to be expressed in creative dance, in art, in writing? Lower school children take especial pleasure in putting it all together for a parents' night. In short, the opportunities for *using* knowledge are nearly endless—and all are potentially educative in the cooperatively-managed classroom.[119]

The *evaluation of knowledge* is also of central concern to the pragmatically-oriented educator. Again, knowledge involves doing and undergoing or, if you will, evaluated doing. Naturally, the type of evaluation used depends upon the type of knowledge-claim being advanced, the purposes of those involved and the setting in which it was developed.[120] District-wide curriculum projects, for example, should be experimentally evaluated—and this involves extensive planning in consultation with research methodology specialists long before school implementation. The thoroughgoing commitment to evaluation of which we are speaking, however, goes far beyond such extensive and formal projects. It involves the student's forming the habit of checking the results of his science experiment with his laboratory

---

[119] To make an implicit point explicit, opportunities for educators to use knowledge are just as important as for the student. An era of accelerated change demands constant reconstruction of generalizations concerning such phenomena as the curriculum, instructional strategies and discipline.

[120] For a most suggestive treatment of this problem, see Burton, Kimball and Wing, *Education for Effective Thinking*, Chapter VIII.

partner and/or other teams working on related experiments. At the end of a problem-solving unit it involves teacher and students reviewing the problem definition and the criteria of "working." It calls upon the whole classroom community to develop the habit of taking part in the evaluative process, perhaps asking and discussing their answers to questions such as the following: Did the idea work? If not, why not? What difficulties developed? Was it a matter of inadequate definition, team member inadequacies, insufficient resources, sloppy procedures? How might we have handled them more successfully? Which procedures worked best? Such evaluation best prepares the class for meaningful generalization activities—or for a more knowledgeable return to the stage of hypothesis construction and selection.

In conclusion, the optimal use and evaluation of knowledge claims is neither simple nor mechanical. Success demands that certain attitudes be developed among all members of the school community. Students as well as administrators and teachers must develop the willingness and the skill to raise searching questions—and be reinforced for doing so. An ability to recall facts must never be considered sufficient, for their use is necessary to the enrichment of present living—and tomorrow depends upon today. Contextual and generalized knowledge claims, even when verified, must be treated as tentative resources for, and not as determiners of, decision-making. The community must become committed cooperatively to developing common purposes to which problem-solving activities can contribute. And the entire community must become aware of, and resistant to, time-habituated remnants of a far different educational system such as fixed schedules, standardized examinations and static subject-matter to be learned and stockpiled for a future day.

4. The Appropriational Theory of Knowledge and Truth

There are, the existentialist maintains, different realms of knowledge, the chief distinction lying between knowledge of the world we inhabit and knowledge of the self. In parallel fashion, there are different modes of knowing appropriate to these realms, experimentation being especially appropriate to the former as is intuition to the latter. Nevertheless, several factors caution us against establishing dichotomies too strict and inflexible, e.g.: 1) Intuition and other knowing modes (such as revelation for some existentialists) may suggest possibilities for coming to know this world, just as reason has its role in developing self-knowledge. 2) Furthermore, each individual has the responsibility consciously to "appropriate" that knowledge of both realms—produced by any mode of knowing—as is necessary to his making choices or decisions concerning the nature of both self and other.

Opportunities for appropriation can be increased in quality and in quantity only when both objective and subjective possibilities are available for self-choosing. Objective possibilities, for instance, are opened by mathematical and scientific studies. Also vital are the fine arts, history, language, philosophy, physical education and religion.[121] Such information *about* the self and other human beings—such as might be obtained through a psychology course or through testing—provides additional possibilities for appropriation, although the danger of such information being interpreted as knowledge *of* the self are great and must be consciously and continually resisted.

With regard to developing subjective possibilities, Existentialism appears to have a dual emphasis. Quite clear, of course, is its emphasis on resisting the objectification of the self and—almost as strong—the objectification of other individuals. There is some indication, however, that subjectively approaching objects in the world other than beings can also open new possibilities for self-appropriation, e.g., a work of art, a mineral fragment or a tree.[122] In this same train of thought, Austin Patty suggests that a poem can be so approached. As an artist, for example, the teacher

> *could wonder aloud or introspect aloud about the choice a poet made as regards subject or vocabulary; he could raise questions of creative choice—how the poet adapted the world and its possibilities to his will or how the poet's will makes meaning in the life of the poet the poem is. . . . If the teacher becomes identified in mutual introspection with the existence of the poet the poem is, he acts as an artist per se in the classroom. He remains in every way authentic, since he is still choosing meaning in his existence. All this, of course, is not objectifying the poem, but subjectifying it. What is more important, the teacher-artist reveals his introspection in such a way that reciprocity is honestly called forth, reciprocity of authenticities, reciprocity of introspections.*[123]

Patty also notes that the poem would also be subjectified were the focus on questions which allowed the student to react "to it in an authentic way: choose to make meaning in his own existence in the

[121] As early as Chapter 3, however, we saw that existentialists differ widely as to the extent to which the child should be involved in content, methodological and rate decisions. Suggestions for an appropriate student role range from "having a voice" to "having control."

[122] See Diamond, *Martin Buber: Jewish Existentialist*, pp. 23–38.

[123] "Existential Teaching," pp. 333–334.

presence of the poem."[124] For the existentialist, then, the subjective approach seems clearly designed 1) to create additional possibilities for human beings through *mutual* introspection, and 2) to create additional possibilities for the self in those cases when an inanimate object makes mutuality impossible.

Specific content and instructional strategies will depend upon the age and developmental level of the student. For example, basic skills and responsibility-awareness goals will generally receive greater emphasis in working with children than with adults. Conversely, crises-creation and an awareness that new choices and directions are *always* open will generally receive greater emphasis in working with adults than with children.[125] In all cases, however, the accent is on keeping education open as a ready source of possibilities for appropriation in the self-choosing of the active, interested, authentic human being.

As we come to the close of our formal treatment of Epistemology, several observations which have slowly been taking form may now properly be made explicit. In the first place, Metaphysics—the philosophical area perhaps least open to scientific experimentation—is, at the very least, systematically interwoven with Epistemology. Our assumptions as to basic reality, for instance, have been seen to be correlated with almost every epistemological assumption. The same point could be made with regard to our assumptions concerning human nature and free will or determinism. In many private schools, assumptions as to God and faith occupy a similar relationship. This suggests, at the very least, that the heavy belief component of metaphysical assumptions must be scrutinized with the greatest of care by the teacher who, by definition, is deeply involved in questions of teaching and learning.

Secondly, the relationship between nonphilosophical factors and teaching and learning are obvious and demand constant and continuing attention. Contemporary sociology can tell us much, for instance, about variations in the needs of different socioeconomic and ethnic groups. Philosophical responses to the pedagogically vital question of what should be taught need to be reviewed in light of such information. Historical factors are as involved in this question as in the problem of how teachers and administrators can best ensure that what should be taught is learned. The reformer who would joust with

---

[124] *Ibid.*, p. 334.

[125] For an interesting comparison of educational goals, content and strategies appropriate to the child, youth, adolescent and adult—based on a study of Buber, Jaspers, Kierkegaard and Sartre—see Bedford, *Existentialism and Creativity*, pp. 320–330.

long-entrenched curricular and role patterns would do well to know what he is up against—as well as what strategies have met with success in the past.

In all teaching and learning questions, however, psychological factors are central. True, there are difficulties in moving from studies of animal learning to human learning. In the remaining decades of the twentieth century, however, research in educational psychology promises to give us power of a magnitude which makes *Walden Two* or *1984* pale by comparison. However, this research will not release us from the responsibility to make decisions as to how these powers will be used. Nor, given the past record, will it always explicitly separate fact from belief. Philosophically-knowledgeable educators in the field and in institutions of higher learning will bear heavy responsibility in making these decisions and for separating psychological fact from belief.

Furthermore, the present realistic-orientation of philosophical behaviorism needs careful scrutiny. It is hypothesized that one major factor accounting for program failure will be found in marked philosophical dissonance between the assumptive structure of a program or strategy and that of the teacher who must implement it. This suggests that the teacher's frame of reference must be overcome—or that the program must be employed only by teachers who are in essential agreement with its assumptive base—or that program goals and strategies must be made sufficiently flexible to allow alternative approaches for teachers of different philosophical orientations. A case in point is the present approach to programmed instruction. In its present form, many educators find it unbearably sterile and teacher-centered. But this reaction tends to distract us from the possibility of altering the approach so as to retain major advantages while minimizing unacceptable elements. For example, greater student-student and teacher-student interaction can be incorporated, and more time can be scheduled for what Wilson calls "contested truth" and "open exploration."[126]

Finally, there is a great need for the teacher to specify his own epistemological assumptions and delineate their fact and belief components. For example, what are the beliefs involved in *your* assumption concerning "mind"? To what extent are they supported or questioned by fact? And what does this say to you as a professional educator?

[126] *Cf.* L. Craig Wilson, *The Open Access Curriculum* (Boston: Allyn and Bacon, Inc., 1971), Chapter I, especially figures 2 through 5.

Suggestions for Further Reading

The Nature and Basic Problems of Epistemology

AYER, A. J., *The Problem of Knowledge.* Baltimore: Penguin Books, 1956.

HUNNEX, MILTON D., *Philosophies and Philosophers.* Rev. and enlarged ed. San Francisco: Chandler Publishing Company, An Intext Publisher, 1971. Part II (outline of the nature, basic problems and significant alternatives of Epistemology).

MORRIS, VAN CLEVE, *Philosophy and the American School: An Introduction to the Philosophy of Education.* Boston: Houghton Mifflin Company, 1961. Chapter III.

SCHEFFLER, ISRAEL, *Conditions of Knowledge: An Introduction to Epistemology and Education.* Keystones of Education Series. Chicago: Scott, Foresman and Company, 1965. A stimulating treatment of Epistemology from the analytic perspective.

SHERMIS, S. SAMUEL, *Philosophic Foundations of Education.* New York: American Book Company, 1967. Chapter VII.

Epistemological Assumptions and Their Expression in Educational Policies and Practices

BECK, CARLTON E., *Philosophical Guidelines for Counseling.* 2nd ed. Dubuque, Iowa: Wm. C. Brown Company Publishers, 1971. Numerous articles deal explicitly with Epistemology and counseling, especially with the more existentialistically-oriented counseling.

BEDFORD, MITCHELL, *Existentialism and Creativity.* New York: Philosophical Library, 1972. Study based on the writings of Buber, Jaspers, Kierkegaard and Sartre; Chapter V (Existentialism and education).

BODE, BOYD H., *How We Learn.* Boston: D. C. Heath and Company, 1940. Chapters I–IV, VII–IX, XI, XIV and XVII (four theories of mind).

BRAUNER, CHARLES J., and HOBERT W. BURNS, *Problems in Education and Philosophy.* Foundations of Education Series. Englewood Cliffs, N.J.: Prentice-Hall, Inc., 1965. Chapter II.

BROUDY, HARRY S., *Building a Philosophy of Education.* 2nd ed. Englewood Cliffs, N.J.: Prentice-Hall, Inc., 1961. Chapters V, XII and XIII (a classical realist on reality and knowledge and the curriculum).

BROWN, L. M., *General Philosophy in Education.* New York: McGraw-Hill Book Company, 1966. An analytic approach; Chapters V (knowing) and VI (mind).

BRUBACHER, JOHN S., *Modern Philosophies of Education.* 4th ed. New York: McGraw-Hill Book Company, 1969. Chapter XI (comparative treatment of "epistemological aspects of method").

BURTON, WILLIAM H., ROLAND B. KIMBALL and RICHARD L. WING, *Education for Effective Thinking: An Introductory Text.* New York: Appleton-Century-Crofts, Inc., 1960.

BUTLER, J. DONALD, *Idealism in Education.* Philosophy of Education Series. New York: Harper & Row, Publishers, 1966. Pages 55–67.

DEWEY, JOHN, *Democracy and Education: An Introduction to the Philosophy of Education.* New York: The Macmillan Company, 1916. Paperback ed.; New York: The Free Press, 1966. Chapters III, XX and XXV.

——, *Experience and Education.* The Kappa Delta Pi Lecture Series, 1938. New York: Collier Books, A Division of the Crowell-Collier Publishing Company, 1963. Classic treatment of the pragmatic view of experience; criticism of classical assumptions and misunderstandings of the pragmatic position expressed in the Progressive Education Movement.

——, *How We Think.* Rev. ed. Boston: D. C. Heath and Company, 1933.

——, *The Quest for Certainty: A Study of the Relation of Knowledge and Action.* New York: Minton, Balch & Co., 1929. Paperback ed.; New York: G. P. Putnam's Sons, 1960. Chapters I–II (older theories), IV (experiencing and knowing), V–VI (function and test of valid ideas), VII–VIII (theories of objects of knowledge) and IX–XI (mind and methods of knowing).

——, *Reconstruction in Philosophy.* Enlarged ed. Boston: The Beacon Press, 1948. Chapters IV and VI.

Greene, Maxine, ed., *Existential Encounters for Teachers.* New York: Random House, 1967. Part III.

——, *Teacher as Stranger: Educational Philosophy for the Modern Age.* Belmont, Calif.: Wadsworth Publishing Company, Inc., 1973. Chapters V, VI and VII.

HULLFISH, H. GORDON, and PHILIP G. SMITH, *Reflective Thinking: The Method of Education.* New York: Dodd, Mead & Company, 1968.

KNELLER, GEORGE F., *Existentialism and Education.* New York: Philosophical Library, Inc., 1958. Science Editions paperback ed.; New York: John Wiley & Sons, Inc., 1964.

LAWSON, DOUGLAS E., "Changing Concepts of the Mind," *Phi Delta Kappan,* XX (1937), pp. 42–49.

MORRIS, VAN CLEVE, *Existentialism in Education: What It Means.* Philosophy of Education Series. New York: Harper & Row, Publishers, 1966.

NAUMAN, ST. ELMO, JR., *The New Dictionary of Existentialism.* New York: Philosophical Library, 1971. Especially note entries under "Knowledge," "Reason" and "Subjectivity."

PAI, YOUNG, *Teaching, Learning, and the Mind.* Boston: Houghton Mifflin Company, 1973.

PATTY, AUSTIN, "Existential Teaching," *Educational Theory,* XVII, No. 4 (October 1967), pp. 329–334. Points of contact between knowledge of being-in-itself and knowledge of being-for-itself; excellent treatment of subjective approach to objects.

Skinner, B. F., *The Technology of Teaching.* New York: Appleton-Century-Crofts Educational Division, Meredith Corporation, 1968. A behavioristic approach to education based on many assumptions consistent with contemporary Scientific Realism.

Smith, M. Daniel, *Theoretical Foundations of Learning and Teaching.* Waltham, Mass.: Xerox College Publishing, 1971. A review of behavioristic research which bears on education.

Thomas, Lawrence G., "Implications of Transaction Theory," *Educational Forum,* **XXXII,** No. 1 (January 1968), pp. 145–155. Contemporary pragmatic approach to "objectivity" and "frame of reference."

———, "Response to the Presidential Address," *Educational Theory,* **XVII,** No. 4 (October 1967), pp. 295–297. Contemporary pragmatic approach to "frame of reference."

For an excellent working bibliography of other readings on Epistemology and the relationship between it and the nature and aims of education, curriculum, school organization and policy, and teaching-learning, see Harry S. Broudy *et al.,* eds., *Philosophy of Education: An Organization of Topics and Selected Sources.* Urbana: University of Illinois Press, 1967. This bibliography was supplemented in 1969 (Christiana M. Smith and Harry S. Broudy, eds.) and 1971 (Ronald P. Jeffrey, ed.).

PART *IV*

Axiology and American Education

6

Axiology: Its Nature, Function, Concepts and Assumptions

The children departed and several sets of papers corrected, Kevin Jones, fourth grade science teacher at the Otter Hills Lower School and President of the district "local" of the American Federation of Teachers, is about ready to leave for home. Suddenly he hears a knock on his classroom door. Opening it, he is confronted by Alice Trotter, the school's senior secretary. Most upset, she explains that she has come confidentially to Mr. Jones as an AFT representative. The secretaries throughout the district are horrified with their deteriorating work conditions and the fact that they haven't even received a cost-of-living increase for three years. In some schools, state labor laws are barely being honored, and additional secretaries are not being hired to handle the fast-mounting work load. She wonders if they ought to seek the union's help in arranging a collective bargaining election, that is, themselves form a local of the union and thus gain more "clout" with the administration.

Mr. Jones knows the secretaries are going to have to make a choice—it's either that or just "drifting along" with the situation. Drifting probably won't make it any better and will surely increase their sense of frustration. But he also feels that he as one human being can't tell another "to what" or "for what" she ought to obligate herself. That commitment can only be made freely by the individual in question—whatever form it might take. Keeping these data in

181

mind, try to outline the conversation between Mr. Jones and Ms. Trotter which follows her request for advice.

In the second version of this incident, Mr. Jones is no more willing to tell Ms. Trotter what she ought to do than he was in the first. He does, however, have quite a different view of obligation. In brief, the secretaries should follow that course of action which critical inquiry indicates is most reasonable. As we know from our epistemological studies, this involves a cooperative exercise in "intelligence" or "minding behaviors" on the part of the secretaries, wherein the problem is sharply defined, all relevant factors are considered and the most likely plan of action is selected from among viable possibilities. Given these new data, try to outline the conversation which ensues. Parenthetically, do you see any role for Mr. Jones after the conversation terminates? If so, describe his possible activities and their rationale.

Let us now turn to an incident involving Verna Lothridge, Vice-Principal of the Gold Creek Middle School. Jim Chang, a seventh grader, has just been sent to her office for "talking back" to his math teacher. This is pretty surprising, for Jim is known as one of the most "sandpapered" youngsters in the school. He is, as one would suspect, terribly upset. For about ten minutes, he tells Ms. Lothridge how badly he feels about what he has done, that he really thinks it was "sinful," etc., etc., etc. Although she finds his oversensitivity somewhat painful, Ms. Lothridge truly likes Jim and thinks him sincere. On the other hand, she feels that certain behaviors (as well as things, ideas and processes) are either inherently valuable or inherently evil— and insubordination definitely falls under the latter category. All things considered, how do you feel she will handle Jim's case?

Shifting gears, we find ourselves back in the Vice-Principal's office. Jim Chang is there under the same circumstances, and his response is just as it was. This time, however, Ms. Lothridge rejects the notion that *anything* is "inherently valuable." Rather, values are developed out of feeling-guided choices, that is, if a behavior is chosen it is thereby *made* valuable. Given this assumption—and Jim's reaction to the incident—how do you think she will handle the case this time?

In these two examples we find ourselves deep in axiological alternatives. In the first, we were confronted by different assumptions about obligation; in the second, by different assumptions about what values are and where they are to be found. By way of a "next step" in developing more adequate solutions to the problems posed above, let us turn directly to a more systematic consideration of the nature and functions of Axiology. (Let us also remember the interrelatedness of human concerns that dictates constant reference to other theory. Such is the path not only to building understanding, but also to forming a personal philosophy of education.)

A.   Axiology: Nature and Function

In this chapter and that which follows, we shall be dealing with Axiology, the general theory of value. As we shall see in Chapter 7, it is not
only an especially important area of study—for we as educators face
value questions every day—but it also represents an area of great
professional confusion. Most of us generally feel far more comfortable
in dealing with book reports or turtles than we do in directly facing the
question of whether such activities are worthwhile. Sorry: This time
such questions cannot be avoided.

Before turning to questions of value and education, however, the
present chapter must deal with the various dimensions of Axiology and
their function in human activity. We must ask what a value is and
where it can be located. How does one validate a value-claim? (Perhaps our study of epistemology can offer us some help with this
problem.) And once validated, is there any way in which we can
classify our values into groups and order them in terms of importance?
After all, in education our limited resources usually demand that we
be as concerned with setting priorities among good things as we are in
distinguishing that which is worthwhile from that which is not.

Having worked on these problems, we shall then turn to ethics, a
subdivision of Axiology which deals with values as they are related to
human conduct.[1] We shall be looking into the meanings of words
such as "good" and "bad," "right" and "wrong," and "moral" and
"immoral." The problem of moral "principles" or "standards" will come
up, as will their function in guiding human behavior. (This topic will
undoubtedly involve us in metaphysical matters, for the question of
man's freedom to act on human moral standards is surely of vital
concern.) Our study will also take us into views concerning the nature of obligation and the assistance that conscience may afford us
in doing what we "ought" to do. Finally, we shall inquire into the
goals of a moral life, the development of means to those ends and the
problem of how progress in living morally is to be determined.

As you realized quite some time ago, the notion of "schools" of
philosophy is of limited use in philosophizing. Nowhere is this more
the case than in dealing with axiological problems. Our very first
concept, for instance, will find many realists maintaining that values
are *objective*, that they exist inherently as properties of certain acts,
ideas, objects and processes. Other realists, however, will argue that
this is simply not the case. Values are *subjective;* they rest on the
preference of a human being for a given existent. If he doesn't feel

---

[1] Aesthetics, another subdivision of Axiology, which deals with the principles of
beauty and with value judgments about what is beautiful, will not be developed
in this text.

positively toward it, the existent is valueless and that's the end of the matter. Still other realists, however, will disagree again, claiming that values are *contextual*—that the value of an existent depends strictly upon its relationships with other things desired in a given context of time, place and people. True, in most cases the more classical philosophers are drawn to axiological objectivism; the existentialists, to subjectivism; and the pragmatists, to contextualism. Nevertheless, the notable exceptions bid us be wary.

On the theory that that which is faced is less foreboding than that which is avoided, the time has come to confront these difficulties directly and sort them out.

B. Axiological Concepts and Assumptions

1. Value: Its Nature and Locus

A. VALUE AS A PROPERTY OF OBJECTIVE REALITY. In the classical tradition, value generally refers to a property or a quality which is a constituent of, or resides in, the various elements of objective reality such as acts, ideas, objects and processes. Unaffected by contextual change, it is this "built-in" quality which allows us to speak of an inherently valuable painting or educational policy. Some commentators suggest that value may represent a "tertiary quality," which though vital in its own right does not form part of the essence of the object itself. It will be remembered from our epistemological studies that "primary qualities" such as shape are as necessary to the very existence of the object as are "secondary qualities" such as taste (even though the latter depend to some extent on the perceiving subject).[2]

In any case, values as unchanging, a priori qualities are discovered, not created, by the subject. Only our knowledge of them is relative. Even if we are not aware of them, however, they exist in God and/or in natural reality. As such, they are not affected by our preferences, our environmental conditions or our behaviors in coming to know

[2] *Cf*. Risieri Frondizi, *What Is Value? An Introduction to Axiology*, trans. Solomon Lipp (Lasalle, Ill.: Open Court, 1963), pp. 5–8.

Perhaps it is this notion of "tertiary qualities" which partially influences Broudy's claim that while objective, values are found in "the relation between the structures of things and the structure of human nature." (See Harry S. Broudy, *Building a Philosophy of Education*. 2nd ed. (Englewood Cliffs, N.J.: Prentice-Hall, Inc., 1961), p. 139.) His position does represent some departure from the assumption which sees value as residing *in* the elements themselves, although it too is clearly within the classical tradition.

them. In the last analysis, values *demand* our preference or desire and our interest, for it is their presence which makes an existent good. The authority of values, then, is in its own way just as great as the authority of truth as determined by scientific inquiry.[3]

Inasmuch as the classical position has historically held that the presence of value does not represent a phenomenon open to scientific verification, it is interesting to observe many scientists being drawn to the assumption of "value as a property of objective reality." Solomon, for instance, notes that studies in the behavioral sciences are increasingly pointing to either

> *an invariant factorial structure of moral values and ethical judg-*
> *ments across cultural boundaries . . . or to high cross-cultural*
> *similarity in need and goal structures.*
>
> . . .
>
> *That which is* desirable *for mankind in order to function op-*
> *timally is becoming increasingly clear as studies of human be-*
> *havior progress. Behavioral scientists may be approaching the*
> *uncomfortable point in time when it will no longer be possible*
> *to be ethically neutral regarding deviation from the human*
> *values, the attainable traits, and the attainable social reality,*
> *which research illuminates.*[4]

Needless to say, such a conclusion represents quite a shift from the ethical relativism of the "Ruth Benedict era" in cultural anthropology.

In this same connection we may also note the writings of the so-called "Vienna Circle," a group of psychoanalysts much influenced by theistic Existentialism. Representing the more orthodox wing of this movement, Caruso sees neurosis as involving making absolute that which is relative (as contrasted with psychological health, which does not confuse the two). He writes:

> *Neurosis is what it is because it cannot agree with the absolute*
> *character it has itself assigned to relative values. In its negative*
> *aspect, therefore, neurosis appears as a metaphysical lie inherent*
> *in the neurotic's life. In its positive aspect it represents an at-*
> *tempt to unmask this very lie, in order to re-establish orthodoxy*
> *of life, a true relationship to the hierarchy [order] of values.*
> *Neurosis is simply devoid of all purpose or meaning unless it is*
> *at one and the same time a flight from the absolute and a yearn-*
> *ing for the absolute.*[5]

[3] Philip H. Phenix, *Education and the Common Good: A Moral Philosophy of the Curriculum* (New York: Harper & Brothers, Publishers, 1961), p. 10.

[4] Lawrence N. Solomon, "A Note on the Ethical Implications of Values Research," *Journal of Humanistic Psychology*, X, No. 1 (Spring 1970), pp. 30–31.

[5] Igor A. Caruso, *Existential Psychology: From Analysis to Synthesis*, trans. Eva Krapf (London: Darton, Longman & Todd Ltd., 1964), p. 101.

B. VALUE AS A CREATION OF SUBJECTIVE CHOICE. For the existentialist, that which is valuable is *made* valuable by choosing it. This is best understood as essentially a variation of the "subjectivist" position in Axiology wherein the locutions "*x* is a value" or "*x* is valuable" mean that the enunciator is simply claiming that he desires *x* or feels positively toward *x* and, perhaps, suggests—without exerting pressure—that others might seriously consider the possibilities of *x* in their own lives. Certainly no claim is being advanced that *x* is a property of any objective reality or that its acceptance is incumbent upon another individual other than through his own free choice.

It must be noted that axiological subjectivism is not confined to existentialists—nor are all existentialists strict subjectivists. For example, theistic existentialists such as Martin Buber and existentialists drawn to Marxism often illustrate truly perplexing combinations of subjectivism and objectivism. On the other hand, the neo-realist Ralph Barton Perry, despite his arguments against "*vicious* relativism"[6] (italics added), seems in essential agreement with this position when he writes:

> *That which is an object of interest is* eo ipso *invested with value. Any object, whatever it be, acquires value when any interest, whatever it be, is taken in it; just as anything becomes a target whenever anyone whatsoever aims at it.*
>
> . . .
>
> *A value acquires existence when an interest is generated, regardless of any knowledge about it. A value will cease to exist when its own sustaining interest is destroyed or altered* . . .[7]

And in like measure, Louis Raths, despite his argument that thinking appears much earlier in life than valuing,[8] also stands basically in the subjectivist camp, writing:

> *If children—or adults, for that matter—are to develop values, they must develop them out of personal choices.*
>
> . . .
>
> *Values [are the product of a three-part process]:* . . . *CHOOSING: (1) freely, (2) from alternatives, and (3) after thoughtful consideration of the consequences of each alternative; PRIZING: (4) cherishing, being happy with the choice, and (5) willing to*

---

[6] Ralph Barton Perry, *General Theory of Value: Its Meanings and Basic Principles Construed in Terms of Interest* (New York: Longmans, Green and Company, 1926), pp. 127–131.

[7] *Ibid.*, pp. 115–116 and 140.

[8] Louis E. Raths, Merrill Harmin and Sidney B. Simon, *Values and Teaching: Working with Values in the Classroom* (Columbus, Ohio: Charles E. Merrill Publishing Co., 1966), p. 201.

affirm the choice publicly; and ACTING: (6) doing something with the choice, and (7) repeatedly, in some pattern of life.[9]

For Raths, values must be distinguished from "value indicators" which may or may not signify the formers' presence, e.g., (stated) goals or purposes, attitudes, interests, feelings, beliefs or convictions, worries and activities (which may be forced).[10]

Finally, we may note the strong accent on the "immediacy" of the valuing experience in the subjectivist position. The existentialists in particular tend to agree with Carl Rogers, who views the valuing process of the mature person as "fluid, flexible, based on this particular moment, and the degree to which this moment is experienced as enhancing and actualizing."[11] Raths's greater emphasis on extended inquiry into consequences strikes a somewhat different tone, although in his accent on action as revealing choice he is surely at one with the existentialistic tradition.

C. VALUE AS A PRODUCT OF CONTEXTUAL INQUIRY. The contextualist position occupies something of a "middle ground" between axiological objectivism and axiological subjectivism.[12] On the one hand, contextualists and objectivists agree that value judgments have a more "objective" base than the emotion-guided choices of the subject. On the other, contextualists and subjectivists agree that the genesis of values is to be found in human desires rather than the presence of a quality existing a priori in acts, ideas, objects and processes independent of the subject.

Pragmatists, as axiological contextualists, submit that directly experienced desires and likings provide "candidates" for value, but are not values in themselves. Functioning as necessary though not sufficient conditions for value, their own value-status has yet to be determined. We decide whether a desire is "desirable," i.e., *worthy* of being desired (or a value-candidate is "valuable," i.e., worthy of being valued) only by tracing out the relationships between the desire in question and other variables within a given context of time, place and people. Not every desire is desirable—only those which we judge so

[9] *Ibid.*, pp. 35 and 30.

[10] *Ibid.*, pp. 30–33.

[11] Carl R. Rogers, *Freedom to Learn* (Columbus, Ohio: Charles E. Merrill Publishing Co., 1969), pp. 248–249.

[12] *Careful!* This descriptive statement does *not* carry a hidden value judgment. In the series "1 . . . 2 . . . 3," for example, "2" is not the best answer just because it occupies the middle position; either "1" or "3" may be correct. (This warning is promoted by the Western tradition of the "Golden Mean," the tendency in a pluralistic culture to value moving toward the center for societal stability, and the author's desire not to indoctrinate his own biases.)

in terms of their demonstrated contextual relationships. Values, then, are found neither in existents per se nor in our emotion-guided choosing of an existent, but in the relationships between existents within a given context. To say that "x is a value" or that "x is valuable" means that the transactional relationships between x and other existents in a given context have been traced out and x has been judged worthy of choice *within that context*.[13]

For a common sense example which may clarify this assumption, let us turn to a new edition of a long-loved book which catches our eye in the university bookstore.[14] The objectivist would claim that value represents a quality inherent in the book itself. Were this not so, we could discern neither the book's value nor its value relative to other goods. Thus we would have no objective basis for deciding whether to purchase it. The subjectivist, on the other hand, would say that its value depends on our feelings. If we do not feel that value on examining the book, it is valueless. If we do, choosing to purchase or not to purchase it will involve reference to criteria discussed later in this chapter under the assumption of the "hierarchy of individual decision."

The contextualist faces a quite different set of problems. True, they begin with his desire for the book, but that simple fact does not make the book desirable. To determine the desirability of the book, contextual inquiry is necessary. Of course, that may not take place. The individual may fall back on such phenomena as impulse or authority. But, faced with conflicting desires and interests (i.e., longer-term and more inclusive dispositions), he may turn to the behaviors discussed in Chapter 4 under the assumption of "mind as purposeful, problem-solving behavior." If reinforced for such behavior, he will develop the habit of asking questions such as the following: "How about my strong feelings for Lois and the possibility of taking her to that Saturday evening concert in the city?" "How about that clutch problem on the car—and that new student-teaching fee: seventy-five dollars! And Dad just finished paying three-fourths of the tuition bill!" "What of my aesthetic excitement over a really fine example of leather binding— and the tremendous pleasure afforded *over the years* by the few fine editions which I do own? And how about the fact that I already have an inexpensive edition of the book?"

Well—perhaps the point is clear enough by now. Although my desire for it may not change, the book will—or will not—be judged desirable-valuable in the present context. This will involve reference

---

13 *Cf.* John Dewey, *The Quest for Certainty; A Study of the Relation of Knowledge and Action* (New York: Minton, Balch & Co., 1929); (Capricorn Books Ed.; New York: G. P. Putnam's Sons, 1960), Chapter X.

14 *Cf.* Frondizi, *What Is Value?*, pp. 128–140.

not only to my desire for the book, but also to the harmony of the given desire with other valued interests and the ways in which the consequences of acting in one way or another might serve "to expand, not contract, the totality of significant experience, meaning and activity."[15] In another, future context, of course, the question of the book's value may be answered quite differently.

All of this is not to deny that generalizations about what is valuable do develop over time. Like all generalizations, however, they are based on only a sample of past mediations of human experience. They are, therefore, best treated as (important) resources for moral decision-making, rather than as absolute directives. Furthermore, reliable generalizations about any facet of human experiencing demand the corroboration of others, who, though concerned with similar problems, have made judgments in different contexts and within different frames of reference. We shall return to this point in discussing the "morality of critical inquiry."

2. Value Judgments: Validation

A. VALIDATION THROUGH TRADITIONAL MODES OF KNOWING. We have seen that the "objectivist" tradition in axiological theory holds that values exist in a realm different from that of facts. And yet it is maintained that human value judgments are true or false even though most objectivists claim that they cannot be defined or verified through experimental procedures. Rather than to experimentation, the objectivist turns to a variety of more traditional, nonexperimental procedures for their validation.

The validation mode which seems most frequently cited is that of emotional intuition through which we immediately discern the value quality inhering in an existent. This process parallels that of sensory perceiving and refining through which we develop knowledge of this world. Unlike the latter process, however, it yields knowledge even more direct and certain. Although difficult to describe clearly in words, the notion involves atuning our being with that force referred to by the idealist as Absolute Mind. Other objectivists suggest that the process is perhaps a bit less direct, that slowly over time—perhaps millennia—insights into value develop and are validated by the very fact that generations of human beings live by them and accept their claim upon them.[16] Other objectivists emphasize validation through

---

[15] John L. Childs, *Education and Morals: An Experimentalist Philosophy of Education* (New York: Appleton-Century-Crofts, Inc., 1950), p. 167.

[16] *Cf.* Arnold Horowitz, "Experimentalism and Education," *Educational Forum*, I (May 1937), pp. 412–413.

accepting God's will as received through direct revelation or inter-preted by reputable authorities.[17]   Many Roman Catholics emphasize the primary role of "conscience" both in discerning moral values and standards and in validating value judgments, a point which will be considered at length later in this chapter.[18]   In all these cases, of course, reason should supplement the primary validation mode when-ever possible.   In short, then, a scientific ethics as such is impossible. To say that "x is valuable" or "x is a value" means that an appropriate agent (e.g., emotional intuition, custom, revelation, reputable author-ity or reason) certifies that x does in fact possess the property or quality referred to as "value."

A handful of objectivists do take a somewhat more benign view of experimentation as a validational mode—especially in connection with "instrumental" as contrasted with "consummatory" values.[19]   Experi-mentation, for instance, may help us to understand the environmental and psychological conditions under which individuals achieve insight into the realm of values.[20]   Other philosophers such as Lawrence Thomas, while not given to this assumption, suggest additional uses to which science might be put by the objectivist.   For instance, scientific inquiry might be most helpful in locating reputable authorities and in determining the mean or median of expert judgments of value.   Once established, we could then comparatively determine the value-level of others, the adequacy of a school building or a curriculum, or even the proper achievement of pupils.[21]   Thomas also notes that science might aid in identifying the psychological and social correlates of those gifted with intuition or speculative reason, as well as the consequences of each validational mode upon the morale and actions of those less gifted.[22]   Finally, philosophers committed to the objectivist position might contribute in at least two ways to a scientific exploration of those values held to be means to inherently good ends or goals:

> First, they can help develop precise, operational definitions of the inherently good ends so that the informed public in general

[17] Cf. John L. Mothershead, Jr., Ethics: Modern Conceptions of the Principles of Right (New York: Holt, Rinehart and Winston, 1955), pp. 179–188.

[18] See James H. VanderVeldt and Robert P. Odenwald, Psychiatry and Catholicism (New York: McGraw-Hill Book Company, Inc., 1952), pp. 24–25.

[19] For details pertaining to this distinction, see the discussion of classifying and ordering values according to the assumption of "the hierarchy of the given," which occurs later in this chapter.

[20] See Broudy's treatment of this possibility in Building a Philosophy of Education, pp. 138–140.

[21] Lawrence G. Thomas, "Prospects of Scientific Research into Values," Educational Theory, VI, No. 4 (October 1956), p. 197.   Quoted by permission of the author and Educational Theory.

[22] Ibid., p. 198.   Quoted by permission.

and scientific researchers in particular can know when they have been reached or approached more closely. Thus, what is meant by good citizenship and how it can be expressed in degrees of attainment? . . . Second, philosophers can help develop precise, operational definitions of the means judged valuable to those ends so that researchers can manipulate them objectively and experimentally. Thus, what is meant by a knowledge of history or a study of foreign language? What do they mean in terms of specific content, specific teaching methods, and specific learning situations?[23]

In all concerns where science might possibly be involved, however, it does seem necessary to point out that its role for the objectivist would—at best—be contributory. All of the scientific data in the world provide no substitute for that basic insight into values which lies well beyond the realm of science.

B. VALIDATION THROUGH AUTHENTIC CHOICE. Earlier discussions have clarified the qualities of authenticity: consciousness of freedom and responsibility, awareness of the capacity to mold reality in the face of change, capacity subjectively to appraise both the moment's facticities and its possibilities, and commitment to self-knowledge and self-actualization. When a desired existent is spontaneously chosen by the authentic man, there is no need for further "validation" of his judgment. The "desired" becomes the "desirable" (that *worthy* of being desired) by the very fact of choosing. We need turn neither to nonempirical modes of knowing nor to experimental inquiry, for other than by our own choice they hold no power. Furthermore, while we must be open to possibilities emanating from any source, choice is far more a matter of immediate internal experience than it is of external proof or consensus.

Free, undetermined, unjustifiable other than by appeal to choice itself, our value judgments open us to anxiety. Although we can always choose anew, we have no way of knowing how our choices will turn out. And yet it is in facing-grasping-accepting anxiety through *risking* choice—in a meaningful sense, choosing ourselves—that we gain the courage to continue on the path of becoming.

C. VALIDATION THROUGH EXPERIMENTATION. We have seen that the pragmatist understands values to be the products of active, intentional transactions between desires (i.e., value candidates) and other variables within a given context (e.g., other desires, established interests, reality factors). These transactions can be initiated by the organism when conflicting desires or altered needs born of new

[23] *Ibid.*, p. 199. Quoted by permission.

developmental stages or environmental factors block action based on established habit patterns. On the basis of critical inquiry, the desire in question is judged contextually desirable or undesirable in terms of its efficacy as a means in dissolving the action blockage and freeing the individual to continue to expand, harmonize and give meaning to his experience—that is, "to grow."

The pragmatist does not feel that "values" are so different from "facts" that value claims must be validated by reference to traditional modes of knowing. As Lepley observes, ". . . valuative statements are [not] inherently different from scientific propositions as denoting cause-effect relations. . . ."[24] Nor can the claim that "x is (contextually) valuable" be validated by producing even reliable scientific data about what people merely desire—although most attitude and interest measures go no further. Therefore, the pragmatist suggests that we return to the procedures of experimental science to help establish that knowledge of relationships upon which value judgments depend. Dewey emphasizes the rationale for this decision:

> A moral that frames its judgments of value on the basis of consequences must depend in a most intimate manner upon the conclusions of science. For the knowledge of the relations between changes which enable us to connect things as antecedents and consequences is science.[25]

By way of an example, let us sit in on a faculty meeting where several art teachers have vigorously proposed that an annual "art fair" be held in conjunction with National Education Week. Other teachers have questioned the desirability of such an event. If an ensuing discussion (e.g., of the feasibility of holding the event, the needs and rights of teachers in other departments and the many other factors which will undoubtedly be brought up) does not shake the desire of the art teachers—and frustration brings decision-making to a halt—how might we validate (or invalidate) the value of the proposed event? Thomas suggests that three major questions of fact need to be considered:

> The first asks, what are the relationships, perceived by the person or the group, which make the object appear worth having or enjoying? . . .
> The second . . . is whether the perceived relationships actually work or function as the subjects believe they do or will. . . .
> The third . . . is how much the object at hand, when its perceived relationships are acted upon or tested factually, is actually desired or wanted now in the light of experienced relation-

24 Ray Lepley, "The Identity of Fact and Value," *Philosophy of Science*, **X**, No. 1 (January 1943), p. 129.
25 *The Quest for Certainty*, p. 274.

> *ships. In other words, has the original desired object become in fact desirable when the judgments of its worth have been acted upon, experienced, actually known?*[26]

Thomas maintains that these questions can be asked meaningfully only within a specified frame of reference and that this requirement includes the identification of those interests judged to be relevant to the existent in question. In our case, discussion may establish that the interests of the art teachers include providing opportunities for students to translate theory into practice, motivating them to spend more time on art projects, interesting more students in electing art courses and securing increased parent and district support for their program. When critically examined and expressed in behavioral terms, these interests now constitute the possible ends to which the proposed art fair is hypothesized as a means. For research purposes, they will be

> *judged good only in relation to antecedent conditions—i.e., in relation to the means chosen. In the light of such factors as the time and energy required to exploit the chosen means . . . , these consequences are anticipated as enjoyable or worth having.*[27]

It is entirely possible, of course, that the science teachers will grant the value of the art fair (in terms of its consequences for the art department) but insist that the *basic* question concerns whether it is valuable in terms of the obligations incumbent upon the entire faculty. In this situation Thomas maintains that rational decision-making necessitates constructing a more common frame of reference which encompasses the major interests of all parties involved.[28] To the degree that such a common frame of reference *cannot* be constructed, the possibilities for rational decision-making will be diminished. The group will be forced to turn away from consensus toward compromise, co-existence or compulsion (in decending order). As our earlier discussions have indicated, however, the desire will always be to keep communications

[26] "Prospects of Scientific Research into Values," pp. 200–201. Quoted by permission.

[27] *Ibid.*, p. 202. Quoted by permission. Thomas carefully notes that *"their* consequences—the results after reaching such an anticipated end [e.g., securing increased parent and district support for the art program] are not part of the present research problem. The [instrumental] worth of the ends in view is ignored, left unchallenged, or taken for granted. If at some later time, doubt arises as to whether one or two of them are desirable in terms of *their* consequences and associations [e.g., the effect upon the science program of pouring more money into the art department], then they themselves should become objects of investigation in a new frame of reference of other interests." *Ibid.* Quoted by permission.

[28] *Ibid.*, pp. 202–203. Paraphrased by permission. For a discussion of the steps in building a group frame of reference, see the assumptions of "objectivity as intersubjectivity" and "frame of reference as self-in-becoming" in Chapter 4.

open and to increase the points of contact between the parties. Thus, at a later date it may again be possible to strive for a higher level of rationality as the sanction for decision-making. When an acceptable frame of reference *can* be constructed cooperatively, however, the question of what "ought" to be done as regards the art fair can readily be answered. In terms of the interests included in the common frame of reference, the art fair *should* be held if the answers to the three questions of fact posed earlier in this section are in the affirmative.[29]

Finally, it is important to note that the validation of value claims for any existent must involve more than researching the questions posed above and the reproduction of such experimentation by others in similar situations. It is also necessary to determine whether the subjects will really *act* on their value judgments, a task which may be made possible by the "action research" proposed by Talcott Parsons and Clyde Kluckhohn in *Toward a General Theory of Action*, ed. Talcott Parsons and Edward A. Shils (Harper Torchbook ed.; New York: Harper & Row, Publishers, 1962). As Dewey states,

> In empirical fact, the measure of the value a person attaches to a good end is not what he says about its preciousness but the care he devotes to obtaining and using the means without which it cannot be obtained.[30]

3. Values: Classifying and Ordering

A. THE HIERARCHY OF THE GIVEN. As is the case with all other dimensions of reality, the classicist holds that order is a basic principle in the realm of values. Their classification and arrangement into a hierarchy exist as a "given" which is deeply woven into the very texture of reality and to some extent can be known by man. In this section, therefore, we must survey how one can gain knowledge of the a priori classifications and ordering, the general principles by which values are rank ordered and discoveries concerning specific values classes and their relative importance.

For many idealists emotional intuition is not only essential to discovering the presence of value but is also the means by which we apprehend the hierarchical arrangement of values. In the act of "preferring" one value over another we gain intuitive knowledge of its superiority. The idealist maintains, and consistently so, that we prefer a good existent *because* it is valuable; our preference does not create

29 *Ibid.*, p. 203.

30 John Dewey, *Theory of Valuation*, International Encyclopaedia of Unified Science, II, "Foundations of the Unity of Science," No. 4 (Chicago: University of Chicago Press, 1939), p. 27.

its superiority. Nor must we think that this is a logical matter even
though preference *may* take place at the conscious level and be
accompanied by reflection. Finally, we must distinguish between
preferring on the one hand and "choice" or "judgment" which clearly
rest on a priori, intuitive knowledge of the superiority of one value as
compared with its alternatives.[31]

Other classicists, as we might suppose from earlier discussions, place
a greater accent than do idealists on logical reasoning and other modes
of knowing in discerning value classifications and their proper ordering. Aided by law and God's assistance, for example, the Roman
Catholic moral theologian Karl Hörmann maintains that the hierarchy
of values is "perceptible to man because it corresponds to the order of
being in his *rational* nature with its bodily and mental inclinations"
(italics added).[32] Reinhardt is no less adamant in his accent on
reason, writing:

> As long as reason has a chance to deliberate, and in the meas-
> ure in which it can exercise its function, to that extent man will
> be able to estimate the relative value of particular goods in view
> of the Absolute [God-established] Norm. And though human
> passions may strongly lean toward those goods which satisfy
> man's sense appetites, the ensuing acts will no longer be necessi-
> tated, but will possess the character traits of varying degrees of
> freedom.[33]

Our second problem concerns the general principles which seem to
underlie the relative positions of values in perceived hierarchies,
knowledge of which may give us no little assistance in making choices
and judgments. On these principles axiological objectivists stand in
relative harmony: 1) The intrinsic or consummatory value—that which
is valuable in itself—stands higher than the extrinsic or instrumental
value, whose importance lies in providing a means to something
higher. 2) The ultimate or permanent value stands higher than the
value which is proximate or transitory. 3) The value which helps man
to fulfill his nature stands higher than the value which is merely
pleasurable. Hence, 1) God stands higher in the hierarchy of values
than does money; 2) salvation, higher than the value of completing a
diet; and 3) obedience to moral laws, higher than sensual pleasure.

In considering these principles, four additional points need to be
kept in mind. First, we are dealing with continua and not with dis-

[31] *Cf.* Frondizi, *What Is Value?*, pp. 92–95.

[32] Karl Hörmann, *An Introduction to Moral Philosophy,* trans. Edward Quinn
(Westminster, Md.: The Newman Press, 1961), p. 78.

[33] Kurt F. Reinhardt, *A Realistic Philosophy: The Perennial Principles of Thought
and Action in a Changing World* (Milwaukee: The Bruce Publishing Company,
1944), p. 139.

crete categories. For the coin collector, a particularly fine specimen may have considerable intrinsic value. He values it for *itself*—perhaps more than for what it would bring in the marketplace. Nevertheless, we may maintain in general that money possesses extrinsic value. All of the legalistic arguments conjurable by the "classroom lawyer" cannot shake our brute knowledge of this truth. Secondly, we also observe that intrinsic values are more likely to be ultimate and nature-fulfilling than they are proximate and merely pleasurable. The point, once again, is that we are dealing with general principles and not with airtight categories. Thirdly, the classicist is *not* suggesting that existents having lower value be held in contempt. Far from it! The value of money in fostering the higher values is immense. The problem arises when we confuse the two—when we treat the lower as more valuable than the higher.[34] Finally, inasmuch as not all choices are between goods, these principles suggest that when one is faced with two evils, one would discern and choose the lesser evil.

The last point under this assumption requires that we consider what has been discovered about specific values classes and their relative positioning in the hierarchy of a given reality. Again, classicists are in marked agreement. Time and space allow the briefest summary of but two orderings, that of the idealist Max Scheler and the Roman Catholic Karl Hörmann. In ascending order, for example, Scheler places the pleasant and unpleasant values, the vital values (including the aesthetic values, the values of the just and the unjust, and the values of pure knowledge of the truth), and the values of the holy and the profane (religious values).[35] This schema is to be compared with that of Hörmann, who writes:

> *We can distinguish . . . a) external values (food, home, cloth-ing, and other external possessions), b) vital values (health and strength), c) social values (order in the state, peace, social wel-fare), d) spiritual values (truth, beauty), e) moral values (the good), [and] f) religious values (the sacred). . . . The lower ends or values form the condition for the realization of the higher and exist for the sake of these. They are summed up in moral value, which in the fullest sense is man's realization of himself and this—when we look deeply into it—coincides with the acquisition of religious value or assimilation to God. When there is a conflict between values at different levels, the right solution is to give priority to the higher value. . . . All values must in the last resort be at the service of moral value, which essentially is the same as religious value: martyrs, who give their lives for God, are acting rightly. It is perverse on the other*

[34] Though scarcely a "serious" example, it is difficult for a person of my generation not to think of the "sin" of the Walt Disney character Scrooge McDuck, whose greatest pleasure lay in wallowing in his money-bin!
[35] Frondizi, *What Is Value?*, p. 101.

> *hand to sacrifice a higher for a lower value: thus we cannot in-*
> *fringe the moral law even if we think by so doing to aid life.*[36]

Such is the axiological foundation of the objectivist as he faces the difficulties of living a moral life. It should not be concluded, however, that certainty is always his lot—or that rules for conduct will always be clear. Where secure knowledge is available, consistent action *should* follow. But sufficient knowledge is not always available, nor is man always guided by it when it is. These are difficulties which all men share. We shall consider the classical answers when we turn to their ethical assumptions later in the present chapter.

B. THE HIERARCHY OF INDIVIDUAL DECISION. Axiological sub-jectivism extends little hope for developing a general hierarchy or ordering of values. Human experience is far too individual and sub-jective a thing for that. Nevertheless, it does seem conceivable that an individual, desiring to make a choice from among goods in a par-ticular and limited situation, might be able to construct a temporary ranking. True, it would be highly relative to the situation. Born with interest, it most assuredly would die with interest. Procedural clues are found in Ralph Barton Perry's criteria of "intensity," "preference" and "inclusiveness" from his *General Theory of Value* and "duration" from his *Realms of Value.*

Let us take a commonplace example and imagine that we desire to purchase a suit. On examining the racks, we turn up a navy blue suit and a dark gray tweed suit, both of which are of interest. Perry's criteria might lead us to ask (rhetorically) questions such as the fol-lowing: "How much does the blue suit arouse my interest as compared with the gray suit?" "How *frequently* have I desired to purchase a blue suit—or how *long* have I desired to purchase a blue suit—in comparison with a gray suit?" "Given a teacher's budget, on how many different occasions might the blue suit be appropriate as com-pared with the other?" "All things considered, which do I prefer?" Given a relative similarity of answers to the first two questions, the fact that a dark gray tweed suit shows chalk dust less than a navy blue suit and yet is appropriate to many evening affairs might lead you—all things considered—to prefer the tweed. That, however, would be your affair, for the standard of inclusiveness is not binding other than as you make it so—and for yourself alone.

Note well that in the preceding example we were confronted by a quite idiosyncratic decision. I was not choosing for you, nor you for me. Most subjectivists would claim that rank ordering is properly an individual concern. For instance, Frankel writes:

[36] *An Introduction to Moral Philosophy,* pp. 78–79.

> *Existential analysis, then, does not interfere in the ranking of values; it rests content when the individual begins to evaluate; what values he elects is and remains the patient's own affair. Existential analysis must not be concerned with what the patient decides for, what goals he sets for himself, but only that he decides at all. . . . Continuation of the treatment beyond that point, so that it intrudes into the personal sphere of particular decisions, must be termed impermissible. The physician should never be allowed to take over the patient's responsibility; he must never permit that responsibility to be shifted to himself; he must never anticipate decisions or impose them upon the patient. His job is to make it possible for the patient to reach decisions; he must endow the patient with the capacity for deciding.*[37]

Frankel does add that in some instances the doctor may have to help the person "determine his preference," . . ."clarify . . . where his true wishes lay . . ."[38]

Rather than leading to anarchy, some writers in the subjectivist tradition suggest that an open and general admission that value ranking is an individual affair might lead to quite beneficial and even surprising consequences. In the first place, our simple confidence in the individual could do much to create an environment in which he would feel free to construct and reconstruct unique hierarchies appropriate to his personal experience. Secondly, free to be himself, he could become more sensitive to the common needs which all men exhibit, including the need for accepting-relationships with others. Thus he might produce rankings both more socialized and containing more shared elements.[39] Today our view of American pluralism as beneficial has soured and given way to a disturbingly high level of antagonism and repression. Could it be that the benefits of permitting a marked rise in individual decision-making power might more than compensate for the anxiety occasioned by the effort?

C. THE HIERARCHY OF THE SITUATION. Having no assumption of a pre-existent, orderly, independent reality to which to refer, the contextualist properly maintains that any rank ordering or hierarchy of values will be situational. That is, it will be relative to a particular context of time, place and people. The objectivist's absolute ranking of intrinsic (consummatory) values above extrinsic (instrumental) values, for instance, is viewed as particularly indefensible. Our com-

[37] Viktor E. Frankel, *The Doctor and the Soul: An Introduction to Logotherapy,* trans. Richard and Clara Winston (New York: Alfred A. Knopf, 1955), p. 270.
[38] *Ibid.,* pp. 270–271.
[39] *Cf.* Carl R. Rogers, *Client-Centered Therapy: Its Current Practice, Implications, and Theory* (Boston: Houghton Mifflin Company, 1951), p. 524.

ing discussion of ends and means under the assumption of "growth as its own end" will indicate that an existent when viewed as a proximate end (i.e., a goal, aim, purpose) has intrinsic value. When achieved, however, it may come to be viewed from quite another perspective, namely, as a means to some further goal and, hence, assumes extrinsic value. There is no absolute ranking here, for the nature of the value changes with the situation. The contextualist also maintains that it is difficult to conceive of *any* existent that would not possess instrumental value in that achieving it would only open new possibilities for achievement—for growth. Even our present God-idea, for example, may be instrumental in leading us forward to a higher, more refined structure of ideals and achieved goods.

In those situations which are quite personal, e.g., the selection of a suit discussed in the preceding section, it is entirely possible that the subjectivist's criteria of intensity, duration, inclusiveness and preference will function quite nicely in establishing action priorities. But the pragmatist is also concerned with quite another situation: that in which a group, initially holding seemingly different interests, must set priorities. This is, it must decide on the order in which it will seek to achieve and/or maintain a variety of perceived goods. The setting of educational policies, of course, usually places us in just such a situation. Given this problem, we again face the task of trying to achieve a more common frame of reference—one that incorporates the major values of the interested parties—through developing behavioral definitions of important terms and engaging in the other activities discussed earlier. This is the optimally rational path to establishing a hierarchy of values. As we saw in the discussion of "validation through experimentation," failure foreshadows other, progressively less rational ranking procedures, e.g., compromise, coexistence and compulsion.

Finally, it should be added—as in similar cases which have come before—that generalizations about what is more valuable than something else do develop on the part of both individuals and groups. As resources for decision-making, it is entirely proper (if not necessary) that we consult these resources. We err only in thinking that they reflect an exterior, unrefinable reality, rather than the fruits of man's experience which must be refined as further experience is undergone and evaluated.

4. Morality

A. THE MORALITY OF SEEKING AND CONFORMING TO OBJECTIVE GOOD. The moral question for the classicist arises when experience

presents alternatives in a setting where man is free to choose. In short, man must decide what he *ought* to do in a situation which includes both standards of the right and specific contextual variables. Phenix captures the classical mood when he argues that

> the moral enterprise makes sense only if there are objective ex-
> cellences that invite the loyalties of men and constitute the
> standard and goal of human endeavor. It is not claimed that
> anyone knows what the ultimate good is, nor that it is always
> actually possible to secure agreement about moral questions.
> But it does seem clear that any serious concern to discover and
> to do what is right rests on the premise that there are objective
> standards of worth upon which universal agreement is in prin-
> ciple possible.[40]

He goes on to argue that objective moral standards do not allow men to fulfill their moral responsibility by simply applying the most appropriate rule in a legalistic manner. Neither, however, does the fact that contextual variables must be taken into consideration in making specific moral judgments imply that values are subjective and relative to the judgment maker. Rather, Phenix maintains, "the moral enterprise presupposes the potential universality of judgments about values that are individually objective."[41]

Believing that the only alternative to constant clashes of opinion irresolvable other than by force lies in the development of standards for guiding human decision-making—and that such "objective excellences" do exist—the classicist has vigorously sought their explication. Actually, what is involved in this quest should not be underestimated. If moral standards could be defined we would then have reference points most useful in deciding the morality of a contemplated action prior to its implementation. The classicist has turned—as we have seen—to his beliefs about God, as well as to time-honored tradition. He has turned to folkways and to law. Increasingly, many scientific realists have turned to the behavioral sciences. And they have turned to philosophy. If Hörmann's argument that "moral value . . . man's realization of himself . . . coincides with the acquisition of religious values"[42] is accepted, then a variety of classical positions with regard to the nature of moral standards must be seen to coalesce. For instance, Henderson, committed to the assumption that man's fundamental nature and needs are unchanging, writes:

> To treat one's self or others as an end is to promote the develop-
> ment of the best possible personality. This is not a formula

[40] *Education and the Common Good*, p. 5.
[41] *Ibid.*, pp. 5–6.
[42] *An Introduction to Moral Philosophy*, p. 78.

*which can be applied without thought.   It takes intelligent and
conscientious study of a situation to determine what is right
to do.*[43]

Broudy defines the morally right act as one which is freely chosen
because it is seen as right, one which gives attention to the means of
carrying it out and one which

> *contributes to some rationally chosen goal or end, some hope or
> welfare, satisfaction, or happiness.   It is evil if it frustrates such
> a hope.   To be morally right, therefore, an act must be intended
> to fill not any claim, but a claim to some good in life.*[44]

Without exception, the classicists cited are agreed that the task of
seeking and conforming to objective good is both morally necessary
and viciously difficult.   Our efforts to perceive the good, specifically to
formulate the right and to act appropriately can be, and are, constantly
frustrated by a host of existential variables.   Most of these are only
partially under our control.   We are, for instance, frustrated by the
finite limits of human vision in the face of reality's depth and richness.
We may be ignorant of the good—or inattentive when confronted by
it.   We may fail to exercise our reason or err in implementing our
intentions.   Passion (e.g., fear to the point of panic), an intransigent
environment or our own self-centeredness may dull our best efforts.
And in extreme cases psychopathic states or deeply engrained evil
habits may blind even our search for the good, let alone our efforts to
conform ourselves to it.[45]   Yet the good exists.   And man is constantly
confronted by it, as well as by the necessity to decide what he ought to
do.   The classicist bids him to turn to the fruit of man's insight and
reason, to exert his best efforts to act morally and, when tripped by
obstacles expected or unexpected, to pick himself up, learn and continue on the path of self-realization.

B. THE MORALITY OF AUTHENTICITY.   At first glance the ethical
theory of Existentialism can appear extreme—if not absurd—to the
late twentieth century American.   In essence, its radical individualism
and its violent attacks on the entire foundation of Western thought
seem oddly inappropriate given the complexities of life in a mass
technological culture.   But slowly its very radicalism and violence
open our eyes to the *possibility* that America may be suffering from

[43] Stella Henderson, *Introduction to Philosophy of Education* (Chicago: The University of Chicago Press, 1947), p. 113.

[44] *Building a Philosophy of Education*, p. 236.   Quoted by permission of the publisher.

[45] See Hörmann's discussion of the "Impairment of Human Acts" in *An Introduction to Moral Philosophy*, pp. 102–109.

what Jaspers calls "false peace of mind." We begin to see that the old "morality of seeking and conforming to objective good" and the new, "scientific" "morality of critical inquiry" are similar in that they subject the individual to external control. So subjected, modern man is relieved of full responsibility for his actions. So subjected, he becomes passive at a time in history when society's very survival demands his full involvement. At this point, having sensed their justification, we may find the radicalism and violence of existentialistic arguments somewhat less objectionable. And we may stand ready to consider their positive alternatives with a less jaundiced eye.

The existentialist, in sum, calls upon us to risk taking a chance on the individual man. Nauman captures the gist of the "morality of authenticity," writing:

> The individual is the only center for the choice of the good. No rules or commandments or laws have any ethical significance unless they are chosen by the individual. This choice is completely free. Man is free to choose his own nature. Man alone is responsible to choose what he is to become, and this is his choice alone. Objective advice on moral matters cannot be given, as choice and value are subjective.[46]

"Self-examination and not social obedience," writes Kneller, "is the first lesson in moral behavior. The child must be saved, not for traditional religious ends but from his own unexamined self and from those who interfere with the free exercise of his own moral choice."[47] We cannot ask more of man than that he know himself and then, in the full light of his free intellectual and emotional self, choose decisively and spontaneously. In the last analysis, we shall know what he really values only as reflected in how he actually lives his life.

Authentic morality demands that man free himself from external ideals. Submission to external and preconceived ideals is no less dangerous than submission to unchosen moral standards or to being treated as an object by the Other. Both weaken man's ability and resolve to focus on his concrete, individual, human tasks. Then, too, "the true value of man lies, not in the species or type that he approximates, but in the historical individual, for whom no substitution or replacement is possible."[48]

The individual who frees himself from the external standards im-

---

[46] St. Elmo Nauman, Jr., *The New Dictionary of Existentialism* (New York: Philosophical Library, 1971), p. 75.

[47] George F. Kneller, *Existentialism and Education* (New York: Philosophical Library, Inc., 1958); (Science Editions paperback ed.; New York: John Wiley & Sons, Inc., 1964), pp. 84–85.

[48] Karl Jaspers, *The Perennial Scope of Philosophy,* trans. R. Manheim (New York: Philosophical Library, 1949), p. 69.

posed by objective good, empirically-guided "intelligence" or the Other does open himself to anxiety. The feelings encountered are not unlike those experienced in first leaving home for college—or the security of the airplane for that initial "free-fall." The point is that in so doing one *regains control* of his own experience and finds—sometimes to his surprise—that value systems are

> *not necessarily something imposed from without, but . . .*
> *something experienced. The individual discovers that he has*
> *within himself the capacity for weighing the experiential evi-*
> *dence and deciding upon those things which make for long-run*
> *enhancement of self (which inevitably involves the enhance-*
> *ment of other selves as well).*[49]

Let us look again at the concluding words of Carl Rogers as just quoted: ". . . long-run enhancement of self (which inevitably involves the enhancement of other selves as well)." The existentialist position on one's moral responsibility to others finally rests on one's responsibility to self. Would that we had a social order that allowed the individual to develop without repression! But we do not—and the school is its agent. Better, many existentialists say, to *leave* society in one way or another in order to *fulfill* authentic moral responsibility as best one can, than to be crushed. Neill, realistic as always, sums up the case rather well:

> *An American visitor, a professor of psychology, criticized our*
> *school on the grounds that it is an island, that it is not fitting into*
> *a community, and that it is not part of a larger social unit.*
>
>   •   •   •
>
> *My answer is that I am not an active proselytizer of society: I*
> *can only convince society that it is necessary for it to rid itself of*
> *its hate and its punishment and its mysticism. Although I*
> *write and say what I think of society, if I tried to reform society*
> *by* action, *society would kill me as a public danger.*
>   *If, for example, I tried to form a society in which adolescents*
> *would be free to have their own natural love life, I should be*
> *ruined if not imprisoned as an immoral seducer of youth. Hat-*
> *ing compromise as I do, I have to compromise here, realizing*
> *that* my *[roman added] primary job is not the reformation of so-*
> *ciety, but the bringing of happiness to some few children.*[50]

On the other hand, it must be noted that there are existentialists (individualistic as always!) for whom *social involvement* provides the general arena for significant choice. Buber and Marcel stand as prime

[49] Rogers, *Client-Centered Therapy*, p. 150.
[50] A. S. Neill, *Summerhill: A Radical Approach to Child Rearing* (New York: Hart Publishing Company, 1960), pp. 22–23.

examples, although we may add the Italian existentialist Nicola
Abbagnano, who maintains:

> Only in his existential connection with the community does man
> discover himself, the other, and finally the ultimate meaning of
> the determinations of his finitude, i.e., his birth, his death, his
> problematic and temporal constitution, and his freedom. Out-
> side the coexistent community, man loses his own individuality,
> and therefore, his freedom, since there is no freedom which is
> not freedom for a task in which man defines himself. Conse-
> quently, implicit in every task is a cooperation and solidarity
> with other men.[51]

C. THE MORALITY OF CRITICAL INQUIRY. Morality for the contextualist finds its genesis in the brute fact that experience cannot be
mediated by the human being without encountering endless frustration
and blockages of action. After defining the locus of the problem, he
must consciously overview all of the relevant variables involving self
and other, construct alternative plans of action, choose, act, evaluate
and generalize. If successful, equilibrium is restored and energy is
freed for continuing activity. The situation becomes "moral" when
incompatible desires, habits or goals—or inadequacies in his behavioral repertoire—challenge man intelligently to guide the coordination
of all environmental variables in coming to a choice and entering upon
appropriate action. To accept the challenge and to institute what has
variously been called "critical inquiry," "reflective thinking," "intelligence" or "minding behaviors" represents the very essence of moral
goodness.

The morally good act, then, "is the result of a morally good choice.
A morally good choice is one that is not an immediate response to
habit or impulse but that is mediated by the exercise of intelligence."[52]
Although he writes in a different ethical tradition, Perry provides an
interesting parallel, asking:

> But could we not show that a moral judgment is objectively
> sound not in the sense that it is true, i.e., correct as against its
> contraries and for anyone, but rather in the sense that its author
> reasonably makes such judgment or holds such moral opinion?
> It would be his judgment act that would primarily be justified,
> because he had gone about forming his opinion reasonably or
> in accordance with a 'morally reasonable' procedure binding on
> everyone. The content of his judgment would be justified only
> by derivation from that fact, and it would not necessarily be the
> judgment that others would reasonably make on the same sub-

---

[51] Gari Lesnoff-Caravaglia, *Education as Existential Possibility* (New York: Philosophical Library, Inc., 1972), p. 42, citing Nicola Abbagnano, *Esistenzialismo
positivo* (Torino: Taylor, 1948), p. 12.
[52] Mothershead, *Ethics,* p. 143.

*ject, although they very well might, and his reasonableness
would no doubt have persuasive weight for others if it were
made known to them.*[53]

"Ends," writes Dewey, "are determinable only on the grounds of the
means that are involved in bringing them about;"[54] ". . . the experimental way of thinking . . . would place *method and means* upon the
level of importance that has in the past, been imputed exclusively to
ends. . . . It is impossible to form a just estimate of the paralysis of
effort that has been produced by indifference to means."[55]

Not surprisingly, the contextualist insists that "reasonableness" or
"intelligence"—call it what you will—deeply involves the individual in
the affairs of the human community. Values are located in relationships; relationships are explicated through transactional behaviors.
Increasingly, the reliability of our generalizations concerning the valuable demands cooperative inquiry with others in increasingly wider
spatial and temporal circles. Factors such as race, sex, nationality,
ideology, socioeconomic status, variable aptitudes and historical period
are first transformed from marks of superiority or inferiority to mere
differences and then are gradually seen to provide richer resources for
human inquiry. Thus we mount a direct effort to define and secure
those environmental conditions under which such inquiry can be
undertaken openly, profitably and enjoyably. And thus indirectly we
lay the foundation for our own individual good. Morality for the
contextualist, then, can never be an "either-or" situation as regards the
individual and the social; a deep-seated commitment to "both-and"
guides his actions.[56] Whatever the deficiencies of his ethical theory,
moral selfishness is clearly not one of them.

Our study of pragmatic positions in Metaphysics and Epistemology
has indicated that evaluated human experience can give rise to generalizations of considerable worth in future problem-solving. This is
also the case in Axiology. By way of example, Dewey is quick to
admit that

> *there is no need to deny that a general and abstract conception
> of health finally develops. But it is the outcome of a great num-
> ber of empirical inquiries, not an a priori preconditioning 'stand-
> dard' for carrying on inquiries.*[57]

[53] Thomas D. Perry, "Moral Autonomy and Reasonableness," in *Theories of Value
and Problems of Education,* ed. Philip G. Smith (Urbana: University of Illinois
Press, 1970), p. 210.

[54] *Theory of Valuation,* p. 53.

[55] *The Quest for Certainty,* p. 279.

[56] *Cf.* R. E. Mason, *Educational Ideals in American Society* (Boston: Allyn and
Bacon, Inc., 1960), pp. 243–244. Also see the liberal assumption of "dynamic association" in Chapter 8 of this text.

[57] *Theory of Valuation,* p. 46.

Moral "principles" (or to use the more common term, moral "stand-ards"), then, must be understood as instruments for analyzing a particular problematic situation. The right or the wrong of one's action, however, is judged not merely by conforming to the principle, but by the exercise of intelligence throughout the entire problem-solving process—from definition to generalization.

Saying this, we must still be careful not to underestimate the poten-tial value of moral generalizations. They may, for example, give rise to "ideals" wherein the good as experienced is transformed into a view of the "still better" and, as such, assumes a powerful motivating poten-tial. Moral principles, like hypotheses, often suggest possibilities for action, especially when the variables of a particular situation are so numerous and complex as to confuse our efforts to find a pattern and develop a plan of action. They may warn us against precipitous action based on impulse, habit or custom. And we may find that they actively facilitate the exercise of intelligence in that they organize man's experience concerning the major variables that he has found usually require consideration if plans of action are to predict the consequences of acting upon them.[58]

We may conclude by noting the observation that for the contextual-ist "the good is always a process, not the Good as some fixed state to which we aspire."[59] Never a remote ideal, a momentary enjoyment or a possession fixed and absolute, it is, rather, that process by which intelligence "provides for an orderly, harmonious, unified release of energy in action."[60] Rucker writes:

> *Our notions of the good and of virtue will evolve in the process of their realization. Ethics, like everything else for Dewey, is a search, not a prize, and we are moral or immoral men as we do or do not consciously apply our intelligences to that search.*[61]

5. Obligation and Conscience

A. THE OBLIGATION TO FOLLOW CONSCIENCE TOWARD THE GOOD. Classical theory holds that lawful reality is characterized by the presence of objective values and behavioral standards. It also holds, however, that these values and standards are not always easily dis-

[58] Dewey and Tufts, *Ethics*, p. 309.

[59] Darnell Rucker, "Dewey's Ethics, Part Two," in *Guide to the Works of John Dewey*, ed. Jo Ann Boydston (Carbondale: Southern Illinois University Press, 1970), p. 123.

[60] Edward C. Moore, *American Pragmatism: Peirce, James, and Dewey* (New York: Columbia University Press, 1961), p. 264.

[61] "Dewey's Ethics, Part Two," in *Guide to the Works of John Dewey*, ed. Boyd-ston, p. 125.

cerned and that even when they are reasonably clear, a host of existential conditions may impair man's conformity to them. And yet, when their reality is even perceived as possible, they obligate man to try to understand and act so as to fulfill their claims upon him. Note the important parallel which exists between the physical and moral realms: How "intelligent" would we count the man who knew of the law of gravitation and yet opened a window on the eighty-fifth floor of a New York City skyscraper and stepped out! In like measure, how "moral" would we count the same man who knew and accepted the standard against killing and then committed suicide? Clearly, we are obligated to the perceived good. The present question, of course, concerns the aids available to us in its perception.

Beyond reason and the demands of one's human nature, most classicists argue that man also has a "conscience" which aids him in discerning and following the right.[62] Existing as a God-imparted power or simply as a part of man's naturalistic endowment, it comes into play when man is faced with distinguishing both the presence and the degrees of moral goodness or evil in a contemplated act. The "true," "correct" or "healthy" conscience will signal a conflict between his desires and his duty, warn of the evil lurking beneath seemingly innocent pleasures, sensitize him to the right and wrong in the situation and impel him to seek the right. After the decision—and those classicists who hold the assumption of the "free self" warn that even the workings of a healthy conscience may be disregarded by man—conscience judges the rightness or wrongness of the act and induces feelings of approval or guilt.[63]

Classicists differ as to the degree to which we may have confidence in conscience's promptings. Henderson writes:

> *No man's conscience tells him infallibly what is right or wrong. For that we need the insights of our keenest thinkers, those who have learned the most about human nature and its needs. Human thought, human experiences, human suffering—sometimes bitter indeed—help us to learn what is right.*[64]

Even those most confident of the powers of a "true" conscience, however, are not unaware of the aberrations which can be occasioned by a "false" conscience.[65] Due to environmental factors and/or con-

---

[62] Some classicists argue that conscience is primarily a function of the intellect. Others, however, maintain that it is an expression of man's entire ethical personality. Thus it encompasses his feelings and his will, as well as his intellect. See VanderVeldt and Odenwald, *Psychiatry and Catholicism*, p. 21.

[63] *Ibid.,* p. 20.

[64] *Introduction to Philosophy of Education*, p. 97.

[65] For a discussion of the various forms of a "false" conscience, see VanderVeldt and Odenwald, *Psychiatry and Catholicism*, pp. 21–23.

stitutional defects such as original sin, conscience may be mistaken.
For those classicists who emphasize the primary role of conscience in
discerning moral values and standards, however, man is *obligated* to
follow its promptings as long as he acts in good faith (i.e., as long as
he has tried with all his power to develop a "true" conscience) and his
conscience leaves no doubt as to the right.   VanderVeldt and Odenwald maintain that under these conditions

> *he is bound to follow his conscience and he is morally responsi-*
> *ble for his actions in the same measure as his conscience tells*
> *him.   If his conscience is ignorant of the law, that law, morally*
> *speaking, does not exist for him; if his conscience gives a false*
> *interpretation of the law, he must follow the erroneous pathways*
> *marked by it; if his conscience minimizes or aggrandizes an ob-*
> *ligation, that obligation decreases or increases for him in the*
> *same proportion.*[66]

The penalties of not following conscience—resulting in the "bad"
conscience—are spelled out by Caruso:

> *Modern psychology has shown . . . that no dynamic psycho-*
> *logical current can be annihilated; if it is covered up or repressed*
> *it will appear by devious ways and transform the unbearable*
> *bad conscience into aggression—either into aggression against*
> *the ego, which may lead to self-torture, to Kierkegaard's 'sick-*
> *ness unto death,' or into aggression against the surrounding*
> *world, and in particular against those of its representatives who*
> *play some part in the disturbed mental life.   This aggression in*
> *its turn heightens the pangs of conscience, and the aggressive*
> *person is thus caught in a vicious cycle.*[67]

B. THE OBLIGATION OF FREE COMMITMENT.   In an interesting
and helpful treatment of existentialistic ethics, Professor Mothershead writes:

> *Duty is not already there to be done.   Obligation is instated by*
> *free human commitment.   Since we and our world are what*
> *they are by virtue of our free choices, it follows that we are*
> *wholly responsible for ourselves and our world.   This is one cir-*
> *cumstance which makes our freedom awful.*[68]

Once again we see the existentialist place responsibility for all dimensions of living squarely upon the individual human being.   His only
escape from meaninglessness is to accept the inevitable frustrations
and loneliness of becoming and take up the burden of deciding

[66] *Ibid.*, p. 25.
[67] *Existential Psychology*, p. 28.
[68] *Ethics*, pp. 305–306.

specifically *to* what and *for* what he will be responsible. Existential-ism offers few guidelines indeed, refusing to answer

> *the question of 'to what' a person should feel responsible—whether to his God or his conscience or his society or whatever higher power. [In like measure it refuses] to say what a person should feel responsible for—for the realization of which values, for the fulfillment of which personal tasks, for which particular meaning to life. On the contrary, the task . . . consists pre-cisely in bringing the individual to the point where he can of his own accord discern his own proper tasks, out of the con-sciousness of his own responsibility, and can find the clear, no longer indeterminate, unique and singular meaning of his own life.[69]*

For some theistic existentialists, man is assisted in commitment-making by his conscience which, though fallible, does fulfill quite traditional functions. Other existentialists feel that conscience strictly represents the internalized voice of a repressive society and must be trans-formed.[70] All, however, stress man's necessary obligation: *to choose.* And the ultimate choice is not between choosing good or choosing evil, but—much more difficult and all-encompassing—between choos-ing the authentic life or the Shoel-like hell[71] of unauthenticity.

C. THE OBLIGATION TO BE INTELLIGENT.   John Childs, in an argu-ment entitled "The Obligation to Be Intelligent," strikes a note that perhaps deserves greater emphasis than it has thus far received in our study of axiological contextualism. He writes:

> *Tolerance is a great virtue, but tolerance does not imply moral indifference. Tolerance, moreover, is but one of the many values comprehended in what we call our democratic way of life, and educators can be intelligent about education in and for democracy only as they are intelligent about the various human attitudes and practices which make this life of freedom and tol-erance possible.[72]*

Contextualists in general—and pragmatists in particular—are often accused of having no substantive loyalties, of being concerned only

[69] Frankel, *The Doctor and the Soul*, p. 269.

[70] *Cf.* Nauman, *The New Dictionary of Existentialism*, pp. 19–22.

[71] Shoel, the "hell" of the Hebrews—like the afterworlds of the Babylonians, Egyp-tians, Homeric Greeks and many other ancient peoples—was a dreary place of dust and dismal shadows to which all men went forever on death. Its inhabitants were scarcely conscious and incapable of any emotion. "Unauthenticity" is more akin to this dim, gray, shadowy existence than it is to the hot, red, actively punishing Christian hell. For further notes, see the topic "Underworld" as indexed in E. O. James, *The Ancient Gods* (New York: G. P. Putnam's Sons, 1960).

[72] *Education and Morals*, p. 14.

with process and of advocating a methodology which crumbles under the attacks of those who *really* know what they want and feel no particular need to be especially rational in securing it. This is seen especially true in times of extreme internal and/or external pressure, e.g., the years since the later 1930s. Believing this to be the case, various groups have split off from the pragmatic camp. For instance, the leader of the self-styled "crisis philosophy" referred to as Reconstructionism has written:

> *Education as means is only strong when education as an end is strong. We need to know what we want, where we want to go, what our objectives are. Then we can begin to work out ways by which to achieve them. Here is one of the points at which the reconstructionist modifies the progressivist philosophy. The latter emphasizes that ends emerge out of the means we use: if we develop effective means, the ends will eventually come into view. The reconstructionist philosophy emphasizes more strongly that means are also shaped by the ends we decide upon and commit ourselves to. That is, if we are clear about where we are going, we will be more likely to develop the necessary processes by which to get there To be sure, ends and means are necessary to each other. Nevertheless, education should now concern itself much more deeply and directly than hitherto with the great ends of civilization.*[73]

To some extent this criticism is correct. But to some extent it also represents a loss of faith in intelligence. What is the meaning of this seeming paradox?

Surely, Dewey always held a deep suspicion of all absolutes. We need look no further than the assumption of "basic reality as the experience of individuals-in-society" or of "value as the product of contextual inquiry" to discern the reasons. Experience means change; the value judged good in one context may become bad when unreflectively transferred to another. Intelligence exists to bring *all* contextual factors into play and effect a resolution of the blocked situation and a freeing of energy. This involves not only guiding modifications of the self but also of every other physical and social variable. In discussing Dewey's ethics, Mothershead concludes:

> *We are moral beings, not because in some cosmic sense we ought to be, but because, as a matter of fact, we must be. Our failure to acknowledge obligation is not wickedness but ignorance of the social character of our existence.*[74]

[73] Theodore Brameld, *Education as Power* (New York: Holt, Rinehart and Winston, Inc., 1965), p. 38.
[74] *Ethics*, p. 145.

Traditions, customs and unevaluated institutions—all supported and given status and prestige by a priori theories—cloud our vision.[75] Man finds it difficult to see clearly that his obligation must be to an *absolute process*, intelligence, and not to some *substantive absolute*, be it the Good or a particular political or economic system.

At the same time and as strange as it may inherently seem, Dewey can also write:

> *The practical problem that has to be faced is the establishment of cultural conditions that will support the kinds of behavior in which emotions and ideas, desires and appraisals, are integrated.*[76]

It is suggested that Dewey's position, while often difficult to maintain, is not inconsistent. Obligating ourselves to intelligence in decision-making does not free us from seeking those cultural conditions conducive to its expression. It does not take a B. F. Skinner to tell us that the absence of such conditions will result in the behavior being extinguished. It is also true that democracy—at least in its "liberal" form as developed in Chapter 8—seems to offer the best hope of creating and maintaining these conditions. But the good can always become the better. And experience brings change. The present institutions and values of democracy must always be undergoing reconstruction lest their promise turn sour. Thus a premature fixing of ends—however "great" they may appear at the moment—can only shackle the operations of intelligence. And here, to be blunt, "premature" is taken to refer to any point prior to the extinction of life itself.

We must not think that intelligence will always succeed. Even when guided by conscience (understood as the learned habit of reflectively considering all conditions and consequences in making a moral decision), it will often fail. Sometimes the obstacles will be too great; sometimes the variables too many for today's man to comprehend, let alone to integrate. Sometimes, as we have seen, consensus-building will fail and survival will temporarily demand compromise, coexistence and even compulsion. Ofttimes indeed, the most irrational faith for late twentieth century man *will* appear to be a faith in human rationality. Yet the pragmatist must ask: "What gives us any better hope of constructing meaning in the world?" "If I must make a choice, what better basis for it?" And with no little "fear and trembling" he will put his blue chips down on intelligence and accept its direction. Any other act will be viewed as inescapably wrong and ultimately immoral.

[75] *Theory of Valuation*, p. 61.
[76] *Ibid.*, p. 65.

6. Ends, Means and Progress

A. GROWTH TOWARD AN ULTIMATE GOAL. Neither life generally
nor education in particular is a goal-less enterprise. The notion that
either phenomenon could exist without goals is clearly contrary to
common sense. True, the basic ends (i.e., aims, goals, purposes) of
life and education cannot be established by experimentation. However, our studies have already indicated that the classicist posits *other*
modes of knowing that carry their own validity. In general, classicists
maintain that educational goals are absolute and universal and can
be discerned only through metaphysical study, particularly the study
of human nature. Even the theistic classicist can accept this strategy,
believing in the last analysis that self-realization coincides with the
acquisition of religious values. According to Fleshman, for example,

> *Self-realization is the aim in ethics and education. The end of*
> *life must be a development in character. . . . The final problem*
> *in ethics and the ultimate aim in education must be tested in*
> *terms of the realization of the rational self. The supreme law*
> *of every educational process is to make the best of self possible.*
> *The pupil is to develop his own personality to the fullest extent*
> *and in doing so he is to assist in the development of other per-*
> *sonalities associated with him. The duty to self and duty to*
> *others are coordinated by the profound world principle that*
> *each individual pupil is a part of the eternal consciousness and*
> *that pupils are fellows by virtue of a common relation to the*
> *Infinite Mind.*[77]

When we turn to human nature, Broudy writes, we see that it "has a
structure that is everywhere the same, and that this structure demands
for its preservation the forms of action characteristic of the 'good' life,"
namely, self-perfection whose forms are self-determination, self-realization and self-integration.[78] Finally, Henderson notes, "We can find
the basis of morality in our own natures, in the conduct necessary to
realize our best potentialities and the kind of society in which man
could live as man."[79]

Thus we may conclude that the ultimate goal of education lies in
guiding man's realization of his potential powers. It is for this
purpose and this purpose alone that we control learning, and it is our
ideals of human character and association that provide the measure by
which we judge specific educational means. Did we not have such an
ultimate goal, it would be impossible to distinguish between mere

[77] Arthur C. Fleshman, *The Educational Process* (Philadelphia: J. B. Lippincott
Company, 1908), pp. 125–126.
[78] *Building a Philosophy of Education*, p. 39. Quoted by permission.
[79] *Introduction to Philosophy of Education*, p. 114.

change and improvement. Indeed, "without an ultimate guiding principle, our immediate solution can be only immediate adjustment, expedience, and muddling through."[80]   Finally, without absolute, fixed ends we are defenseless in the face of contending opinions. There is simply no way to distinguish between the moral worth of a Schweitzer and a Hitler.

It must be noted that classicists are in some disagreement as to the *means* by which we are to achieve our ultimate goal. One extreme is exemplified by Adler, who argues that "educational means *in general* are the same for all men at all times and everywhere."[81]   By contrast, Horowitz, while maintaining that "the 'why' and 'what' [of education] are, ultimately, [fixed] beyond empiricism and attainable by reason alone," grants that means "must be verified experimentally and tested constantly in practice, constantly modified and made more efficient."[82] Nevertheless, all classicists seem to agree that the means chosen must be morally good; the end, however good in itself, can *never* justify evil means.[83]   Given knowledge of the proper ends of education and access to a variety of morally sound means, the problem then comes down to deciding which means best contribute to the realization of the ends. With the possible exception of the Alderian, the classicist usually begins with some self-evident and authoritative principles and deductively works out his answer. Occasionally, when he concludes that the problem is open to empirical investigation, he may employ experimental tests. Examples of each of these procedures will be given in Chapter 7.

"Progress" does not present an insurmountable problem for the classicist. Given experts capable of discerning the absolute, universal ends of education which exist in an ideal realm, in the mind of God or in the very nature of physical reality—and popular acceptance of expert authority as the very foundation of freedom—progress is measured in terms of how far the child advances toward these ends.[84] How far, for instance, has he advanced in freely determining his own life style in view of his possibilities? How far, in realizing his own cognitive, affective and psychomotor potentials? And how far, in integrating his life on the basis of self-knowledge and knowledge of

[80] Horowitz, "Experimentalism and Education," pp. 408–409.

[81] Mortimer J. Adler, "In Defense of the Philosophy of Education," in *Philosophies of Education*, The Forty-first Yearbook of the National Society for the Study of Education, Part I, ed. Nelson B. Henry (Bloomington, Ill.: Public School Publishing Company, 1942), p. 222.

[82] "Experimentalism and Education," p. 413.

[83] Hörmann, *An Introduction to Moral Theology*, p. 116.

[84] *Cf.* Lawrence G. Thomas, "The Meaning of 'Progress' in Progressive Education," *Educational Administration and Supervision including Teacher Training*, XXXII, No. 7 (October 1946), p. 387. Quoted by permission of the author.

the world about him? The answers—not as yet always quantifiable—provide a measure of his progress.

B. GROWTH IN SELF-DIRECTION. "Maturing," writes Perls, "is the transcendence from environmental support to self-support" (italics removed).[85] Marcel, however, points out that self-direction does not necessarily entail a perverted egocentricity, a complete lack of concern for the good of the Other. He writes, "If, however, we make an honest enquiry, experience will force us to the paradoxical conclusion that the more I am able to preserve this intimacy with myself, the more I shall be capable of making real contact with my neighbor . . ."[86] The relevance of this quotation to our own culture should not go unnoticed. As our population grows, as one open vista after another—from Arizona to Maine—gives way to tract-housing and industrial plants, as the opportunity for intimacy with oneself gives way to increasingly manic "doing," we actually find ourselves diminished in being, less capable of meaningful contact with anyone. More and more we "exist," breathing oxygen and giving off carbon dioxide, but few would claim that we truly "live." Thus a re-establishment of contact with ourselves and a reclaiming of conscious control over our own life-directions are prerequisite not only to individual but to social progress.

In explicating the basic ends or goals of Existentialism, then, it seems necessary to inquire into just what is meant by such global notions as self-support, self-direction and a contact with ourselves that opens real contacts with the Other. One especially detailed and promising treatment is found in Carl Rogers's concept of the "fully-functioning person." Rogers maintains that such a person is:

> 1) *able to live fully in and with each and all of his feelings and reactions;* 2) *making use of all his organic equipment to sense, as accurately as possible, the existential situation within and without;* 3) *using all of the data his nervous system can thus supply, using it in awareness, but recognizing that his total organism may be, and often is, wiser than his awareness;* 4) *able to permit his total organism to function in all its complexity in selecting, from the multitude of possibilities, that behavior which in this moment of time will be most generally and genuinely satisfying;* 5) *able to trust his organism in this functioning, not because it is infallible, but because he can be fully open to the consequences of each of his actions and correct them if they prove to be less than satisfying;* 6) *able to experience all of his feelings, and . . . afraid of none of his feelings;* 7) *his own*

---

[85] Frederick S. Perls, M.D., Ph.D., *Gestalt Therapy Verbatim*, comp. and ed. by John O. Stevens (Moab, Utah: Real People Press, 1969), p. 28.
[86] Gabriel Marcel, *Homo Viator*, trans. Emma Craufurd (London: Victor Gollancz Ltd., 1951), p. 131.

> *sifter of evidence, but . . . open to evidence from all sources;*
> *8) completely engaged in the process of being and becoming*
> *himself, and thus discovers that he is soundly and realistically*
> *social; 9) liv[ing] completely in this moment, but learn[ing]*
> *that this is the soundest living for all time; and 10) a fully func-*
> *tioning organism, and because of the awareness of himself which*
> *flows freely in and through his experiences, he is a fully func-*
> *tioning person.*[87]

Turning to the means by which such a person might be developed, we find something of a problem. The literature of European Existentialism is almost paranoid in its view that society—almost by definition—is repressive and that, in one way or another, the individual who would be authentic must insulate himself from it.[88]   Given the devastation visited upon Europe by two world wars and the utter failure of rationality which attended them, we need not be especially surprised.   Indeed, we have seen the influence of such a view in our own culture in recent years as "opting out" has become a much-discussed and, for some, a viable alternative to "staying with the herd." At the same time, we have seen many European existentialists insist that coming into a meaningful, a "real," relationship with the Other is a necessary (though not sufficient) step in achieving personal authenticity.   And in this culture we have witnessed the rise of communes, both theistic and nontheistic.

There is a difference between the Europeans and most American theorists (at least of the older generations) who could be said to be oriented to Existentialism. The latter are markedly less pessimistic about the possibilities of developing a nonrepressive society—or at least less repressive subcultures. Perhaps their greater optimism is culture-bound and unrealistic. It *is* true that American culture—at least prior to the years of our involvement in Vietnam—has been markedly optimistic. It is also true that the value placed upon the group has always been high in this culture, in spite of the counter-weight placed on the "rugged individual." Be that as it may, writers such as Raths and Rogers are not nearly so negative about the possibility of group-means as are, say, Kierkegaard and Sartre. Raths's value-clarifying method, for example, is *set* in the classroom. Rogers speaks often and at length of the potential value in *group* therapy. To illustrate, he writes:

> *Values are raised, in plenty, by members of the group, and this*
> *rich and varied expression of ways of life offers to the individual*
> *member of a group many alternate perspectives without any re-*

---

[87] *Freedom to Learn,* p. 288.

[88] See Nauman, "Society," in *The New Dictionary of Existentialism,* pp. 155–159.

quirement that he commit himself. The values being expressed are relevant to the individual speaking; the listeners are free from pressure to accept or reject; they can use the material as they perceive it to be meaningful to themselves. In addition, the kinds of values expressed in a group represent something of a cross section of the values of the culture in which the individual lives, with considerably more variance than could be held by the therapist alone. The very diversity of values expressed is an important factor, it is believed, in creating a climate in which the final choice is left truly with the individual.[89]

Rogers does emphasize that the therapist's role in group work, as in individual therapy, must uphold "the primary value of the individual's right to determine his own way of life."[90]   The community may be necessary, but the individual is its focal point.   We shall return to this problem in Chapter 7 when discussing possibilities suggested for educational policy and practices.

The "measurement" of progress toward becoming a "self-directive" or "fully-functioning" person presents more problems than were encountered in discussing the means to that end.   In the first place, it will be remembered that the existentialist denies the efficacy of experimental inquiry in dealing with the inner person.   Secondly, the existentialist maintains that change is a basic principle of reality and, thus, victories won in today's battles will have to be sought anew in tomorrow's.   Efforts to datafy progress in knowledge of being-for-itself are simply misguided.   Only the individual concerned can judge when progress has occurred—even though he does well to consider data produced in the realm of knowledge-in-itself.

On the other hand, existentialistic theory is strangely optimistic as to the "possibility" of human progress.   Man is *not* born inherently evil or predisposed to evil; he *can* achieve self-worth; and wrong choices *can* be made anew.   We would do well to contemplate the agreement among Kierkegaard, Jaspers and Sartre to the effect "that man has everything to gain in this life and absolutely nothing to lose, and thus one might as well be involved in the life process actively."[91]

C. GROWTH AS ITS OWN END.   Over time each of us finds those little, sometimes insignificant, things that give momentary pleasure— that add a little spice to the daily round of activities.   The author, for instance, is often pleasured by book and chapter titles.   Take the title of the first chapter of Ernest Bayles's *Pragmatism in Education:*

[89] *Client-Centered Therapy*, pp. 292–293.
[90] *Ibid.*, p. 292.
[91] Mitchell Bedford, *Existentialism and Creativity* (New York: Philosophical Library, 1972), p. 281.

"Pragmatism: Relativity Taken Seriously." Beautiful. Actually, that's as appropriate a beginning for this section as any, for it does raise some serious questions as to how one possibly can find goals in the midst of constant flux. After all, if you don't know where you're going, how do you start?

We might suspect that the pragmatist has an answer—and he does. Goals don't exist to be "found." All we do find in a situation are "experienced satisfactions and anticipated enjoyments—which can be combined in new patterns and projected as possible ends of the current activity."[92] Given an environment that reinforces such behavior, the pragmatist turns to the possibilities of human experience as his raw materials and *constructs* goals through the cooperative exercise of intelligence. These goals, as Dewey notes, are as endless and varied as transactions between man and environment can make them. He maintains that classical thought

> *must abandon the notion of a predetermined limited number of ends inherently arranged in an order of increasing comprehensiveness and finality. It will have to recognize that natural termini are as infinitely numerous and varied as are the individual systems of action they delimit; and that since there is only relative, not absolute, impermeability and fixity of structure, new individuals with novel ends emerge in irregular procession. It must recognize that limits, closures, ends are experimentally or dynamically determined, presenting like the boundaries of political individuals or states, a moving adjustment of various energy-systems in their cooperative and competitive interactions, not something belonging to them of their own right.*[93]

Keeping the tentative end in view, the pragmatist returns his focus to the situation at hand. Moral standards and other generalizations of human experience are used as tools to analyze the situation in terms of possible means of reaching the end. The very construction of a tentative end (the end-in-view) also allows us to examine the situation and locate additional means and probable obstacles, as well as to arrange the means in the order in which they may best be used.[94] Thomas writes:

> . . . *a tenuous and tentative [transaction] is created between presently available means and projected ends, each influencing*

[92] Thomas, "The Meaning of 'Progress' in Progressive Education," p. 389. Quoted by permission.

[93] John Dewey, *Experience and Nature.* 2nd ed. (Chicago: Open Court Publishing Co., 1926); (paperback ed.; New York: Dover Publications, Inc., 1958), p. 395.

[94] John Dewey, *Democracy and Education: An Introduction to the Philosophy of Education* (New York: The Macmillan Company, 1916); (paperback ed.; New York: The Free Press, 1966), p. 102.

and modifying the other. A desirable end is always a feasible end, though of course not all feasible ends are desirable. When the [transactive] relationship has become as stable as intellectual analysis can make it, the time has come for action on the means-ends hypothesis—i.e., to test out whether doing 'this' will actually accomplish 'that'.[95]

Note the necessary interrelatedness of ends and means: The end-in-view actually serves as a means to locate means of reaching it![96] Dewey goes so far as to argue that any end

is merely a series of acts viewed at a remote stage; and a means is merely the series viewed at an earlier one. The distinction of means and ends arises in surveying the course of a proposed line of action, a connected series in time. The "end" is the last act thought of; the means are the acts to be performed prior to it in time.

. . .

Means and ends are two names for the same reality. The terms denote not a division in reality but a distinction in judgment.[97]

A review of the art fair example posed earlier in this chapter lends support to Dewey's contention. Remember that initially the art fair was proposed as a goal. Later, following analysis, it came to be viewed as a means of reaching other goals, i.e., the behaviorally-stated teacher interests. Achieving *these* goals would, of course, lead to still other possibilities both in terms of ends and means. And so it goes, *ad infinitum.*

The desirability or the value of each end-in-view is determined according to the procedures suggested under the assumption of "validation through experimentation." This is obviously a never-ending process, one involving growth itself, which eliminates the need for an ultimate end to ensure direction. "The need for such certainty," Thomas notes, "is eliminated when one's process of making evaluations includes an independent and objective way of testing and improving one's value judgments continuously."[98]

How, then, are we to understand "progress"? One thing may be said with reasonable certainty: It means an increase in the number and complexity of *problems* with which human beings will have to deal

---

[95] "The Meaning of 'Progress' in Progressive Education," p. 392. Quoted by permission.

[96] Dewey, *Theory of Valuation*, p. 53.

[97] John Dewey, *Human Nature and Conduct: An Introduction to Social Psychology* (New York: Henry Holt and Company, 1922), pp. 34 and 36.

[98] "The Meaning of 'Progress' in Progressive Education," p. 395. Quoted by permission.

intelligently.[99] It also means, however, an increase in the meanings available as resources for new problem-solving. *Culturally,* we may look for a growth in intelligence as a quality of human action and a development of the will and capacity of citizens to take part in cooperative decision-making and implementation.[100] *Individually,* we may look for the person to exhibit more knowledge of different means for realizing his purposes, greater knowledge of the probable consequences of teaching his goals and more dependable knowledge of what he really wants as his goals. Progress, then, is a way of living.

As Thomas summarizes it,

> *Progress is judged . . . not by approaching closer to certain pre-established ends, but by growth in the ability of persons to evolve new means-ends relationships on a wider, deeper, and richer scale. Direction is found, not in a fixed, ultimate end for all human living, but in the method of using criticized human experience as the source and test of values.*[101]

In truth and "in reality there is nothing to which growth is relative save more growth."[102]

Nowhere more than in Axiology have we found support for Colin Greer's argument that the public schools have failed to produce a homogeneous society.[103] Indeed, the value structure of American culture is far more akin to a piece of conglomerate than to any igneous rock conceivable! It will be interesting to see the different possibilities suggested for this nation's educational activities by such theoretical diversity.

[99] Dewey, *Human Nature and Conduct,* p. 286.

[100] Ephraim Vern Sayers and Ward Madden, *Education and the Democratic Faith: An Introduction to the Philosophy of Education* (New York: Appleton-Century-Crofts, Inc., 1959), p. 223.

[101] "The Meaning of 'Progress' in Progressive Education," p. 396. Quoted by permission.

[102] Dewey, *Democracy and Education,* p. 51.

[103] Colin Greer, "Public Schools: The Myth of the Melting Pot," *Saturday Review,* LIII (November 15, 1969), pp. 84–86 and 102.

7

Axiological Assumptions and
Educational Possibilities

There are several ways in which we might proceed in this chapter. One, for instance, would be similar to the path taken in the two earlier chapters on education, Metaphysics and Epistemology. Therein, we speculatively considered each assumption in terms of its various possibilities for the curriculum, instructional strategies, organization, administration and professional personnel of the American school. It would not be impossible—or necessarily unfruitful—to choose this path in the present discussion. For instance, the assumptions of axiological *objectivism* do suggest that the curriculum must be developed in light of certain absolute ends of man and that it might be so sequenced as to lead the child, step by step, to these ends. The notion that the curriculum must consist of a solid study of the arts and sciences and that value distinctions may be made between the so-called curricular and extracurricular subjects—even between the "fine" and "practical" arts—is suggested. We could argue that the child should be evaluated-graded in terms of how close he approximates what he "ought" to know. We could develop a strong argument for the hierarchical arrangement of school decision-making and personnel. Finally, we could surely cast some additional light on the emphasis that classicists have historically placed on the moral character of the teacher.

Turning to axiological *subjectivism*, the emphasis on spontaneous choice and the "hierarchy of individual decision" helps us better to understand why the curriculum must be chosen by the child—and why that which is chosen *is* his curriculum and his path to self-actualization. The rise of the so-called "open schools" and "free universities" and their frequent isolation from more established educational "systems" represent phenomena not difficult to understand given theory presented in the preceding chapter. Nor are the possibilities presented by an I-Thou relationship between teacher and student or the teacher's role in helping the child to clarify his preferences without theoretical support.

Finally, we might turn to axiological *contextualism.* In the theory presented in Chapter 6 we find additional reasons for the pragmatist's refusal automatically to value core courses higher than electives. Support is found for instructional strategies such as multidimensional evaluation (i.e., grading based on factors such as student-teacher conferences, effort and citizenship—in addition to subject-matter achievement). Reasons are found for the emphasis on means as well as ends, efforts to develop a democratic classroom environment and direct instruction in using generalizations in decision-making. And the assumptions we have considered do suggest cooperative decision-making in moral matters, less authoritative teacher and administrator roles, and viewing childhood as a life stage valid in its own right (rather than merely as a preparation for adulthood). Additional support is to be found for initiating study on the basis of the students' present interests and experience whenever possible.

Two basic reasons suggest that another path is to be preferred. In the first place, many if not most of the points mentioned above have already received substantial support from related metaphysical and epistemological assumptions and will be tightly summarized in Chapter 9. Secondly—and perhaps more important—today's American education is as aware of the need for "moral education" as it is confused by just how to go about it. Taken together, these factors suggest that a somewhat more narrow examination of the axiological assumptions presented in Chapter 6, in terms of their possibilities for public school programs in moral education, is appropriate even to an introductory text.

A. Axiological Objectivism and Moral Education

Over the years, axiological objectivists have posed a variety of strategies by which the child could be motivated to translate his knowledge of inherently good acts, ideas, objects and processes into moral behavior. Many of these procedures can be observed in today's American school; others, as we shall see, are now looked upon with some disfavor. The latter point is more important, for objectivists should not be criticized for procedures which in the main they have discarded of their own volition.

A common emphasis is found in the provision of inspiring models either in person or through literature. For example, we read:

> But, above all, the educated will, through contact or communion with moral geniuses, store up enthusiasm for all that is noble and morally beautiful.
>
> . . .
>
> If not in the immediate environment of the child, in the records of the past there can be shown to him the true patriots. . . . If contemporary events of public life frequently offer to the young the spectacles of opportunism, corruption, and ineptitude, history has preserved for them brighter pictures. . . . The youthful heart is hungry for the latter; they give the young hope, great hope, as well as the desire to accomplish great things.[104]

Fixed, permanent values should be made "so accessible to the growing person that education ceases to be a training merely outwardly imposed, and instead becomes an individual decision, a genuine acknowledgement of these values."[105]

Objectivists have also called for appealing to the child's conscience and/or attempting to persuade his reason concerning the need for moral action. Lectures and teacher-guided discussions have pointed to specified behaviors strongly sanctioned by reputable authorities and/or made obligatory by the moral law. A related practice builds on peer pressure. In one form, students are provided with a special period of the day for self and group evaluation. They discuss and judge their own behavior and receive suggestions from their peers.[106]

A blend of inspiration, instruction and training appears to dominate most objectivist programs for moral education. Stella Henderson, for instance, illustrates each of these three elements, writing:

> Children must learn what is right and what is wrong; they must learn to love the right and to hate the wrong; they must form habits of right conduct.[107]

[104] Michael Demiashkevich, An Introduction to the Philosophy of Education (New York: American Book Company, 1935), pp. 303–304. In the same vein, also see Herman H. Horne, Philosophy of Education. Rev. ed. (New York: The Macmillan Company, 1927), pp. 181–186.

[105] Caruso, Existential Psychology, p. 130.

[106] James Raths, "A Strategy for Developing Values," Educational Leadership, XXI (May 1964), p. 510.

[107] Introduction to Philosophy of Education, p. 346.

For Henderson, the second of these points is both the most difficult to achieve and the most crucial for character education. The chances for success depend on the school's ability to ensure that the child

> *1) has a legitimate way to satisfy his needs and reasonable wants, 2) fails to obtain satisfaction from unacceptable ways of gratifying needs or from any attempt to satisfy an unreasonable want, and 3) becomes aware of the needs of his higher nature.*[108]

As we have seen earlier, Harry Broudy views the good life as involving the achievement of self-determination, self-realization and self-integration through developing the habits of acquiring, using and enjoying truth. In order to develop these habits, the school must turn to knowledge preserved in the humanities, the sciences and the fine arts. Therein the student will find knowledge about social problems, ordered values to aid him in systematically developing action alternatives and resources for developing the skills of moral reflection.[109] Broudy sees the secondary school as the locus for studying value norms and man's experience with moral reflection and for reorganizing knowledge so as to make it relevant to current social problems. It is also the time when students can become more sensitive to their own values, the values of others, conflicts between value hierarchies and dependable value syntheses. "Wisdom," writes Broudy, "comes as one tries to use the concepts of the disciplines and the insights of the arts to make the problems of life intelligible."[110] Success in moral education, of course, is not guaranteed. Only the individual human being can acknowledge the claims of knowledge about the good life as incumbent upon himself and act with moral responsibility.

It cannot—and should not—be denied that many objectivists have resorted to external control in trying to ensure correct habit formation. Not infrequently the behavioral choices of the child have been limited, sometimes directly and sometimes more insidiously, by reinforcing only authority-sanctioned choices. A familiar behavioral management principle reads: "When you wish to increase the frequency of a behavior employ a strengthening consequence and use it immediately and consistently."[111] External control has also led others to view the teacher's role in helping the student improve his moral behavior as fivefold: 1) ensuring that he is informed as to what he

---

[108] *Ibid.*

[109] Harry S. Broudy, *The Real World of the Public Schools* (New York: Harcourt Brace Jovanovich, Inc., 1972), p. 163.

[110] *Ibid.*, p. 164.

[111] John T. Neisworth, Stanley L. Deno and Joseph R. Jenkins, *Student Motivation and Classroom Management: A Behavioristic Approach* (Lemont, Pa.: Behavior Technics, Inc., 1969), p. 8.

ought to like or do; 2) sensitizing him to be suspicious of what he initially *wants* to do, inhibiting his desires in terms of what he now knows he *ought* to do; 3) disciplining the child who after reflection will not do what he knows he ought to do, so as to secure proper behavior; 4) providing opportunities for proper behavior in order to build behavioral habits; and 5) hoping that the child over time will move beyond the stage of mere "socialization" (i.e., unconscious action in accord with habit) and consciously choose the proper action. Even under conditions of external control, however, this latter step is seen as necessary to truly "moral" behavior.

The question of external control in moral education does represent an issue facing the axiological objectivist. The force of the problem increases with the degree to which the objectivist is certain that he knows the truth of the matter at hand. His answer will also depend to some extent on his metaphysical assumptions as to human nature and free will. Believing in free will, for instance, he may feel constrained to stand by as the individual chooses error—at least insofar as that choice does not harm others. Horne asks—and answers:

> *Why then teach ethics? Because, though knowledge does not insure right action, there can be no right action without knowledge. Because, too, knowing the right, through the motor-tendency of ideas, is at least a temptation to do it.*[112]

The determinist, on the other hand, may well decide to exert "the control [which] always rests in the last analysis in the hands of society"[113] and engineer those contingencies which will ensure the "right" choice. As in Skinner's *Beyond Freedom and Dignity*, the act may be justified by pointing out that inasmuch as all behavior is controlled, it is best controlled intelligently and in the interests of enhanced living or even societal survival. If this involves undemocratic decision-making by "managers" and "Planners," so be it.[114]

B.   Axiological Subjectivism and Moral Education

To the possible surprise of some readers, the task of suggesting a program for moral education consistent with the assumptions of axiological subjectivism is not really insurmountable. To mention but

---

112 Herman H. Horne, *Idealism in Education* (New York: The Macmillan Company, 1923), p. 137.

113 B. F. Skinner, *Walden Two* (New York: The Macmillan Company, 1948), p. 109.

114 *Ibid.*, pp. 259–276.

a handful of sources, the writings of the European existentialists, European and American psychologists oriented toward Existentialism, A. S. Neill, and the American educators Maxine Greene and Louis E. Raths provide a not insubstantial base.[115]   At this point in our studies, the picture they paint is relatively clear: Man is thoroughly disoriented by the pressures of war and a mass technological society, by spatial mobility, the disintegration of the family and the very pluralism of American culture. He has lost contact with himself. His only hope lies in regaining control of, and taking personal responsibility for, his own experience. Neither the anxiety nor the positive potential inherent in such a step must be underestimated—especially in the most sensitive tasks involved in valuing.

Louis Raths points out that the task of doing *something* about moral education has—not uncharacteristically—been dumped on the schools. Though mindful of the disorientation and confusion of the schools, themselves a primary social agent, he has accepted this task and sharply defined his starting point:

> *Since each person's experiences are different, we cannot be certain what values, what style of life, would be most suitable for any person. We do, however, have some idea about what processes might be most effective for obtaining sound values.*[116]

Furthermore, as noted in Chapter 6, values develop out of personal choices. Carl Rogers speaks to the benefits of such a position, writing:

> *Because the values are perceived as originating in self, the value system becomes more realistic and comfortable and more nearly in harmony with the perceived self. Valued goals appear more achievable.*[117]

Raths's support for Rogers's position is indicated by Gray, who refers to the sense of clarity and direction and the proud enthusiasm of the person confident of his own values. By contrast, the individual who is confused as to his values (perhaps having accepted them from others) tends toward apathy, flightiness, inconsistency, drifting, overconformity, overdissention and posturing.[118]   *Thus a total rejection of indoctrination and a commitment to explicating and implementing processes*

---

[115] One could also turn to British and American "language analysts," although this tack lies outside the confines of the present text.

[116] Louis E. Raths, Merrill Harmin and Sidney B. Simon, "Helping Children to Clarify Values," *NEA Journal*, LVI (October 1967), p. 13.

[117] *Client-Centered Therapy*, p. 195.

[118] Farnum Gray, "Doing Something about Values," *Learning, The Magazine for Creative Teaching*, I, No. 2 (December 1972), p. 16.

*by which each person may create his own values become hallmarks of
the subjectivistic approach to moral education.*

As contrasted with traditional approaches which have only shaped
behavior, attitudes and interests, Raths's process-approach to value
creation[119] pivots on the notion of "clarifying strategies." Herein the
teacher's function is twofold: 1) to create a climate in which the
student dares to disclose himself, and 2) to respond to students in
ways which call upon them to determine what they truly value. James
Raths suggests that maintaining an accepting, nonjudgmental attitude
toward the student—other than in extreme cases involving threat to
life or limb—will go far toward fostering the desired climate. The
teacher must also indicate his concern for each student by listening to
him and remembering his ideas. With a gradual building of mutual
trust and respect—and a deliberate structuring of opportunity for
expression into courses—students will come to express their attitudes
and other behaviors normally well hidden from the Other. The
teacher, functioning as a catalyst, will then be able quietly to turn their
attention to what they are saying and doing as (possibly) contrasted
with what they are really ready to choose, publicly defend and act
upon.[120]

A variety of situations are ripe for clarifying behavior—indeed, all
situations where conflict and confusion pose real problems for students
and toward which they will express preference present opportunities.
Gray notes the potentialities in politics, religion, work, leisure time,
school, love and sex, family, material possessions, culture, personal
tastes, friends, money, aging and death, health, race, war and peace,
and rules and authority.[121] Usually directed to an individual student
in informal situations (e.g., classroom, hallways or playground), *brief*
exchanges gently prod the student to use the seven valuing processes
in examining the means he is creating in the world.[122]

This general position is essentially in agreement with Greene, who
calls for setting up school environments which make it difficult for the
student to maintain "peace of mind" and which focus through literature, the arts and "crisis situations" on engaging the student in con-
frontations in which he is urged to take a stand. Greene and Raths do

---

[119] The distinction between "values" and "value-indicators" such as "attitudes"
and "interests" is noted in Chapter 6 under the assumption of "values as the creation of subjective choice." For an extended development, see Raths, Harmin and
Simon, *Values and Teaching*, pp. 30–33.

[120] "A Strategy for Developing Values," pp. 511–512. There is demonstrably an
atmosphere of "reflection" in the Raths approach which is at odds with the usual
existentialist accent on "spontaneity." Such phenomena are frequently observed
when ideas are translated from one cultural context to another.

[121] "Doing Something about Values," p. 16.

[122] Raths, Harmin and Simon, "Helping Students to Clarify Values," pp. 13–14.

differ somewhat, in that the former feels that the student who evades his responsibility to choose should be taken to task.[123]   Raths, in contrast to Greene, calls for a more catalytic or mirroring role for the teacher; e.g., he may state his views but only after the students have expressed theirs.   For Greene, the teacher must also function as a free, positive subjectivity and thus generate additional possibilities for students in I-Thou encounters. The issue, of course, centers on what procedure will best motivate the student to develop his own resources, to "make the transition from environmental support to self-support." At the moment when he feels threatened and frustrated, Perls is probably correct in suggesting that

> the child [will start] to mobilize the environment by playing phony roles, playing stupid, playing helpless, playing weak, flattering, and all the roles we use in order to manipulate our environment.[124]

Whether the teacher decides to refuse to answer a student question, to ask a clarifying question in return or to try to shake the student out of his lethargy would seem to depend in part on the environment which has been created in the classroom.   Whatever the alternatives considered, the teacher—no less than the student—must surely accept his responsibility for choice and action.

Raths, Harmin and Simon suggest a variety of methods, each essentially involving responding to student behavior in such a way as to motivate the student to consider what he actually values. (Some of the strategies, to be sure, can be used with groups, but the focus is always on the individual's response.)   Neither time nor space permit an adequate development of these methods, but the interested educator should turn without fail to their basic text for a most stimulating discussion and many practical examples. You will find a thorough discussion of methods such as the "value sheet," the "value-clarifying discussion," "role-playing," the "contrived incident," the "zig-zag lesson," "devil's advocate," the "value continuum," "thought sheets," "weekly reaction sheets," "open-ended questions," "coded student papers," "time diary," "autobiographical questionnaire," the "public interview," the "decision-making interview," "voting," the "five-minute [student] quote without comment," "student reports" and "action projects."[125]

The teacher unfamiliar with this approach is advised to begin by

[123] Maxine Greene, *Teacher as Stranger: Educational Philosophy for the Modern Age* (Belmont, Calif.: Wadsworth Publishing Co., Inc., 1973), pp. 280–282.
[124] *Gestalt Therapy Verbatim*, p. 36.
[125] *Values and Teaching*, Chapters VI and VII.

building the requisite classroom environment and working to minimize any tendency to moralize. Then he may initiate the direct process by trying those methods which are felt to be most in tune with one's own personality. It would probably also be wise to turn first to those situations where the teacher's feelings are positive or at least neutral and in which the students have no reason to suspect indoctrination. Raths's process-approach is not easy to learn—nor is it therapy for the disturbed child or a substitute for the teacher's other responsibilities. When understood as a continuing process of informally stimulating value activity, however, it does offer an exciting approach to moral education for the public school.[126]

C. Axiological Contextualism and Moral Education

In Chapter 6 we considered at some length the contextualist's assumption of the "morality of critical inquiry." Given this base, we might suspect that moral education will at least involve the fullest possible development of reflective thinking or minding behaviors. And so it does—but especially as regards the crucial problem of making defensible value judgments in a pluralistic culture. Our task in this section, then, is relatively straightforward. After the briefest focus on the terms "moral" and "spiritual," we shall turn to an elucidation of specific possibilities, goals, problems and procedures of moral education as viewed from a pragmatic vantage point, a vantage point which stands in marked contrast to those of both axiological objectivism and subjectivism.

We have seen that in mediating experience, the organism enters into transactive relationships—involving both doing and undergoing—with other existents in his life space. Through his response to a life situation and a thoughtful consideration of the counter-response of others, both an individual's self-construct and the meaning he ascribes to other existents is gradually shaped or molded. The moral and spiritual are to be understood as *qualities of the response* to the actual life situation. A response is moral when it is guided by reflective thinking, thinking which takes into account all possible antecedent variables, alternative plans of action and possible consequences. This thinking also commits us, of course, to evaluating the consequences resulting from the response and generalizing any contextual knowledge. The term "spiritual," on the other hand, is best understood as involving a

---

[126] Raths, Harmin and Simon, "Helping Students to Clarify Values," p. 15.

special emphasis on two aspects of morality: 1) conscious reference to man's highest ideals and capacities in guiding the response, and 2) a commitment to continue to refine these ideals as a means of both unifying the self and continuing the search for a better life for all mankind. In a situation involving uncertainty or conflict, immorality consists of abandoning the response to the forces of expediency, impulse or unexamined habit, rather than guiding its expression through reflective thinking.[127]

When critical intelligence is so understood, as Dewey put it, "the teacher . . . will find every subject, every method of instruction, every incident of the school life pregnant with moral possibility."[128] Or, to quote Madden, reflective thinking

> can and should be the characteristic feature of the school cur-
> riculum. It should be the basis of every school activity to which
> it is applicable, and should characterize the relations of pupils to
> one another, of pupils to teachers, of teachers to administrators,
> and of school to community.[129]

Any response situation, then, which involves members of the school community carries moral and spiritual potential. What happens to these possibilities, of course, depends upon the sensitivity of those concerned and their willingness and skill cooperatively to make explicit and to actualize that which initially is merely implicit and potential.[130]

In its broadest terms, moral education is designed to sensitize individuals to, and facilitate the explication and actualization of, the value potential inherent in response situations. These tasks are seen to involve the achievement of two distinct but interrelated goals; i.e., the development of critical intelligence on the one hand, and the development of an integrated and dynamic self-community structure on the other.

The development of critical intelligence as the chief tool of moral decision-making clearly involves certain skills, opportunities, attitudes and knowledge. The skills of reflective thinking have already been discussed under several headings (including the assumption of "mind as purposeful, problem-solving behavior") and will not be re-examined here. Suffice it to say that these skills are requisite both to making

[127] Cf. William Clayton Bower, Moral and Spiritual Values in Education (Lexington: University of Kentucky Press, 1952), pp. 76–77.

[128] John Dewey, Moral Principles in Education (Boston: Houghton Mifflin Company, 1909); facsimile ed.; New York: The Wisdom Library, A Division of Philosophical Library, 1959), p. 58.

[129] Ward Madden, Religious Values in Education (New York: Harper & Brothers Publishers, 1951), p. 187.

[130] Bower, Moral and Spiritual Values in Education, p. 77.

rational value judgments and to resolving the value conflicts which must be expected in a pluralistic culture. Such skills obviously demand opportunities for *all* school personnel, individually and co-operatively, to make moral and spiritual choices, evaluate the consequences and generalize contextual knowledge. This is the method by which we create new values, build the habits referred to as "conscience" and develop and refine moral standards and spiritual ideals so vital to continuing growth. John Childs expresses the pragmatic attitude to moral standards taken as guides to action, writing:

> *In brief, unless education is to serve outmoded and reactionary ends, it must accept responsibility for defining the kind of behaviors which now should be associated with such traditional and basic moral categories as "honesty," "unselfishness," "chastity," "loyalty," "equality," "responsibility," and "freedom." The present has deep continuities with the past, but it also has its significant discontinuities. The discontinuities, moreover, are as real as the continuities. Education, during this period of social transition and strain, will not promote democratic interests, if it seeks to make "moral absolutes" out of historic rights and forms of human conduct.*[131]

The pragmatic attitude, then, not only involves a call for the *transmission* of our culture's moral and spiritual heritage, but also a call for its *re-examination* and, as necessary, its *reconstruction* so as to keep it alive and growing.

Finally, the development of critical intelligence does not denigrate knowledge, even though it comes as a by-product of solving problems of current import to the community. Indeed, knowledge developed through minding behaviors provides resources of inestimable value in continuing to learn. For example, the experimental studies of the Harvard psychologist Lawrence Kohlberg (based on the earlier work of Dewey, Durkheim and Piaget) have suggested that in all cultures the development of moral judgment passes through three levels which include six, invariantly sequenced stages, as follows:

PRECONVENTIONAL LEVEL
At this level the child is responsive to such rules and labels as good or bad and right or wrong. He interprets these labels in purely physical or hedonistic terms: If he is bad, he is punished; if he is good, he is rewarded. He also interprets the labels in terms of the physical power of those who enunciate them—parents, teachers and other adults. The level comprises the following two stages:
  Stage 1: punishment and obedience orientation. The physical consequences of action determine its goodness or badness re-

---

[131] *Education and Morals,* pp. 30–31.

gardless of the human meaning or value of these consequences. Avoidance of punishment and unquestioning deference to power are valued in their own right, not in terms of respect for an underlying moral order supported by punishment and authority, the latter being stage 4.

Stage 2: instrumental relativist orientation. *Right action consists of that which instrumentally satisfies one's own needs and occasionally the needs of others. Human relations are viewed in terms similar to those of the marketplace. Elements of fairness, of reciprocity and equal sharing are present, but they are always interpreted in a pragmatic way. Reciprocity is a matter of "you scratch my back and I'll scratch yours," not of loyalty, gratitude or justice.*

CONVENTIONAL LEVEL

At this level maintaining the expectations of the individual's family, group or nation is perceived as valuable in its own right, regardless of immediate and obvious consequences. The attitude is one not only of conformity to the social order but of loyalty to it, of actively maintaining, supporting and justifying the order, and of identifying with the persons or group involved in it. This level comprises the following two stages:

Stage 3: interpersonal concordance or "good boy–nice girl" orientation. *Good behavior is that which pleases or helps others and is approved by them. There is much conformity to stereotypical images of what is majority or "natural" behavior. Behavior is frequently judged by intention: "He means well" becomes important, and one earns approval by "being nice."*

Stage 4: "law and order" orientation. *Authority, fixed rules and the maintenance of the social order are valued. Right behavior consists of doing one's duty, showing respect for authority and maintaining the social order for its own sake.*

POSTCONVENTIONAL LEVEL

At this level there is a clear effort to reach a personal definition of moral values—to define principles that have validity and application apart from the authority of groups or persons and apart from the individual's own identification with these groups. This level again has two stages:

Stage 5: social-contract legalistic orientation. *Generally, this stage has utilitarian overtones. Right action tends to be defined in terms of general individual rights and in terms of standards that have been critically examined and agreed upon by the whole society. There is a clear awareness of the importance of personal values and opinions and a corresponding emphasis on procedural rules for reaching consensus. Other than that which is constitutionally and democratically agreed upon, right is a matter of personal values and opinion. The result is an emphasis both upon the "legal point of view" and upon the possibility of making rational and socially desirable changes in the law, rather than freezing it as in the "law and order" stage 4. Outside the legal realm, free agreement is the binding element of obligation. This* *is the "official" morality of the U.S. government and the Constitution.*

Stage 6: universal ethical principle orientation. *Right is defined by the conscience in accord with self-chosen ethical principles, which in turn are based on logical comprehensiveness, universality and consistency. . . . At heart, these are universal principles of justice, of the reciprocity and equality of human rights, and of respect for the dignity of human beings as individual persons.*[132]

Passage through these stages can be accelerated, slowed or even brought to a halt, depending on the interaction of the individual's ways of mediating or structuring his experience and the structural features of the environment itself. It also depends upon a reorganization of cognitive-affective elements which can be achieved only by the individual. This reorganization can be stimulated by external agents, but it cannot be controlled by them. Passage from lower to higher levels allows the individual to achieve a more stable equilibrium and to use his moral judgments to control his behavior and thus handle moral problems in a more efficient and consistent manner.[133]

What a potential boon this experimental data provides the pragmatist, when he considers that *in 1897* Dewey had written:

> *All conduct springs ultimately and radically out of native instincts and impulses. We must know what these instincts and impulses are, and what they are at each particular stage of the child's development, in order to know what to appeal to and what to build upon. Neglect of this principle may give a mechanical imitation of moral conduct, but the imitation will be ethically dead, because it is external and has its centre without, not within the individual.*[134]

---

[132] *Cf.* Lawrence Kohlberg with Philip Whitten, "Understanding the Hidden Curriculum," *Learning, The Magazine for Creative Teaching,* I, No. 2 (December 1972), pp. 11–12. Reprinted by special permission from *Learning, The Magazine for Creative Teaching,* December 1972. Copyright 1972 by Education Today Company, Inc.

[133] With the exception of the treatment of Kohlberg's six stages, this (fragmentary) summary is based on Lawrence Kohlberg, "Stages of Moral Development as a Basis for Moral Education," in *Moral Education: Interdisciplinary Approaches,* ed. C. M. Beck *et al.* (Toronto, Canada: University of Toronto Press, 1971), pp. 23–92. Other accounts can be found in Kohlberg, "Education for Justice: A Modern Statement of the Platonic View," in *Moral Education: Five Lectures,* intro. Nancy F. and Theodore F. Sizer (Cambridge: Harvard University Press, 1970), pp. 57–83; and Kohlberg, "From Is to Ought: How to Commit the Naturalistic Fallacy and Get Away with It in the Study of Moral Development," in *Cognitive Development and Epistemology,* ed. Theodore Mischel (New York: Academic Press, 1971), pp. 151–235.

[134] *Moral Principles in Education* (1909), pp. 47–48. This book represents an elaboration of an article entitled "Ethical Principles Underlying Education," first published in the *Third Yearbook of the National Herbart Society* (Chicago: The Society, 1897), pp. 7–33. The quotation appears verbatim in the 1897 article.

Once again we note a phenomenon encountered earlier in discussing the interrelatedness of ends and means under the assumption of "growth as its own end." Namely, intelligence viewed from one perspective as an end of moral education can, when viewed from another, provide us with the very means of realizing it.

Beyond developing critical intelligence, it has also been suggested that achieving the tasks of moral education depends upon developing an integrated and dynamic self-community structure. This goal involves individuals cooperatively using their critical intelligence to construct increasingly comprehensive and integrated patterns of meaning as regards both their social reality and their own characters. These are clearly related tasks. Madden writes:

> By helping to create a community he helps create a self, for he finds in the life of the community his life role, his mind, and the materials for building and enriching his personality.[135]

The desideratum, then, is the insightful, reflective person who has a deep understanding of culture and self, and who possesses the attitudes, knowledge and skills requisite to keeping both dynamic. Thus we create the individual and the society which can enjoy realized values and yet exercise firmness and restraint in controversy. Thus we create the individual and the society which can develop symbols and ceremonies in order to celebrate their achievement and aspirations, excite others to investigate their dedication and build a vigorous—a religious—commitment to continue a never-ending task.[136]

These being the goals of a contextualist moral education, we must now turn to the procedures by which they can be realized, as well as to some mention of the problems which may confront us along the way.

Surely one of the greatest of these problems will center on the creation of an appropriate school environment. Few contextualists would agree that the goals of moral education outlined above could possibly be accomplished in one course—especially in a "special" course in ethics. Rather, as Smith points out,

> What is needed . . . is an educational-social climate in which the whole process of formal schooling may develop as part of a progressively enlarged and refined pattern of meaning. . . . Under such a perspective, subject matter does not remain a compartment by itself where it may be viewed as more or less interesting in its own right and more or less valuable as a means to something else. On the contrary, it may become for the student, as it already has for the teacher, an integrated part of

[135] *Religious Values in Education*, p. 185.
[136] *Ibid.*, pp. 186–187.

> *the complex web of meanings by which reality is structured. It thus enriches both fact and values and increases control over the course of subsequent experience, while personality and character emerge in the process.*[137]

Indeed, Kilpatrick goes so far as to write that

> *the cultivation of a really constructive atmosphere is perhaps the first crucial task of school and teacher—an atmosphere of friendly group relationships to open the pupil's heart to constructive thinking and acting. Out of this can come the easy exchange of helpful ideas, the feeling of hearty acceptance of responsible effort, and a growing regard for good standards of workmanship and proper behavior toward others.*[138]

These are obviously schools which show a deep respect for individual and cultural differences by refusing to *impose* a moral code on their members.   They are also schools structured so as to facilitate the fullest participation of all their members in the pursuit of justice.   As Kohlberg notes, "Schools with atmospheres perceived by students as at their stage or lower lead to less moral advance than do schools whose atmospheres are perceived at a higher stage."[139]

The contextualist believes that the optimal environment is created by involving all members of the school community—in all phases of their contact—in posing value claims (i.e., hypothesized values), experimentally testing whether they are contextually valuable and generalizing situational knowledge so as to produce more reliable moral principles and more refined ideas.   In one sense, the whole school becomes a center for examining moral conflicts and learning how to make rational value judgments.   There are several factors which should be considered in implementing such a plan.   First, moral issues of real concern to the participants must be involved, and—as Raths has pointed out—alternative solutions must be available for choice and action.   Secondly, a social setting is indicated, for a group—especially if it includes educators as well as students—will include individuals working at different stages of moral judgment. Under cooperative conditions, they will suggest additional relationships between desires as possibilities for testing and thus provide opportunity for moral standards of greater reliability and applicability

137 Philip G. Smith, *Philosophy of Education: Introductory Studies* (New York: Harper & Row, 1965), pp. 194–195.
138 William H. Kilpatrick, *Philosophy of Education* (New York: The Macmillan Company, 1951), p. 367.
139 "Stages of Moral Development as a Basis for Moral Education," in *Moral Education*, ed. Beck, p. 83.

to be developed.[140]   Note the opportunities for moral development as Student A suggests that desire x is related to interest y in that the two result in greater school order (Stage 4)—and is met by Student B's question as to whether excessive stability doesn't discourage trying to develop more creative relationships between people (Stage 5).

After listening in order to determine at which judgmental level the students are generally operating, Kohlberg suggests that they be exposed to "moral conflict situations for which [their present] principles have no ready solution."[141]   Additional conflict is introduced by teacher challenges and by involving participants in discussion and argument.[142]   As the process continues, the teacher (or in the case of older students, the group itself with minimal assistance) helps them work through the "ambiguity, contradiction and complexity" occasioned by their groping toward a higher judgmental stage at the same time they are still concerned with what the "laws, roles, and previous commitments [of earlier stages] require [them] to do."[143]   Thus stimulated and guided, the students may intuitively grasp the nature of the next higher step and begin to reorganize their experience accordingly.[144]   In this connection it is interesting to note that Kilpatrick maintained that for the best growth

> . . . the young must get the idea of the next advance. To bring an idea to conscious awareness is usually an essential prerequisite to getting it accepted as a principle of behavior. And to get this conscious awareness two things seem necessary, a practical experience of the new principle and the naming of it.[145]

Finally, we must agree with Kohlberg that indoctrination is not involved in this process. He argues:

> Following Dewey and Piaget, I shall argue that the goal of moral education is the stimulation of the "natural" development of the individual child's own moral judgment and capacities, thus allowing him to use his own moral judgment to control

[140] The group factor, of course, provides an additional advantage in that only about fifty percent of any one individual's ideas are usually expressive of his major stage; the rest express the stage he has just left behind and the stage into which he is moving. Kohlberg, op. cit., p. 38.

[141] "Education for Justice," in Moral Education, intro. Sizer, p. 82.

[142] Ibid.

[143] Kohlberg with Whitten, "Understanding the Hidden Curriculum," p. 13. Quoted by permission.

[144] Kohlberg, "Education for Justice," in Moral Education, intro. Sizer, p. 82.

[145] Philosophy of Education, p. 368.

> *his behavior. The attractiveness of defining the goal of moral education as the stimulation of development rather than as the teaching of fixed rules stems from the fact that it involves aiding the child to take the next step in a direction towards which he is already tending, rather than imposing an alien pattern upon him.*[146]

Behavior is obviously a necessity. If knowledge is to result, educator and student-initiated discussions and cognitive-affective reorganization must result in action. And this must be action which the student personally feels is appropriate to the moral conflict situation and essential to his own purposes. (It will be remembered that for the pragmatist knowledge is *produced* by evaluated action; only hypotheses exist *prior* to action.) The student who is able to anticipate at least some of the major consequences of his contemplated action and is willing to accept them *must* be allowed to act, evaluate and generalize. There are, of course, two general category exceptions. One is found in those situations where the child's lack of experience with a given phenomenon does not enable him to foresee consequences, e.g., the toddler who has just "discovered" the hot stove. In these instances, the educator—be he parent, teacher or whoever—must view the experience as maleducative and (humanely) stop it—period. The second case is found in those situations where social conventions and/or laws prohibit the behavior. For instance, certain experiences simply *cannot* take place in the tenth grade biology classroom as a result of the "sex education" unit—foreseen consequences and agreement to live with them or not! In these instances, the educator must resort to "vicarious experiencing," e.g., a discussion of "what might happen if . . ." *Direct* experience will just have to await another day. These two categories notwithstanding, the predisposition of the pragmatist is to allow action whenever possible—this is really the basic point at issue.

There is little doubt, given our culture's pluralism and the fact that most of us are working with children and adolescents, that action will result not only in value conflict resolution but also in value dissonance. This point brings us to the vital role which the teacher occupies in contextualist moral education. Neither society's agent for ensuring internalization of its moral codes nor a mere catalytic agent, she does have superior and more extensive experience than her students in analyzing conflict situations. Furthermore (hopefully), she will be operating at a higher level of moral judgment than the students, which entails her understanding of the characteristic problems and thought-action modes of the earlier stages. Hers is the role of stage-setter,

[146] "Stages of Moral Development as a Basis for Moral Education," in *Moral Education*, ed. Beck, p. 71.

guide and coordinator, but not that of the sole authority.[147]   Hers is
the role of helping students to work through value dissonance by
taking them back through the stages of decision-making and trying to
find out exactly where the trouble arose.[148]   And hers is the role of
helping students to add needed resource for moral decision-making
from home, church and other educative institutions.   Hopefully, she
will inspire their greatest efforts and highest thinking in pointing out
the moral possibilities in all aspects of the school's life.   Hopefully, she
will help them distinguish between questions of morality where men
may properly differ and conformity to a minimal set of democratically-
derived behavioral guidelines.   Here, we maintain, the very survival of
the institution demands behavioral conformity, although they certainly
should learn how to change these guidelines in a democratic manner.
As Thomas notes, such an approach

> *requires a teacher of broad knowledge, great versatility, deep
> understanding of children, and much capacity for coöperative
> planning.   The task of selecting and preparing such teachers
> should be neither underestimated nor ignored.*[149]

One final question remains: How can such a moral education program
possibly be carried on within a school which has other educative
responsibilities?   Surely the contextualist is not suggesting that we
cease teaching multiplication facts, the correct and graceful use of the
English language or the skills of football!   Kilpatrick suggests a twofold answer that is not without appeal:

> *First, the character stressed . . . as the aim of education is
> the intelligent character, one able to think adequately before it
> decides to act.   Thus to think intelligently the individual must
> have a wide range of effective knowledge, and this the school
> must help him get.*[150]

However, Kilpatrick maintains, we must distinguish between knowledge as resources for problem-solving and knowledge for its own sake.
Knowledge of the first type is entirely consistent with the goals of

[147] Thomas, "The Meaning of 'Progress' in Progressive Education," p. 398.
Quoted by permission.

[148] Although not altogether consistent with the contextualist position, the forty-first
yearbook of the NCCS provides most interesting chapters on the objectives of value
analysis, teaching strategies and procedures for value analysis, and resolving value
conflicts.   See Lawrence Metcalf, ed., *Values Education: Rationale, Strategies, and
Procedures,* 41st Yearbook (Washington, D.C.: National Council for the Social
Studies, 1971).

[149] "The Meaning of 'Progress' in Progressive Education," p. 399.   Quoted by
permission.

[150] *Philosophy of Education,* pp. 368–369.

moral education. Thus school time and energy involved in its pursuit fulfills a dual purpose and is not caught between conflicting demands. He writes:

> *The new school wishes* as much knowledge as possible *of the sort to help life go on better, to make life more meaningful, to deal with life more intelligently. The new way intends accordingly to have knowledge learned on the basis of its present functioning in the life of the learner. It believes that knowledge is easier and better learned this way and is far more likely to be used, and that knowledge better learned and used in life furnishes the best basis for further learning.*[151]

In looking back over the last two chapters, one senses that something considerably more momentous than "character development" is involved in questions of value theory and moral education. Indeed, we are really talking about the very survival of the species and the quality of life it will enjoy *even if* it survives. Some commentators argue that the former concern is basic. For example, Skinner writes, "Survival is the only value according to which a culture is eventually to be judged, and any practice that furthers survival has survival value by definition."[152]

Each of the axiological positions considered in this section of *Philosophy and Schooling* has dealt with the question of survival, at least by implication. However, each has argued that we must also attend to the quality of life which will accompany survival if our efforts are to be deemed worthwhile. One stance finds morality in seeking and conforming to the permanent values. Given such guides, we best ensure both survival and the Good Life. The second challenges us to take a chance on the individual man, to foster his authenticity and have faith that creativity sufficient both to survival and life-quality will flow from such a strategy—if, indeed, either is possible. The third suggests that we teach a process by which man's moral decisions and commitments can be continually reconstructed as experience confronts him with change, and identifies morality with involvement in this process. All three stress that a worthwhile survival is possible but that the outcome depends, at least in part, on man's actions.

For better or worse, each educator must make his choice from among alternative possibilities viable in our culture. The hour grows late for twentieth century man. We face the challenges of an increasingly urbanized and organized civilization, as well as those challenges

[151] *Ibid.*, p. 369.

[152] B. F. Skinner, *Beyond Freedom and Dignity* (New York: Alfred A. Knopf, 1971), p. 136.

posed by a "knowledge explosion" which has put tools in our hands frightening both in number and in power. We face challenges arising from internal pressures generated by a pluralism gone sour, and external pressures from a world which no longer must acknowledge American sovereignty. And we face the challenges posed by the crying need to develop individuality in a mass society.

Where do you stand—and what do you intend to do about value education?

Suggestions for Further Reading

The Nature and Basic Problems of Axiology

FRANKENA, WILLIAM K., *Ethics.* Foundations of Philosophy Series. Englewood Cliffs, N.J.: Prentice-Hall, Inc., 1963.

FRONDIZI, RISIERI, *What Is Value? An Introduction to Axiology.* Trans.
Solomon Lipp. Lasalle, Ill.: Open Court, 1963.

MOTHERSHEAD, JOHN L., JR., *Ethics: Modern Conceptions of the Principles
of Right.* New York: Holt, Rinehart and Winston, 1955.

*Axiological Assumptions and Their Expression in
American Educational Policy and Practices*

BOWER, WILLIAM C., *Moral and Spiritual Values in Education.* Lexington:
University of Kentucky Press, 1952. Chapters VI, VII, VIII and IX–
XIV.

BROUDY, HARRY S., *Building a Philosophy of Education.* 2nd ed. Englewood Cliffs, N.J.: Prentice-Hall, Inc., 1961. Chapter II and Part II.

CHILDS, JOHN L., *Education and Morals: An Experimentalist Philosophy of
Education.* New York: Appleton-Century-Crofts, Inc., 1950.

DEWEY, JOHN, *Democracy and Education: An Introduction to the Philosophy of Education.* New York: The Macmillan Company, 1916. Paperback ed.; New York: The Free Press, 1966. Chapters III, VIII, XVIII
and XXVI.

——, *Experience and Nature.* 2nd ed. Chicago: Open Court Publishing Co., 1926. Paperback ed.; New York: Dover Publications, Inc.,
1958.

——, *Human Nature and Conduct: An Introduction to Social Psychology.* New York: Henry Holt and Company, 1922. Part III, Sections
6 and 9.

——, *Moral Principles in Education.* New York: The Wisdom Library,
A Division of Philosophical Library, 1959.

——, *The Quest for Certainty: A Study of the Relation of Knowledge
and Action.* New York: Minton, Balch & Co., 1929. Paperback ed.;
New York: G. P. Putnam's Sons, 1960. Chapter X.

——, *Theory of Valuation.* International Encyclopaedia of Unified Science, Vol. II, "Foundations of the Unity of Science," No. 4. Chicago:
University of Chicago Press, 1939.

DEWEY, JOHN, and JAMES H. TUFTS, *Ethics*. Rev. ed. New York: Henry Holt and Company, 1932. The first edition of 1908 is also well worth considering.

FLETCHER, JOSEPH, *Moral Responsibility: Situation Ethics at Work*. Philadelphia: The Westminster Press, 1967. An interesting account by a Christian contextualist.

————, *Situation Ethics: The New Morality*. Philadelphia: The Westminster Press, 1966.

FRANKEL, VICTOR E., *The Doctor and the Soul: An Introduction to Logotherapy*. Trans. Richard and Clara Winston. New York: Alfred A. Knopf, 1955. An account of a Christian existentialist.

FROMM, ERICH, *Man for Himself: An Inquiry into the Psychology of Ethics*. New York: Rinehart and Company, Inc., 1947.

GREENE, MAXINE, *Teacher as Stranger: Educational Philosophy for the Modern Age*. Belmont, Calif.: Wadsworth Publishing Company, Inc., 1973. Chapters VIII, IX and X; oriented toward Existentialism but contains extremely fair treatments of pragmatic and analytic approaches.

HANDY, ROLLO, *The Measurement of Values: Behavioral Science and Philosophical Approaches*. St. Louis: Warren H. Green, Inc., 1970. Advanced but most useful summary of measurement techniques appropriate to different conceptions of value.

————, *Value Theory and the Behavioral Sciences*. Springfield, Ill.: Charles C. Thomas, Publisher, 1969.

HÖRMANN, KARL, *An Introduction to Moral Philosophy*. Trans. Edward Quinn. Westminster, Md.: The Newman Press, 1961. A Roman Catholic approach.

HORNE, HERMAN H., *The Democratic Philosophy of Education: Companion to Dewey's Democracy and Education, Exposition and Comment*. New York: The Macmillan Company, 1932. Comparison of idealistic and pragmatic views.

KILPATRICK, WILLIAM H., *Philosophy of Education*. New York: The Macmillan Company, 1951. Chapters VIII, XI, XII and XXV.

MADDEN, WARD, *Religious Values in Education*. New York: Harper & Brothers Publishers, 1951. Chapters V and VII; pragmatic approach.

METCALF, LAWRENCE C., ed., *Value Education: Rationale, Strategies, and Procedures*. 41st Yearbook. Washington, D.C.: National Council for the Social Studies, 1971.

PERRY, RALPH BARTON, *General Theory of Value: Its Meanings and Basic Principles Construed in Terms of Interest*. New York: Longmans, Green and Company, 1926. Subjectivist approach of a neorealist.

PETERS, R. S., *Ethics and Education*. Keystones of Education Series. Glenview, Ill.: Scott, Foresman and Company, 1967. An analytic approach.

PHENIX, PHILIP H., *Education and the Common Good: A Moral Philosophy of the Curriculum*. New York: Harper & Brothers, Publishers, 1961. Chapter I (contrasting pragmatic and realistic positions).

PIAGET, JEAN, *The Moral Judgment of the Child*. Trans. Marjorie Gabain. Glencoe, Ill.: Free Press, 1948.

RATHS, LOUIS E., MERRILL HARMIN and SIDNEY B. SIMON, *Values and Teaching: Working with Values in the Classroom*. Columbus, Ohio: Charles E. Merrill Publishing Co., 1966. A classic subjectivist view of values and education with excellent examples.

ROGERS, CARL R., *Client-Centered Therapy: Its Current Practice, Implications, and Theory*. Boston: Houghton Mifflin Company, 1951. Practices suggestive for education; representative of nontheistic Existentialism.

————, *Freedom to Learn*. Columbus, Ohio: Charles E. Merrill Publishing Company, 1969.

San Jose State College Associates in Philosophy, *In Quest of Value: Readings in Philosophy and Personal Values*. San Francisco: Chandler Publishing Company, n.d. Selection of articles dealing with value questions and science, Naturalism, Pragmatism, Marxism, Existentialism, Freud, Neo-Thomism, ethical relativity, linguistic analysis and Liberalism.

SMITH, B. OTHANEL, WILLIAM O. STANLEY and J. HARLEN SHORES, *Fundamentals of Curriculum Development*. Rev. ed. New York: Harcourt, Brace & World, Inc., 1957. Chapters IV and VI–XIII (values and the curriculum).

SMITH, PHILIP G., *Philosophy of Education: Introductory Studies*. New York: Harper & Row, 1965. Chapter VII.

THOMAS, LAWRENCE G., "The Meaning of 'Progress' in Progressive Education," *Educational Administration and Supervision*, XXXII, No. 7 (October 1946), pp. 385–400.

————, "Prospects of Scientific Research into Values," *Educational Theory*, VI, No. 4 (October 1956), pp. 193–205.

VANDERVELDT, JAMES H., and ROBERT P. ODENWALD, *Psychiatry and Catholicism*. New York: McGraw-Hill Book Company, Inc., 1952.

For an excellent working bibliography of other readings on Axiology and the relationship between Axiology and the nature and aims of education, curriculum, school organization and policy, and teaching-learning, see HARRY S. BROUDY et al., eds., *Philosophy of Education: An Organization of Topics and Selected Sources*. Urbana: University of Illinois Press, 1967. This bibliography was supplemented in 1969 (Christiana M. Smith and Harry S. Broudy, eds.) and 1971 (Ronald P. Jeffrey, ed.).

PART *V*

Social Philosophy, Ideologies and American Education

8

Social Philosophy and Ideologies: Nature, Function, Concepts and Assumptions

For the moment imagine that you are the most vital educator in our society: a parent. Your idealistic teenager has just turned to you at the dinner table and exclaimed that 1) there can be no social justice until the black man has a fair chance to obtain all cultural benefits, and 2) in our town a necessary first step consists of breaking up segregated schools through extensive busing. You are convinced that the State exists to secure justice and order. As far as you are concerned, justice means being free to do the work for which you are best suited, receiving rewards commensurate with your work and being spared constant interference from others—especially the State. Social injustice, which involves receiving undeserved rewards, leads only to irresponsibility and lessened effort. Respond to your teenager.

Respond to your teenager once again. This time, however, assume that you honestly believe that justice refers to an act, idea or process which increases the power of a human being to take part in creating and enjoying a society in which he can truly be an individual. This power demands that inequalities be corrected and the conditions which produced them be eliminated. One can't pretend that the individual whose potential has been stifled for generations can take such a human role. Fitting people for cooperative social planning, implementation and evaluation, then, need not lead to irresponsibility, but to increased effort, greater responsibility and a richer and more secure society.

You have just accepted the chairmanship of a large high school English department. Although you haven't particularly noticed much change in people (at least for the better!) over your fifteen years of teaching, you do retain some faith that limited social progress is possible under certain conditions. One basic condition is that individuals must have an opportunity to define and compete for their personal goals as long as the competition doesn't become excessive and interfere with the rights of others. True, the successful must develop restraint and remember that they have some responsibility to those less able. At the first departmental meeting the five tenth-grade English teachers ask how much coordination is to be required between the teaching of their sections during the coming year. Please respond.

The high school is the same, and the chairmanship has still been accepted. This time, however, you are convinced that the key to progress lies in a cooperative definition, planning, implementation and evaluation of common goals. Responsible change based upon deliberation and discussion, the harmonization of interests through the development of a more common frame of reference, common use of the scientific method and expert resources, and the generation of new rights and responsibilities, offers us the best chance to grow both as a group and individually. Respond to your colleagues under these conditions.

These problems lead us directly into a consideration of social philosophy and its relevance to educational policy and practice.

A.   Social Philosophy: Nature and Function

We have seen that general philosophy may properly be defined by pointing to its *activities* (speculating, synthesizing, prescribing and analyzing), to its *content* (subsumed under the headings of Metaphysics, Epistemology and Axiology) and to its basic attitudes. Social philosophy draws upon the activities and related attitudes of general philosophy, but its content centers on the variables of man's associative living.[1] The content of social philosophy, then, includes studies dealing with concepts such as the nature and function of the state, the relationship between the individual and society, the nature of freedom, the nature of justice and equality, the nature of community and the

---

[1] Parallel points could be made with regard to the "Philosophy *of* History," "Philosophy *of* Religion" or "Philosophy *of* Science."

nature and possibility of social progress. The social philosopher is deeply concerned with questions of the origin, structure and purposes of the State; the competency of the common man; the duties, responsibilities and selection of leaders and followers; and the nature and relationship of law, authority, rights and responsibilities. He studies the meaning and limitations of freedom within a social order, relationships between justice, equality and freedom; the operational definition of equality (that is, are we to understand equality to involve "identical" or "differentiated" treatment of men?); the meaning of true community or fraternity and the means of bringing it about; and the problems, possibilities and means of achieving social progress.

In considering these and related questions, the social philosopher soon encounters a phenomenon with which heretofore we have not had to deal—at least not explicitly: the *ideological* explanation. Nettler suggests that the common theme of ideological explanations is their "group-supported patterning of beliefs of inadequate empirical warrant, where such beliefs are energizing, in attack or defense of values, and comprehensive"[2] [italics removed]. Note these criteria: group-supported and comprehensive, inadequate empirical basis and used to motivate. Thus far it seems that the basic purpose of philosophical synthesis, speculation and analysis has been *understanding*, rather than *motivating* adherents to go out and "win the world" to "the cause." True, norm development and prescription are facets of what we mean by philosophy. It is also true that understanding in the world as we know it involves developing comprehensive syntheses of fact and belief. Nevertheless, the emphasis on group acceptance, faith and zeal which characterizes ideological thinking goes well beyond that evidenced in general philosophy or the application of philosophy to the clarification of other human pursuits. Given the fact, however, that the social philosopher must deal with ideological thinking in his search for an understanding of social processes and institutions, let us turn briefly to a more adequate treatment of its nature and function.

Contemporary interpretations of ideology are heavily encrusted with earlier meanings. The eighteenth century French followers of Condillac, for example, conceptualized ideology as a scientific substitute for metaphysics which would allow men to build a society of reason upon truths discovered by sensory observation and generalization. Napoleon, despairing of these French philosophers who opposed his imperialistic ambitions, contemptuously dismissed ideology as impractical and unrealistic—too "theoretical" for a "practical" world. Marx and Karl Mannheim accentuated the negative connotation of

[2] Gwynn Nettler, *Explanations* (New York: McGraw-Hill Book Company, 1970), p. 117.

the term by maintaining that ideological thinking is necessarily prejudiced-distorted (to the point of falsehood) by virtue of its genesis in given space-time contexts which "determine" its content.[3]

For the purposes of this text, we shall view ideological thinking in a somewhat broader context which includes the following points. Ideological thinking: 1) arises from man's efforts to understand and act in a highly complex social environment which he does not fully understand and which he only partially controls; 2) is drawn out of a specific cultural base and is deeply rooted over time in the basic desires, hopes, fears and contradictions of that base; 3) includes assertions which—on the basis of empirical demonstration—are variously true, doubtful, unproved or unprovable; 4) tends to be less interested in developing understanding on the basis of empirical demonstration than in a capacity to unite individuals and groups, offer satisfying explanations of social processes, articulate social ills and desiderata, justify actions and attitudes, and motivate enthusiasm and social action. (Statements *are* "ideological," Plamenatz maintains, on the basis of such capacity and not because they include doubtful, unproved or unprovable—as well as true—elements.);[4] and 5) tends to simplify complex social interactions, consciously or unconsciously select and use facts and beliefs to achieve its objective, and be most resistant to change.

Ideological thinking is not a phenomenon encountered by social philosophers alone. For instance, it permeates treatises on orthodox religion which show far less interest in the empirical justification of their tenets than a desire to unite men under religious symbols, explain the relationship of the Divine and natural orders, explicate natural failings and the remedies open to those who are strengthened by God's grace, inculcate and enforce approved actions and attitudes, and motivate enthusiasm and social action. Salvation is as common a goal of ideological thinking as it is of thinking labeled "religious."[5]

When ideological thinking and science are compared, it is probably necessary to make some distinction between the theory of science and its applications. In its theory, contemporary science surely strives far more rigorously than does an ideology for an understanding of the natural order on the basis of empirically demonstrable facts. Uniting men and groups, developing explanations resting on correlated fact and belief, and motivating enthusiasm and specific social action are

---

[3] See Karl Mannheim, *Ideology and Utopia*, trans. Louis Wirth and Edward Shils (London: Routledge & Kegan Paul Ltd., 1936), pp. 62–67.

[4] John Plamenatz, *Ideology* (New York: Praeger Publishers, Inc., 1970), p. 31.

[5] Naturally, these comments are offered in a descriptive and not a derogatory sense. The fact that religion makes use of ideological explanations does not speak either to religion's truth or its falsity—unless one accepts the notion of ideology as "impractical" or "false," which this author tends to view as "open questions."

generally beyond the pale. Nor, though both are public, does science appear to be as given to the tendency to select and simplify facts, the use of language to arouse emotions or the solicitation of public acceptance as is ideology. In its application and popularization, on the other hand, the scientist has been known to slip into ideological thinking. Skinner, for example, writes,

> The free inner man who is held responsible for the behavior of the external biological organism is only a pre-scientific substitute for the kinds of causes which are discovered in the course of a scientific analysis.[6]

Empirically demonstrated fact or hypothesis? Is its purpose understanding or a call to the colors? Turning to another example, Professor Goff writes,

> The continuing task of education, then, is the encouragement of social emancipation, the restoration from morbidity of thought which yields to bigotry, and the advancement of liberalism as decreed by law that has as its sustaining ground the Constitution of our country.[7]

Again we may ask: Empirically demonstrated fact or hypothesis? Does its purpose lie primarily in understanding or in a call to the colors? Many more examples can be marshalled to suggest that the tendency to use (carefully selected) facts in order to arouse emotion and commitment does not appear to be completely foreign to "scientific" writing.[8]

It is, nevertheless, in examinations of social processes and institutions that we see ideological thinking reach its fullest expression and power. Such thinking has spawned many an "ideology," which—like the " 'schools' of philosophy"—represents groupings of individuals who hold reasonably consistent assumptions concerning the concepts of social philosophy. In America today, we observe the battle between Conservatism and Liberalism for the hearts—and votes—of men. We hear echoes of Marxism and Neo-Fascism. Sargent suggests we ought to look at the ideologies of "The New Left" and "Anarchism."[9] Given

[6] B. F. Skinner, Science and Human Behavior (New York: The Free Press, 1953), p. 447.

[7] Regina M. Goff, "Culture and Personality Development of Minority Peoples," Negro Education in America, Sixteenth Yearbook of the John Dewey Society, ed. Virgil A. Clift et al. (New York: Harper & Row, Publishers, Inc., 1962), p. 150.

[8] Excellent examples will be found in Nettler, Explanations, pp. 182–183 and 189–190.

[9] Lyman T. Sargent, Contemporary Political Ideologies (Homewood, Ill.: The Dorsey Press, 1969), pp. 149–157 and 159–178.

the limitations of time and space, our study will concentrate on the assumptions and educational significance of American Conservatism and Liberalism. We shall be examining the degree to which each exemplifies ideological thinking. In addition we shall be asking how *effective* these two movements are as ideologies. Do they promote a feeling of belonging, participation and a sense of personal involvement in social processes and institutions, a feeling that ways can be found to realize desired goals and a faith that members will gain success and opponents will meet defeat? Do they provide for leadership, a rallying point for people ready for self-sacrifice and a rationalization of social institutions and relationships between men and society? Finally, do they provide some experiential confirmation of their outlooks, goals and suggested means, and do their members receive adequate rewards for loyalty and service?[10] It is to these questions that we now turn.

B. Social Philosophical Concepts and Ideological Assumptions

1. The State and the General Welfare

A. STATE AND GENERAL WELFARE: THE LIMITED STATE. The contemporary American conservative sees the role of the State (normally understood as, though not restricted to, the federal government) to be quite limited, albeit not unimportant in the modern world. In negative terms, it tries to stay out of the way of individuals freely building their own good. As a function of this role, it referees the competition of individuals who in seeking their own interests sometimes threaten those of others. This is not to say that the State should markedly interfere with natural competition; even so, there are times when economic or political bullying must be checked so as to protect the minimal conditions for true competition. In more positive terms, the State provides a bulwark against external assault and internal disorder. It stands as a symbol of our national unity. The rights of the more talented among our citizens are recognized, rewarded and protected by government; the extremes of majority rule and social

[10] Other comments concerning the criteria of an effective ideology will be found in Hadley Cantril, *The Politics of Despair* (New York: Basic Books, Inc., 1958), Chapter IV; W. Y. Elliott, "Ideas and Ideologies," *Political Thought since World War II*, ed. W. J. Stankiewicz (New York: The Free Press of Glencoe, 1964), pp. 25–30; Gaetano Mosca, *The Ruling Class;* trans. H. D. Kahn; ed. and rev. with intro. by Arthur Livingston (New York: McGraw-Hill Book Co., Inc., 1939), Chapter VII; and Plamenatz, *Ideology*, pp. 143–144.

leveling are resisted. Opportunity for exercising individual freedom is enhanced as it protects the right to private property. We may also note that the State is expected to provide moral leadership in keeping alive a taste for our historic traditions, including,

> *the constitution—interpreted in a given manner— . . . private property, the free market, the protection of agriculture, the maintenance of national defense and the system of government, the idea that the United States is a Christian nation, and the maintenance of local autonomy and popular control over schools . . .*[11]

And, finally, in the most extreme cases the federal government may render limited humanitarian aid to those afflicted by natural and man-made disaster, be it tornado, flood or fire—unemployment, illness or (in our society) old age.

As for organization, the conservative supports the tripartite federal structure established by our Constitution, feeling that balanced, diffused and restricted power best reflects human nature and offers the greatest assurance that individuals may continue to enjoy both freedom and justice within order. In point of fact, for our people this form of government may well be the most acceptable, although other forms (e.g., monarchy or aristocracy) may also provide the desired balance of order, justice and freedom.[12] Although this structure stands as the chief agent of society, we must always remember that government "is something like fire. Under control, it is the most useful of servants; out of control, it is a ravaging tyrant."[13]

Several reasons come to mind when we ask why the role and structure of government are so defined. Kirk argues that "government is instituted to secure justice and order, through respect for legitimate authority; if you ask from government more than this [e.g., that it promote happiness], we begin to imperil justice and order."[14] The conservative also argues that the greatest amount of wealth is produced when the economy is under least restriction. The general welfare, then, is promoted when a limited government, actively insisting on little more than fair play, works in harmony with the natural instinct of individuals to seek their own good through their own

[11] Francis G. Wilson, "The Anatomy of Conservatives," *Political Thought since World War II*, ed. Stankiewicz, p. 344.

[12] Russell Kirk, "Prescription, Authority, and Ordered Freedom," *What Is Conservatism?*, ed. Frank S. Meyer (New York: Holt, Rinehart and Winston, 1964), pp. 36 and 39.

[13] Clinton Rossiter, *Conservatism in America* (New York: Alfred A. Knopf, Inc., 1955), p. 34.

[14] Kirk, "Prescription, Authority, and Ordered Freedom," *What Is Conservatism?*, ed. Meyer, p. 33.

efforts. An astute observer of twentieth century America—though not a conservative—John Dewey caught the sense of this contention when he wrote:

> *The earlier economic individualism had a definite creed and function. It sought to release from legal restrictions man's wants and his efforts to satisfy those wants. It is believed that such emancipation would stimulate latent energy into action, would automatically assign individual ability to work for which it was suited, would cause it to perform that work under stimulus of the advantage to be gained, and would secure for capacity and enterprise the reward and position to which they were entitled. At the same time, individual energy and savings would be serving the needs of others, and thus promoting the general welfare and effecting a general harmony of interests.*[15]

B. STATE AND GENERAL WELFARE: THE ACTIVE STATE.   Liberalism, writes Ramsay Muir, involves

> *a readiness to use the power of the State for the purpose of creating the conditions within which individual energy can thrive, of preventing all abuses of power, of affording to every citizen the means of acquiring mastery of his own capabilities, and of establishing a real equality of opportunity for all. These aims are compatible with a very active policy of social reorganization, involving a great enlargement of the function of the State.*[16]

David Spitz underscores the notion that "the liberal plea for collective or state action is not a call for totalitarianism but a call for individual freedom. . . . The concern of the liberal is not with collectivism but with individuality, the development of personality, to which collective action is but a means. In the modern world it is a necessary means."[17]

These two quotations suggest that the American conservative and the American liberal differ not so much as to their goal of producing stable productive individuals as they do concerning the proper means thereto. (This easy generalization, however, should not obscure the possibility that markedly different means may give rise to quite different products!) For the conservative, the means are primarily individualistic; for the liberal, the social conditions of twentieth century America demand the active intervention of man's creation, the State, so

[15] John Dewey, *Individualism Old and New* (Capricorn Books ed.; New York: Minton, Balch and Company, 1930), pp. 76–77.

[16] Ramsay Muir, "Liberalism," *Chamber's Encyclopedia*, 1923–1927 ed.; quoted in Rossiter, *Conservatism in America*, p. 59.

[17] David Spitz, "A Liberal Perspective on Liberalism and Conservatism," *Left, Right and Center*, ed. Robert A. Goldwin (Chicago: Rand McNally & Company, 1965), p. 24.

as to secure the necessary conditions under which individualism can take root and flourish. Deeply engrained selfish habits and concentrations of economic and political power are all too common in our society. Institutional defects today exist which are well beyond the power of any individual to correct. Such conditions necessitate collective social action if individual development is not to be restricted, warped or made impossible. The liberal, therefore, is confronted by the problem of how the action of the State can be planned and executed so as to facilitate the fullest individualism.

The liberal believes that social action so designed must arise out of cooperative policy planning, implementation and evaluation on the part of as great a proportion of the citizenry as possible. The citizens' powers in this process are not restricted merely to the more passive role of advising elected leaders, consenting to their proposals or at stated intervals passing upon the adequacy of their leadership. Rather, through wide and continuing involvement in every facet of problems touching upon their interests, theirs is the responsibility to take an active and intelligent role in policy matters. In a complex society it is through this involvement or participation that we consciously create additional shared interests. Consequently we create additional opportunities for individuals to develop their potential, as well as the sense of security and tolerance requisite to the expression of human differences. Sayers and Madden point out that social action so conceived creates offices and roles to facilitate cooperative activity. It creates organizations and procedures to ensure the expression of varied interests concerning questions for which a group solution is necessary. Laws are viewed as necessary social instruments for facilitating cooperative activity based on shared goals.[18] The purpose of social organization, then, is not to restrict human activity but to provide the means by which individuals together can set their goals and be about reaching them. Social institutions and processes are evaluated on the basis of how well they foster such activity.

On the basis of these considerations, the liberal believes that a conscious effort to seek the general welfare is prerequisite to the development of full individuality. No human being, he concludes, can possibly develop his unique potential when fellow citizens are plagued by fear, poverty, ignorance and other social ills. These poisons subtly permeate the whole society. The opportunity and the means to define and develop one's own individuality is surely a by-product of cooperative efforts to eradicate such ills and to create a society in which open intelligent interaction supports the distinctive development of each of its citizens.

[18] *Cf.* Ephraim Vern Sayers and Ward Madden, *Education and the Democratic Faith* (New York: Appleton-Century-Crofts, Inc., 1959), pp. 79–82.

2. Individual and Society

A. INDIVIDUAL AND SOCIETY: THE INDIVIDUAL WITHIN TRADITION.

> The Conservative realizes . . . that man's development, in both
> its spiritual and material aspects, is not something that can be
> directed by outside forces. Every man, for his individual good
> and for the good of his society, is responsible for his own development.
> The choices that govern his life are choices that he
> must make; they cannot be made by any other human being, or
> collectively of human beings.[19]

The author of this statement, Senator Goldwater of Arizona, goes on to
define politics "as the art of achieving the maximum amount of freedom
that is consistent with the maintenance of the social order."[20]
We see in these two quotations the basic problem which conservatives—of
various orientations—face in reconciling individual and society.
On the one hand, the goal is the development of the free,
independent, self-controlled individual. On the other, the conservative
is necessarily concerned with social order. In the world-as-it-is, it
is order built on tradition and authority that controls for defects in
both human nature and environment, that promotes justice and that
makes it possible for each individual to use his freedom in developing
his potential without undue interference from others. Freedom and
order, then, are mutually dependent concepts. Without freedom, man
is but a slave; without order, the exercise of freedom is futile.

Given this view, it is not impossible to understand why the conservative
has little confidence in man unguided by tested authority and
tradition. Reinforcing this lack of confidence is the fact that contemporary
American Conservatism is normally given either to the
assumption that human nature is "inherently evil" (or predisposed to
evil) or "inherently superior or inferior."[21] In either case, natural
inclinations must be checked in both the individual's interests and
those of his follow citizens. A good example is found in his inclination
to seize and expand power. As the English Roman Catholic Lord
Acton wrote in protesting the growing power of the Papacy, "Power
tends to corrupt, and absolute power corrupts absolutely."[22] Educa-

---

[19] Barry M. Goldwater, *The Conscience of a Conservative* (A MacFadden Capitol
Hill Book; New York: MacFadden-Bartell Corporation, 1961), p. 12.

[20] *Ibid.*, p. 13.

[21] An extended discussion of these two assumptions and educational policies and
practices consistent with them will be found in Chapters 2 and 3.

[22] John E. E. Dalberg-Acton, *Essays on Freedom and Power* (Glencoe, Ill.: The
Free Press, 1949), p. 364.

tion, motivation, restraint and reward are necessary best to ready man—especially the common man—for self-government, but they will never perfect either the individual or the social institutions he creates. His spiritual and intellectual defects—not to speak of his insurmountable limitations with regard to knowledge and control of the natural world—render senseless such utopian hopes.

As in any productive reconciliation of individual and society, there must be leadership. Even in the case of inherently evil human nature—and more so in the case of a society containing a limited number of those with "superior" natures—there exist individuals who are blessed with a clearer view of the public interest and a greater natural ability to understand the necessities of authority and tradition. In business and in other social pursuits they have competed, and in winning have proved their capacity for leadership. Denied opportunity to exercise this capacity and gain further rewards (by a society which does not understand either the limitations of man or the road to progress), they will naturally react with bitterness. Both their fellow citizens and society generally will suffer irreparable loss. Perforce they must not confuse their freedom with license. They, like all men, must observe each individual's inalienable human rights. Theirs, however, is a special responsibility to preserve tradition and human order, to offer moral leadership which will inspire men to pursue their own interests individually and in voluntary association with their fellows. They, like all men, must be restrained by our constitutional tradition of balanced, diffused and restricted power, as well as by the fear that their fellow citizens will revoke their influence and rewards if they transgress the bounds of lawful authority.

We see, then, individual and society reconciled through a general commitment to order, justice and freedom. Other than in cases where extreme cruelty or injustice force minimal control, natural stratifications and other distinctions between men are recognized and maintained. Social unrest is minimized by an appropriate division of authority, labor and rewards. Conditions are thus created in which each individual—be he follower or leader—can seek his own good through fair competition within the law and in so doing maintain and enhance the right of others to pursue their happiness within society.

B. INDIVIDUAL AND SOCIETY: THE INTERDEPENDENT SOCIETY. As suggested under the assumption of the "active state," the American liberal maintains that there is no necessary—or profitable—antagonism between the individual and the social whole. The development of a rich individuality requires social organization. Effective social organization requires the development of human beings who are more aware of their distinctive differences and more skilled in devoting their resources to the common (and, indirectly, their own) good.

Although some liberals hold to the assumption that human beings are by nature good, the great majority maintain a more restricted faith, that is, that man in cooperation with his fellows is capable of learning to construct the interdependent relationship of society and true individuality.[23]   To illustrate the dominant position, we turn to John Dewey, who writes:

> The foundation of democracy is faith in the capacities of human nature; faith in human intelligence and in the power of pooled and cooperative experience. It is not belief that these things are complete but that if given a show they will grow and be able to generate progressively the knowledge and wisdom needed to guide collective action.[24]

Unlike the conservative, the liberal does not believe that there are limitations to the development of such a human nature inextricably buried in the very constitution of man. Such limitations as do exist, he suggests, are explainable by reference to a multitude of factors, including physiological, psychological and environmental variables. For example, severe mental retardation, psychoses or cultural deprivation can and do limit development. In principle, however, even these maladies are susceptible to control and "cure." For one not so afflicted, increasing skill in the use of "creative intelligence" to develop individuality can (more easily) be learned through disciplined study, application and evaluation in a social setting.[25]

The importance of the social setting to the development of individuality is emphasized by Dewey. He admits that

> . . . it is true that social arrangements, laws, institutions are made for man, rather than that man is made for them; that they are means and agencies of human welfare and progress. But they are not means for obtaining something for individuals, not even happiness. They are means of creating individuals. Only in the physical sense of physical bodies that to the senses are separate is individuality an original datum. Individuality in a social and moral sense is something to be wrought out. It means

---

[23] An extended discussion of the assumptions of human nature as "inherently good" and as "constructed and evaluated transactionally," including possibilities for consistent educational policies and practices, will be found in Chapters 2 and 3.

[24] John Dewey, "Democracy and Educational Administration," an address before the National Education Association, Feb. 22, 1937; published in *School and Society*, April 3, 1937; reprinted in *Intelligence in the Modern World*, ed. Joseph Ratner (New York: Random House, 1939), p. 402.

[25] For an operational definition of "creative intelligence," see the discussion of "mind as purposeful, problem-solving behavior" in Chapter 4.

initiative, inventiveness, varied resourcefulness, assumption of responsibility in choice of belief and conduct. They are not gifts, but achievements.[26]

The details of a desirable social setting are set forth under the assumption of the "active state." To summarize and extend that discussion, cooperative participation and mutual responsibility for consequences provide the necessary means. Social instrumentalities (e.g., offices, roles, organizations, procedures and laws) are developed through these means in order to build personalities. Given the hypothesis that the achievement of one man's good depends upon the ability of all to function to the limit of their capacities, great attention is focussed on the common welfare. Artificial hierarchies based on "custom, tradition, prejudice, superstition, and other nonrational sources, such as race, color, ancestry, property (particularly landed and inherited property) and religion"[27] are generally eroded when they are found to limit maximal human functioning. In deciding such matters, tradition is a resource, but—being based on only a sample of past human experiencing—it can never tell us what we should do in a new, specific context of time, place and people. Final authority for social decisions is placed in the cooperative disciplined inquiry of the citizenry. The obvious desideratum is a strong stable society which is—at one and the same time—based on, and productive of, opportunity for all its members constantly to expand and express their abilities.

When temporary and related to the fulfillment of cooperatively planned goals, there is clearly a place for leadership in a setting where individual and society are interdependent. William Heard Kilpatrick suggests that democratic leadership can and does take many forms. Nearly every citizen can assume some leadership role in promoting a cooperative problem-solution. True, the role assumed will differ from topic to topic and from person to person. There is, for example, the leadership based on the interest and concern of an individual that something be done to solve a problem. This type of leadership may enthuse others and lead to other leadership possibilities. If the problem is sufficiently complex and popular sentiment for a solution is developed, men who have wide practical experience in solving problems of the workaday world (e.g., a local business leader or politician) may be induced to become involved in the effort. Their administrative ability and their sensitivity to what can and what cannot be "sold" to the general public will be of great value. They also have access to a third type of leader, the man of expertise or specialized knowledge,

[26] John Dewey, *Reconstruction in Philosophy.* Enlarged ed. (Boston: The Beacon Press, 1948), p. 194.

[27] *Cf.* James Burnham, *Suicide of the West* (New York: The John Day Company, 1964), pp. 129–130.

and can lend needed support to securing his involvement.[28]   However vigorous, leadership so understood is clearly designed to facilitate a more productive participation on the part of the followers.   It does not exist to gain and protect power, but to give power to the people.   Its rewards lie in seeing people grow—seeing one's followers themselves being delegated authority when their expertise develops and is recognized as needed by the group.   As with all human behavior, its skills and its appeal are learned.   The principle of "one man, one vote" and the open evaluation by the citizenry of the leader's effectiveness in promoting its participation provide safeguards against other patterns of leadership all too available in our culture.

Given cooperative efforts toward such goals, the liberal remains confident that the necessary interdependence of individual and society can be achieved to the profit of all concerned.

3. Freedom

A. FREEDOM: FREEDOM WITHOUT LICENSE.   "In the *moral* realm," writes Meyer, "freedom is only a means whereby men can pursue their proper end, which is virtue . . . in the political realm freedom is the primary end."[29]   We may follow Senator Goldwater's lead in suggesting that a more balanced expression of the conservative position calls for modifying the Meyer statement as follows: ". . . in the *political* realm 'the maximal amount of freedom that is consistent with the maintenance of social order'[30] is the primary end."   Be this as it may, the demand that political activity maximize opportunity for freedom is clearly a basic conservative tenet.

"Freedom" in conservative thinking refers *both* to the absence of restrictions or undue "meddling" *and* to the opportunity to fulfill one's own personality, to pursue virtue and the like.   Both positive and negative elements in this meaning are qualified by the notion that the right to express one's freedom must not interfere with similar rights of others.   Although not "granted" by society, it may be protected and extended by the State (as the chief agent of society) through maximizing opportunities for its expression.   It does this by fulfilling its proper functions which are outlined under the conservative assumption of "the limited state."   It may be helpful at this point to emphasize the

[28] *Cf.* William Heard Kilpatrick, *Education and the Social Crisis* (New York: Liveright Publishing Corporation, 1932), pp. 33–36.

[29] Frank S. Meyer, "Freedom, Tradition, Conservatism," *What Is Conservatism?*, p. 15.

[30] Goldwater, *The Conscience of a Conservative*, p. 13.

especially important role of the State in increasing freedom through protecting property rights. Rossiter goes so far as to suggest that:

> *Property makes it possible for a man to be free. True independ-*
> *ence can never be enjoyed by one who must rely on other per-*
> *sons or agencies—especially government—for food, shelter, and*
> *material comforts. Property gives him a place on which to*
> *stand and make free choices; it grants him a sphere in which he*
> *may ignore the state.*[31]

In conclusion, we may ask why freedom should be protected and extended in these ways. The conservative's answer is twofold: Given man's nature, the necessity of order within both man and State and the power-potential of modern government, *either* a more active approach *or* a more laissez-faire approach on the part of the State would undoubtedly fail. Either individual freedom would be stamped out by a centralized power complex brooking no rivals, or it would cease to exist under conditions of chaos. Secondly, the very importance of freedom justifies expending the effort and running the risks of defining and implementing the (difficult) middle course between the dual errors of activism and permissiveness. Sutton sketches freedom's central importance to man's associative life, writing,

> *The virtue of freedom is that individuals acting on their own*
> *initiative to further their own interests, act with efficiency, en-*
> *ergy, determination, and spontaneity to a degree that is never*
> *present under any other social arrangement.*[32]

B. FREEDOM: FREEDOM AS POWER. Given his strong belief in an active state and the correlative relationship of individual and society, it is not surprising that the American liberal rejects any understanding of freedom which focusses on the "right" to be left alone. On the contrary, freedom refers to the *power* of citizens cooperatively to design and build a society which fosters the development of the richest, most varied kinds of personalities. It refers to their opportunity to enjoy the results of their efforts in as many different ways as there are individuals. Freedom, then, is as significant for the development of society as for the development of the individual. Sayers and Madden explicate this distinction:

> *Freedom conceived as outside a social system exists positively in*
> *the degree that social organization is lacking, and decreases in*

[31] Rossiter, *Conservatism in America*, pp. 38–39.

[32] Francis X. Sutton *et al.*, *The American Business Creed* (Cambridge, Mass.: Harvard University Press, 1956), p. 169.

> *amount as social organization develops. The [liberal] concept of freedom, on the contrary, holds it to be a function of effective social organization. Freedom conceived in this latter way is a social result. Instead of a pre-existent absolute right, which is man's either by natural or by divine endowment, freedom becomes in this view, a [power] that men must achieve by means of special modes of association.*[33]

These "special modes of association" are just those to which the liberal refers when he proposes organizing society on the basis of cooperative participation and mutual responsibility for the consequences. Rather than attributing freedom to the individual isolated in a mass technological society, these interactive modes provide for the motivation, the secure structure and the skills needed by man if he is creatively to express his unique differences within society.

Critical participation or involvement—call it what you will—is clearly the basic component in achieving freedom as power. The individual who "opts out" of rational social involvement in cooperation with his fellow citizens *cannot be free.* If anything dismays the liberal contemplating the contemporary social scene (and much does!), it is the cry of many Americans in their late teens and twenties: "Hey, man, I just want to be left alone to do my own thing." Sayers and Madden put the case bluntly:

> *People must possess an ethical willingness and patience continuously to inquire into, to examine, and re-examine, their differences, and to reconstruct their beliefs and purposes. Only thus can there be achieved the continuing "community" of outlook or "consensus" and the perfecting of co-operation that are essential to democratic freedom.*[34]

Freedom so conceived does involve more than desire, more than patience and willingness. The individual must learn the difficult skills of critical thinking[35] and learn how to use them in working through problems in cooperation with others. In this setting man can develop more knowledge of different ways to achieve, greater knowledge of the probable consequences of reaching and a more dependable knowledge of what he really wants as his goals. The limits of such freedom are found not in a negativistic refusal to interfere with the same rights for others, but in the responsibility we bear for our influence on others.

---

[33] *Education and the Democratic Faith*, p. 59.

[34] *Ibid.*, p. 63.

[35] See the discussion of "mind as purposeful, problem-solving behavior" in Chapter 4.

4. Justice and Equality

A. JUSTICE AND EQUALITY: JUST REWARDS. Justice, the conservative maintains, demands that "every man be free to do the work for which he is best suited, and that he receives the rewards which that work deserves, and that no one meddle with him."[36] Such a definition of "justice" clearly depends upon a proper understanding of "equality." Man *is* equal in an ultimate moral sense. His moral equity entails his being treated only as an end and never merely as a means. It confers upon him the right to develop his talents up to the very limits of his potential. It gives him the right to identical treatment before the law. Finally, it gives him a right to a voice in electing his potential representatives and to expect that the polity will protect him from tyranny. In all other senses, however, men are demonstrably unequal. "Social organization is complex and always includes a variety of classes, orders, and groups. Differentiation, hierarchy, and leadership are the inevitable characteristics of any civil society."[37]

The crux of social injustice lies in treating identically men whose labors merit differential treatment. Nobility is sacrificed to mediocrity; the leaders are frustrated and withdraw into boredom; the common man, lacking necessary leadership, sees a deterioration in the quality of his civilization and in his material wellbeing.[38] Lacking external motivation, he quickly finds it easier to look to the source of undeserved rewards for his sustenance rather than to his own efforts. Bitterness and discord follow; new inequalities rise weedlike out of the ashes of those temporarily vanquished by compulsive social engineering.

It must be reiterated that Conservatism is well aware that gross injustice can result from vigorous competition for individual goods. Such injustice must surely be controlled in the interests of freedom. What disturbs the conservative is the liberal's mania for attempting to level all social differences. He has little taste for such exercises in egalitarianism. If he evidences caution in deciding that a given situation involves injustice, it is because he lives in a society where social planners are compulsively scrutinizing everything from education to tax structure in an attempt to destroy the natural aristocracy upon which depends the common good.

True equality depends upon educating the common man to the

---

[36] Russell Kirk, *A Program for Conservatives*. Rev. ed. (Chicago: Henry Regnery Company, 1962), p. 168.

[37] Samuel P. Huntington, "Conservatism as an Ideology," *Political Thought since World War II*, ed. Stankiewicz, p. 358.

[38] Kirk, "Prescription, Authority, and Ordered Freedom," p. 34.

principles of justice and to the details of his natural endowment, removing the obstacles to individual effort, and then allowing him to decide for which rewards he will strive. Leaders, in like measure, must be educated into the ideal of service and be subjected to periodic elections. Legislation must ensure that the economically strong do not dominate or exploit their fellow citizens.[39] Responsibility coupled with rights, affirms the conservative, represents the clear road to justice and equality.

B. JUSTICE AND EQUALITY: EGALITARIANISM. In the thinking of contemporary American Liberalism, justice is the quality of an act, idea or process which increases the power of human beings to create and enjoy a society which facilitates individuality. So defined, justice is necessarily closely interrelated with liberal assumptions concerning equality and freedom. As we have seen, social diseases such as poverty and ignorance spread epidemiclike throughout a society and markedly reduce the opportunity of *all* citizens to realize their social and personal goals.

Justice demands that we work to correct inequalities and eliminate the conditions which produced them. The liberal acceptance of this responsibility is exemplified in the 1944 "State of the Union" message in which President Franklin D. Roosevelt declared:

> *We cannot be content, no matter how high the general standard of living may be, if some fraction of our people—whether it be one-third or one-fifth or one-tenth—is ill-fed, ill-clothed, ill-housed, and insecure.*[40]

Observable inequalities there are. In housing, in schooling, in employment, as in nearly every other area of our associative life, countless numbers of people have fallen victim to decades of having been given the "same" opportunity to succeed as . . . the son of a millionaire or a college professor. Full blame cannot be placed on the ill-fed black child of the ghetto who profits little from lessons designed for suburban middle-class white children. Full blame cannot be placed on the slum dweller who fails to break the long-standing cycle of poverty, crime and despair. Full blame cannot be placed on the 23-year-old unskilled automobile worker who, overcome with the meaninglessness of his work and the near hopelessness of ever leaving the production line, responds with frustration, aggression and lessened social concern.

[39] Herbert Hoover, *American Individualism* (Garden City, N.Y.: Doubleday, Page & Company, 1923), pp. 42–43 and 51–56.

[40] Cited in Eugene J. McCarthy, *A Liberal Answer to the Conservative Challenge* (A MacFadden Capitol Hill Book; New York: MacFadden-Bartell Corporation, 1964), p. 40.

It is absolutely farcical to pretend that we achieve "equal" opportunity by lining up both Olympic gold medal winner and the untutored citizen at the starting line of a race and then treating them "identically." In truth, we thus ensure that most citizens will be prevented from making their potential contribution to the building of a new society and a true individuality. Such pretense is neither in our own interest nor in the interests of our brothers. Rather, justice demands that we work with them to cure their sickness, aid in their recovery and facilitate their need contribution to our common tasks. The result will be an increase, not a decrease, in opportunity and power for all. The result will be richer visions of the society to be built, inasmuch as new voices will be included in the definition of common purposes and means.

The cure of physical illness demands added concern, added resources and added effort. It may, for example, call for special diets not needed by the healthy. In educational terms, we must work with the socially sick to determine what is needed to allow them to resume growing or—more difficult after decades or centuries of neglect—to *begin* to grow. "Head Start" programs, federally funded work-skill-development programs, new suburban public housing and—yes—even the "busing of little school children" may well be needed.

It must be noted that the purpose of all this effort is *not* the molding of Americans into robots who differ only in their serial numbers. Personality development will always be affected by environmental micro-climates, let alone genetic factors which may or may not be controlled in the future. Furthermore, democracy does not require or even desire *identical* contributions from its citizens. It does demand that individuals have a real opportunity to define, develop and provide their unique contributions to the common good and, hence, to their own good. Competition is sick when it destroys such opportunity by treating men like horses in that all but those who "win, place and show" are seen as "losers." It even goes beyond sickness when it holds them in perpetual bondage. Better, the liberal says, to restrict competition to seeing who can make the most distinctive contribution to societal betterment. Better that social worth be defined along a multitude of scales than be attributed only to those who win the races of intelligence, power and wealth. When variety is itself seen as potentially valuable and differences which give rise to creative contributions are rewarded, we provide the conditions for developing an increased desire for even more self-expression and growth.

Can we really claim that healing our brothers and helping them to develop that power-freedom needed to play their role in creating a richer society will work to the disadvantage of the healthy? Can we really claim that leaders with *more* opportunities to serve will find *fewer* rewards? Can we really claim that societal stability will be lessened by involving all citizens actively in achieving common social purposes, including those who are now relegated to the periphery of society? In each case the liberal answers in the negative, contending that freedom can be increased and justice served only in an egalitarian society.

5. Community

A. COMMUNITY: VOLUNTARY ASSOCIATION. The conservative views "community" as a complex of voluntary associations (e.g., family, church, union, professional organization, school and town) in which man can develop a needed sense of belonging, security and opportunity to further his interests in the complex impersonal world of the late twentieth century. The realization of such a community does depend, it is true, upon the balanced presence of order, justice and freedom. Its goals are not automatically realized upon the mere desiring, nor can social legislation secure their full expression. Furthermore, such a community cannot be realized by subordinating the individual to a theoretical "common good." On the contrary, it must realize that the general welfare will be promoted only by recognizing the right of individuals to join freely with others of similar interests in order to create wider opportunities for reaching their own goals.

The potential benefit of such association are many. For example, matters of the heart—including a heightened desire for peace, sensitivity to human misery and the courage to be different, that is, to express one's unique individuality—can surely be developed only under such conditions. To think that such attitudes can be legislated is (at best) futile. The basis is also laid for rehumanizing our mass society by restoring dignity and function to the common man. Finally, in the voluntary association of true community we see the strongest bulwark against the encroachments of collectivism, foreign and domestic. The free man working in harmony with his brothers whom he personally knows as human beings can do far more to resist such evils than ever was achieved by a centralized bureaucracy. Insulated from the wellsprings of human emotion and action, the centralized State must view such voluntary associations as rivals, act to stamp them out and hence open the culture to a decay which numbers its days as surely as those of a tree deprived of its roots. On balance, such decay is far more difficult to combat, far more deadly to the health of the community, than are the occasional selfish excesses of individuals.[41]

---

[41] *Cf.* Kirk, *A Program for Conservatives,* pp. 156–161.

B. COMMUNITY: DYNAMIC ASSOCIATION. Focussing on several related questions may help us to understand the meaning of "community" which stands as a keystone of contemporary Liberalism. First noting what the liberal means by "society," we shall look at the relationship between society and a sense of "community" or "fraternity." Finally, we shall inquire into how this sense is developed, as well as how it is maintained in a world of change.

The liberal notion of society is indebted to studies by many investigators in disciplines which range from anthropology through philosophy, political science and psychology, to sociology. Representative is the following definition offered by Professor John Dewey:

> Society is of course but the relations of individuals to one another in this form and that. And all relations are interactions, not fixed molds. The particular interactions that compose a human society include the give-and-take of participation, of a sharing that increases, that expands and deepens, the capacity and significance of the interacting factors.[42]

Dewey points out, however, that "no amount of aggregate collective action of itself constitutes a community," that a sense of community or fraternity develops only when the possibilities of cooperative action "are perceived and become an object of desire and effort," that learning to be human involves developing over time through "the give-and-take of communication an effective sense of being an individually distinctive member of a community; one who understands and appreciates its beliefs, desires and methods and who contributes to a [continuing] conversion of organic powers into human resources and values."[43]

Several conditions beyond the mere fact of associative living are thus necessary for the *achievement* of a sense of community. Each human being, for example, must have a differentiated opportunity[44] to share in determining the conditions and goals of his own labors. Furthermore, the society—especially the pluralistic society—must foster the most open communication and vigorously protect dissent. Only under these conditions can individuals feel sufficiently secure publicly to identify their interests and cooperate with others of different persuasions to develop some consensus with regard to shared goals

[42] Dewey, *Individualism Old and New*, p. 85.

[43] John Dewey, "Communication and Communal Living," *Intelligence in the Modern World*, pp. 387 and 389.

[44] Equal in the sense of "differentiated" is being contrasted with equal in the sense of "identical." As we have seen, differentiated treatment may be necessary to give two individuals a truly equal chance to contribute their best to a common task, especially if the conditions of the two were markedly unequal prior to their entering upon the task at hand. Marked inequality, the liberal maintains, militates against unique, creative contributions.

and the means necessary to reach them.[45]   Finally, the liberal maintains that the individual must become committed to the absolute necessity of evaluating his "beliefs, desires and methods" in terms of their efficacy in promoting the kind of society which frees human potential for continuing growth.   When necessary, this commitment must afford the courage, patience and skills to reconstruct social consensus under changed conditions of time, place and people.   We may note that the liberal characteristically turns to "education in the 'method of intelligence'" as the process of developing and maintaining these conditions in a world of change.   We shall note the details of this process in the next chapter.

The liberal desideratum is a sense of brotherhood felt only by those of all classes, races and ability-levels who are committed to a society whose goals and processes they have had an indispensable part in shaping.   This commitment is to a society which provides opportunity for each of them to grow in uniqueness and power.   Theirs is an allegiance strengthened by the conscious awareness that the power and the instrumentalities needed to maintain such happy social conditions under conditions of change lie in their hands.   The liberal assumption that community depends necessarily upon a dynamic association of individuals questions whether brotherhood can ever be achieved under the more passive voluntary association favored by conservatives.   Does the mere fact of voluntary association for the purpose of making one's interests a social possibility create the bonds necessary for long-term allegiance on the part of many, very different peoples?   Doesn't the level of competition and suspicion required by conservatives even in this association militate against a development of consensus?   Does it create the conditions which facilitate gaining reasonable rewards for all members of such a social unit?   Does it create flexibility in time of stress and change?   The liberal faults the conservative notion of community on all of these grounds, doubting that necessary social bonds, rewards or flexibility can be created and maintained under such conditions.

6. Social Progress

A. SOCIAL PROGRESS: PROGRESS THROUGH "COMPETITIVE INDIVIDUALISM."[46]   The conservative refuses to take a Pollyanna attitude

---

[45] Contrast this with James Burnham's view that non-liberals may maintain that "unrestricted free speech in relation to political matters . . . expresses, like unrestricted academic freedom, the loosening social cohesion and the decay of standards, and condones the erosion of the social order," in *Suicide of the West*, p. 128.

[46] "Competitive individualism" is a term used frequently by Sayers and Madden in their text *Education and the Democratic Faith* as a substitute for "Conservatism"

toward the difficulties which militate against social progress in today's world. Twentieth century man has built up many a parasitic habit under decades of liberal encouragement. Inherently predisposed to evil (or in number predominately of an "inferior" nature), most human beings are ignorant—and, worse, their reasoning powers are limited. Man is lonely in the natural world, being a creature of both the natural and supernatural orders. He is also subject to the "fallout" of defective social institutions and a physical environment which at best is no more than neutral to his purposes.

In spite of such a painfully realistic appraisal of man's condition, the conservative still maintains that *some* optimism as to the possibility of social progress is justified—if certain conditions prevail. Man, for instance, must be allowed to define and compete for his own goals both individually and in voluntary association with his peers. The individual must be educated to the accumulated wisdom of the species as contained in tradition and law. Those who are successful in competition must not only be educated into habits of service to their fellow men but also restrained if they occasionally treat them with excessive brutality or indifference. As we have seen, leaders must be rewarded and rule by popular majorities; if any attempt to rule contrary to our Constitution, they must be opposed. In all, the possibility of social progress depends in large measure upon man being afforded this training and protection and then allowed either to run the race and win appropriate rewards or to give up and suffer the consequences which naturally come to the "also-ran."

Government, to be sure, has a role in facilitating this possibility. Excesses born of individual competition must be checked. Both hard-won truths and new conditions must be considered in directing inevitable change into constructive channels. The efforts of would-be utopian social engineers who would disrupt time-tested governmental structures and procedures and even lead us toward a surrender of national sovereignty to international bodies must be halted. Such efforts should be ignored when possible, and when necessary countered by mobilizing the disapproval of both leaders and followers. All in all, it is probably safer to tolerate *minor* injustices than to attempt to control *all* injustice by massive social manipulation. Given the human condition, such efforts are doomed to ultimate failure and generally lead only to different (and, often, greater) injustices, especially for our most worthwhile citizens. In matters of change, then, the role of government and individual alike is to take only measured

---

or (another common, if inaccurate, label) "Democratic Capitalism." When paired with "cooperative individualism" (their substitute for "Liberalism" or [the more accurate] "Democratic Socialism"), it does seem quite helpful in indicating important similarities as well as basic differences between these two American ideologies.

and well-considered steps which maintain a continuity with that tradition and law without which progress is impossible. After all, the conservative muses, this isn't the worst of all possible worlds. Indeed, with all of its shortcomings the United States has given great gifts to many other nations and to mankind as a whole. Our nation and mankind would be much the worse were social planners unleashed to spread decay within.

Human nature is *not* perfectible—at least in this life. Under optimal conditions, however, desirable human qualities such as patriotism, restraint, love of law and order, compassion, reverence for God and God's purposes for men, and that contentment which comes from being at peace with oneself and one's place in the cosmic scheme can surely be enhanced. In the hands of each individual citizen rests the only possible key to social progress.

B. SOCIAL PROGRESS: PROGRESS THROUGH "COOPERATIVE INDIVIDUALISM." In agreement with the conservative, the liberal does believe that social progress is possible, albeit difficult and tenuous under conditions of modern living. We have seen that he also agrees with the conservative as to the social goal being the development of full individuality. Our study has indicated, however, that American conservatives and liberals part company on the question of the necessary means to this end. The liberal clearly feels that Conservatism's preference for lightly-checked competition leads only to the development of levels of inequality and conditions of tension which actually lessen the opportunity and power necessary to achieve individuality. He does see how the betterment of all can ultimately rest on the exploitation of the many by the few. Searching for the means requisite to the development of individuality, he refuses to accept wider accessibility to the fruits of competition, e.g., electricity or "muscle cars," as a viable substitute for the possibilities opened by a deeper and more pervasive sense of community.

The liberal alternative is contained in the assumption of "cooperative individualism" in partnership with experimental science. Resting his proposals on a faith in the potential remediability of human difficulties through the systematic use of reason, the liberal calls for the clarification of human interests through deliberation and discussion. When faced with competing interests, he desires the cooperative participation of all concerned in building more common outlooks, purposes and plans of action, as a basis for common action. This more common base may often be difficult to achieve, especially in times of crisis or under conditions of deeply-seated interests. There will clearly be times when less than general consensus will be possible. At best, the situation may call for an agreement to co-exist coupled with defensive behavior on the part of contending individuals and groups. At worst, the democratic majority may have to act on the basis of compromise, excommunication and/or compulsion. However necessary these behaviors may be on a temporary basis, the goal is to keep the problem out in the open and return to a search for a wider consensus at the first possible moment.[47]

The liberal's assumption also demands that new human rights and responsibilities be defined and instituted and existing policies and procedures be reconstructed in the light of changing existential conditions. In all things the liberal would depend upon the resources of experimental science and scientists—limited only by the norms of a democratic society—to provide data and skills requisite for more careful inquiry, planning, implementation and evaluation. Benne and Muntyan suggest five democratic norms[48]: 1) "The engineering of change and the meeting of pressures on a group or organization toward change must be collaborative." So conceived, collaboration involves divergent interest groups who are equally convinced that their interests provide the necessary raw materials for change and that the common interest will incorporate the best interests of all concerned under existing conditions. Collaboration also necessitates reference to scientific resources and the skill of scientists who have expertise in the problem area. 2) "The engineering of change must be educational for the participants." Success in a particular instance should lead to heightened capacity for handling later demands. 3) "The engineering of change must be experimental." The true liberal eschews the "bandwagon" approach and insists on the most searching, experimental test of the efficacy of the proposed policy of practice. 4) "The engineering of change must be task-oriented, that is, controlled by the requirements of the problem confronted and its effective solution, rather than oriented to the maintenance or extension of the prestige or power of those who originate contributions." The goal is to secure the best solution and minimize the confounding influence of those who suggested it—be they leaders or followers, adults or children. 5) "The engineering of change must be [focussed on the general welfare], yet provide for the establishment of appropriate areas of privacy and for the development of persons as creative units of influence in our society."

Competition tends to be restricted to seeing who can make the most distinctive contributions to the general welfare, and to self-competition directed at developing new personal insights and skills conducive to

---

[47] Kenneth D. Benne and Bozidar Muntyan, *Human Relations in Curriculum Change* (New York: The Dryden Press, 1951), pp. 296–304. Also see R. Bruce Raup *et al., The Improvement of Practical Intelligence.* Rev. ed. (New York: Harper & Brothers, Publishers, 1950), p. 231.

[48] Benne and Muntyan, *Human Relations in Curriculum Change*, pp. 307–316.

the same end. In the final analysis, many liberals extend the logic of cooperation far beyond small-group or national concerns, hypothesizing that the building of a world community is both necessary and theoretically possible given similar dedication and processes. True, progress under normal conditions—at any social level—is slow. Progress so secured, however, has widespread support and increases the capacity of all citizens for achieving and maintaining the social conditions prerequisite to individuality in the future.

The ideal democratic character established through these processes has been described as "integrated," "socialized" and "objective."[49] It is integrated in that its sense of selfhood can exist in spite of the change which characterizes human experience. Such integration allows an individual to define and act on principles and yet be free to refine his beliefs when confronted by new demands. Such integration allows him to press his full being—including both his dreams and his knowledge of reality in a given context—into an expansion of human nature. It is socialized in that it fully realizes that individual and social whole are interdependent and yet distinguishable, that the tenuous, spiral-like balance and improvement of these two facets of existence is necessary to the improvement of either. Finally, the ideal democratic character is objective in that it rests firmly upon intersubjective processes that have demonstrated their worth in defining the ever-changing reality which is man out of the dynamic tension between that which he is and that which he may become.

Let us now turn to a consideration of how educational policies and practices might be influenced by these assumptions.

---

[49] See Raup *et al., The Improvement of Practical Intelligence,* pp. 254–265.

9

Ideological Assumptions and Educational Possibilities

As in previous sections dealing with relationships between metaphysical, epistemological and axiological assumptions and educational practice, it is admitted that ideological assumptions in themselves do not determine practice. According to this view, however, they do represent one of several variables necessarily considered in attempting to understand professional behavior. The foundation for this argument was developed in the first chapter.

In at least two ways, however, this chapter does differ from others which have suggested possibilities consistent with theory for professional decision-making. The first variation is introduced by the fact that Conservatism and Liberalism are more than formal ideologies which speak explicitly to the major questions of associative living in America. They are also more general frames of reference which under various labels and over the centuries have influenced the development of schools of philosophy, as well as many other cultural phenomena. For example, you have probably already realized that both philosophical Realism (with the possible exception of some voices in contemporary "Scientific Realism") and philosophical Idealism tend to be relatively "conservative" in orientation. The assumption of philosophical Pragmatism, on the other hand, are far more "liberal" in tone and intent.[50] Given this fact, we may properly correlate the assump-

---

[50] It is interesting to note that the extremely individualistic assumptions of Existentialism tend to be rejected at important points by both American conservatives and American liberals. Unlike advocates of the "New Left," who ideologically-

271

tions of these schools with the more formal ideological assumptions considered in the preceding chapter in order to suggest richer possibilities for decision-making.

The projected syntheses of conservative and liberal assumptions also prompt a minor change in organizational format. Heretofore, with the partial exception of Chapter 7, we have examined each assumption rather generally in terms of its possibilities for practice, noting when appropriate the effect of its interaction with other philosophical assumptions and nonphilosophical factors. Larger and more complex groupings of ideologically-related assumptions suggest that we may now be able more specifically to examine the groupings as to their potential resources for solving professional problems. Accordingly, our discussion will be organized into a consideration of potential ideological resources for dealing with problems of the curriculum and its organization; educational strategies, technology and materials; educational structure; educational administration; and education as a profession. In some sense, then, this chapter may be viewed as a summary of some of the practical possibilities which the author feels are suggested by philosophical theory.

A.   The Curriculum and Its Organization

1. Conservative Views on the Curriculum and Its Organization

American conservatives have traditionally looked upon the curriculum as a course of study based on the rich wisdom of the race, coherently related and logically ordered. The curriculum stresses that substantive content and those intellectual skills and values which are so vital to both individual and societal health as to be required of all students. Following (and extending) a thorough grounding in the "Three Rs," many conservatives have called for an emphasis on the so-called "generative subjects."[51]   Core studies in English, foreign languages,

---

speaking are probably best placed within but at the far left of Liberalism, existentialists often appear most given to the ideology of "Individualistic Anarchism." For an interesting discussion of the "New Left" and "Anarchism" as ideologies, see Sargent, *Contemporary Political Ideologies*, Chapters VII and VIII, especially pp. 171–175.

[51] *Cf.* Arthur E. Bestor, "Education for Intellectual Discipline," *Philosophies of Education*, ed. Philip H. Phenix (New York: John Wiley and Sons, 1961), pp. 36ff.

history, mathematics and science are especially valuable in that they discipline the mind and equip it with the intellectual skills and content prerequisite to solving contemporary problems efficiently and humanely. Furthermore, these subjects offer rich opportunities for inculcating the historic values of American culture; e.g., the idea of the limited State, individual rights and responsibilities, law and order, the idea of justice, constitutional government, private property, the free market and national defense. Their "usefulness" is not limited to an "intellectual elite"; rather, their importance lies in their demonstrated power to lead all students to the full meaning of humanness.

For those who have mastered both foundational skills and the common core as best they can given their abilities, there is room for well-designed and well-taught electives. Some conservatives would insist that these electives be restricted to the boundaries set by traditional liberal studies; others, in an attempt to ensure equality of opportunity, would allow students of lesser ability some prevocational electives. All stress the need for rigor in presentation and expectation.[52] The subject-matter of elective and core courses alike should be organized according to logical principles developed by specialists in the respective disciplines, sequenced in terms of scope and depth by discipline specialists working with specialists in human growth and development, and then presented to the child as efficiently as possible.

Finally, it must be noted that the primary task of the school is to discipline the mind of the young through transmitting the cultural heritage. That social change which is necessary and proper is possible only when it can be based on such knowledge, skills and attitudes. "For everything there is a season, and a time for every matter under heaven."[53] For the student, the school years are a time for learning—not for active involvement in social change for which a proper foundation has not yet been laid.

2. Liberal Views on the Curriculum and Its Organization

For the liberal the curriculum potentially includes *all* experiences under the jurisdiction of the school—ranging from playground activities through cooperative development of classroom behavior standards to more traditional studies in the arts and sciences. Emphasized are those experiences through which the impulsive behavior of the immature organism can be transformed into habit patterns adequate to

[52] *Cf.* Wingo, *The Philosophy of American Education,* pp. 85–87.
[53] Eccles. 3:1 (RSV).

construct and reconstruct the social means to personality development. A wide range of experiences has this potential; surely no one study is *inherently* more valuable than another. In specific terms, the value of any study lies in the increased problem-solving skill it engenders in the student. Generally speaking, of course, its value lies in the use to which it is put in "civilizing" the student, that is, increasing his ability to become a unique, productive human being in a social setting.

Obviously, skill and commitment to the processes of open, critical inquiry must be developed. Nevertheless, as a mill must have grist, so must mind[54] have content and skill resources available to bring to problem-solving. No less important to the liberal than to the conservative are learnings dealing with the child's cultural heritage and the basic skills of communication. Furthermore, the student must become knowledgeable with regard to the causes and cure of social illness, the purpose of social instrumentalities, the interdependence of the individual and the social whole, the nature of human potential and democratic norms for leadership. The goal, however, is functional decision-making power and that increased enjoyment of life which flows from such power. Such learning is not developed merely as a preparation for the future or for purposes of mental discipline. Indeed, traditional studies can lose their value when considered apart from the use to which they can be put in solving problems encountered by the student in his ongoing experience. Finally, we may observe that the constantly changing contexts within which human problems arise demand new data and new arrangements of data for problem solution. Of necessity, liberally-oriented curricula in responding to this phenomenon tend to be somewhat short-lived. Today, for instance, we may emphasize history and geography; tomorrow we may correlate history, geography, anthropology, economics, political science, psychology and sociology.

The liberal feels that a curriculum adequate to these goals must be ordered *psychologically* (with a view to the child's experience) rather than according to the "logical" structure posited by subject-matter specialists. Curriculum planners begin with the experiential base of children in a specified context, e.g., American middle class, urban-dwelling, nine-year-olds in 1975. They attempt to understand both the limitations and the potential of this experience and then to provide cognitive, affective and psychomotor experiences which increase the child's ability and commitment to solve new problems. Note that the initial pedagogical starting point for organizing the curriculum does lie in the experience which the child brings to the classroom. The

---

[54] The assumption of "mind as purposeful, problem-solving behavior," an assumption detailed in Chapter 4, is quite consistent with the liberal position.

study of an American history class which has just had a field trip to Valley Forge may be quite different from one which is formed of children living on a Navaho reservation. Nevertheless, the child must be helped to widen and synthesize his experience, for he must develop that knowledge and skill necessary to solving the problems of the adult world. There are at least two important points here: Firstly, the child is not simply presented with a pre-existent, pre-ordered curriculum. Rather, his experiences and the modes of learning appropriate to his developmental stage are considered in organizing school experiences. In the second place, the goal is not to "adjust" the child to pre-existent knowledge. Rather, school experiences are so designed as to result in transactions between the child and culture in which both are shaped. For example, note that the child is not led merely to understand and accept a definition of democracy laid down by the "Founding Fathers." Rather, experiences are designed to enable him to develop both a definition of democracy appropriate to his context of time, place and people, and a personal commitment to that definition. Rather than being confronted with ordered, synthesized adult knowledge, the child is gradually helped himself to order and synthesize knowledge as needed for solving problems he faces at each developmental stage.

The liberal feels that the school is necessarily involved in questions of social change—although, like the conservative, he questions whether it should become directly involved as a social institution in a specific program of change. True, the policy and procedural decisions it makes will greatly affect the student's view of such concepts as community, equality, freedom and justice. To be consistent with its ideological base, however, a mature Liberalism must treat its own assumptions concerning such concepts as just that—*assumptions* and not simply "common sense." Exposed to the competing assumptions of Conservatism and other ideologies, as well as those of the liberal, the student must through critical inquiry and in a social setting define and assert his own frame of reference. The liberally-oriented school cannot indoctrinate—even liberal assumptions! The liberal's commitment is to the betterment of our society and an increasingly meaningful definition of and allegiance to basic social concepts through critical inquiry—not to the indoctrination of any one set of definitions however palatable at a given time and place to a given set of liberals. The risks inherent in continually, democratically reconstructing experience are great—as is well known by anyone who has ever worked on a school committee. The liberal feels, however, that the risks inherent in attempting to freeze experience in terms of the meanings given it by any group are even greater.

B. Educational Strategies, Technologies and Materials

1. Conservative Views on Educational Strategies, Technology and Materials

The emphasis of conservatively-oriented teaching is clearly upon the mastery of those learnings which are essential to human well-being and social stability. Much compromise is possible when this basic claim is admitted. There are those conservatives, for instance, who emphasize the inherent order of subjects and insist that the child must approach essential learnings as they are structured by specialists within the various disciplines. History, then, is properly studied according to a chronological approach which rests heavily on reading and teacher presentation. Other conservatives, we may note, have argued that pedagogical order must be determined on the basis of how the child naturally learns. They have argued that modifications in a given subject's "logical order" must be effected on the basis of what developmental psychology tells us about the learning modes appropriate to different stages in human development.[55] In this case, there may be a far greater emphasis on sequencing the scope, depth and pacing of presentations and on "discovery" techniques, involving much discussion and inductive reasoning, than in the former approach. In *each* case, however, it will be noted that the emphasis is on mastering truths which existed *prior to* the learning experience. The discovery of new truths is not likely to occur before doctoral studies; in those rare cases where this does happen the truth was there to be discovered in the first place. Once again, the dispute does not center on *what* is to be taught but, rather, on *how* it may best be presented so as to secure the most complete adjustment of the child to pre-existent truth. Any and all specific materials or technological devices are so evaluated.

In all we hear a demand for rigorous standards of achievement and an insistence that promotion must be based on that achievement. We hear a call for making the child aware that schooling is a serious affair, that "study is hard work." There is a demand for individual competition, restrained only in clear cases of excessive zeal. Minor excesses are best ignored. Grades and other rewards for successful competition in things intellectual and moral, identify and reinforce talent—and remind the talented that effort must not cease. Assistance is given to

---

[55] For examples of the latter position, see Mortimer Adler, "The Order of Learning," *The Philosophy of Christian Education* (American Catholic Philosophical Association, Proceedings of the Western Division, 1941), pp. 119–122; and Jacques Maritain, *Education at the Crossroads* (New Haven: Yale University Press, 1943). Both works are cited in Sayers and Madden, *Education and the Democratic Faith*, pp. 386–387.

the less able, but such aid is strictly limited to that which will help them help themselves. On occasion, voluntary grouping (e.g., committees) is permitted in the classroom. "Group-think," however, is restricted by differentially rewarding the efforts of individuals within the group according to their objective worth.

As we see, the teacher retains basic control over classroom activities, looking in turn to the supervisor and the principal for her guidance. Hers is the primary motivational responsibility. Hers is the job of providing a moral example. Hers is the task of balancing individual rights and responsibilities within tradition and order. To her falls the sometimes difficult chore of resisting the liberal biases of so many professional educators and publishers which permeate the materials and strategies offered for classroom use.

2. Liberal Views on Educational Strategies, Technology and Materials

Of central importance to the liberal educator is the arrangement of a school environment wherein the habits of critical inquiry—along with potentially useful content and skill resources—can be learned through cooperative planning, problem-solving, evaluation and generalization. Every strategy, technological device or set of materials used by the educator is directed to these goals. To put it another way, every social instrumentality is directed to securing increased opportunity, equality, justice and freedom.

As one might suppose, a problem-solving format is widely supported by pedagogical liberals. Problematic situations are probably most useful when they arise naturally out of the ongoing activity or experience of the students. Nevertheless, the skilled teacher may sometimes create such situations herself. Beyond their use as motivational devices, for instance, the bulletin board displays, the tables covered with interesting project possibilities or the field trip which greets students on the first day of a unit can be viewed as creating problems for them to define and solve. Naturally, these problems must be appropriate to the children's developmental level and background. They must be challenging without being frustrating; the resources for their solution must be either available or securable. Once defined by the entire class or a work committee, the problem must be examined by the group in order to ascertain whether necessary learning habits and other resources are indeed in hand. Alternatives, at the border of the student's immediate experiences, may be introduced by the teacher. When necessary the group may have to be assisted to develop new goals and/or needed means.

It must also be emphasized that the evaluation and generalization stages of the problem-solving process are every bit as important as those which precede them, i.e., definition, hypothesis-construction and choice, and action. In short, the activity has to take the child beyond mere "doing" or reaching a solution that momentarily "works." Inquiry habits must be strengthened, refined or reconstructed. As a result of the activity taken as a *whole,* the child must be more able than he was at its inception to organize and synthesize his content and skill knowledge, more able to explicate and move toward his ideals. The proximate desideratum, of course, is a solution based upon group consensus regarding the nature of the problem and the means to its solution. As we have seen, temporary but necessary retreat into compromise, excommunication or compulsion must be balanced by a protection of minority positions and efforts to restore a cooperative setting. A longer-term view suggests that the desiderata must also include increased student power in developing group frames of reference and a heightened sense of community based on more shared interests and means.

The liberally-oriented teacher has a wealth of resources available for implementing this format. Naturally, traditional content and learning skills provide necessary resources. Democratic norms and leadership skills are also important. In addition, however, the resources of the entire school and nonschool communities are available to the knowledgeable and committed teacher. For an example, we might turn to a unit on "Afro-American history and culture" taught to sixth graders some years ago in a school where both the black population and the tension-level were fast increasing. The entire community was involved. The principal, informed of the unit's purposes, suggested many program possibilities. The (black) school librarian provided a wealth of books—of various reading levels—for classroom use. The (white) district supervisor personally conducted a fascinating art lesson. A doctoral student in a nearby university—the author—supplemented committee work on black history. Another graduate student appeared in his national garb and talked with the students about modern Africa. Delightful native folk dances and songs were incorporated into the physical education and music programs. Scrapbooks provided opportunities for exercises in the language arts. The point should now be clear: no one subject, no one strategy or set of materials, is inherently valuable. The widest range of resources is useful in promoting problem-solving based on but extending and relating student experience. The use of such resources to unite school and community is one significant by-product.

Technological devices present something of a problem to the liberal. On the one hand, in many subjects they do provide excellent opportunities for added useful drill which simply cannot be provided by an overburdened classroom teacher. On the other hand, contemporary programmed books and machines appear to be dedicated in the main to teaching a pre-existent body of facts and interpretations with greater efficiency than otherwise would be possible. Remedial tracks are commonly provided only when the student makes an "error." You are correct if you suspect that a simple ingestion of facts is not going to be accepted by many liberals as synonymous with learning. Rarely in real-life problem-solving is one presented with an answer sheet in which one answer is right, one is pretty close and the other three are clearly incorrect. On the contrary, three (or more) answers may be correct at any given stage of the solution process. The answer chosen determines the additional problems to be faced by the student as he moves closer to problem-resolution. There is no real reason—other than the temporary ascendency of more conservative and traditional assumptions in American culture and, hence, in American education—why machines, especially computers, could not be programmed to give small groups of students more realistic experiences in problem-solving. The task—an exciting one indeed—still lies before us.

The question of evaluation is more straightforward for the liberal, particularly as to differential rewards. School rewards (e.g., grades, certificates and other signs of approval) are based on their hypothesized power to increase the ability and motivation of the student to strive for social and individual goals. This means that the student's background must be taken into account, that no mechanical "system" is appropriate to reward-giving. By way of an example, let us imagine a twenty-five point range of individual starting points in a class (represented by a scale ranging from point five to point thirty). The curriculum guide desires all students to be at point thirty-five by the end of the term. One student progresses from point seven to point twenty-one; another, from point twenty-eight to point thirty-two. Which student receives the higher grade? Consistent with his theory, the liberal could argue in terms of both relative power increase and motivational effect that the student who reached point twenty-one should receive the higher grade. (How different this would be from many schools where administrative policy absolutely forbids assigning any grade above "C" to a child in a "basic skills" section!) Furthermore, he could find it completely reasonable to ensure that the child who started at point seven was given opportunity for—and was motivated toward using—supplementary assistance.

It is possible that the preceding discussion obscures (at least) one significant point. It would seem quite consistent for a liberal to prefer downgrading most interpersonal competition, including competition for grades. Instead, he would emphasize the creation of a cooperative environment in which students could safely share their knowledge rather than jealously guarding it out of fear that sharing would result in being assigned a lower position on the grade curve come the test. Vital interest in solving a problem of real personal interest and competition directed to making the most significant contribution possible to solving the problem (rather than in outshining one's colleagues) would provide basic motivation and minimize disciplinary problems. Pass-fail grading fits neatly into such a system. The point of the preceding discussion, then, was more to suggest a way for the liberal to coexist with an entrenched grade system than to outline the situation most amenable to his ideology.

In all of this, the teacher stands as the epitome of the democratic leader who possesses specialized knowledge and expertise in helping students to express, widen and synthesize their experience. The teacher is not valueless—not without standards—nor does she believe that the child should dominate the classroom any more than she should. On the contrary, she is dedicated to creating (and maintaining) a cooperative, democratic environment in which knowledge is developed and in which the expression of each member's interests—including her own—lead to a heightened sense of community.

C. Educational Structure

1. Conservative Views on Educational Structure

Given their curricular and instructional biases, it does not seem strange that the structural concerns of pedagogical conservatives are directed jointly to protecting (and extending) talent and to ensuring effective cultural transmission. Several strategies seem consistent with the theory we have been considering. For instance, the notion of authority-sequenced learning experiences suggests a preference for the familiar traditional grade progression. Departmentalization can increase with the growing knowledge of the child. Naturally, acceleration is possible for those who demonstrate talent, although the mastery requirement prevents any "automatic pass" based on nonacademic factors such as age or "effort." A judicious use of tracking and homogeneous ability grouping facilitate that competition upon which progress depends. As noted earlier, voluntary grouping in conservatively-oriented classrooms is not out of the question, but the accent remains upon individual achievement. In turn, this emphasis suggests that the physical classroom itself be organized so as to inhibit mutual student interference and to facilitate transmission. The focus is upon the teacher who is there to teach. The arrangement of desks and other classroom equipment—as well as the design of the school plant itself—reflects this focus.

Having said all this, we must remember that there are conservatives who take a more positive view of psychological findings concerning child development. For these conservatives, individual differences and sequential learning modes may call for a nongraded structure (especially in the earlier school years). Provisions may well be made for considerable teacher-student and student-student interaction of a less tightly-structured, less deductive variety. In this variation as in the former, however, ability must be extended through rewarding achievement. The essentials of culture must be transmitted, however different the path to their understanding. The structural goal remains the provision of conditions under which they may be most efficiently learned.

In terms of Conservatism and structure, mention should also be made of the potential of a strong private school system. Select college-preparatory schools offer exciting opportunities to train especially promising leaders. Both independent and church-related schools provide competitive alternatives to the public school—and to the benefit of both. Albeit slowly, many conservatives appear to be moving toward the conclusion that their potential importance to our overall educational system necessitates increased financial assistance. Given our constitutional separation of church and state, this development promises to be of great interest in the last quarter of the twentieth century.

2. Liberal Views on Educational Structure

In seeking to operationalize his ideological theory, the liberal has historically placed heavy emphasis on questions of educational structure or organization. Questions of both "vertical" structure and "horizontal" structure have received attention.[56]

---

[56] The terms "vertical" and "horizontal" are defined by John Goodlad and Kenneth Rehage in "Unscrambling the Vocabulary of School Organization," *National Education Association Journal*, LI, No. 8 (November 1962), p. 34. Quoted by permission of the NEA and John I. Goodlad.

> Schools are organized to serve specific functions. They must classify students and move them upward from a point of admission to a point of departure. *Vertical* organization serves this function. Schools must also divide the student body among available teachers. *Horizontal* organization serves this second function.

"Nongraded" or "ungraded" programs are receiving considerable attention from contemporary liberals, especially in view of the needs of children just entering upon formal schooling.[57] True, the growth patterns of all living organisms are uneven—but this is especially so in the earliest years. With just cause, many black parents have railed against a system which ability-types their children as early as the second grade and then places them into lower-tracked groups in such vital subjects as reading. With just cause, they have argued that the handicaps their children bring to school render indefensible such early decisions and that in many cases they comprise a barely concealed expression of racial prejudice. With just cause, they have argued that their children's handicaps and the attitude of many teachers toward teaching such sections make it far easier to get in than to get out, and that five or six years of such "instruction" leads to nothing more than the development of functional illiterates and potential dropouts. Today we are hearing an argument—which cuts across racial, ethnic and socioeconomic lines—that school structure must be adapted to uneven physical, emotional and intellectual growth patterns, especially when this unevenness is reinforced by cultural factors. We are hearing the argument that the early school years—at the very least— must provide an environment less dominated by the pressure of constant grade hurdles. The nongraded plan, which commonly groups children earlier assigned to grades 1, 2 and 3, provides one answer. Stressed are opportunities for: 1) self-competition (rather than interpersonal competition), 2) variable progress in different subjects (rather than an emphasis on grade standards which may result in a child's nonpromotion due to inadequate learning in merely one subject area), 3) increased emotional health (rather than feelings of pressure or boredom with preset curricula), 4) speaking to individual human differences (rather than treating children as statistics), 5) flexibility in grouping, especially under conditions of team-teaching (rather than the more limited and inflexible grouping patterns open to the single teacher who must deal with an entire class) and 6) greater cooperative activity among the faculty (rather than the isolation encouraged by

---

Confusion arises from a failure to differentiate between vertical and horizontal aspects of school organization. Grading, multigrading and nongrading are the vertical organization plans from which to choose. The horizontal pattern may be determined by grouping children homogeneously or heterogeneously, by organizing the curriculum so as to emphasize the separateness of subjects or the interrelationships among them, by having self-contained or departmentalized classrooms, or by using any one of many possible patterns of interclass grouping.

[57] Non- or ungraded programs are not, of course, particularly recent developments in American education, even though they are of contemporary import. A succinct history of these programs will be found in Hillson, *Change and Innovation in Elementary School Organization,* pp. 294–295.

departmentalization or being assigned to one group for each and every day of the school year).[58] The possibility remains that such a program—freed of a gross overemphasis on achieving subject-matter competency—would be preferable in terms of both content-skill learning and emotional and physical development well beyond the early school years.

In terms of horizontal structure, several options appear to be consistent with liberal theory. Already mentioned has been the notion of combining a nongraded format with team-teaching. In a time of fast-increasing knowledge and pressures upon the school to increase class size, this combination might fulfill one of the most important goals posed by earlier progressives for the self-contained classroom:[59] the correlation rather than the compartmentalization of subject matter. In those situations where conditions force a more traditional organizational plan, liberals have expressed the strongest preference for maintaining heterogeneous grouping.[60] There has been a gradual retreat from calling for blanket heterogeneous grouping. Today, even in the most liberally-oriented schools, students in science, mathematics and language arts are commonly grouped homogeneously. Support remains, however, for preserving at least some heterogeneous grouping, perhaps within the social studies (where citizenship education demands contact with all social strata), homeroom or the expressive arts. In all, the liberal has strongly supported working with children in small groups (e.g., committees) in an effort both to develop richer problem-solutions and to facilitate the growth of community.

The physical organization of the school reflects the liberal's goals and favored means. Classrooms assign space to committee tables and permit easy contact with fellow students and staff. Shelves and cases are provided to house the extensive store of resource materials and equipment needed for learning. Lounges for staff and students provide opportunities for informal contact and learning. The buildings themselves are likely to contain movable walls which permit quick rearrangements of space for varied cooperative activities.

If the public school ever realized its full potential, many liberals might well allow the natural (i.e., nonlegislated) death of private schools. In truth, we need the interaction of all our people if a viable society is to be maintained and strengthened. Until that day, how-

---

[58] *Ibid.*, pp. 295–296.

[59] The self-contained classroom is one in which the teacher works with the same group of students in most subjects and for the entire school day. Occasionally—less frequently earlier in the century—the teacher receives some assistance from specialists in subjects such as the fine arts and physical education.

[60] Heterogeneous grouping is to be contrasted with homogeneous grouping, in which an effort is made to group children of more similar "ability," "achievement," "interests" or the like.

ever, most liberals may continue to call for supporting and maintaining independent and church-related schools as a buffer against public school failures, as an arena in which experimentation may be carried out more easily than is allowed by bureaucratic controls of the public system and as a creative source of ideas different from those reinforced within the "system."

As a final structural note, we must remember that the liberal is firmly committed to the school as an instrument of justice and equality for all. Gross inequalities between students of different economic, ethnic, racial or religious backgrounds are seen as potentially dangerous to the general welfare and, hence, to self-development. The complicated, miserably difficult problems of division suggest to many liberals that the traditional neighborhood school may have to go if quality education for all is ever to be realized. The notion of area or citywide "educational parks" to which children may, when necessary, be bused offers one option which must be considered carefully in the decades ahead.

D. Educational Administration

1. Conservative Views on Educational Administration

Historically, American conservatives have supported local control of the schools as a buffer against the potential power of a centralized, bureaucratic State. Over the years, however—especially with the development of the superintendency—a natural administrative hierarchy has developed. While opposing the growing and impersonal influence of the federal government and at times even that of a (state) department of public instruction, conservatives have called for a strong role for local administrative specialists. True, this role is limited by the conservative's belief in individual rights and his necessary concern for the widest possible public support. After all, citizens must pass on bond issues and teachers and students can mount wasteful protest activities. In fact, superintendents, supervisors and principals have long evidenced suspicion of those who would interfere with their control over the running of daily school affairs. Tension between administrators on the one hand and community figures, parents, teachers and students on the other seems to be quite common.

The administrator, in the conservative view, is clearly more than a "facilitator." Indeed, his is the special responsibility to control for defects in his subordinates.   Program decisions have to be made; once made, their classroom implementation has to be monitored.   Individual effort must be inspired throughout the system under the administrator's jurisdiction.   His is the direct responsibility for examining the character of those who would teach and the achievement of those who are teaching.   He also has the strongest responsibility for ensuring that policy decisions—necessarily involving the input of those outside the local area and/or lacking professional training—reflect professional knowledge and commitment.

Teachers clearly have a right to an identical opportunity to demonstrate their skill.   Because of their specialized training, that school system is probably best served which also permits them to make "recommendations" concerning professional problems of concern to the entire academic community.   Furthermore, they surely have a right to be evaluated only by knowledgeable peers and supervisors.   (What teacher, possibly having several years experience, should be forced to have his work evaluated by an immature eighteen-year-old?   What teacher should be forced to submit himself to the *publication* of such "evaluations"?   In like measure, however, what administrator should be forced to submit to *teacher* evaluations?)   The responsible administrator will ensure these rights, even though he properly insists that the implementation of policy and the control of necessary resources remain in his hands.   Actually, the conscientious teacher whose proper rights are protected will have little desire to interfere with administrative prerogatives.   He has more than enough to do as it is!

Student behavior is subject to a no-nonsense approach by administrators and teachers alike.   Students are in school to build that foundation of knowledge, skills and values which is prerequisite to responsible social change.   It is ridiculous to maintain that they have the "right" to interfere with those given the task of promoting their success.   As a result, certain adult rights (e.g., the full legal protection of "due process") are properly closed to them until maturity and knowledge can guide brute instinct.   It must be underlined that the conservative is not calling for an unfeeling, authoritarian or inhumane rejection of *proper* student rights, e.g., the right to be well-counseled, well-taught and properly disciplined.   The student clearly must be taught, for instance, how limited government works.   Many conservatives, however, would insist that a role-playing model—similar perhaps to the American Legion-sponsored Boys' or Girls' State—represents the most reasonable solution.   No few educational conservatives look upon the liberal-inspired student government model with distrust and/or disdain.   In the end, they feel, it must either manipulate the student or pit him against teacher and administrator.

2. Liberal Views on Educational Administration

The liberal views of educational governance and the role of professional leaders are probably already reasonably clear given our earlier discussion of the leadership role in connection with liberal assumptions concerning the individual and society. Nevertheless, several summary statements and related commentary may help to bring administrative possibilities suggested by liberal theory into sharper focus.

The administrator clearly stands at the center of efforts to define and reconstruct school policy and practice. Given his experience and organizational position, he is a vital figure in helping members of the school and the wider communities cooperatively to work through perceptions colored by their various frames of reference toward a greater area of shared meanings. Consensus is the goal; a resort to compromise, excommunication and/or compulsion represents some degree of process failure and is subject to the same limitations outlined earlier. In the last analysis, the liberal prefers that the administrator's authority be vested in the resources and skills he brings to extending the power of all, rather than in the legal charge accompanying his position. It would be an unfortunate error, however, to suppose that this view of administration is in any way invalid or inconsequential.

The administrator, in fact, is confronted by the widest range of leadership possibilities. Due to his training and his greater freedom to assign time and energy to synthetic activities, both professional problems and possibilities may well occur to him which go unseen by others interested in the school. This is probably especially true in matters financial, although it often may be true in program and personnel matters as well. He has the possibility of helping members of all segments of the community to qualify for an increasing voice in deciding matters of school policy and procedure. As decisions are reached cooperatively and democratically, he also faces the responsibility of interpreting them to the school, the wider professional and general communities. Of course there will be times in a pluralistic society when he simply cannot gain acceptance of the most carefully constructed position. Who, however, is in the better position both to secure a meaningful reconstruction of the position and to maintain school morale during the process: the administrator who has shared power *with* people, or the one who has attempted to exercise power *over* them? Within the bounds of democratic norms, then, the opportunities for vigorous administrative leadership are both vital and extremely varied.

The liberal maintains that the role of the teacher, the student and even the general citizen in educational governance is different from that of the professional administrator only in degree and not in kind.

Even their limitations are much the same: a commitment to democratic norms and the ability, interest and effort to become conversant with the issues. Rather than crying that the teacher (let alone the student) does not have the time to discern the issues, the liberally-oriented administrator is busy creating instrumentalities by which the interested individual can develop such competency. Rather than jealously guarding " 'his' prerogatives," the liberally-oriented administrator is busy creating situations where meaningful transactions can take place between individuals concerning matters of common concern. Information sheets and other background materials, classroom discussions, role playing, meetings, the development of strong teacher and student councils having an input to an "administrative council"— all offer possibilities to the administrator who does not feel he is the sole repository of Absolute Truth in education. As Sayers and Madden point out so well, the attitude of the administrator is the key variable. Given a positive attitude, many deficiencies in maturity, training, time, willingness or access to needed information may be minimized. Given a positive attitude, the administrator is in a unique position to help teachers, students and concerned citizens alike better to assume their rightful voice in school decisions, to help all concerned develop skill in and commitment to democratic decision-making and to go far toward ensuring more productive decisions.[61] The latter point should not be lost even on more conservative administrators—although they may think the price is still a bit high.

E.   Education as a Profession

1. Conservative Views on Education as a Profession

Pedagogical conservatives and liberals alike are fully committed to the development of a mature teaching profession. In this development, questions concerning needed standards, the development of a distinctive body of knowledge and skills, an organization sufficient to exerting necessary social pressure in line with the profession's needs and a sense of social obligation and commitment are all of concern. Conservatives have suggested several possibilities with regard to answering these questions.

Many contemporary conservatives still echo Robert Hutchins's cry that teacher "training" must *follow* a solid liberal "education."[62] They

[61] *Cf.* Sayers and Madden, *Education and the Democratic Faith,* pp. 423–424.
[62] See *The Higher Learning in America* (New Haven: Yale University Press, 1936).

have railed against teacher college programs that replace needed studies in the arts and sciences with a plethora of "methods" courses, maintaining that many such programs confuse knowledge of how to teach with knowledge of the subject which is to be taught.[63] Pedagogical conservatives have consistently called for an emphasis on the arts and sciences components of teacher education programs. A common proposal is that these be accompanied by a severely limited number of special methods courses—wider in scope at the elementary level than at the secondary. Some work is suggested in educational psychology; most work in history, philosophy and sociology is to be completed in the appropriate arts and sciences departments rather than under the guise of philosophy or history or sociology of education. All methods work is to be rigorously tied to clinical or field experiences, possibly in the senior year or perhaps better in a fifth year of study for which the Master of Arts in Teaching (M.A.T.) might be awarded. Conservatives have also demanded that such programs give more attention to questions of value education and religious education than has been the rule throughout most of the present century. Of late—though with no little fear concerning the preservation of liberal studies—they have been giving a great deal of attention to performance- or competency-based teacher education programs which base their professional content on a specification of the minimal knowledge and skills needed by teachers in the field.[64]

The attitude of more conservative educators to professional organizations has been especially interesting. In fact, their attitudes have not been inconsistent with their attitudes toward organizations in the wider political sphere where associations of "big business" have received considerable approbation. After all, these represent the societies of the successful and are generally necessary to sociocultural well-being. Associations of labor (even "big labor"), on the other hand, are suspect. Their strength finally rests on the follower who, unguided by the natural aristocracy of talent and wealth, grasps for

[63] One immediately thinks of James Conant's *The Education of American Teachers* (New York: McGraw-Hill Book Company, Inc., 1963). Contemporary "professional issues" anthologies commonly include articles reflecting similar positions. For example, examine the contents of Leslie A. Fiedler and Jacob Vinocur, eds., *The Continuing Debate: Essays on Education* (New York: St. Martin's Press, 1964); Harold Full, ed., *Controversy in American Education.* 2nd ed. (New York: The Macmillan Company, 1972); Jean Grambs *et al.*, eds., *Education in the World Today* (Reading, Mass.: Addison-Wesley Publishing Company, 1972); and Howard Ozmon, ed., *Contemporary Critics of Education* (Danville, Ill.: The Interstate Printers & Publishers, Inc., 1970).

[64] See the series of papers on performance-based teacher education prepared under the auspices of the American Association of Colleges for Teacher Education (AACTE). Especially interesting are the reservations expressed by the classical realist Harry S. Broudy in the fourth paper, *A Critique of Performance-Based Teacher Education* (Washington, D.C.: AACTE, 1972).

ever-increasing material rewards for himself at the expense of needed corporate profits.[65] It is not surprising that "teacher unions" have met with tremendous resistance from the conservatively-oriented. Evidencing a great suspicion of "teacher power," they have historically favored professional organizations which include administrators along with teachers and have vigorously fought teacher militancy within these groups. As might be supposed, both teacher "strikes" and "sanctions" have been much criticized.

Conservative theory appears to suggest "merit pay" plans over the so-called "salary scales" and the elimination of unrestricted tenure provisions which make it (functionally) impossible to remove incompetents. Again, the most likely *ideological* rationale lies in a desire to reward achievement. And, as we have seen, competition is based on achievement. We may also suspect that merit pay systems and the elimination of unrestricted tenure provisions generally provide a much increased voice for the administration in controlling the vital reinforcers of salary and retention—a phenomenon not out of keeping with conservative preferences.[66]

2. Liberal Views on Education as a Profession

As we have seen, interest in the development of a mature profession cuts across ideological lines. Heavily influenced by nonphilosophical factors, differences between educational liberals and conservatives often appear to be more matters of degree than of kind. To illustrate, both the conservative and the liberal are agreed that the person who would teach at any level must be solidly grounded in the substantive and skill resources of subject-matter. Both generally agree that the lower grade teacher must have a fairly inclusive exposure to the full range of curricular and methodological possibilities appropriate to this level. Both generally agree that the upper grade teacher must have a much deeper understanding of his area of specialization. When they differ, we usually sense a conservative emphasis on traditional subjects as somehow possessing pedagogical power in themselves. Hence, at the doctoral level the student who is preparing to become a college

[65] The changing attitude of American conservatives toward those *leaders* of the great labor unions (who often have much more in common with the cultural, financial and political interests of corporate moguls than with their own rank and file membership) represents an interesting development in late twentieth century America.

[66] In all fairness, it must be admitted that *any* salary and retention policy could (theoretically) be developed and controlled cooperatively by the entire academic community. In some instances it has been, but heightened administrative control under merit pay and limited tenure situations seems more the rule than not.

instructor in English may take but one course (if that) explicitly concerned with teaching English. The minimal "methods" requirements
for prospective high school teachers are often nearly as limited.

The pedagogical liberal has several definite reservations concerning
such practices. In the first place, familiarity with the content and
inquiry skills of a given discipline does not necessarily mean that one
can teach the material to others, especially if their more limited experience and less mature learning skills differ from those of the teacher.
Secondly, higher education has historically been a bastion of more
conservative pedagogical outlooks. In traditional arts and sciences
departments, one may study under quite a few instructors who indicate very little interest indeed in applying the content and skills of
their disciplines to problems encountered in daily living. "The pursuit
of pure Truth" is no empty slogan in higher education! In fact, it was
the disinterest of many institutions of higher education in applicatory
concerns which in part led to the formation of normal schools and,
later, of teacher colleges. Today, generally reunited with liberal arts
institutions, colleges and departments of teacher education—including
their faculty and students—still remain suspect in the eyes of many of
their colleagues. Our concern for theory applicability and the "hows"
of instruction are viewed as more appropriate to "training" than to
"education"; our possible contributions to the search for Truth are seen
as limited by such "peripheral" concerns.[67] Finally, the liberal holds
that an explicit correlation of the teacher candidate's knowledge and
skills is necessary if he in turn is to lead his students to developing
their own syntheses.

The rough outline of several liberal alternatives to conservative
views of teacher education may now be attempted. Entrance criteria
into teacher education programs must be raised, although they must
take into account the candidate's commitment to teaching the young
and his psychological and physical health, as well as his previous
academic achievement. Evaluation of achievement, health and attitude must continue throughout the program. Explicit and thorough
attention must be given to the methods of critical inquiry and synthesis, as well as to the necessary resources and skills of subject-matter.
If this can all be done in four years, fine; often a five-year program
will be necessary. There is, however, much to be said for beginning

---

[67] Naturally, the applicability concern of professional educators is not one factor
which decreases their stature in the eyes of arts and sciences colleagues. The
individual who passes himself off as an "educational sociologist"—or an "educational philosopher"—and has only minimal training in sociology or philosophy has
limitations in making the kinds of contributions which would increase his status
with university colleagues—or students. Furthermore, the general weakness of our
admission policies raises many questions for those in the sister professions such as
law and medicine.

work in teacher education as early as the sophomore year of college. Guided sequenced work in the field—as an observer, teacher aide and intern—should accompany theory courses no matter in which department or college they are taken.   Placing clinical experiences in the senior year or in the fifth year runs the strong risk of missing necessary opportunities to develop correlations between theory and practice.   Additional seminars should be provided to correlate and develop the pedagogical significance of learnings developed throughout the program, especially in arts and sciences courses.   Another possibility, of course, lies in team-teaching arts and sciences courses heavily enrolled with teacher candidates.   Very useful cooperative efforts have been undertaken, for example, by colleagues in mathematics and mathematics education, in science and science education. The stress is clearly on the evaluation and generalization of knowledge—not on mere activity alone.   Performance-based programs, therefore, which simply stress the relatively individualized study of a pre-existent curriculum are of little interest to liberals.   *If* the program allows for group activities which create opportunities for transactional relationships to develop, *if* opportunities for student choice and input are written into the program and *if* evaluative measures go well beyond the objective paper-and-pencil variety, the liberal's interest begins to increase.[68]   In other words, the definition of and commitment to "professionalism" comes only with involvement and mutual responsibility.   "Taking courses" or meeting pre-existent competency requirements leads to little more than a degree.

For the liberal, professional organizations are only a means and not an end.   Their instrumental value is high when they provide security and a heightened sense of community.   Most liberals—at least theoretically—would probably prefer an organization which promoted cooperative planning and implementation by all individuals concerned with the school.   Unfortunately, the managerial model of administration, the strength in this culture of a view that posits human nature as inherently defective (especially when the human beings involved are teachers or students) and the prevalence of the conservative definition of leadership, often militate against such an organization.   Liberal educators, therefore, have taken full part in confrontation politics when needed to force compromises on salary and working conditions from the power structure.   In the main this has been done reluctantly and efforts have been made quickly to restore effective working arrangements with administrators and boards of education.

Basically the same points could be made with regard to salary plans

[68] The competency-based program which is suggested in the student manual accompanying this text provides an example of efforts to bring such programs more in line with liberal assumptions.

and tenure questions.   There is nothing in the liberal position which suggests a preference for stepped salary scales (as contrasted with merit pay proposals) or blanket tenure plans.   As noted earlier, either stepped salary scales or merit pay plans *could* be established and implemented by the entire school community.   Where salary and retention decisions can be made cooperatively, there is little need for detailed, protective, legal agreements.   Where they cannot, the educator must be protected from those habituated to power—and profit-grabbing.

Throughout these two chapters dealing with "social philosophy, ideologies and American education," differences between conservative and liberal assumptions have necessarily received detailed attention.   At this point in our study, however, the demands of a balanced treatment suggest that we emphasize important similarities between our nation's dominant ideologies.   We shall see that these do seem to provide some foundation for a distinctive "American ideology."

*American conservatives and liberals seem united in their love of country—in the high valuation they place on its past accomplishments, its present potential and its future promise.   This point should not be obscured by the ostentatious flag-waving of many contemporary conservatives or the liberal's deep reservations about our nation's actions in the Vietnam affair.

*American conservatives and liberals seem united in seeing the social goal as lying in the development of full individuality.   This point should not be (completely) obscured by their differences over the necessary means to its realization.

*American conservatives and liberals seem united in their acceptance of democratic decision-making.   This point should not be obscured by the conservative's preference for allowing leaders to make many decisions once input has been secured from their followers—nor by his occasional penchant for secrecy in the actual decision-making process.   Nor should it be obscured by the liberal's predisposition to greater openness, his insistence on extending an important voice to the masses—sometimes without adequately preparing them to exercise a meaningful role in reaching a decision.

*American conservatives and liberals seem united in their preference for measured social change.   Change is slowed *both* by the conservative's deference to tradition *and* the liberal's accent on a decision-making model which includes serious reference to tradition as an "antecedent variable."   For the liberal, change is further slowed by the sheer weight of disconfirming data necessary significantly to alter an experiential generalization.   This point should not be obscured by ideological rhetoric; its proof may be seen in the reactions of a Franklin Roosevelt when the general public views a social possibility as departing radically from "our way of doing things."

*Finally, American conservatives and liberals seem united in their qualified optimism with regard to the possibility of social progress. This point should not be obscured by their many differences over human potential or the means of maximizing it.

There will be schools in which the conservatively-oriented educator would find it difficult to teach; there will be schools in which the liberally-oriented educator would meet similar frustration. The points sketched above, however, suggest that there will be far more schools in which individuals of good will but dissimilar ideological orientations can make significant contributions with reasonable comfort.

Part V

Suggestions for Further Reading

The Nature and Basic Problems of Social
Philosophy and Ideology

CANTRIL, HADLEY, *The Politics of Despair.* New York: Basic Books, Inc., 1958. Chapter IV (ingredients of a lasting faith).

JOHNSON, HARRY S., "Ideology and the Social System," *International Encyclopedia of the Social Sciences.* Ed. David L. Sills. New York: The Macmillan Company and The Free Press, 1968. Pages 76–85 (meaning, sources, types, focusses, importance, control).

MANNHEIM, KARL, *Ideology and Utopia.* Trans. Louis Wirth and Edward Shils. London: Routledge & Kegan Paul Ltd., 1936. See especially Parts II ("Ideology and Utopia") and IV ("The Utopian Mentality").

MOSCA, GAETANO, *The Ruling Class.* Ed. and rev. with an introduction by Arthur Livingston; trans. H. D. Kahn. New York: McGraw-Hill Book Company, Inc., 1939. Chapter VII.

NETTLER, GWYNN, *Explanations.* New York: McGraw-Hill Book Company, Inc., 1970. Chapter VI (criteria of ideology, truth as utility, traces of ideology among scientists, test of ideological explanation).

PLAMENATZ, JOHN, *Ideology.* New York: Praeger Publishers, Inc., 1970. (Uses of word, functions of, backgrounds in Kant and Hegel, social conditioning of ideas, Marxist concept of "class ideology," political uses of ideology).

SARGENT, LYMAN T., *Contemporary American Political Ideologies: A Comparative Analysis.* Homewood, Ill.: The Dorsey Press, 1969. Introduction (definition) and Chapters IV (Democracy), VII (The New Left) and VIII (Anarchism).

SHILS, EDWARD, "The Concept and Function of Ideology," *International Encyclopedia of the Social Sciences.* Ed. David L. Sills. New York: The Macmillan Company and The Free Press, 1968. Pages 66–76 (meanings —as distinguished from outlooks and creeds, systems and movements of thought, and programs; ideological positions; change; functions; truth and ideology—relations with science; the end of ideology?).

STANKIEWICZ, W. J., ed., *Political Thought since World War II.* New York: The Free Press of Glencoe, A Division of the Macmillan Company, 1964. Pages 25–30 (criteria of ideological survival) and Part IV, Sections 2 (Conservatism) and 3 (Liberalism).

SUTTON, FRANCIS X. *et al.*, The American Business Creed. Cambridge, Mass.: Harvard University Press, 1956. Chapter I (characteristics of ideology).

Ideological Assumptions and Their Expression in
Educational Policy and Practices

BELL, DANIEL, ed., *The Radical Right. The New American Right.* Expanded and updated; Anchor Books edition. Garden City, N.Y.: Doubleday & Company, Inc., 1964. Essays which contrast Conservatism with extremist movements on the far American political right.

BENNE, KENNETH D., and BOZIDAR MUNTYAN, *Human Relations in Curriculum Change.* New York: The Dryden Press, Inc., 1951. Part IV ("Democratic Ethics and the Management of Change"; modes of social control evaluated in light of democratic ethics; the necessary correlation of social change skills with democratic norms).

BRUBACHER, JOHN S., ed., *Eclectic Philosophy of Education: A Book of Readings.* Englewood Cliffs, N.J.: Prentice-Hall, Inc., 1951. Selected readings which compare positions on many topics of social philosophical concern; e.g., "Democratic Education," "Education and the Production and Ownership of Wealth," "Nationalism and Education," "The School and Social Progress" and "Freedom as Method."

BURNHAM, JAMES, *Suicide of the West: An Essay on the Meaning and Destiny of Liberalism.* New York: The John Day Company, Inc., 1964. Chapters VII (balanced and, at times, telling criticisms of Liberalism by a confirmed conservative—who understands the liberal!) and IX (liberal and conservative orderings of values compared).

COHEN, CARL, ed., *Communism, Fascism, and Democracy: The Theoretical Foundations.* New York: Random House, Inc., 1962. Pages 584–590 (freedom), 590–600 (society) and 631–689 (democracy as a way of life).

CURTI, MERLE, *The Social Ideas of American Educators.* Rev. ed. Patterson, N.J.: Littlefield, Adams & Co., 1963. Chapter XV (Dewey).

DEWEY, JOHN, *Democracy and Education.* New York: The Macmillan Company, 1916. Free Press paperback edition, 1966. Chapter VII (various relationships between the individual and society).

————, *Individualism Old and New.* New York: Minton, Balch and Company, 1930. Capricorn Books edition, 1962. The kind of individualism (rights and responsibilities) appropriate to a mass, corporate, technological society.

————, *The Public and Its Problems.* New York: Henry Holt and Company, 1948.

————, *Reconstruction in Philosophy.* Enlarged ed. Boston: The Beacon Press, 1948. Chapter VIII (possible relationships of the individual and society; implications of these relationships).

GOLDWATER, BARRY, *The Conscience of a Conservative.* A Macfadden Capitol Hill Book. New York: Macfadden-Bartell Corporation, 1950. A conservative politician comments on aid to education, labor, taxes, civil rights, agriculture and the welfare state.

GOLDWIN, ROBERT A., ed., *Left, Right and Center: Essays on Liberalism and Conservatism in the United States.* Chicago: Rand McNally & Company, 1965.

HOOVER, HERBERT, *American Individualism.* Garden City, N.Y.: Double-day, Page & Company, 1923. Excellent treatment of the libertarian tradition in Conservatism in terms of its early modification by economic factors.

KARIER, CLARENCE J., "Liberalism and the Quest for Orderly Change," *History of Education Quarterly,* XII, No. 1 (Spring 1972), pp. 57–80. Twentieth Century Liberalism: the major sources of its weakness and a more realistic assessment of its strengths.

KILPATRICK, WM. HEARD, *Education and the Social Crisis.* Kappa Delta Pi Lecture Series. New York: Liveright Publishing Corporation, 1932. Chapters IV (democratic planning) and V (democratic education; liberal view of indoctrination).

————, *Philosophy of Education.* New York: The Macmillan Company, 1951. Chapters IX and X (respect for personality).

KIRK, RUSSELL, *A Program for Conservatives.* Rev. ed. Chicago: Henry Regnery Company, 1962. Conservative answers to the problems of the heart, mind, social boredom, community, social justice, wants, order, power, loyalty and tradition.

McCARTHY, EUGENE J., *A Liberal Answer to the Conservative Challenge.* A Macfadden Capitol Hill Book. New York: Macfadden-Bartell Corporation, 1964.

MEYER, FRANK, ed., *What Is Conservatism?* New York: Holt, Rinehart and Winston, 1964. Twelve conservative spokesmen (e.g., Russell Kirk, F. A. Hayek, Wm. F. Buckley, Jr.) speak to conservative assumptions.

O'NEILL, WILLIAM, *Readin, Ritin, and Rafferty! A Study of Educational Fundamentalism.* Berkeley, Calif.: The Glendessary Press, 1969. Max Rafferty quotations on ideological themes, together with an interesting—though not always objective—commentary.

RATNER, JOSEPH, ed., *Intelligence in the Modern World: John Dewey's Philosophy.* New York: The Modern Library, Random House, Inc., 1939. Chapters V (the modes of societal life) and VII (intelligence in social action).

RAUP, R. BRUCE *et al.,* *The Improvement of Practical Intelligence: The Central Task of Education.* New York: Harper & Brothers, Publishers, 1950. Chapters XII and XIII (democratic planning and the ideal democratic character product).

ROSSITER, CLINTON, *Conservatism in America.* New York: Alfred A. Knopf, Inc., 1955. Basic conservative assumptions, evaluation of American Conservatism in terms of its ideological purity, history of American Conservatism.

ROTH, ROBERT J., S. J., *John Dewey and Self-Realization.* Englewood Cliffs, N.J.: Prentice-Hall, Inc., 1962.

SAYERS, EPHRAIM VERN, and WARD MADDEN, *Education and the Democratic Faith: An Introduction to the Philosophy of Education.* New York: Appleton-Century-Crofts, Inc., 1959. Liberal conceptions—briefly but clearly contrasted with conservative and other ideological conceptions—of cooperation and/or competition (pp. 35–50 and 73–85), equality (pp. 51–56), freedom (pp. 57–69 and 86–95) and leadership (pp. 96–102). See Part II for educational policies and practices seen consistent with assumptions.

SCHULTZ, FREDERICK M., "Community as a Pedagogical Enterprise and the Functions of Schooling within It in the Philosophy of John Dewey," *Educational Theory*, **XXI**, No. 3 (Summer 1971), pp. 320–337.

WINGO, G. MAX, *The Philosophy of American Education*.   Boston: D. C. Heath and Company, 1965.   Chapters III ("The Conservative Tradition"), IV ("Essentialism: The Conservative Tradition in Education"), V ("Philosophical Idealism in the Conservative Tradition") and VI ("Realistic Philosophy and the Conservative Tradition").

PART *VI*

Applied Philosophy
of Education

10

Philosophy of Education and Professional Problem-Solving

In a way the title of this sixth part of our studies, "Applied Philosophy of Education," is somewhat misleading. After all, Chapters 3, 5, 7 and 9 have each involved us in speculatively examining philosophy in terms of its possibilities for educational policy and practice. In addition to reading, other course activities have engaged us in this same task. The present chapter, then, basically involves an *intensification* of our efforts to use philosophical resources in professional problem-solving. Naturally, this intensification is made possible by the content, skill and attitudinal base thus far developed. Secondly, it also entails a *shift of emphasis* from perceiving general applicational possibilities to working out applications in specific situations. And these, of course, are exactly the situations which confront educators.

There are two foci with which we shall be especially concerned: 1) How can we develop defensible inferences concerning philosophical assumptions which appear to be influencing observed (or described) behavior? 2) How can we employ philosophical resources (in the light of nonphilosophical factors) to generate possibilities for solving specific professional problems? Each of these foci will involve an introductory discussion of procedures and problems and a guided exercise. Additional problem-solving exercises will then involve you actively and personally in using every bit of knowledge, skill and insight developed in our work together, as well as in other nonphilosophical studies foundational to professional education. Hopefully, these activities will provide a meaningful and appropriate introduction to this text's concluding chapter: "Building and Using a Personal Philosophy of Education."

A. Finding Reasons

In the very first chapter, "philosophical assumptions" were defined as the conceptual outcome of tentatively taking a position with regard to alternative meanings of a given philosophical concept. It was noted that they generally include both facts and beliefs and, like beliefs, tend to become highly intertwined one with another within one's frame of reference. It was also maintained that they generally influence one's thinking and occasionally even serve as critical factors in determining what happens in educational situations.[1] Geiger reminds us:

> It should be superfluous to note that "assumption" here implies nothing illegitimate. The popular use of the term in which "assume" is placed in contradistinction to "know" is deceptive. Assumptions are vital in all fields of human knowledge. Without them science—and common sense as well—would have neither foundation nor source. But their operation must be made articulate. We must become conscious of them, and more sensitive.[2]

Ennis makes the same demand, writing: "It is important to be clear about what we are looking for when we search for assumptions, and to be clear about how we can tell that one has been located."[3]

What we are looking for is the premise (or premises) which serve as a reason for a given conclusion, point of view or behavior. If the assumption is stated explicitly, there is generally no great problem. For instance, we have no trouble locating the premise in the library-posted statement: "Inasmuch as people will steal you blind given half a chance, purses and other personal possessions should not be left unattended." More often, however, there is a problem in that assumptions are rarely stated. "They are the kind of thing," writes Ennis, "that we are talking about when we say that someone implicitly based his conclusion on a certain assumption or that he ought to accept it in

[1] See Chapter 1, footnote 28 et passim.

[2] George R. Geiger, Philosophy and the Social Order: An Introductory Approach (Boston: Houghton Mifflin Company, 1947), p. 56.

[3] Robert H. Ennis, "Assumption-Finding," in Language and Concepts in Education, ed. B. Othanel Smith and Robert H. Ennis (Chicago: Rand McNally & Company, 1961), p. 162.

order to accept the conclusion."[4]   Many individuals are not aware of the reasons for their conclusions or behaviors; sometimes, especially in a pluralistic culture, one is quite aware of them but realizes all too well that honesty will offend some power group.   Hence the premises are either unstated or cloaked in euphemisms.   The result?   We are simply faced with the statement, "Purses and other personal possessions should not be left unattended."   Or, we may observe teachers monitoring the halls before school, between classes and until the last student has left the building in the afternoon.   We wonder what criteria could possibly allow us reasonably to infer that the verbal or monitoring behavior had been motivated by a given philosophical assumption or assumptions.

Scheffler makes the search for such criteria more difficult when he observes that an individual's

> *beliefs hang together and exercise mutual influence upon one another, that they are, furthermore, in delicate interaction with his aims and attitudes.   A single belief therefore cannot be attributed to a person simply on the basis of his response dispositions under given overt circumstances, no matter how varied these dispositions are taken to be.   For the single belief is judged, in part, by reference to other beliefs and goals we assume the person to have; these other beliefs and goals color the circumstances under which the particular response is taking place.*[5]

The situation is further complicated by the fact that not all beliefs are philosophical in nature; one's belief structure encompasses historical, psychological and sociological elements as well.   Sensing that Scheffler is correct, we probably do best to agree that in a transactional situation no criteria whatsoever will allow us logically (or otherwise) to *prove* that a given assumption or assumptions did in fact motivate the behavior.   Rather, assumption-finding is more a "non-logical (not illogical), imaginative process,"[6] or, again to quote Scheffler,

> *Belief attribution, in short, looks more like abstract theoretical hypothesizing in the realm of science than like description of relatively low-level physical traits.*[7]

---

[4] "Assumption-Finding," in *Language and Concepts in Education*, eds. Smith and Ennis, p. 163.

[5] Israel Scheffler, *Conditions of Knowledge: An Introduction to Epistemology and Education;* Keystones of Education Series (Chicago: Scott, Foresman and Company, 1965), p. 86.

[6] Joe R. Burnett, "Some Observations on the Logical Implications of Philosophic Theory for Educational Theory and Practice," in *Philosophic Problems for Education,* ed. Young Pai and Joseph T. Myers (Philadelphia and New York: J. B. Lippincott Company, 1967), p. 34.

[7] *Conditions of Knowledge,* p. 86.

Given this conclusion and the difficulties which force it upon us, why do we continue to search for the reasons, including philosophical assumptions, underlying observed or described behavior? Several purposes come to mind. In the first place, we want to become more aware of our own predispositions—at times in order to control their expression (e.g., so as not to indoctrinate our students), and at other times in order to translate them more consistently and effectively into action. Secondly, however, we also want to become more aware of the factors which motivate others to action. Thus we may increase the effectiveness of our communication with them. Furthermore, if a problem necessitates a cooperative solution, we are more adequately prepared to attempt a shared frame of reference. Determining our own assumptions has occupied us implicitly throughout our studies; the task will be given explicit attention in the next chapter. Inferring the assumptions of others, however—especially when we must generally rely on their verbal reports and other behaviors as a base for making hypotheses—presents quite another problem. And it is to this problem that we now turn.

1. The Criteria of Assumption-Finding

Having given up any attempt at "proof," we must obviously reconstruct our task. Our charge must now be viewed as one of increasing the reliability of an hypothesis that an individual's assumption(s) provide an acceptable reason for observed or described behavior. True, this reconstruction itself rests upon certain presuppositions which will not themselves be questioned in this text. For instance, we shall assume that means-ends relationships can be constructed in mediating experience. We shall also assume that commonalities in human problem-solving behavior allow us to make generalizations about it. And finally, we shall accept the assumption of rational behavior, i.e., that people usually intend the most probable consequences of their actions—even though they may err in estimating the actual consequences which follow a given action.[8]

The basic argument is that the reliability of our inferences or hypotheses with regard to the presence and function of specific assumptions is increased in proportion to the care with which we individually and cooperatively take the following criteria into account:[9]

[8] Hobert W. Burns, "The Logic of the 'Educational Implication,'" in *Philosophic Problems for Education*, ed. Pai and Myers, p. 45.

[9] No attempt to rank order these criteria is implied by the listing as given. To be sure, there *may* be a hierarchy, but it is assumed that any such ordering will be related to the given context.

1. *The freedom of the individual(s) observed to act in ways consistent with his or her assumption(s).* That is, is there a relative lack of observable restriction or compulsion? Is there, for example, a teacher's manual or a school "policy" which mandates certain behavior, e.g., monitoring the halls? What behaviors are being reinforced by the environment? What effect does *your* presence seem to be having on the observed?

2. *The consistency of the observed behavior with the inferred assumption.* Is the behavior generally consistent with what you infer to be the individual's assumption(s)? What *should* the individual have assumed given the observed behavior? Would holding the (inferred) assumption increase the probability that behavior of the type observed would occur? Does the assumption in question seem to provide a likely or even a necessary reason for the behavior? Assuming rationality of action, Scheffler warns us in this regard that when behavior and inferred assumption diverge,

> *we need to decide whether to postulate weakness of will, or irrationality, or deviant purpose, or ignorance, or bizarre belief, or insincerity, and the choice may often be difficult.*[10]

Scheffler's warning makes sense. If we have reasonable evidence concerning environmental conditions and are beginning to form some notion of the individual's frame of reference, a markedly inconsistent action should be treated with caution. An isolated instance of rigid, external control of a student may well be the result of that short-term "irrationality" occasioned by coming down with a cold or having had an argument with one's spouse or superior. We need not jump to the assumption that the instructor holds human nature to be inherently evil.

3. *Any facts and nonphilosophical factors (i.e., historical, psychological, sociological or reality factors) seen relevant to the situation.* This criterion involves judging whether the inferred philosophical assumption(s) provide the primary (or even an important) reason for the observed behavior. For example, social class differences between teacher and students which often result in value conflict may be a far more important factor in determining a given classroom's environment than the teacher's philosophical assumptions. In like measure, factors in the history of a given region—e.g., the influence in America of Scots-Irish Calvinism born in colonial times but continuing to this day in certain areas—may subtly but firmly shape a school's disciplinary expectations. In such cases, the reliability of hypotheses concerning the philosophical assumptions of the teacher is markedly reduced.

[10] *Conditions of Knowledge,* pp. 89–90.

This is not to say, of course, that the teacher could not possibly hold the assumption. It is to say that the philosophical factor will be difficult to identify in the presence of other strong influences. Consistency factors may cause an abnormally intensified effect; inconsistency may cause dissonance. In both cases, separate and distinct causal factors are difficult to identify within ongoing transactions. The moral? Go slow—assemble all available evidence—and consider it with care prior to making a judgment.

4. *The possibility that philosophical assumption x may provide a more adequate explanatory principle than philosophical assumption y.* Undoubtedly we should seek the most simple and direct hypothesis which will account for the observed behavior. Then, too, the possibility for sound judgment in this matter can only be increased as one becomes more knowledgeable about the philosophical theory to which one is turning for an explanatory principle. The possibility may also be increased if one is aware of the "connections" between theory and practice originally suggested by the formulator(s) of that theory.[11] Nevertheless, it does not appear absolutely essential to have read Plato to understand the assumption of "ideas as archetypes of existents." Nor must we feel constrained by the theory-practice "connections" suggested by Plato in, say, the *Republic.* We may agree that if the student has had opportunity explicitly to consider the contemporary relevance of Plato's assumptions and prescriptions and is aware of the original context in which they were developed, this background might well be helpful in judgment-making. Studied for its own sake, its usefulness appears suspect.

5. *An adequate exposure to the observed's behavior patterns, preferably under varied conditions of time, place and people.* Obviously, one cannot spend an hour or two in a teacher's classroom and hope to develop very defensible inferences as to the assumptions underlying his behavior. Nor can one determine the teacher's assumptions merely by asking him what he had in mind when he did such and such—although this need not preclude us from doing so in conjunction with other analytic activities. Again, inferences are not defensible on the basis of verbal behavior alone. The transactional mediation of experience gradually modifies even the firmest of assumptions; the teacher may be unaware of his reasons or (justifiably) defensive about revealing them. In short, at this time it is most difficult to generalize about the meaning of "an adequate exposure." In a situation containing so many complex and transacting variables, contextual judgment probably remains our best guide.

[11] *Cf.* Burnett, "Some Observations on the Logical Implications of Philosophic Theory for Educational Theory and Practice," in *Philosophic Problems for Education,* ed. Pai and Myers, p. 34.

These criteria are not "foolproof" nor can they be applied mechanically. Indeed, as a student in an introductory course, you are likely to encounter several severe difficulties in applying them. These difficulties will demand a high level of cooperative work with the instructional staff if they are to be minimized. Consider the following: a) Given a rough, intuitive, five-point reliability scale (e.g., highly probable, probable, possible, unlikely, highly unlikely), no *claim* beyond "possibility" seems defensible for an inference which does not take *all five* assumption-finding criteria into account. This is not to say that one couldn't advance *hypotheses* as to greater reliability under controlled conditions (e.g., receiving assurances that one or more of the criteria had been fulfilled) and with knowledge of the purposes and limitations of the exercise.[12] b) It doesn't take a "Renaissance Man" to fulfill criterion number 3, but a willingness to ask questions of specialists—expecially one's instructors in other educational foundations courses—is demanded. No one can know everything; your instructor will himself be asking many questions of his colleagues. Questions might commonly take the form: "Does your specialization suggest any good reasons for the subject behaving this way?" or, "Do you see any factors in this situation which might explain why the subject behaved in the way observed or described?" If it is at all possible for a good nonphilosophically-based reason to exist, it would probably be best not to advance a claim greater than "possible" for the philosophical inference.[13] c) The first and fifth criteria demand a field experience in which you can observe and work with one educator over some time and in a variety of settings. That is, observe his work in a "homeroom" setting, in the courses he teaches, in his sports or other extracurricular activities, and try to talk with him informally—perhaps over a cup of coffee in the teachers' lounge.[14] d) If you have not had some background in academic philosophy, be especially careful in coming to conclusions as to matters relating to criteria numbers two and four. When in doubt, consult with the instructor.

At this point, you may well be wondering whether assumption-finding is an appropriate activity for predoctoral students. The an-

[12] *Note to professional colleagues:* Different student populations should probably be exposed to quite different demands for inference defensibility. For example, it may be enough simply to expose the first-year undergraduate to one set of variables involved in professional decision-making and to give him some practice in working with the criteria. By contrast, the needs of the inservice teacher or the doctoral student may suggest considerably higher demands.

[13] *Note to professional colleagues:* We might facilitate such activity by providing team-led workshops and/or common team-supervised field experiences.

[14] *Note to professional colleagues:* This is not to preclude such activities as exposure to a variety of school environments, observations of school board or PTA meetings, or analyses of written documents. Should inferences regarding guiding assumptions be desired, however, point (a) should be remembered.

swer is a qualified "yes." Several reasons for this answer have already been discussed at the close of the introductory section entitled "Finding Reasons." In addition, it is important to underline the notion that our primary goal in engaging in assumption-finding activities is not certainty, but *making our judgments more rational*. If the flux of human experience prevents us from "proving" that a given assumption was instrumental to a certain behavior, it most surely does not prevent us from making our inferences more defensible—or obtaining a wealth of personal and professional insights in the process.

2. *An Exercise in Finding Reasons*

What we really need at this point is opportunity to spend some time together observing in a mutually interesting educational setting, quietly and reflectively considering philosophical possibilities in the situation and working out inferences about assumptions which could reasonably be held to have influenced observed behavior.

Given the limitations of a textbook, however, about the best that can be done is to introduce you to Mrs. Sandra Evers, a highly effective and especially well-liked middle school teacher. But let us be serious: The limitations of space and the written word will not *really* permit an adequate exposure to her behavior patterns—and surely not under varied conditions of time, place and people. We shall merely assume—for the purposes of this exercise—that such exposure did take place and that her behavior was generally consistent with that observed in the incident which follows. Furthermore, you will have to accept my word that the school environment is both supportive of her teaching area (language arts) and does allow her freedom to express her assumptions in her various professional activities. (Remember these two assumption-finding criteria—numbers one and five—when you personally get involved in field observation, and make sure they are covered.) After reading the videotape script which follows, let us see if we can do a bit better on criteria numbers two, three and four.

A QUESTION OF VALUES

(Mrs. Evers's language arts classroom is not unlike the other twenty-two classrooms in the Louviers Middle School—that is, in most respects. There are the usual desks, bulletin boards, windows, lockers and all the rest. The most striking difference is to be found at the rear of the room.   There Mrs. Evers has created what she smilingly refers to as the "meditation corner."   The corner is carpeted; a vase of flowers and an array of colorful book jackets usually rest on a table placed under the window; and a bookcase refinished by former students holds a good many volumes having special appeal to early adolescents. Several comfortable chairs complete the attractive and inviting scene. Students are allowed to browse before class begins, often after "seat assignments" are completed, and Tuesdays and Thursdays after school. At times—and this particular day is one of them—the students enter class to find Mrs. Evers sitting in a chair in the corner.   Putting their books down on their desks, they walk back to join her—some quietly to sit on chairs, more on the floor.)

Mrs. Evers: Last night I was reading an account of the riots.   Did you see it when you worked on your newspaper assignment?

Kelly: Yes, Mrs. Evers—even though I had a hard time getting the newspaper away from my dad.   Boy, was he mad!   He was walking up and down in the family room, waving the paper and yelling that the whole bunch of those traitors should be shipped off to Russia.   He told me that if he had refused to join the army—let alone started a riot or burned the flag—they would have thrown him in jail, or worse.

Melissa: I don't know, Kelly.   My brother is home from college.   He read the article too and said that everyone just had to be free to do his own thing—that was what our country was all about.   I don't know what to think.

Mrs. Evers (taking a well-worn text from the table beside her):   Relax for a few minutes and listen carefully to two things I'm going to read you.   The first, entitled "Song of the Settlers," is by Jessamyn West.

1   *Freedom is a hard-bought thing—*
2   *A gift no man can give,*
3   *For some, a way of dying,*
4   *For most, a way to live.*

5   *Freedom is a hard-bought thing—*
6   *A rifle in the hand,*
7   *The horses hitched at sunup,*
8   *A harvest in the land.*

9   *Freedom is a hard-bought thing—*
10   *A Massacre, a bloody rout,*
11   *The candles lit at nightfall,*
12   *And the night shut out.*

13   *Freedom is a hard-bought thing—*
14   *An arrow in the back,*
15   *The wind in the long corn rows,*
16   *And the hay in the rack.*

17   *Freedom is a way of living,*
18   *A song, a mighty cry.*
19   *Freedom is the bread we eat;*
20   *Let it be the way we die!*[15]

(Noting that her students are deeply attentive, Mrs. Evers continues:)
And finally, Elias Lieberman's "I Am an American." Pay especial attention
to the second stanza.

I am an American.
*My father belongs to the Sons
    of the Revolution;*
*My mother, to the Colonial
    Dames.*
*One of my ancestors pitched tea
    overboard in Boston Harbor;*
*Another stood his ground with
    Warren;*
*Another hungered with Washington
    at Valley Forge.*
*My forefathers were America in
    the making.*
They spoke in her council halls;
They died on her battle-fields;
They commanded her ships;
They cleared her forests.
Dawns reddened and paled.
*Staunch hearts of mine beat fast
    at each new star*
In the nation's flag.
*Keen eyes of mine foresaw her
    greater glory.*
The sweep of her seas,
The plenty of her plains,
*The man-hives in her billion-
    wired cities.*
*Every drop of blood in me holds
    a heritage of patriotism.*
I am proud of my past.
I am an American

A   I am an American.
B   *My father was an atom of dust,*
C   *My mother a straw in the wind,*
D   *To his serene majesty.*

15 From *A Mirror for the Sky*, copyright 1946, 1948, by Jessamyn West. Reprinted by permission of Harcourt Brace Jovanovich, Inc., and Russell & Volken-
ing, Inc. First published in *The New Yorker*.

E   One of my ancestors died in the
         mines of Siberia;

F   Another was crippled for life by
         twenty blows of the knout.

G   Another was killed defending his
         home during the massacres.

H   The history of my ancestors is
         a trail of blood

I   To the palace-gate of the
         Great White Czar.

J   But then the dream came—

K   The dream of America.

L   In the light of the Liberty torch

M   The atom of dust became a man

N   And the straw in the wind be-
         came a woman

O   For the first time.

P   "See," said my father, pointing to
         the flag that fluttered near,

Q   "That flag of stars and stripes
         is yours;

R   It is the emblem of the promised
         land.

S   It means, my son, the hope
         of humanity.

T   Live for it—die for it!"

U   Under the open sky of my new
         country I swore to do so;

V   And every drop of blood in me
         will keep that vow.

W   I am proud of my future.

X   I am an American.[16]

(Silence greets Mrs. Evers's reading of the two poems—the kind of silence that signifies an impact which all teachers seek to achieve, although few do and then only on rare occasion. Finally, there is a stir in the group.)

Mrs. Evers: These two poems tell us a good deal about the meaning of "freedom," don't they? Really, Kelly, it's not surprising that your father was so upset. He went to war and paid a high price for the gift of freedom. Your brother, whom I knew well, paid the highest price in Vietnam. Why should your father stand still when other people won't pay their fair share? After all, don't they have the same obligations he has—whether they like it or not?

[16] Elias Lieberman, "I Am an American"; copyright 1918, 1946; originally appeared in *Everybody's Magazine* (July 1916), then included in *Paved Streets* by Elias Lieberman (Boston: Cornhill Company, 1918); reprinted by permission of Mrs. Rose K. (Elias) Lieberman.

Kelly: I don't think I understood before . . .

Mrs. Evers (seeing Linda's raised hand):   Yes, Linda.

Linda: Somehow, I liked the other poem better.   Maybe it's because we climbed up in the Statue of Liberty last summer—almost to the Liberty Torch—and saw Ellis Island where the immigrants came into America.   I liked the idea of the flag standing for freedom.   How can people burn anything that valuable—like they did in Washington?

Mrs. Evers (nods her head in agreement with Linda, pauses and speaks): Sometimes seeing what an idea such as freedom really means allows us to understand the reasonableness—or the unreasonableness—of the other person's actions.   (Pause.)   Let's take a closer look at our two poems.   Beth, get those dittoed sheets off my desk and pass them around.   (Pause for distribution and overview.)   We've read quite a bit of poetry this year, class. Why does the first poem, "Song of the Settlers," make us stop and think? Cindy?

Cindy: Well, it's not just one thing—but there *are* the rhymed words at the end of the even-numbered lines.

Mrs. Evers: Agreed—on both counts.   Brian?

Brian: The regular rhythm?   Three beats to a line, I think.

Mrs. Evers: Very *good*, Brian!   Beth?

Beth: The parallel line structure . . .

Mrs. Evers: No question about that.   Does anyone see anything else? (Pause.)   Look closely now.   We haven't discussed this point.   (Pause.) Yes, Carol.

Carol: Look at the first lines of each of the first four stanzas—lines 1, 5, 9 and 13: "Freedom is a hard-bought thing."   They all begin that way.   But then look at the first line of the last stanza—line 17: "Freedom is a way of living."   I think—it makes you stop and think—just because it's different.   Is that correct, Mrs. Evers?

Mrs. Evers: That's correct indeed, Carol.   Nicely said.   You see, class, here we have a splendid example of the poetess using a *number* of ways to communicate with us.   We may understand her message by trying to *feel* what freedom really means.   Of course we may also understand the truths of her message by analyzing the poem until we begin to feel that the parts somehow fit together.   It's not easy, but you are doing very well.   (Pause.) And how about the second poem?   (Pause.)   Craig?

Craig: I'm confused, Mrs. Evers.   I don't see rhymes; I don't see parallel structure; I don't feel any special beat; I don't see that different kind of thing Carol saw—yet I liked this poem too.   I'm not sure why . . .

Mrs. Evers: Well, one thing we know for sure, Craig.   The things we saw in the other poem may *contribute* to a poem's power, but they're not absolutely *necessary*.   Why?   Because you still feel the power of "I Am an American."   Right?

Craig: Right!

Mrs. Evers: We're surely going to have to talk more about "blank verse." I think, however, that we've done just about enough "analyzing" for today. Let's finish up by simply talking about the language of this poem.   Do you see anything interesting in lines B, C and D, Jeff?

Jeff: Yeah. He's comparing his father to an "atom of dust" and his mother to a "straw in the wind" to show that in Russia they didn't count for much.

Mrs. Evers: Yes. These are two good examples of what we call "metaphors." By the way, Jeff, how did you know he came from Russia?

Jeff: Oh, a book I read a couple of weeks ago was all about the Czars and sending guys to Siberia and that kind of stuff.

Mrs. Evers: Good enough, Jeff. Perhaps you'd like to tell the class about the book some day soon. (Pause.) Does anybody know what a "knout" is—line F? (Pause.) No? That's a special kind of whip used to punish prisoners. It's not difficult to see why Lieberman's father and mother dreamed about coming to America. (Pause.) Well, one more point for today: What is an "emblem"—Line R? (Pause.) Linda? (Pause.) No? Anyone? (Pause.) Werner.

Werner: It's a sign for something else. Like my scout badge—in the poem, the flag stands for America, for freedom.

Mrs. Evers: That's it, Werner. Actually most important things are like that. Freedom, for example, can't be heard or touched. Rather, we *see* the flag which stands for it. (Pause.) Well—for tonight's homework, I'd like you to try to write a poem about freedom. Keep it short—just try to put your feelings into words. We'll talk about it tomorrow.

Although we have assumed that you have indeed observed Mrs. Evers in a variety of settings and that her behavior was generally consistent with that observed in this incident, we do not have the specifics from those other settings. Thus lacking full data relevant to criterion number 5, we are probably prohibited from hypothesizing an extremely high degree of possibility for our inferences. We do know, of course, (if only by fiat) that she is free to act in ways consistent with her assumptions (criterion number 1). Let us, therefore, list those assumptions which Mrs. Evers might conceivably hold and then appeal to the remaining three criteria to see what kind of a case can be developed for at least a sampling of the listing.

It is hypothesized that Mrs. Evers *possibly* holds the following assumptions:

Basic Reality: Creative, purposeful, spiritual energy;

Ideas: Archetypes of existents;

Experience: Contact with a given reality;

Objectivity: Alignment with a given reality;

Frame of Reference: Limitation-to-Be-Transcended;

Knowledge and Truth: The consistency theory;

Value/Its Nature and Locus: Property of objective reality;

Value Judgments/Validation: Through traditional modes of knowing;

Morality: The morality of seeking and conforming to Objective Good;

Obligation and Conscience: Obligation to follow conscience toward the Good;

Ends, Means and Progress: Growth toward an ultimate goal;

Individual and Society: The individual within tradition; and

Freedom: Freedom without license.

It is also hypothesized that she holds that human nature is *either* inherently evil *or* inherently good. And, although there is considerably less evidence, she may view mind or soul as an immaterial entity and believes that values are classified and ordered according to the hierarchy of the given. Available evidence does not appear to support any additional (positive) inferences.

Confining our attention to those assumptions initially hypothesized as reasonably defensible, let us select two of them for a more detailed analysis, namely, Mrs. Evers's assumptions concerning the concepts "human nature" and "ideas."

First, let us examine the inference that Mrs. Evers assumes that human nature is either inherently evil (or predisposed to evil) or inherently good. In both cases we would expect to see a consistent use of "external control" behaviors—in the first case, to control evil inclinations; or in the second, to control the perverting influences of the environment. We do see these behaviors, however humanely and subtly expressed. Who has created the meditation corner and "allows" the students to browse through it? Who gives the assignments? Who "directs traffic" in the room, e.g., through her physical location when the students enter the room and as regards Beth? Who is the source of authority, the person who says, "Right," "Very *good,*" "No question about that" and "That's correct indeed"? Although the atmosphere is far from repressive, there is not one significant instance of cooperatively-controlled or student-controlled behavior in the script. In short, the second criterion (i.e., consistency of observed behavior and inferred assumption) does appear to be fulfilled. It will be noted, however, that the lack of specific information based on an extended behavioral sample (criterion number 5) prohibits us from distinguishing between the two assumptions in question.

It could conceivably be argued that Mrs. Evers holds human nature to be either inherently superior or inherently inferior. (Note criterion number 4.) And yet, were this the case would we not expect to see a more extensive use of external control with the inherently *inferior* child? Is it not true, for example, that students in an elective advanced chemistry course (as compared with those in a low section of the required basic course) are usually subjected to much less external control? And is this not as much a matter of the teacher trusting their superior judgment as it is a matter of their (supposedly) having learned certain procedures and the use of basic equipment? The level of verbalization, the quality of response to content and analysis questions, and the type of homework assignment given the students at the close of their class suggest that they are *markedly superior*. Thus in this instance, the degree and consistency of external control exhibited lead us to reject the alternative hypothesis.

In terms of criterion number 3 (concerning the primacy of philosophical or nonphilosophical factors), it might be argued that the historical demand for "keeping students under control" and/or the brute reality factor of having to have control in a classroom containing thirty or more early adolescents really provide the *primary* reason for the teacher's behavior. Not so. True, throughout history control has always been emphasized and is surely a contemporary reality factor. But there are different types of control, e.g., external control, cooperative control, internal or self-control. Thus as long as there *is* effective control *of some kind* and we know that the teacher is free to implement her assumptions, we may assume that in the given context these historical and/or reality factors are not as vital determiners of behavior as are the philosophical assumptions of the teacher.

Given but the sketchiest indications of criteria 2, 3 and 4 concerns—dictated by space requirements alone—the case for this first inference is becoming quite substantial. Indeed, Mrs. Evers quite possibly *does* hold the assumption that children are by nature either inherently evil or inherently good.

In the second instance, it was inferred that the instructor assumes that ideas are archetypes of existents. Criterion number 2 suggests that we might expect to observe the teacher behaving as if the child already possesses the idea and that if properly stimulated it can often be brought to the conscious level. So led out, the value of the idea will be grasped intuitively and the child will possess a key vital to understanding phenomena in the confusing sensory world. Finally, we might expect to observe the teacher helping the child to see how the idea is "objectified" in existents and how he must penetrate beneath "sensory accidents" to perceive it. Indeed, each of these behaviors is observable.

Note Mrs. Evers's skillful provision of experiences which will stimulate the emergence of the idea of freedom, e.g., the initial newspaper assignment, the almost casual question about the riots, the poem reading and consequent analytic activity, and the end-script home-work assignment. Note her comment to Carol about understanding the poetess's message by trying to feel or intuit what freedom means (in addition to attempting to understand through achieving consis-tency between ideas). Note her question concerning why the first poem *makes* us stop and think—as if, were we ever to stop for a moment in this blaring, jarring world, we just might find Truth within ourselves. Then, turn to Linda's rejection of burning the flag once she realizes its value as a symbol for freedom—or Kelly's comment, "I don't think I understood before. . . ." Note Mrs. Evers's comment that grasping the meaning of freedom allows us better to understand the reasonableness or unreasonableness of actions. Watch this teacher work with her students in coming to know what the idea means to others and how it is objectified in common existents such as the flag and other emblems. Note her direct comment that most important things can't be sensed—that we sense only existents in which they are objectified. Do these points not make a case for the contention that observed behavior and inferred assumption are sufficiently consistent to fulfill the second criterion of assumption-finding?

Passing over criterion number 4 (for reflection fails to locate another philosophical assumption which would better explain Mrs. Evers's behaviors), we come to the third criterion. Are there any facts or nonphilosophical factors in the situation which might offer a more adequate explanatory principle than the inferred philosophical as-sumption? An examination of historical, reality and sociological fac-tors fails to uncover such a principle. Psychological data is available, however, which may place our inference in some jeopardy.

Rusk reminds us that Friedrich Froebel, perhaps best remembered as the father of the kindergarten, believed that

> . . . *the mind unfolds from within according to a pre-determined pattern. 'All the child is ever to be and become, lies, however slightly indicated, in the child, and can be attained only through development from within outward.' The pattern followed is that known as pre-formation according to which the germ con-tains in miniature the fully developed plant or animal, point for point.*[17]

Froebel's notion of preformationism not only represented a long-established philosophical theory, but one which still finds contempo-rary expression and in a variety of disciplines. For instance, a striking analogue (i.e., a parallel development) is found in contemporary

[17] Robert R. Rusk, *The Doctrines of the Great Educators*. 3rd ed. (New York: St Martin's Press, 1965), p. 270; Rusk quotes Froebel, *The Education of Man*, trans. W. N. Hailman (New York: D. Appleton & Co., 1909), p. 68.

psychology's "maturational theory," especially as it concerns cognitive and moral development.[18]   The analogue contains the notion that we must turn to the child's natural endowment (including his genetic structure, innate ideas, etc.), rather than to the environment, for the primary causal factors which will explain his development.   Were this argument defensible, of course, our philosophical inference would be subject to no little difficulty, for it would be quite reasonable to hypothesize that Mrs. Evers's behaviors were based on psychological rather than philosophical assumptions.   At the very least, confusion would ensue and the reliability of the philosophical inference would be sharply reduced.

An adequate (let alone a thorough) examination of the defensibility of this psychological position is beyond the confines of this text.   It may be suggested, however, that such study would undoubtedly involve reference to at least three psychologists: Lawrence Kohlberg, Jean Piaget and Noam Chomsky.   Kohlberg's position, introduced in Chapter 7, appears inconsistent with preformationism due to his awareness of the degree to which environmental and genetic factors interact to shape behavior.   Piaget does feel that we biologically inherit certain broad capacities (i.e., "functions") for mediating experience in producing knowledge.   However, he sharply denies that our natural endowment contains innate ideas or the germ of specific behaviors (i.e., "content") or that it contains ways of organizing our experience (i.e., "structures") which characterize the various stages of cognitive development.   For instance, he writes:

> Maturation simply indicates whether or not the construction of a specific structure is possible at a specific stage.   It does not itself contain a preformed structure, but simply opens up possibilities—the new reality still has to be constructed.[19]

Finally, some examination of Chomsky's writings suggests that he indeed holds a place for innate ideas and, at the very least, stresses man's natural endowment more highly than either Kohlberg or Piaget. Man's mind contains innate structures and principles which are not only the basis for language learning but also determine in large part how he will interpret experience.   Maturational processes themselves

---

[18] The author is most indebted to Dr. Frank Murray, Professor of Educational Psychology at the University of Delaware, both for this insight and his kind provision of related resource materials.   Any errors of interpretation which follow, however, are obviously the sole responsibility of the author.

[19] Jean Piaget, Remarks in Response to Harry Beilin, "Developmental Stages and Developmental Processes," in *Measurement and Piaget: Proceedings of the CTB/ McGraw-Hill Conference on Ordinal Scales of Cognitive Development,* ed. Donald Ross Green, M. P. Ford and G. H. Flamer (New York: McGraw-Hill Book Company, 1971), p. 193.

are genetically determined. Experience is needed to bring these structures, principles and processes into operation, but the course of experience will be heavily determined by the given.

Any conclusion, given the presence of the psychological analogue, must be tentative and subject to further inquiry. It does not appear, however, that the Kohlberg or Piaget positions reduce the reliability of the inferred assumption. In Chomsky's case the possibility for reliability reduction exists, but proof will have to await further explication of his own position on innate archetypal ideas. It is not at all certain, for instance, that "freedom" would necessarily be included among them. Furthermore, few psychologists accept strict preformationism. Chomsky's "psychology" really finds its natural home in traditional philosophy rather than in the behavioral sciences. Tentatively, then, we may assume that Mrs. Evers quite possibly does hold the inferred philosophical assumption.[20]

3. Additional Resources for Finding Reasons

In this section you will encounter four additional videotape scripts designed for assumption-finding. As in the script just considered, you may assume that the teacher (or each participant in the script entitled "The Principal's Advisory Committee") is free to express his or her assumptions. You may also assume that you did extensively observe the teacher or participant outside the situation in question and that observed behavior was generally consistent with that described. (As in the script partially analyzed, however, you do not have access to the specifics of the extended observations.)

Using the text in conjunction with the "Philosophical Concepts–Assumptions Checklist" that follows on the following four pages,[21] and following the directions of your instructor, 1) develop hypotheses as to

[20] Advanced students who wish to pursue this argument might turn to several sources. Relevant works by Kohlberg have been noted in Chapter 7. For Piaget, see: John H. Flavell, *The Developmental Psychology of Jean Piaget* (New York: Van Nostrand Reinhold Company, 1963); Donald Ross Green *et al.*, eds., *Measurement and Piaget;* and Frank B. Murray, ed., *Critical Features of Piaget's Theory of the Development of Thought* (New York: MSS Information Corporation, 1972). For Noam Chomsky, see: Chomsky, *Cartesian Linguistics: A Chapter in the History of Rationalist Thought* (New York: Harper & Row, 1966); Chomsky, *Language and Mind* (New York: Harcourt, Brace & World, 1968); and Chomsky, *Problems of Knowledge and Freedom:* The Russell Lectures (New York: Pantheon Books, A Division of Random House, 1971).

[21] The "Philosophical Concepts–Assumptions Checklist" may be reproduced without permission for use with *Philosophy and Schooling* by Charles D. Marler, but may not be reproduced for any other purpose without the written consent of the publisher.

which assumptions are "possibly held" by the teacher or participant in question, and 2) attempt to defend the reliability of your inferences.

THE GREAT DAYLILY DISSECTION

(The second period bell rings. Hearing it, the fifth graders quickly come to order and wait for their science teacher to begin the day's session. A monitor takes attendance as the teacher speaks, placing the attendance form on the teacher's desk when completed.)

Mrs. Coleman: Good morning! Phyllis, that's quite a flower you have there.

Phyllis: It sure is, Mrs. Coleman. My dad grows some really wild day-lilies. He says this one should be interesting to dissect.

Mrs. Coleman: I look forward to it, too. We'll get to dissections in just a few moments. First, though, let's quickly review the parts of a flower and their function in reproduction. It will help if you remember both what

Philosophical Concepts—Assumptions Checklist

Metaphysics
Basic Reality

The Orderly, Knowable, Sensible World				
Creative, Purposeful, Spiritual Energy				
Experience of Individuals-in-Society				
Experience of the Solitary Individual				

Human Nature

Inherently Evil				
Inherently Good				
Inherently Superior or Inferior				
Constructed and Evaluated Transactionally				
Constructed and Evaluated Individualistically				

Free Will and Determinism

The Free Self				
Basic Determinism				

Philosophical Concepts—Assumptions Checklist (*Cont'd.*)

God and Faith				
The Orthodox God				
The Humanistic God				
The Denial of God				

Epistemology
Mind

Mind or Soul as an Immaterial Entity				
Function of Bodily Processes				
Purposeful, Problem-Solving Behavior				

Ideas

Archetypes of Existents				
Reflections of a Natural, External Reality				
Man-Created Plans of Action				

Experience

Contact with a Given Reality				
Transactional Doing and Undergoing				
Being in the World				

Objectivity

Alignment with a Given Reality				
Intersubjectivity				
Intrasubjectivity				

Frame of Reference

Limitation-to-Be-Transcended				
Self-in-Becoming				

Knowledge and Truth

Consistency Theory				
Correspondence Theory				
Transactional Theory				
Appropriational Theory				

Axiology
Value: Its Nature and Locus

Property of Objective Reality				
Creation of Subjective Choice				
Product of Contextual Inquiry				

Value Judgments: Validation

Through Traditional Modes of Knowing				
Through Authentic Choice				
Through Experimentation				

Values: Classifying and Ordering

The Hierarchy of the Given				
The Hierarchy of Individual Decision				
The Hierarchy of the Situation				

Morality

The Morality of Seeking and Conforming to Objective Good				
The Morality of Authenticity				
The Morality of Critical Inquiry				

Obligation and Conscience

Obligation to Follow Conscience toward the Good				
Obligation of Free Commitment				
Obligation to Be Intelligent				

Ends, Means and Progress

Growth toward an Ultimate Goal				
Growth in Self-Direction				
Growth as Its Own End				

Social Philosophy
The State and the General Welfare

The Limited State				
The Active State				

Philosophical Concepts—Assumptions Checklist (*Cont'd*)

Individual and Society				
The Individual within Tradition				
The Interdependent Society				
Freedom				
Freedom without License				
Freedom as Power				
Justice and Equality				
Just Rewards				
Egalitarianism				
Community				
Voluntary Association				
Dynamic Association				
Social Progress				
Through "Competitive Individualism"				
Through "Cooperative Individualism"				

Dr. Johnson showed us at Longwood Gardens and last night's homework assignment. I'll point to the part on this large chart; you tell me what it is called and what its job is. Phyllis, let's start with you. (Points to part of flower labeled #1.)

Phyllis: That's easy! That's the stem and its function is to support and get food to the flower.

Mrs. Coleman: Very good, Phyllis. (Writes "stem" by #1 and points to #2.) Sandra?

Sandra: That's the sepal, Mrs. Coleman. It protects the flower before it blooms.

Mrs. Coleman: Right. (Writes "sepal" by #2.) Kathy, how about #3?
Kathy: The petal—its color attracts bees.

Mrs. Coleman: Yes. (Writes "petal" by #3.) Kathy, is that the only way bees and other insects are attracted to flowers?

Kathy: Oh, no. The flower's fragrance, its size and shape—nectar—things like that.

Mrs. Coleman: Fine, Kathy. No question about you're having read the homework! (Points to part of flower labeled #4.) Jim?

Jim: The stamen?

Mrs. Coleman: Uhm-hum. (Writes "stamen" by #4.) What's its job, Jim?

Jim: Well—I think it's the male part of the flower.

Mrs. Coleman: OK, Jim.   Now, the stamen has several parts.   Let's see if you can tell us about them.   (Points to the part of the flower labeled #5.) Sam?

Sam: Oh, that's the pollen which fertilizes the ovules and makes seeds.
   (We rejoin Mrs. Coleman's class as they are completing their review of the flower's parts and functions.)

Mrs. Coleman: Very good, Ann!   (Writes "ovule" by #13.   Observing a disturbance, she turns to Jim and speaks firmly but in a friendly way.)   Jim, it's pretty hard to throw spitwads and pay attention at the same time.   If you keep it up, you won't be *ready* to do any dissecting this morning.   Now, would you rather speak to me at recess or act the way science students are supposed to?
   (Jim mumbles, "I'm sorry" and keeps his eyes glued on his desk.)

Mrs. Coleman: Alright, Jim.
   (Jim looks up and grins.)

Mrs. Coleman: Let's get to that dissecting!   Jennifer and Sam are going to give each of you one of the flowers that Phyllis brought to class, and a dissecting kit consisting of a razor blade, a magnifying glass, a dittoed worksheet and a piece of plain white paper.   *Listen now!*   Hands off all equipment until I give you the word.   Touch it and it will be taken away!   (Pause as equipment is distributed.)   Note the list on the blackboard.   *Without touching*, make sure you have everything.   (Pause.)   Have any of you ever taken a flower apart?   (Pause.)   No?   Well, follow directions carefully and I think you'll find it very interesting.   First, take the sheet of plain white paper and put it down right in front of you.   (Pause.)   OK?   Now, take your flower, turn it upside down and shake it—gently—over the paper. What do you see?

Jennifer: It's the pollen, Mrs. Coleman!   Oh, look!

Mrs. Coleman: How does it look under the magnifying glass?   (Pause.) Larry?

Larry: Looks like tiny ping-pong balls to me.   Yellow ones.

Mrs. Coleman: Good.   Now, put your paper aside—don't scatter the pollen —and carefully remove your flower's sepals and petals.   This way . . . (demonstrates.)

Jim: I don't see any sepals!

Mrs. Coleman: Remember what Dr. Johnson showed us, Jim.   The daylily has three petals and three sepals, but the sepals are often the same color as the petals and almost as large.   Look how different your daylily's sepals are from the ones on the chart.   (Mrs. Coleman points out the sepals to Jim and then walks slowly about the room, working with students who need her help.   Pausing by Phyllis's desk, she says):   That's right, Phyllis.   Only pull a little more evenly.   The petal will tear if you jerk too hard.   Good.   (She observes that all the students have removed both sepals and petals.)   Fine. Now, take your worksheet—put your name and the date on it—and draw one of the sepals and one of the petals in the boxes labeled for those parts.

Ann: I really don't see why we have to draw the parts, Mrs. Coleman.

Mrs. Coleman: Why?   Well, drawing helps us to become more exact in our observations.   The more exact we are, the more chance we have to discover the truth about nature's laws. It's all part of the scientist's work. If that's clear, let's continue with the dissection.

(We rejoin the class as they are completing their dissections. Mrs. Coleman is examining Jennifer's worksheet.)

Mrs. Coleman: Are those ovules you have drawn the same as seeds, Jennifer?

Jennifer: No, I don't think so. An ovule has to be fertilized before it can grow into a seed. When the pollen grain lands on the sticky—stigma? (Mrs. Coleman nods.)—a pollen tube grows down the style and into the ovary. Then male cells from the pollen fertilize the female cells of the ovules.

Mrs. Coleman: That's excellent, Jennifer! By the way, would you offer an hypothesis—Do you remember that word?—an *hypothesis* as to what would happen if pollenization did not take place? (Pause.) Yes, Larry.

Larry: I guess pretty soon we wouldn't have any food. There wouldn't be any feed for the cows—Gosh! No ice cream—no steak . . .

(Hearing the horrified tone in Larry's voice, students and teacher alike break into laughter.)

Mrs. Coleman: I'm afraid you're right. And that *would* be pretty bad— for all of us! Well, it's almost time for the bell. *Important announcement, class!* Tomorrow I want each of you to bring in three or four different flowers. Don't forget now—write it down in your assignment books—and put your worksheet in your notebooks. (Pause.) The monitors will now collect the dissecting equipment. Jennifer, carefully place the razor blades and the magnifying glasses on your tray. Sam, place the pieces of paper and the dissected flowers in the trash basket. Try not to spill the pollen. (As Mrs. Coleman continues, Jennifer and Sam begin collecting the equipment. Observing Jim getting ready to try hitting the basket with his wadded paper, she speaks sharply): Jim, I said *Sam* would pick up the paper. No basketball in here! (Returns her attention to the class as a whole.) After we've dissected several different kinds of flowers and talked some more about plant reproduction, we'll be ready for our test.

(Student groans.)

Kathy: Mrs. Coleman, what kind of a test will it be?

Mrs. Coleman: The usual kind, Kathy. There'll be a chart to complete, some matching questions, a few true or false—perhaps a small experiment to complete and write up. If you do your homework and get your facts straight in class, though, there's absolutely nothing to worry about!

DEMOCRATIC PREJUDICE?

(We enter Mr. Ely's eleventh grade social studies classroom and notice the instructor talking quietly with one of his students. The other students, seated at committee tables scattered about the room, are already hard at work.)

Paul: That flu bug really got me down!   Why did I have to miss the class trip through Wilmington?!

Mr. Ely: Well, Paul, I'm sorry too that you missed it—especially when you had made such a contribution to planning it—but, after all, the walking and bus tour was only the first stage of our unit on "problems of the American City."   What can we do about it?

Paul: Oh, don't worry about that, Mr. Ely!   I felt a lot better by Saturday. Three of us spent most of the day looking around!

Mr. Ely: Great!   Have you decided which of the committees you want to work on?

Paul: Well, after Saturday I would still like to work on something having to do with urban renewal.   What a mess!   Is there a group working on that?

Mr. Ely: Yeah.   As a matter of fact, the class set up a finance committee. They're planning a conference with the mayor on the costs of both urban renewal and welfare.   Could you plug your interests into their work?

Paul: Sure.   That's the group where Tom and Sally are working?

Mr. Ely: Right.   Join them and have at it!
(As Mr. Ely checks his attendance book and gathers some folders, Paul goes over to the finance committee table and enters into their discussion.   Mr. Ely finally gets up and begins moving quietly from group to group, working with students in problem-definition, assembling resources for problem-solution and developing plans of action based on committee and individual interests.   The room is a scene of quiet, coordinated activity.   The students and teacher move about freely, working at committee tables, consulting reference books and pamphlets located on well-stocked shelves, and talking with one another about their work.)

Sid: Hey, Mr. Ely, the transportation committee is really stuck.   Can you come over to our table for a minute?

Mr. Ely: OK, Sid.   Let's see what the trouble is.

Mary: Mr. Ely, we've already decided on the problem that we're going to work on.   The new civic center and downtown shopping mall have just got to be connected to the interstate by a feeder route.   But both Sid and Pat are talking about putting it right through that ghetto we saw on the field trip.   Don't these people need low-cost housing more than they need a highway?

Mr. Ely: How about it, Pat?

Pat: Well, Mary's problem is that she gets all excited by one factor and thinks that's the only thing to consider in solving a problem.   If we've learned one thing in this course, it's that you have to consider a *lot* of factors in planning.   Sure, low-cost housing is important!   But we've got two other areas where it can go.   See, here and here on the map.   I just say we've got to consider *other* factors such as the lower costs of the most direct route for the feeder and the fact that the downtown is going to die fast unless shoppers can get to it easily—and things like that.

Mr. Ely: Not easy, is it?   Perhaps in being really honest with each other about what you see as important, you will be able to develop *several* routes for the feeder.   Each should probably take into consideration as many of these factors as possible.   Then, before building that scale model you were talking about and making your class presentation, you'll have a better chance to choose the one route which has the *best* chance of working out under present conditions.

Sid: Wish we could see it built—in Wilmington, that is. All this planning and we'll never know if it would really work.

Mr. Ely: Technically that's true, but don't sell yourselves short. Jim Cary in the City Planner's Office said he wanted to see a copy of your completed report, including your scale model and maps. Reaching *your* goal may give Jim some additional tools to work with. Before I forget it, Mary, you might give his office a ring and see how he is tackling that ghetto problem. Keep with it!

(Mr. Ely raps on the transportation committee's table in order to get his students' attention. When conversation has subsided, he makes the following announcement.)

Mr. Ely: If I remember correctly, we promised the civil rights committee a chance to present their preliminary report today. Ann, you're the chairman. The time is yours.

Ann: Fine, Mr. Ely.

(Ann nods to her fellow committee members. John and Kip begin setting up their audiovisual equipment; Earlene draws the blinds; and Ann moves to the front of the room. The members of the various other committees arrange their chairs in order to see Ann and the projection screen near which she is standing.)

Ann: In the civil rights committee we've been working on a slide and sound presentation entitled, "The Democratic Myth and the American City." Right now we've got more controversy than we know what to do with. We thought if we shared what we had completed, you might help us work through some of our hang-ups. John, if you'll get the lights, I think we're ready to go.

(The class watches a two-minute slide and sound presentation which hits hard at the tremendous gap between democratic theory and the realities of living in a contemporary American city—especially for minority groups.)

Ann: Kip, would you say something about the things that we're arguing about?

Kip: Um . . . I guess some of us feel it's just too prejudiced. I mean . . . here we have a really sore issue and all we're doing is giving the worst side of it. That's not very honest—even if it *is* the "thing to do."

Earlene: Kip, you're crazy! That's the way it is in Wilmington . . . in a lot of cities . . . with a lot of people. If you don't hit the honkies in the suburbs over the head with it, they'll *never* listen!

John: Honkies?!?

Mr. Ely: Whoa now. How about that word "honesty," Earlene?

Earlene: A lot of "honest" people feel that way—"honestly." I'm not the only one!

Sally: Maybe the best way to get the most honest, the most true view is to add up all the honest feelings and see what you've got.

Mr. Ely: How would you know when you had the most honest view?

Sally: Maybe by the way people feel about it . . . after checking out what others thought. Everybody could say . . . about something in it . . . yes, that's the way it is, that's true. I still don't like some parts of it, but I'll live with it because that's the way it really is.

Mr. Ely: You mean "honesty" may be a moral standard, but it doesn't tell you what you have to do before you start doing it. You have to work out what "honesty" means together . . . like the interstate feeder problem that the transportation committee is working on.

Tom: It seems to me that Ann's committee might decide that they wanted to keep their presentation prejudiced . . . in order to force people into thinking. On the other hand, they might want to picture the situation more honestly. I don't know. . . . It really depends on the things they really value and what to get across to certain people at a certain time.

Mr. Ely: Well, that's something to think about . . .

(The passing bell interrupts Mr. Ely's comment. With a smile and a resigned wave of the hand, he dismisses the class.)

THE FREE-FORM CLASSROOM

(It is Monday of the second full week of school. Jane, a student teacher, enters the third-grade classroom to find her supervising teacher, Lois, already at work in the materials area.)

Lois: Hi, Jane. Have you recovered from your first week in the great American public school?

Jane: Do you know I went to bed at eight o'clock on Friday night? And I'm not even doing any teaching yet!

Lois: Would you rather watch a few more days before taking the plunge?

Jane: Please! What's on for today?

Lois: Let's explore free-form paper cutting. Here, help me dish up some paste. (They spoon up blobs of paste onto toweling paper, continuing their conversation as they work.) Seriously, I think these kids have had every teacher-dominated lesson in the curriculum guide—and they've learned . . . oh, they've learned. I'm really having trouble getting them to *say* anything, let alone loosen up and be themselves. This activity should shake them loose if nothing else will! We'll distribute some colored paper, have each child try cutting different shapes, arrange them to suit himself on a backing sheet and—if he wishes—interpret what he's done.

Jane: What are the objectives—balance and design?

Lois: (smiles): Do you think that might be an outgrowth?

Jane: What if you give them the paper and they don't know what to cut? I mean . . . I know you don't want them to imitate—that's not a real art experience—but what if they don't come up with anything?

Lois: What do you feel they *should* come up with?

Jane: Well, you're the teacher, but I do think it's important for them to have a successful art experience.

Lois: Jane, you've got some hang-ups . . . but, welcome to the human community. I think a " 'successful' art experience" is important too. But I don't see how I can anticipate how a "successful" piece of cut paper should look. Don't you think it depends on how each child feels about what he chooses to do and what both process and product mean to him?

Jane: I'm getting the idea. What color paper shall I get out?

Lois: Get a selection of what's available. They can choose what they want.

Jane: Won't that waste a lot of time—trying to decide on colors?

Lois: You think so? The school day is full of wasted time, but I suspect that time spent on personal choice is valuable. You know, *everybody* needs a chance to do his own thing—even the child.

Jane: Sure. Me too. But what will they learn from all this?

Lois: For myself, I'll be satisfied if each child can get all of himself into this simple exercise. You know: really feel it out—be pleased with the sensations and what he creates. There *are* some technical points in art, but we'll get to those as we go along. (Sound of a bell and approaching children.) Here they come! I'll be interested to see how we both feel after class!

>   (As Jane continues to assemble paper and scissors on a large tray, the children rush into the art classroom, some talking—a few greeting the teacher by her first name.)

Lois: Good morning, everybody! Sit wherever you want and let's talk for a few minutes before getting started. One of the things we can do this morning reminds me of something I like to do very very much. I don't know if you have ever done it, but have you ever put your finger on a dusty piece of furniture and traced shapes? Anyone in here ever do that? (In response to grins and affirmative answers, Lois continues): How about a frosty window in the car? Did you ever sit in the back seat and trace your finger around and make shapes? Or, how about in the house? Did you ever trace shapes on a frosty window in the house?

Children: Oh yes! On my bedroom window! On the school bus!

Lois: Running your finger around on the window . . . Did you enjoy it? Well, one of the things we can do this morning is to let our fingers wander with a pair of scissors. Jane is going to come around with a tray; each of you may take a pair of scissors and five or six pieces of paper . . . any color you like. While she's coming around, I'm going to take a pair of scissors and cut any shape I like. (As the materials are distributed and the children are choosing, chattering and beginning to cut shapes, Lois sits on the edge of a student's table and continues): The only thing about the shape, of course, is that in order to cut it out I have to get back to where I started. How about this one?! I think I'll pick another color for my next one. Sometimes I like to cut straight lines—no curves—just a lot of straight lines . . . back and forth. Sometimes it's fun just to not even look at what you are doing. Let your hands and fingers guide you wherever you want them to go. (Observing the children already at work.) Good, go right ahead and start when you get your paper and scissors. (The children are quietly chattering and fast becoming immersed in the activity.) Wow, look at that one! While you are cutting your shapes . . . Oh, I think I'll cut one more. I feel like it . . . While you are cutting your shapes, I am going to take mine, move them around until I like the way they look and then paste them down on a backing sheet.

(As Lois is thinking out loud, Jane is handing out material and talking with the children. Suddenly, Frankie comes up to the teacher.)

Frankie: Lois, could I play with the clay today? I really don't feel like cutting paper.

Lois: You don't want to? That's perfectly all right, Frankie. Get Jane to help you find the clay and then have some fun with it. Okay? (To Jane): Frankie would prefer to do something else . . .

Jane: What would you like to do, Frankie?

Frankie: I want to play with the clay.

Jane (walking over to the materials area with Frankie): Okay, Frankie, here's the clay. Let's go over there and get some room by spreading things out on the floor.

(They walk over to the side of the room as Lois continues.)

Lois: When you have as many shapes cut as you want, go over to the materials area and get a backing sheet and some paste. (As the children continue their cutting, Lois walks over to the materials area, gathers a backing sheet and paste, and returns to her table-corner seat.) It's a lot of fun just to move them around on a piece of paper. You put them one way and get one idea; then you move them around another way and see something else. (Noticing that Renee has put her scissors down and walked over to the window, Lois quietly moves over to her.) Hi, Renee. What do you see?

Renee (shyly): Oh, I'm watching the pretty birds.

Lois: Oh, aren't they pretty? (Renee nods her head.) They truly are. (Lois smiles and continues to walk about the room. Suddenly she stops and exclaims): One thing I know: Everybody in here is different!

(We rejoin the art class as the children are beginning to move about the room in order to secure their backing sheets and paste.)

Lois: Everybody is mighty quiet this morning. Did you play hard this last weekend?

(The children respond to her question absentmindedly, each fully involved in his activity. Mark, Frankie, Annette—all are deeply engrossed.)

(The scene shifts. We see Frankie walking up to Lois.)

Frankie: I want to put my name on my model. May I borrow one of your pencils?

Lois: I don't know if I have a pencil in here with me this morning. I left my purse in my locker and then I came in here without a pencil! Would you believe it? Why don't you go down the hall and ask one of the other teachers for one?

Frankie: Okay, Lois. Thank you.

Lois: Sure.

(The art period is about two-thirds over. Lois, knowing full well the teaching—and teacher—problems one meets in a more traditional school, is speaking):

Lois: How many of you are finished now? (She counts three hands.) How many of you are *almost* finished? (Most of the children raise their hands.) You know why I'm asking! You know we have to fight that old bell!

(Activity continues feverishly. Kathy, Steven and Renee are busy pasting. Annette and Ramona are observed quietly at work. Mark continues cutting paper and talking to himself. Jane and Frankie are seen talking together and smiling as Frankie returns the clay to the materials area.)

Lois: I'm going to bring the tray around, but only for those things you don't want—like little bits of paper and any scissors or paste you're finished with. Only those things you are finished with . . .

(As the art period draws to a close, Lois moves to a position where all of the children can see and hear her.)

Lois: Let's start talking about some of the things we did. Is there anyone who would like to tell us about what he did today? Anyone want to tell us about it? (Pause.) I'll tell you about mine . . . if you want. I'd *like* to tell you about mine . . . as much as I can. I cut a lot of different shapes. I didn't pay too much attention to the colors . . . just the ones that I sort of felt like picking up at the time. And then when I moved the pieces around on the paper and found something I liked, I pasted them down. And I can look at it this way . . . and this way . . . and this way. (Turns art around in all directions for pleasing effects.) It makes me feel good. How about yours, Annette? Would you like to talk about your art?

Annette: Oh, no . . . please . . .

Lois: If you don't feel like it, that's perfectly all right, Annette. You're the best judge. Mark, do you want to tell us about yours?

(Several of the children choose to interpret their creations; several feel theirs is a private thing and decline. Both decisions are equally reinforced.)

Lois: Who else? Steven?

Steven: I have all different shapes . . . and I have a moon . . . and that's all. (Suddenly.) Lois, I don't like Mark's!

Lois: Well, I'm sure there are many good reasons why you don't like what someone else has created, and you surely have a right to feel that way. But Mark is probably the best judge of what *he* likes and what is important to *him*. (Smilingly.) Is that fair enough? (Receiving an affirmative nod from Steven, Lois offers Frankie his chance to tell the class about what he has created in clay.)

Frankie: I made a sub . . . because I like to see subs sink . . . because I've seen a lot of war movies with subs . . . (He loses his train of thought.)

Lois: Do you like it?

Frankie: Uh-huh . . .

Lois: Do you want to keep it?

Frankie: Uh-huh!

(With good humor, Lois turns to her student teacher.)

Lois: I think there is one more in the room that we didn't see.

Jane (surprised):   Ooh!   Mine.   (Laughter.)   Well, I don't know.   I just felt kind of in a curvy mood today.   I just cut out the shapes, put them on a piece of paper.   And it's kind of a happy day outside and green always makes me feel happy . . . so I went and picked some green paper.   And purple makes me feel happy, so I put purple shapes on, too. And, I like mine and I'm going to keep it, teacher.

Lois: I want to keep mine, too.   (Bell sounds.)   And there it is!   You can take your art with you.   Hope you have a happy day!

THE PRINCIPAL'S ADVISORY COMMITTEE

> (Dr. Nelson Farley, principal of Langston High School, is about to call the first meeting of his new advisory committee to order.   The group, chatting informally, is seated around a large table in Dr. Farley's office.)

Dr. Farley: Well, ladies and gentlemen, let's get underway.   The meeting will please come to order.   As you know, the School Board has finally given us permission to form a committee representing all segments of the school community.   They didn't grant our request for a strong "administrative council," but I think you know I intend to treat this advisory committee in much the same way.   After all, I can't very well expect you to take responsibility without sharing some authority.   Now, I think most of you know each other: Mr. Galvan, chairman of the Math-Science Department; Mr. Smythe, chairman of Humanities; Mr. Guest, faculty member-at-large; Miss Gibson, president of the Student Council; and Mr. Porter, student member-at-large.   Unfortunately, Miss Pedwick, chairman of the Department of Fine and Applied Arts, is ill today.   And, of course, you all know my secretary, Miss Hill.   I hope, in addition to serving as the committee's secretary, that she will informally represent the school's support personnel.   OK, Pat?   (Dr. Farley smiles in response to an affirmative nod.)

I had hoped that our first meeting could focus on agenda development, but I'm afraid we've got another job today.   The superintendent is extremely disturbed about last week's demonstrations at McKinley High. Every middle and high school in the district has received a directive to develop guidelines for protest activities and submit them to his office for approval.   So . . . that's it.   Comments?

Leslie Gibson: Our student body is really upset about the suspensions at McKinley, Dr. Farley.   I'd like to suggest that the Student Council be asked to discuss the problem and make some recommendations.   They could also give us a lot of help in talking with the students and even evaluating the effectiveness of the guidelines we finally work out.

Pete Galvan: Just a minute, young lady!   This is an extremely sensitive, explosive issue.   The *last* thing we need to do is get a lot of people involved—especially immature, emotional students.   If we do, our troubles could be a lot worse than McKinley's.   *This* is a democratic body, isn't it?

Let's quietly set up some rules that will control the hotheads and then have the administration lay the law down.

James Smythe: Pete, that's pretty strong.   I think it's clear enough that we have a great bunch of kids here.   With a little guidance, they can see what reasonable protest means and act accordingly.   What's so wrong with Dr. Farley calling a special meeting of the Student Council, presenting the problem and moderating the discussion?   Their feedback might help us quite a bit.

Mike Porter: What's so horrible about letting the Student Council do its own thing?   It seems to me that if we really have an open school, everybody learns, everybody profits.   The students see some things; the administrators see some things; and the faculty see still some other things. We put it all together, compromise a bit, and we have a set of guidelines for protest—or for most anything else—that we can all live with.   We can buy the package because we had a real part in developing it.   You close the door on that kind of cooperation if you keep treating us as if we were still in kindergarten!

Pete Galvan: There's no desire to treat you like a kindergartner, Mike. That would be stupid.   On the other hand, how much more intelligent would it be to treat you like a certified teacher with twelve years of experience?   Look, I'll level with you.   We both want as much freedom as we can get, right?   I've got news for you!   That kind of individual freedom only exists where you've got order.   It's order that controls for defects in people and in the environment.   It's order that allows each person the freedom to develop his potential without unnecessary interference from others.   It's order that allowed a solid academic program to produce three—*three*, mind you!—National Merit Scholarship winners last year.   And it's order that allows us to make what slow progress we finally do make. Don't knock it . . . and forget about opening the protest issue to every Tom, Dick and Harry in the school.   We'd fall apart so fast they'd have the state police in here within a week.

Mike Porter: That's possible.   A lot of kids at Langston have learned not to care.   They probably wouldn't help much.   And quite a few others have learned that when the subject of "order" comes up they're not going to get a thing until they push harder than you do.   They probably wouldn't buy a reasonable approach either.   So maybe you're right.

Tom Guest: Every time people start putting their two cents in, I get an overwhelming urge to do the same thing.   What's so all-fired sacred about the "group"?   Everybody is talking about groups.   Pete has *this* in-group; Jim has this group plus the Student Council—with a "little guidance" from the System, of course; and our two students have their Student Council doing its own thing plus cooperating with this group.   Hell, you've all got the same hang-up!   Why not open the problem up to every single human being in the place?   Why shouldn't each and every student have a chance to express his personal commitment; each and every secretary, hers; and on down the line?   That's how you grow people instead of turnips!

Dr. Farley: Well, I can see that this is a typical education gathering— 50 people and 150 opinions!   (Laughter.)   I'm not sure that we want to get completely sidetracked right now on the question of *who* is going to develop the guidelines.   No matter who does it, you know, we're going to be faced with deciding how to go about it and what the limits are. And once developed, approved and implemented, we're going to face evaluating how all the guidelines accomplish their purpose. We're also going to have to make provisions for those who just won't cooperate. I suspect that the superintendent will be looking for a few suggestions along those lines. Well, then . . . How about the question of how to go about developing the guidelines, necessary limits and that sort of thing?

Pete Galvan: I'd simply say: Be as clear about the issues as you can and state your recommended guidelines in behavioral terms so we can check the results later on. You're only limited by three necessary criteria: 1) Individuals may not engage in protest activities which interfere with the rights of others; 2) Protest activities must not destroy the lawful, orderly environment of the school upon which depends the school's success if not its very existence; and 3) Inasmuch as each individual is equal before the law, each guideline must be binding on each person and to the same degree. There . . . that's a little legalistic, but it ought to do it.

Dr. Farley: Leslie, do you or Mike want to make some countersuggestions?

Leslie Gibson: Maybe we've said too much already.

Dr. Farley: Not at all! If you're going to work with teachers, you'll have to develop a thick hide and a fast tongue. We all have pretty high verbal scores and we'll just talk you to death unless you come right back at us. Don't be afraid . . . we'll listen.

Leslie Gibson: Well, alright. I agree with Mr. Galvan about being clear about the issues, and after his chemistry course I know what he means by behavioral objectives. They're OK, too. But I really don't see the reason for his three criteria. He's really saying that protest activities are OK as long as they don't rock the boat. I'd leave the door completely open and give everybody a chance to come up with recommendations that make sense to them. If they rock the boat, well that's too bad.

Dr. Farley: No more guidance than that? What does it mean, for instance, for a recommendation to "make sense"?

Leslie Gibson: Oh, that just means that the person has thought it out. He's taken into consideration the people here at Langston High—including those who have a lot more reason to protest than we do—his own views, community pressures on the superintendent and the possible consequences of acting on one guideline as compared with another . . . things like that.

Tom Guest: Among other things, Leslie, you seem to be saying that a guideline doesn't "make sense" unless it takes social harmony into consideration. It won't work, for example, unless the community and the students at Langston are reasonably satisfied. Haven't you simply substituted your criterion for the criteria proposed by Mr. Galvan? What happens if an individual just doesn't buy the guidelines that most of the school finally accepts? Is he unreasonable? Immoral?

Leslie Gibson: I'm not really sure . . . but isn't that part of living in any society? You can't do *everything* you want to.

Tom Guest: Then you've lost faith in your "completely open door." Too bad . . . I suspect if you *did* recognize everybody's absolute freedom you'd be amazed how involved and committed they'd become. Oh, there would be some pretty scary protests for a little while . . . until they got fifteen, sixteen or seventeen years of "law and order" out of their systems, and then you'd have a school whose creative accomplishments would exceed anything you ever dreamed of. Too bad . . .

Jim Smythe: I can just see you trying to evaluate the success of your guidelines, Tom. It would set science back into the Dark Ages! I honestly don't think you know the difference between "freedom" and "license." If you are going to evaluate results, you're going to have to specify desired behaviors. Where you don't see them, you tell the offender to "shape up or ship out."

Tom Guest: Don't worry about that, Jim. A lot of students dropped out of school a long time ago. It's just their bodies that are sitting in our classrooms.

Dr. Farley: Perhaps your road to evaluation and control is a little narrow, Jim. I'd like to think in meeting the superintendent's request that we would all learn quite a bit about different ways to reach what we want, about what happens when we take different courses of action . . . perhaps more about what we really want for our school and ourselves as individuals. It's going to be difficult to state those objectives in behavioral terms, but I think we ought to try. I also think that these goals tell us that we must be flexible in disciplining offenders. After all, they might be meeting *some* of our objectives at the same time that they were staging a sit-in in the cafeteria! Let's go slow and work it out.

Uhmm . . . Our time for today is about up. We're faced with some difficult decisions. At tomorrow's meeting, after thinking about the things said here today, will you come prepared to decide four points: 1) Who will develop the protest guidelines? 2) What procedures will we direct them to follow in reaching their recommendations, and what limitations will they be operating under? 3) How is the success or the failure of the guidelines to be determined? 4) How are we to react to violations of the guidelines? How's *that* for a homework assignment?!

B.   Generating Possibilities

1. Taking Philosophical and Nonphilosophical Factors into Account

With this section, the outline and purposes of *Philosophy and Schooling* should begin to become fully visible. You will remember our early discussion which contended that philosophical assumptions in themselves rarely if ever determined (cause) observed educational outcomes (effects). Why? In the first place, they are themselves being shaped by the outcomes. In the second, they are also shaping and being shaped by nonphilosophical factors—which in turn are shaping and being shaped by the outcomes. Here, then, is the full-blown transactional model, a model which accounts for so many failures in researching educational phenomena and developing predictive hypotheses as to student reactions in response to teacher actions.

In the past nine and one-half chapters, we have focussed essentially on philosophical factors. This was proper, for it is really impossible to understand how a philosophical factor transacts with another element without first understanding what is involved in the philosophical factor per se. That is, a knowledgeable synthesis—especially of the complex phenomena involved in teaching-learning—depends upon a careful analysis of its constituent parts. Having attempted one segment of this analysis, however, we must now return to the "real world" of professional decision-making. This is the world where the educator's decisions must take into account both philosophical[22] and nonphilosophical factors operating in a given situation.

The method selected for this stage of our inquiry is the so-called "case-study approach." For those of you who have not encountered this technique in business or legal studies (where it is used extensively), it may prove a bit frustrating at first. For instance, you will be called upon to identify the issue(s) in a professional situation where neither the outcomes are known nor do you even have all of the data leading up to the described incident. A specified "decision-maker" (e.g., a supervisor, principal, class counsellor or superintendent of schools) will be identified, but you will not be given any information about his or her frame of reference. In essence, you will *become* that person.

George and Pauline Perry suggest that several advantages may accrue from such an approach. For instance, you will have to take all sorts of factors into account in coming to a conclusion as to what the decision-maker should do to solve the problem. They believe that in the process of small-group discussions you will begin to gain some insights into the feelings of others. You will also be forced by the very structure of the activity to "get involved," to make a decision. And then, in a less emotion-laden situation than might be the case were such an incident to arise in your own classroom, you will be able to consider peer criticisms. You will also have opportunity to develop a more seasoned judgment and gain extensive experience with the kinds of transactional decision-making skills sorely needed by the effective professional educator.[23]

---

[22] Note, however, that this factor set includes not only the philosophical assumptions of the teacher, but also those of students, administrators, curriculum (including content, structure and materials), the specific school or district as a social institution, and parents and the wider community.

[23] George and Pauline Perry, *Case-Studies in Teaching* (New York: Pitman Publishing Corp., 1969), pp. 4–7.

2. An Exercise in Generating Possibilities

After you have read the case-study which follows, you will find several
questions relevant to reaching decisions in all four studies contained in
this section. In the first instance, the author will suggest some possibilities; in the remaining case-studies, your instructor will help to
establish those procedures most appropriate to your needs.

WHAT DID I DO TO DESERVE THIS?

Lunch was finally over. Mrs. Jaye, three years a teacher but
in her first year at the Berwick School, sighed heavily as
she approached the door to the schoolyard. Three
fights, yelling and arguing all morning, she thought, and
three and one-half hours to go this afternoon. As she
reached for the handle, the door burst open and teacher and
principal nearly collided. Mr. Zanta, face flushed and
breathing heavily, spoke:
     "Mrs. Jaye, I've had it with your class. Their behavior in
this school is unforgivable. Beginning right now, I
want you to deny them all recess privileges until
you get control of them."
     Well, that really does it! She clenched her fists in
her coat pockets and took a deep breath to loosen up the
knots in her chest. Recess privileges indeed! Since when was
a romp in the yard, a drink of water and a chance to go to
the bathroom a privilege! Until *I* get control of them.
How am I supposed to do that: hit them with a club? By
sixth grade, children should have developed some
self-control. Well, I'll call a class meeting and discuss it
with them.
     In the classroom, Mrs. Jaye called for order. "Class, we
have a problem; we need to put our heads together and
come up with some possible solutions. Kenney, you're the
president. Will you please call the meeting to order?"
Kenney sauntered up to the front of the room and
leaned against the blackboard. Someone threw a spitwad; the
class broke into guffaws. "Children, please," Mrs. Jaye
admonished, "that's just what's wrong with this class.
You won't respect each other. Now, I want to discuss with
you your behavior in the yard this morning. There are

so many complaints that I'm being forced to take all your recesses away until we can do something about it."

Phil's chair turned over with a loud crash as he ran to the front of the room and punched Kenney. Two other large boys joined the fracas. Mrs. Jaye pushed her way into the middle, placing her hand on Phil's shoulder.

Taller than his teacher, Phil glared down at her. "Git your hands off me. Don't you never lay a han' on me, you hear —nobody is going to push me around."

"Phil, I wasn't trying to push you around—just stop you from fighting. This is the sort of thing that keeps this class in so much trouble."

"Ain't no trouble . . . He started a fight in the yard an' I'm gonna finish it right now."

"But what about your responsibility to the class? If we can discuss your problem with Kenney, maybe we can work it out as a class."

"Ain't nobody else's business!" Phil slumped in his chair and stared out the window.

"I'm not gonna miss my recesses," muttered Doreen. "I ain't done nothin'; I'll stay home."

"Me too," agreed Wayne. "I don't need to come here. I've already got a job at the mine. I don't need this place."

"Children, we all need this place. We live in the world with lots of people. We have to learn how to get along—make compromises—solve our problems together. What are we going to do about our behavior?"

"Kenney's the problem," Bill volunteered; "I'll solve it after school. Just you wait, Kenney!"

"Children, fighting is not the answer to conflicts."

By now, however, the children were all arguing, laughing or talking together. Mrs. Jaye realized that she was talking to herself. "Thank heavens it's time for music," she muttered as she glanced up at the clock. "Children, it's time to line up for music. Please remember as we walk down the hall that Mr. Zanta is very upset with us. Let's show him how well we can keep our line."

"Don't make no difference now," groaned Joan; "we already lost all our recesses."

"Recess has nothing to do with our behavior, Joan. We should be proud of our class and show others our feelings about ourselves by the way we behave."

Strung out single file, forty-five children made a very long line. When she reached the music room at the head of the

line, Mrs. Jaye held her breath.   Part of the class was still
hidden around the corner.   Mr. Zanta suddenly rounded the
corner with the rest of a thoroughly subdued group.

"Mrs. Jaye," he shouted, "three members of your class
banged on the door to Room 5 where I was observing! Is this
the kind of control you have?   These children have no
respect for your authority.   Turn them right around and go
back to the classroom."   He addressed the class: "The next time
I come by your room I want to see you in your seats with
your books open and your mouths shut!"

Back in the classroom, Mrs. Jaye fought back her anger and
the strongest desire to cry.   "Take out your social studies
books," she commanded.   "Read pages 75–94 and answer
the questions on page 95."   I had hoped to get them into
committees to plan their unit, she thought, but if Mr. Zanta
came down to check and heard all that noise . . . After a
moment or two there was complete silence.   Well at last,
control! Her eyes swept from head to head.   A few of the
children were reading.   Some had put their heads down
on their desks.   Wayne was already asleep.   Just as well . . .
he can't read anyway.   Phil stared out the window across an
open field where a horse was grazing.   Kenney and Bill
glared furtively at one another.   Control . . . respect for my
authority . . . Mrs. Jaye contemplated.   Do I have it now
at this moment?   And it's only late September . . . and
only two o'clock.

After approximately forty minutes she interrupted the
silence.   "Children, since we shall miss recess I'll send five boys
and five girls at a time to the bathroom.   I trust you to behave
in the restrooms, since I have to stay here with the rest of the
class.   If you have any problems remember that your bathroom
monitors are in charge."

The children irritably jostled against one another as they
moved down the hall.   Ramona, a quiet bewildered-looking
child, smiled up at Mrs. Jaye and clung to her hand.   "You're
not mad at me, are you?" she shyly inquired.   Mrs. Jaye
smiled warmly but before she could reply Betty Jean came
running back into the classroom.   "Mrs. Jaye, somebody wrote
on the wall in the boys' room.   Now Mr. Zanta says nobody
in the upper grades will get to see the Christmas movie 'cause
the money will have to go for paint to fix the bathroom."
The noise level rose as the children began to argue among
themselves.

"Children." Mrs. Jaye tried to keep her voice smooth and her words unhurried. "I know you cannot help but care about being punished for doing so many things wrong. Surely if we talk this over quietly we can get many ideas from each other that will give us some guidelines for our behavior. I'm going to ask you as homework to think about all the things that happened today and list your ideas about how to handle our problems."

But they were not listening. Someone in the back of the room began bouncing a ball.

"I ain't comin' tomorrow," muttered Doreen.

"Where's Phil?" asked someone.

"He left," laughed Kenney, "while Mrs. Jaye was talking about homework. I saw him heading across the field."

"I'll git him in the morning," Tom boasted; "I saw him writing on the wall."

Her hands trembled as Mrs. Jaye wrote a note to the principal: "Philip Longstreet has left the building." When she stopped by the office to sign the check-out sheet before going home, the note had been returned to her mailbox. Across the bottom Mr. Zanta had written: "Mrs. Jaye, I have referred your situation to the Central Office. Miss Cornelia Bryant, chief district elementary supervisor, will be in the school tomorrow to observe your teaching and discuss plans for controlling your class for the rest of the term. She will submit a report directly to me and the superintendent. You would do well to give Miss Bryant your full cooperation. signed/James K. Zanta, Principal." Mrs. Jaye looked at the memo, a stunned expression on her face. How *can* I communicate with that man? How can I even communicate with *those children?* This is really *quite* an area: if the kids or the principal don't finish you off, the Central Office will!

QUESTIONS FOR INDIVIDUAL THOUGHT AND PREPARATION FOR SMALL-GROUP DISCUSSION[24]

1. What do you see to be the basic underlying conflict(s) or issue(s) in this case-study? How do historical, philosophical, psychological, reality and/or sociological factors enter into this situation?
2. Identify the character whom you dislike most intensely. Then, try to assume that person's frame of reference and gain a deeper insight into the reasons for his or her point of view and behavior.
3. Specify the character with whom you identify most strongly. Why?

[24] These questions are applicable to all four case-studies in this section.

4. Examine the key statements and other actions of each major character in the study. On the basis of Question #1, suggest "reasons" for his or her behaviors.

5. Assuming that the "decision-maker"[25] holds a) a *classical* or *conservative* frame of reference (and given the nonphilosophical factors identified in Question #1), what do you think he should do? . . . if he holds b) a *pragmatic* or *liberal* frame of reference? . . . if he holds c) an *existentialist* frame of reference?

6. Given your *own* evolving frame of reference, what *specifically* do *you* think the decision-maker should do? (However difficult and tentative your decision, try first to take a general stand and then consciously consider the philosophical assumptions—and nonphilosophical factors—which seem to lead you to that decision.)

7. In speaking to the two preceding problems, you may have come up with four or more different courses of action.

> 7.1 Let us assume that "5a" occurs. What do you think the consequences would be? How do you think the major characters in the study would probably feel and otherwise react to these consequences?
>
> 7.2 Assume "5b" occurs, and consider the same questions.
>
> 7.3 Assume "5c" occurs, and consider the same questions.
>
> 7.4 Assume "6" occurs, and consider the same questions.

8. After completing Question #7, have you changed your mind about what you think the decision-maker should do? If so, why?

In the commentary which follows, it appears neither necessary nor helpful to attempt to speak to all eight suggested questions. Rather, the commentary will be restricted to brief notes on the philosophical and nonphilosophical factors involved in the situation and what they suggest in terms of basic issues.[26] The goal, then, is to help you become involved in the task of generating possibilities without inhibiting your insights or your use of developing skills.

The *historical* elements in the case-study you have just read are many and varied. For instance, one is struck by the lack of professional autonomy on the part of educators generally, but especially on the part of the elementary school teacher. Isolated in a bureaucratic system and often lacking adequate professional assistance, she is still expected to have sufficient knowledge of material and techniques to

---

25 Decision-makers in the four case-studies include the following: "What Did I Do to Deserve This?": Cornelia Bryant; "Odd Man Out": Kinsley Simmons, principal; "You're Damned If You Do and . . . !": Kate Gordonstein, the senior class counsellor; and "The Porcupine Case": Dr. Cooper, superintendent of schools.

26 The purposes of a Department of Educational Foundations within a College of Education have never been more clear than when the author was able to turn to his colleagues for their reactions to "What Did I Do to Deserve This?" Sincere thanks are owed Dr. Robert J. Taggart, Dr. William G. DeColigny, Dr. Anderson Fanta, Dr. Edward Kepka and Dr. Ludwig Mosberg. The author only hopes that he has been equal to the task of accurately interpreting some small portion of their insights.

handle both herself and everyday "minor problems." By "minor problems" we refer to such things as figuring out what to do with forty-five clients who feel put-upon and who do *not* come willingly to her as most clients come to other professionals. We might also notice the historic lack of a clear definition of education as an intellectual enterprise which forces teachers and principals alike to define "success" in such gross and obvious terms as "control." Related to this phenomenon is the bureaucratic nature of education which, over time, has led principals to believe that they are indispensable, in full control of the situation and somehow different from other educators. Naturally, as a member of the power-structure, the principal takes and gives orders, but refrains from openly assisting his "inferiors." Dating back to the 1640s, we also find the strongest sentiment for "local control." This phenomenon does have a positive side, in that the "neighborhood school" is generally viewed as "my school." Unfortunately, it can also result in the unequal distribution of property taxes, considerable differences between pay scales and the number of children per class, and markedly unequal access to paraprofessional and technological assistance. Deeply engrained in the American school system are the ideals of achieving a common core of values and civic-economic self-sufficiency. Woe unto the child who does not view the Protestant-ethic as "common sense"! In like measure, we may feel sorry for the child whose experience does not lead him to value rationality, restraint, compromise and a future-orientation. He may soon find that the ideal of an educated person is obedience rather than rationality. The case-study also illustrates the continuing influence of the Progressive Education Movement (*ca.* late 1800s to World War II) upon the American school. An emphasis on the ideal of the classroom community, democratic group problem-solving and the irresistible power of human reason are all illustrated in this case-study. Unfortunately, an historical phenomenon which still dominates the institutions of teacher education is increasingly passé outside those hallowed walls. Finally, we may feel an historically-based sympathy for the teacher who on the morrow must face the "chief district elementary supervisor." One may hope that her professional association has more power to protect her than most do—or have had in the past.

In terms of *psychological* variables of contemporary interest, much will depend upon the teaching-learning theories of the psychologist in question. For instance, a Skinnerian might ask questions such as the following: "What is reinforcing the students' disruptive behavior?" "What are the specific behaviors which the teacher desires to eliminate, as well as those which she desires to establish?" "What reinforcers are likely to be effective for shaping desirable behaviors?" "How can the classroom be structured to set up the contingencies of reinforcement (contingency management)?" "What are the relative merits of using positive reinforcement rather than punishment as used in this case-study?" Since there appear to be a number of interpersonal conflicts within the class, one might consider conflict resolution and attitude change techniques.

Viewing this case-study from the vantage point of *social psychology* and *sociology*, a number of factors come into focus. For instance, the "social climate" in classroom and school, seen in the general absence of self-esteem and morale and the open hostility which permeates the atmosphere, is hardly conducive to teaching or learning. Part of the problem, of course, lies in the fact that Mrs. Jaye appears utterly unprepared to deal with the environment in which she finds herself. Clinging to habit, she is behaving in ways which have little meaning for her students and which are utterly naive in view of Mr. Zanta's perception of his role and those of teachers and students. Hence, she is suffering some punishing consequences. Unfortunately, the social climate is such as to increase, rather than decrease, dissonance. The bureaucratic structure of the institution, for instance, demands communication "through channels"—and usually from the top down. Educators of different status levels (e.g., administrators, teachers) quickly find that structural contingencies militate against sitting down and working out problems as professional colleagues. The relationships between roles on each level are formally defined in a situation where Mrs. Jaye sorely needs room to negotiate greater congruence of aims, attitudes and role expectations on the basis of informal relationships. Furthermore, the size of her class presents all sorts of problems with regard to the more informal working relationships which she must establish with her sixth graders, not to speak of the principal. These individual and structural conflicts are further lacerated by what seem to be strong social class differences, especially between teacher and pupils. In such an environment it is nearly impossible to develop and enforce workable social norms—other than on the basis of conformity. Mr. Zanta's power displays are obviously inhibiting the development of informal relationships between the two educators and between Mrs. Jaye and her students. Their personality and structural problems may or may not be lessened by the intervention of Miss Bryant. Unless Miss Bryant is a close friend and champion of long-standing, however, Mr. Zanta must feel especially threatened by Mrs. Jaye to involve the Central Office in the dispute.

Passing over "reality factors" which do not appear to be especially significant in this case-study, let us now turn to some consideration of *philosophical* variables. From this vantage point, a *massive* difference in frames of reference appears to exist between the teacher and students on the one hand and the teacher and principal on the other. A detailed analysis of the type pursued in the preceding section of this chapter would be necessary to increase the reliability of our inferences. Nevertheless, we can at least offer the hypothesis that a teacher with a pragmatic-liberal frame of reference is confronted by a principal whose frame of reference is markedly more traditional and conservative. The strongest contrasts appear to exist, for example, in specific assumptions concerning human nature, experience, objectivity, the nature and locus of value, the classification and ordering of values, morality, obligation, ends-means-progress, the individual and society, freedom and social progress. More generally, a philosopher might raise the question of how "moral" it is to try to develop a taste for openness in those whose lives will be relatively closed and subject to restrictions quite consistent with those observed at Berwick. . . . How moral to try to develop a taste for participatory democracy in a society whose majority moves more and more toward restrictive control? Even if the tools were available for achieving such goals—and psychologists suggest they are—how moral . . . ? A philosopher might also raise the issue concerning the weight to be given one's philosophical commitments vis-à-vis nonphilosophical factors in decision-making. Holding a particular philosophical or ideological commitment, how long and how vigorously is one obligated to fight the "system" before one . . . goes into administration . . . or creates one's own school . . . or conforms . . . or leaves the profession? Philosophers ask questions such as these—and they don't appear at all irrelevant to this particular case-study.

Given these factors, it is suggested that the present case-study contains three major issues: 1) how to resolve the multidimensional problems of human beings caught in a web of hostility and conflict; 2) what to do with a teacher who is markedly out of step with the aims, frame of reference and role-expectations of the system, the principal and her students; and 3) how to respond to a system which represents only one viable alternative for the school in American culture.

On the basis of these introductory comments, how about working on the other questions relating to "What Did I Do to Deserve This?" Then, turn to the additional case-studies which follow.

3. Additional Resources for Generating Possibilities

ODD MAN OUT

It was nearly 4:30 on a dark January afternoon as Kinsley Simmons, principal of the Overbrook Middle School, finished

up the midyear evaluation forms for his thirty-two faculty
members. They *weren't* the most "spicy," innovative bunch in
the world, but no one could fault them for lack of effort.
Testing was comfortably above the district averages; rooms
were clean and neat, with colorful displays of student work;
in his two years at Overbrook not a single supervisor had
criticized one of his teachers for serious disciplinary problems.
Yes, there were surely some advantages in coming into a
district with adequate financing and taking over a school with a
good plant, nice kids and a stable professional staff. At times
these advantages almost made one forget the possible disadvan-
tages of such homogeneity. In any case . . . Too bad that
he was having to replace Peggy Moore, one of the Math 7
teachers, at midyear. There's proof for you that the pill
doesn't always work!

Oh well . . .

The interoffice buzzer interrupted his musings. Mrs. Clayton,
Overbrook's secretary for some eighteen years, informed him
that Mr. Morton, the new Math 7 teacher, had phoned
upon arriving in town and would be in his office at nine o'clock
the next morning. Courteous . . . I'll bet *he'll* appreciate
the district policy of two planning days between terms!
Thanking Mrs. Clayton, Mr. Simmons methodically collected
his papers and prepared to call it a day . . . a very
productive day.

Little did Mr. Simmons realize how much "darker" the ninth
of March would be than was that earlier January afternoon!
Flipping the calendar to that particular March day, let's
join a group of Grade 7 teachers in their lounge. Harmony
and stability are scarcely keynotes as Pauline Lanowski, one of
the social studies teachers, is speaking to Betty Gilfours.

"Alfred Morton is a slob! I could stand his long greasy hair
and cowboy boots—after all, he *did* get his M. Ed. at State after
coming out of the service—but I just *will not stand* what he is
doing to our students! Did you know, Betty, that Sally Post
and Les Pfister told me right in front of my class yesterday that
what we were doing was boring?! Right in front of the class!
What am I supposed to do: teach what momentarily catches
their childish fancy or what's in the District Social Studies
Guide? I *did* sign a contract! They were such nice children.
Now, all they want to do is argue. I actually had to ask
them who the teacher was in that class, and I've never had to
do that before in my nine years at Overbrook!"

"Well, Pauline, just be happy you don't have to teach next door to him. Would you believe that his math students make more noise than my typing class? It's unbelievable! It got so bad last Thursday that I went over to the door between our rooms and listened. I'm really not very proud of that . . . The students were all talking at once. It was 'Al this' and 'Al that' . . . by his *first name* they called him! They actually told him what to teach. At one point in the lesson, he became irritated and said, "Well, that's my bag. If you don't like it, put a petition on the principal's desk.' What frightened me was that Kip Chang said that might just be a good idea. What attitudes is he teaching these children?"

Rick Henderson, one of the science teachers and the Grade 7 boys' counsellor, took up the cry: 'Maybe we ought to be just as worried about what he's doing to our program. Sure, many of the kids have become more difficult since Al's been here, but I'm really worried about what will happen to them when they get in Sid Brown's Math 8. You know, Sid really puts it to the kids in eighth grade. Getting ready for high school and all that kind of stuff . . . Sure, Sid knows how to handle eighth graders who get out of line, but what can he do if they haven't really mastered seventh grade content and skills? In the counselling office, I hear parents and even some kids complaining that there's darned little drill in math fundamentals this year and that they rarely know what they *should* be studying because it all depends on what the class thinks is 'relevant' from day to day. Relevant to what?! We're in trouble, gals."

The situation did not improve over the next few weeks; indeed, if anything it intensified. Several teachers had already spoken to Mr. Simmons when the infamous "April Incident" occurred. For years, Dr. Porter Smith, the supervisor of music, had personally prepared all intermediate grade students in the district for the May Sing. It was quite a local event. Parents and children of all ages came from miles around to hear the District Glee Club in the Overbrook Auditorium. The money collected was spent to the dollar for a program in the fine arts which was admired throughout the state. As usual, Dr. Smith had sent around a memorandum on April 19 which set the dates for times and practices. The first practice for seventh graders was scheduled for the afternoon of April 20. He was dumbfounded when that night he received a phone call from Mr. Morton, who quite courteously informed him that his classes had already planned to visit the

Centertown Research Laboratory. Several scientists had volunteered to illustrate the relationship between their research and mathematics. He hoped that something could be worked out with regard to tomorrow's practice. Porter Smith—just as courteously, if a bit coolly—explained that having to work with four middle schools meant a very tight schedule, that he regretted the inconvenience but did want to see all students the next day.

When Morton's students did not appear at the practice, the afternoon recess saw Dr. Smith and eight of Overbrook's senior teachers standing grimfaced at the principal's office door.

The conversation which ensued was not pleasant. The earlier charges concerning attitude, knowledge and skill problems in Mr. Morton's classes were reiterated by all. Furthermore, the senior teachers took pains to let Mr. Simmons know that they represented a consensus of faculty opinion. Dr. Porter Smith had a few things to say about professional cooperation and, by inference, the role of a building principal.

At eight o'clock the next morning, still weary from the pounding administered by some very angry and upset staff members, Kinsley Simmons reached for the interoffice phone and dialed the extension for the Morton classroom.

YOU'RE DAMNED IF YOU DO AND . . . !

The day had come for the last midyear examination. One more test, that last easy semester, a summer of work and fun at the beach, and he—Paul Johnson, National Merit Scholarship winner—would be off either to Stanford or Harvard. How could he miss? He had a sure "A" in calculus; Mr. Foulk, who everybody agreed was the best teacher at Melvayn High, had made the subject come alive.

The two exchanged grins as Paul received his test sheet. Hey, that's it—eight really fair test questions! He had even suggested the rough outlines of one of them himself on the last day of regular classes. Mr. Foulk calmly gave a few instructions, reminded the students that as usual they might share their trigonometric value tables, and wished them well. Paul was soon deeply immersed in the test and quickly finished the first four problems dealing with trigonometric functions and their derivatives. Turning to Ken Linton beside him, he motioned for the tables they had shared throughout the term and which were necessary for deriving the integrals in problems five through eight. Suddenly, he noticed that Ken had written a note on page 7, asking for help with the derivations. Turning his head slightly, he caught a glimpse of Ken's face: tight, apprehensive, choked— terrified. Paul blinked, a worried frown coming over his face. Ken was not only a good friend, but he really had problems: father sick . . . mother dead . . . six brothers and sisters . . . well liked by everyone even if he did have to work after school and on Saturdays . . . just an outside chance to make it into Melvayn State College. But cheating? Paul knew the rules: just once, and you're automatically suspended with the entire term's grades changed to "F." But Ken was a human being . . . After finishing his calculations, he paused for a moment, reluctantly jotted the necessary information below the tables and returned the pamphlet to Ken. His fear and disquietude had only slightly diminished by the time the bell signaled the end of the test. Lucky that he had been ready to answer just about any question blindfolded!

Mr. Foulk quietly asked him and Ken to remain in the room for a moment. His serious expression left little doubt as to what was involved. After the other students had left, Mr. Foulk closed the door and wearily turned to the boys. "Was what I saw a mirage? You know the rules! Ken, I understand some of your difficulties. Why didn't you see me about the test? *I'm human too!* And Paul . . . do you know what you've forced me to do not only to you but to myself?" In low voices, Paul and Ken declined to offer excuses and offered sincere apologies to a man whom they honestly respected. His face ashen, Mr. Foulk asked them to leave, suggesting that there was little more that could be said.

Kate Gordonstein, the senior class counselor, sat reading the instructor's report. On her desk lay the personal folders of the two boys, both of whom she personally knew and liked. Well, no one had ever questioned John Foulk. There were more than a few reasons for his being chairman of the math department. And there were more than a few reasons for the strict rules against cheating. No question about it: once it got to the principal's office, it was all over. What to do . . . Paul . . . Ken . . . the responsibility to the school? Slowly she took the report, attached a "Recommendation to the Principal" form and thoughtfully picked up her pen.

THE PORCUPINE CASE

Miss Norbey, a teacher at the Pullman Elementary School, placed the telephone receiver back on the hook and slowly walked down the hall toward her classroom.   Parents . . . Now, Mrs. Buschell, wife of a School Board member of all people! Well, I'll talk to her this afternoon at 3:15. How did all of this begin? Mrs. Mahoney, the principal, approved my new approach to teaching the fourth grade unit on animals.   Heaven knows, she surely had enough time . . . three weeks . . . to spot any problems in content or procedures. If she didn't like something, why didn't she say so . . . before these phone calls? And if she really did like it, why hasn't she backed me up with the parents? Oh well, I'll try explaining it again myself to Mrs. Buschell this afternoon. Perhaps that's better anyway . . . What a thing to look forward to during five hours of classes: a 3:15 appointment with the angry wife of a School Board member!

As she reached the doorway of her room, Miss Norbey was greeted by five of her students.

"What do we have here?" queried Miss Norbey, trying to smile in spite of her thoughts.

"Look at what Mark Korbis brought in, Miss Norbey," replied Butch.

"Yeah, Miss Norbey, look at these tracks I found in the woods behind our cabin in the Poconos last weekend," said Mark. "I would have told you I was bringing them in, but I wanted to surprise you. Besides I wasn't sure that I had made the casts right; I was afraid they might not turn out. But they did, and my dad drove me to school today so I could bring them in. Look! Here's a possum track and a raccoon's and a dog's—we think it's a German Shepherd 'cuz one lives a mile or so up the road—and this is a rabbit. Here's the best, though: it's a porcupine track!"

"My goodness! You've done a lot of work on that, Mark. Did your father help you with the identifications?"

"Well-l-l, he gave me the books and supplies, but [speaking more quickly] I had to make the casts and find the tracks in the books myself," responded Mark. "Ya know, I really liked that assignment 'cuz it's fun to roam in the woods and see what you can find, and try to find out about animals and stuff. I can't wait to get back up there and work on some of the other things we were talking about, Miss Norbey."

"Mark, why don't you show the class the casts and explain

how you made them," suggested the teacher as the bell signaled the beginning of the first period.

Look at Mark. He's so excited about those castings. He's never been so enthusiastic about anything related to school before. I can't remember when he has ever shown more self-confidence in front of the class. How can my activity approach be so bad if it reaches kids like this one? Now Mark can afford to relax and enjoy science; his grades aren't being based solely on reading and writing as they have been in the past. He *earned* that "A" last week. Actually, any of the children in this class can master the behavioral objectives if they want to. So, why the constant complaints by some of the parents . . . and of all people, Mrs. Buschell, who herself is an ex-teacher?

When Mark finished his presentation, Miss Norbey directed the students to various activities based on individual needs and interests. By the end of the day she had developed renewed confidence in herself and her approach—largely through her observations of many "Mark Korbises."

Soon after the last student had left the classroom, Mrs. Buschell arrived and was greeted cordially by Miss Norbey. After exchanging a few pleasantries, Mrs. Buschell got down to cases.

"We have read the material which you sent home with the children, Miss Norbey, and quite frankly we are deeply concerned about your approach to science. Your paper stated that you hope to see the children 'learn by doing' . . . I think you said by 'actively participating in science.'"

Miss Norbey nodded, allowing Mrs. Buschell to continue.

"We really find it difficult to understand how such an approach can provide our daughter Magdaline with the basic knowledge which eventually will be necessary for admission to any 'proper' college.

"*Try* to understand what I'm saying: Look at the "B" you gave Magdaline on last week's paper . . . That was her first "B" since entering school. And for a fourth grader, I can *assure* you that her paper was thoroughly researched, very well organized and beautifully written. At the same time you gave an "A" to the Korbis boy, whose reading and writing skills are really quite weak . . . By the way, isn't he in that 'slow group' which is reading a full *year* behind grade level?"

Miss Norbey paused a moment, held her temper in check and answered quietly: "I suspect you're raising a number

of important issues, Mrs. Buschell. Let me try to speak to
them honestly. Contemporary scientists do a great
many things in addition to reading and writing. They define
. . . they observe . . . they develop hypotheses . . . they try
out their hypotheses . . . they evaluate the consequences
of action . . . they generalize data . . . and, yes, they
communicate. The approach that I am taking doesn't *exclude*
reading or writing. It simply allows options so that children
who have not yet mastered these skills can receive *some*
reinforcement and thus not be turned completely away from
school activities."

"Excuse me, Miss Norbey," interjected Mrs. Buschell, "but
that is just the point! Children who have failed to master these
skills should not be given the 'option' of learning them. They
should be *required* to learn them . . . in every subject
. . . even if that means drill and objective grading until they
are learned. Pleasant or not, these skills are basic to academic
success. Furthermore, if the child who has developed them
uses them in dealing with scientific topics and is then
penalized for failing to do some additional 'busy work,' I fear
the results. I can understand that there are many things
we don't *like* to do, but we do them because they are part of
our responsibilities. And teaching these skills to all children is
a basic responsibility of every teacher . . . including YOU,
Miss Norbey."

Miss Norbey paused again. "Actually, I hope my encouraging students to study animals in a variety of interesting and
appropriate ways will result in their *desiring* to learn the
skills you mention. After all, observing animals, perhaps
making casts of their tracks and developing some hypotheses
about their behavior in natural settings may so excite the child
that he has a *reason* to read about them. It may even
result in his *wanting* to communicate, in his writing a better
scientific essay than one on 'My Pussycat Sam'—however
well researched, organized or beautifully written. Perhaps I
can encourage the development of such skills by letting my
grades take into account interest, involvement, critical thinking,
independence."

"Miss Norbey, I fear there is really little more I can say
to you . . . personally." With that, Mrs. Buschell quickly
left the room.

As was the custom at Pullman, Miss Norbey mentioned the
conflict with a parent to Mrs. Mahoney. She did decline
to change the grade given to Magdaline Buschell or

her procedures. The principal accepted the report without substantial comment.

A week later, Miss Norbey made her required mailbox check at the conclusion of the day only to find a note from the principal. It read as follows: "Miss Norbey: Several of your students' parents, including some figures very influential in the community, have made an appointment to see the superintendent of schools, Dr. Cooper. They have indicated a desire to discuss ways of 'protecting quality science teaching' and halting what they call your 'experimentation on their children and destructive grading practices.' A formal petition for a hearing has also been presented to Mr. Mark Korbis, Sr., president of the School Board. Given the circumstances, Dr. Cooper has directed you to see him *immediately*. Please leave for the district office as soon as possible. signed/Ann Mahoney"

Wadding the note into a ball, Miss Norbey quickly returned to her classroom and gathered her materials, bag and keys. A few minutes later, a deeply troubled teacher drove out of the parking lot and turned toward the district office.

Toward the close of the first chapter, it was stated that the purpose of *Philosophy and Schooling* was 1) to introduce you to the pedagogically-relevant resources of philosophy, 2) to help you develop some elementary skill in using these resources to clarify and suggest possibilities for your professional activities, 3) to help you explicate your personal philosophy of education and 4) to increase your commitment to making professional decisions based on appropriate facts and rational beliefs rather than upon impulse or expediency.

Obviously, Chapters 1 through 9 spoke to the first part of this overall goal. The present chapter has spoken to the second part more explicitly than the earlier ones. You will also note that for the first time (in the case-studies) you were asked to refer to your *own* frame of reference as a source of possibilities for action. It is this activity that leads naturally to the next and concluding element in these introductory studies, namely, to a more explicit, thorough consideration of how one might go about developing and using a personal philosophy of education.

11

Building and Using a Personal Philosophy of Education

Do you remember the difficulties you had with the first two or three chapters of this text? The technical vocabulary . . . the unfamiliar vantage point from which to view education . . . ? Yet, here we are at the last and, in many ways, the most important chapter of *Philosophy and Schooling*. And you are not only its subject, but, in large measure, its reason for being.

Although it often receives but scant attention, the basic task remaining before us should probably be incorporated in every course of studies. We might speak of this as the "bringing-it-all-together" task, the "stock-taking" task or, perhaps, the "So what?" task. In essence, it consists of what many existentialists refer to as "appropriation." What is there in what we have accomplished together that you want to make part of yourself?

Let us work on the methodological hypothesis that you will be best helped to sort out your answers to this question by a three-part organization, namely, 1) some consideration of the need for an examined, personal philosophy of education; 2) inquiry into the ways by which you might go about developing such a structure; and 3) some parting suggestions as to how you might continue to develop and use this personal and professional instrument. As a personal note, I should also like to offer an additional hypothesis: Your "stock-taking" will be valuable—will make sense to you—only to the extent that you refuse to be talked into *anything* that is not *you*. You are not me . . . nor am I you. This emphasis on your increasing responsibility as our joint work nears its end is not prompted simply by knowledge that it is most difficult to impose anything on another human being (and the assumption that it is immoral when it *is* done).   It also seems entirely appropriate to a pluralistic culture and to a democratic society.   There are many paths to wisdom and, possibly, as many varieties of wisdom as there are paths. Dealing as it does with belief as well as with fact, philosophy does well to acknowledge the lesson of tolerance.   Counts captures this spirit in an article written in 1929:

> *There are many philosophies of education, as there are many philosophies of life, which in my judgment are excellent, and, in a sense, true. . . . Just as the same theme may be variously treated by different artists, and perhaps with equally satisfactory results, so our society to-day may give rise to various educational philosophies at the hands of different philosophers.*[27]

In discussing the philosophical positions which he had developed in his own text, Van Cleve Morris approached the same theme, writing:

> *There is no obligation to believe in any of them, in any combination of them, not even in a wholesome eclecticism that makes room for all of them. In studying philosophy there is only one necessary commitment: to take one's life seriously enough to believe that thought and criticism can be applied to it to make it better, more intelligent, and more civilized.*[28]

A. The Need for an Examined, Personal Philosophy of Education

Each of you *came* to these studies with at least an implicit personal philosophy of education. Oh, yes . . . there might have been some gaps in yours. Perhaps you hadn't developed an assumption about the nature of ideas or the way in which values should be classified or ordered. But when you first looked over the table of contents or the "Philosophical Concepts–Assumptions Checklist," it was pretty clear that you had *some* predisposition toward assumptions concerning human nature, God and faith, objectivity, morality, justice and equality, and most of the rest. Undergraduate and beginning graduate students alike have had ample experiences in home, school, religious

[27] George S. Counts, "Criteria for Judging a Philosophy of Education," *School and Society*, **XXX**, No. 761 (July 27, 1929), p. 107.

[28] Van Cleve Morris, *Philosophy and the American School: An Introduction to the Philosophy of Education* (Boston: Houghton Mifflin Company, 1961), pp. 472–473.

institutions, politics and peer relationships which provide the basis for developing such commitments. But, you see, *that's* just the problem—*that* is the factor which explains the need for a conscious examination and explication of one's own philosophy of education. In a pluralistic culture and at times and under conditions where one's critical powers were not operating at their peak, it is natural and completely understandable that you would have incorporated disparate elements in your view of life, most assuredly including the way in which you look upon education. For instance, there was that great teacher—one of the two best you ever had—and he didn't have a democratic bone in his body! The other one thought traditionalists had horns. There was that upbringing in a very orthodox faith . . . and a most permissive home. Then, following parochial school, there was that first contact with an atheist in that college science class. And now, the freer norms of contemporary young adulthood—and, for some, the experiences of marrying and having a child and feeling that near inexpressible sense of joy and responsibility commingled. . . .

For those of you who have yet to teach, the full impact of this phenomenon may still lie ahead. For those of you already in the field, the point being made may be reasonably obvious. All of us, however, have at least observed the consequences of an unexamined philosophy of education. How about the classmate down the hall who incessantly cries for "relevance" and "direct action"—and yet puts up with irrelevant, boring busy-work in class after class without the slightest protest to organizations which often can effect change? And there's the administrator who

> . . . *develops an opportunistic pattern of operation. He learns to be a manipulator of people and builds personal and professional strength by surrounding himself with satellites and yesmen. Pseudo-democracy, personal charm, favors for his satellites in return for their unquestioning loyalty, fear and confusion for others are some of his tools in trade. Because of his personal characteristics, he quite likely completes the cycle and becomes a satellite himself for some strong political figure in the community.*[29]

Or, there's the coach who emphasizes the "ideals of humanity" in his history class, but on the playing field demands cutthroat competition, places winning above all else and motivates his charges with the battlecry of "Kill 'em, baby!" Or, how about the religious leader who preaches the message of love and tolerance, but ostentatiously walks

[29] Orin B. Graff, Calvin M. Street, Ralph B. Kimbrough and Archie R. Dykes, *Philosophic Theory and Practice in Educational Administration* (Belmont, Calif.: Wadsworth Publishing Company, Inc., 1966), p. 11.

out of a Rotary meeting in the middle of an invited speaker's plea for social justice for workers in the community packing plant? And, finally, what about the teacher who calls for free expression of opinion and then punishes those whose sentiments differ from hers? You and I have seen them all—and I suspect that each of us wants to do a bit better.

A fair question confronts us: Let's suppose that we honestly desire to have as little to do as possible with compartmentalized behavior or behavior based on expediency or opportunism. We want to avoid both the internal conflict born of conscious inconsistency and the confusion in others which ensues from our (often unconscious) communication of conflicting expectations. If all this is the case, how can developing an examined, personal philosophy of education offer any help? After all, a good many (a majority of?) teachers and other educators do *not* hold a conscious philosophy of education—and some of them seem to get by pretty well.

We may suspect that the first point to be made is that at best it will only "help." Educational outcomes are not determined by philosophical factors alone, etc., etc. Nevertheless, the potential value of this assistance is not to be underestimated. Consciously examining the assumptions we now hold allows us to identify consistent and inconsistent elements—and there will be both. Questions can then be raised as to the adequacy of our assumptions, the elements which do represent our current commitments and those which at this point in time must be refined or rejected—or lived with. Given this base, we may become more aware of our own "hidden curriculum," i.e., that which we are communicating to our students in addition to those arithmetical facts or that knowledge of primary and secondary colors. As we integrate philosophical and nonphilosophical factor operational in a given situation, we may often be able to sharpen our awareness of ends and means which are both consistent with our assumptions and can be implemented. In short, as we develop a conscious realization of who we are, where we are going and why— albeit a base which will be refined over time—we begin to see possibilities beyond the moment . . . beyond the end of our nose. This is a base, as Shermis notes, which allows us to clarify both our professional activities and those of our colleagues by asking questions such as,

> What is it that is being proposed? What assumptions support the proposal? What evidence supports the proposal? What consequences are likely to flow from the proposal? What alternatives are there?[30]

[30] S. Samuel Shermis, *Philosophic Foundations of Education* (New York: American Book Company, 1967), p. 277.

It is a base that allows us—if still an undergraduate—to integrate educational foundations courses, curriculum and instruction courses, arts and science studies, and clinical experiences.   If already in the field, it allows us to unify the various facets of our professional activities, including those connected with curriculum, instruction, organization, administration and profession-building.   Gradually we realize *why* we prefer a certain approach to chemistry, an alternate route to discipline or a new policy for student involvement in school decision-making.   Gradually we understand *why* we must oppose Mr. Timkins's proposal at the department meeting or the requirement of a certain course in the teacher education curriculum.   We may even find ourselves able to explain these "whys" to colleagues, students and parents.

There is, of course, no guarantee of success in *any* of these endeavors.   The transactional model emphasizes the complexity of cause-effect relationships far too graphically to allow any such simplistic conclusion.   But in success and in failure there is a stronger notion of the constituents of, including the reasons for, our behavior and, consequently, an ever-firmer base for improving the effectiveness of future effort.   And all of this is surely part of what we mean by the distinction between a " 'professional' educator" and a "technician."

B.   Procedures for Developing a Personal Philosophy of Education

One of the first problems faced by every individual who would develop a personal philosophy of education concerns the question of "consistency."   To what extent can one "pick and choose," or, to put the problem another way, to what extent are we bound by philosophical or ideological "-isms"—or even the assumptions treated in this text?   After all, given this culture—let alone the many subcultures in which each of us has grown up—isn't everyone *naturally* an "eclectic," i.e., one who picks and chooses?

The literature on this question may initially be somewhat confusing.   To cite but two examples, we turn to Graff *et al.* and to Hansen:

> *When one seeks a point of view that reflects honest and consistent values, insights, and understandings and a mode of behavior that results from such a point of view, consistency in philosophical [assumptions] becomes essential.   Eclecticism constitutes a very real barrier to the achievement of this consistency.*[31]

[31] Graff *et al.*, *Philosophic Theory and Practice in Educational Administration*, p. 29.

Much of the homespun "common-sense" philosophy which is so advocated by nonphilosophers as being a superior brand of thinking actually represents a careless and inconclusive kind of hodgepodge of ideas that are not really philosophical at all, but are gratuitously thrown together and labeled "philosophy." Sometimes the eclectic seems to have no conscience about what he believes, and becomes a mere opportunist who appropriates whatever portion of a belief that happens to fit his own feelings or prejudices of the moment. Among alleged eclectics are those also who try to subscribe to two different beliefs which are actually mutually exclusive.

. . .

There is strong evidence for believing that the more systematic the philosophy of education the better the chances that its results—which are bound to occur anyway—will be reasonable, understandable, and defensible.[32]

Careful reading suggests that it is not so much eclecticism per se which is being attached as it is the very real possibility that incompatible assumptions will be combined. This does represent a danger in American culture—and the more inexperienced one is in developing a personal philosophy of education, the greater the danger becomes.

Consider, if you will, the juxtaposition of the "transactional theory" of knowledge and truth and the assumption of the "obligation of free commitment." On the one hand, we have a position that subject and object alike are shaped in transactions and that individual knowledge-claims must be capable of public confirmation if our generalizations are to be made more reliable. We are told that truth refers to an idea that really works—which is quite a bit more than simply saying that an individual sees it as working—and that the verified may force us to give up cherished beliefs. On the other hand, we have an assumption which refuses to specify either "to what" or "for what" an individual must be obligated. Who is to tell this individual that he must feel an obligation to take into account reliable knowledge-generalizations or truth-claims based on specified criteria of "working"? This is not to say that he *couldn't* accept such an obligation, although it is to deny that he *must*. These two assumptions, then, are logically and functionally incompatible.

In a similar vein, consider trying simultaneously to hold that justice and equality are best expressed in the assumption of "just rewards" and the assumption that human nature is "constructed and evaluated transactionally." Here we have the notion that men are not equal other than before God and the law, and that rewarding them other than on the basis of what they produce represents the essence of

[32] Kenneth H. Hansen, *Philosophy for American Education* (Englewood Cliffs, N.J.: Prentice-Hall, Inc., 1960), pp. 269–270 and 277.

*in*justice. The other assumption asks, What if the experience of one group was not such as to develop the more "successful" habits? Are you going to help them by rewarding them only for what their "unsuccessful" habits produced? Or, are you going to motivate them to overcome these habits—to the profit of the entire society—perhaps by giving them a "head start"? And further, doesn't the *individual* competition demanded by the first assumption war with the notion that the habits we refer to as "human nature" are developed in a *social* setting, a setting optimized by cooperative effort? Once again, no way . . .

Are we, then, to conclude that one *is* bound by "-isms," that a responsible eclecticism is impossible? Not necessarily. Consider the assumptions of "the active state" and the "free self." The liberal's view of the State's role in fostering the general welfare does, it is true, call for a high degree of cooperative action. He is concerned that the powerful social forces of the late twentieth century not warp the individual's capacity to have a piece of this action and the profits that accrue therefrom. Especially emphasized is the resultant opportunity to achieve and express one's full individuality. I submit, there is no good reason why one couldn't hold this assumption and also believe in free will. Furthermore, as a secondary point, many liberals do in fact accept this particular belief. And yet, free will is also accepted by idealists (and many realists) who, more often than not, are quite conservative ideologically. The point? A responsible eclecticism *is* possible, although it is not always as easy to achieve as common sense would have us believe. If this point is defensible, we may now turn to the procedures of building *any* coherent, personal philosophy of education.

George Counts, one of the great figures in American education and philosophy, has proposed five criteria by which we might judge the adequacy of a philosophy of education. As we turn to the practical problems of developing such an instrument, his suggestions may have considerable value. Counts writes:

> *A defensible philosophy of education should conform to at least five requirements: it should be systematically empirical in its foundations; it should be comprehensive in its outlook; it should be consistent in its several departments; it should be practicable in its provisions; and it should be satisfying to its adherents.*[33]

By "systematically empirical," Counts means that one's philosophy of education should be based on experience—*all* of one's experience. Although he first mentions scientific experience, Counts is quite aware

[33] "Criteria for Judging a Philosophy of Education," p. 104.

both of the limited scientific data available and of the limitations of any one person in making use of them. Consistent with the argument pursued in this text, he notes that we must also inquire into the realm of belief, especially our metaphysical, ethical and aesthetic beliefs. As these beliefs are correlated with those facts available and meaningful to us—and as both are subjected to continuing reconstruction—we develop an experiential base upon which to build our philosophy.

Counts's second criterion (comprehensiveness) demands that an adequate philosophy of education be relevant to the major activities and problems of education.[34] Among other things, this means that as one develops one's philosophy, one must at least be aware of important phenomena emphasized in the other disciplines foundational to education, especially history, psychology and sociology. A philosophy of education worthy of its name cannot be irrelevant to learning theories, studies of the school as social structure and process, or historical issues such as that of "local control." The task of *synthesizing* philosophical and nonphilosophical factors probably belongs more to "educational theory" than it does to philosophy of education per se—a point argued in Chapter 1 with which Counts seems to disagree. Nevertheless, *taking account of* nonphilosophical factors in building and using a philosophy of education is surely each individual's responsibility.

Passing over the third criterion which underlies the need for consistency between assumptions and facts (eclecticism or no eclecticism), Counts notes that any adequate philosophy of education must be related to the specific context of time, place and people in which it is developed. When it becomes ossified and arrogant, when it fails to maintain a sensitive intimacy with the problems of the day, it will surely go the way of the dinosaur and the dodo bird. Finally, no matter how many of the other criteria it fulfills, a philosophy of education must be satisfying to its adherents. Though more intuitive in nature, this criterion is no less important to adequacy than any of the others.

Specific procedures for developing a personal philosophy of education are difficult to suggest—and absolutely impossible to prescribe. The source of the difficulty is probably attributable to a variety of factors, including the very fact that task and product alike *are* personal, that differences exist in experience and that there are even variations in prefered "inquiry styles." To illustrate, consider how differently some of your friends go about writing a paper. One sits in the midst of crumpled sheets of paper, slowly and meticulously

---

[34] Note the four-part definition of "education" proposed in Chapter 1; i.e., intentional activities (curricular, instructional, structural, administrative and professional), desired educand responses, desired product goals and education as a discipline.

researching and writing and rewriting—almost as if he were putting together a complex puzzle. Another, by contrast, sits quietly—almost as if in a trance. Suddenly there is an absolute flurry of activity and a creative, well-organized paper simply flows into being. Little more is needed beyond the most minor editing and typing. Both papers receive the same grade. The moral? Each person has to find his own style and perfect it over time. The procedures which follow, then, only suggest possibilities. If they work for you, all well and good. If not, extended conversations with your instructor and/or others who have some feeling for you as a unique human being are in order.

You might begin the process by referring to the assumptions set forth in this text. Depending on your present grasp of the material, reread sections of Chapters 2, 4, 6 and 8 as needed—or simply refresh your memory by referring to the "Philosophical Concepts-Assumptions Checklist." Use these short descriptive passages or key phrases as mirrors, turning them this way and that, asking yourself to what extent they reflect you, noting points of agreement and disagreement, and the like. Another beginning point, of course, lies in the method suggested by Professor Thomas. In the latest expression of his approach (1972), he writes:

> Since the most important features of a frame of reference are the facts and values taken for granted, they are the most difficult to identify. The things that we take for granted are the last things we look at or question. Often we have to be irritated, annoyed, or outraged by the suggestions or acts of others to discover the hidden values and beliefs that we have been taking for granted. Instead of indulging our irritation or anger at this stage, we should be wise to take them as clues to recognizing our own frame of reference. Another useful clue is the qualities we praise and the traits we condemn in others. These are often our ideals for ourselves—and sometimes the suppressed tendencies we hate in ourselves.[35]

If successful, we will have explicated at least the outline of our assumptions concerning philosophical concepts of especial importance to education. (Again, it is argued that these philosophical assumptions form but one segment of our total frame of reference.) As we continue to firm up the details of these assumptions, we must also begin to examine their consistency both one with another and with those seemingly relevant facts drawn from as many disciplines as we

[35] Lawrence G. Thomas, "A Model for Making and Testing Value Judgments," in *Philosophical Redirection of Educational Research,* The Seventy-first Yearbook of the National Society for the Study of Education, Part I, ed. Lawrence G. Thomas (Chicago: The National Society for the Study of Education, 1972), p. 250.

are able to understand and correlate.[36]   One approach to this consistency question was illustrated earlier in this section. Simply set the basic details of two or more of your assumptions side by side and reflectively consider whether they can be held simultaneously—in general or under specific circumstances. Discussion with knowledgeable friends may help. Occasionally, even under the best of conditions, a set of assumptions simply refuses to fit together no matter what you seem to do. In such an instance, depending on the importance of those assumptions to you, you might attempt the difficult "autobiographical approach." This consists of looking over your own background (family, where you grew up, school, religious experience, etc.) and attempting to locate the source of conflict. You might find, for instance, that one contending element came out of early humanistic religious training, whereas the other was influenced by the more orthodox religious position to which you now subscribe. Even if you are successful in identifying the source of difficulty, however, you still face some hard decisions. All that is being claimed is that a philosophical "wrestling match" held in the light of day is a bit less frightening than one held in absolute darkness.

With your tentative philosophical assumptions in hand, and taking account of seemingly relevant nonphilosophical factors, you may now imaginatively construct some plans of action for solving a specific educational problem. For the undergraduate this may involve deciding between a rural, suburban or urban setting for the required field work in that "science methods and materials" course you will be taking next term. Or, it might involve deciding between registering for a regularly scheduled elective or planning an independent study project. Or, perhaps, you are really nervous about facing discipline problems in your student teaching and would like at least to go into the classroom with a tentative *modus operandi*. For the inservice teacher the possibilities are nearly endless. There are the activities of that new unit which really do demand different evaluative procedures than those with which you—and your students—are familiar. There's the field trip to the natural history museum. Who will be involved in planning it? What will go on once you arrive? How will the activities be evaluated once you return to the classroom? Or, there's that rather uncomfortable relationship between you and the other third grade teacher. If only it could be warmed up . . . The possibilities for cooperative activities . . . sharing materials . . . new ideas . . .

If you have developed some sensitivity to the author's frame of reference, you have probably already guessed the remaining steps . . .

[36] Here is another good argument for taking your introductory work in educational history, psychology and sociology at approximately the same time as you are getting into the philosophy of education.

Right! Choose and try out the most likely hypothesis. Evaluate the realized consequences of having acted upon it. Use the resultant contextual knowledge to refine-reconstruct the assumptions which now constitute your examined, personal philosophy of education. And do it again and again and again. Gradually you will come to realize that a personal philosophy of education is either a vibrantly living and growing thing that permeates one's personel and professional life, or it is lifeless and superfluous and, perhaps, even dangerous.

If you experience many frustrations and occasional failures—especially at first—do remember that some of the greatest individuals we refer to as "human beings" have been at this sort of thing for several thousand years. Also remember the assumption that morality is found in the care you personally bring to the philosophy-building process, not in the results or even in what others think of the results. As an educator of fifteen years, however, I will hazard this hypothesis: The results—both for you and for those who are your professional responsibility—will more than justify your best efforts.

C. Where Now? Suggestions for the Continuing Development and Use of your Personal Philosophy of Education

Some possibilities for the continuing development and use of your personal philosophy of education have been explicitly noted in this chapter; other chapters are heavy with implicit possibilities. Although there is neither desire nor need simply to repeat this material, several parting suggestions do seem in order.

Speaking first to the undergraduate student: pay attention to the philosophical assumptions which appear to be held by instructors in other courses and outside-school youth activities. These models offer possibilities—both positive and negative. Take a long look at instructional materials discussed in your "curriculum and instruction" courses. Upon what philosophical assumptions do they seem to be based? How do these assumptions square with yours? Is there any possibility of effecting a compromise between the methods suggested in the accompanying "teacher's manual" and the methods you would find more comfortable given your own frame of reference? Bring these points up in class; talk about them with your instructors; analyze some of them in a paper.[37] Secondly, take some part in your student council, especially if it is directly connected with your department,

---

[37] This is an especially important point. There is growing evidence for the hypothesis that teacher-material dissonance is an important variable in program failure.

school or college of education. If your courses are indoctrinating fellow students, albeit unconsciously, the council can do a good deal to ensure that alternative models (of teacher behavior, materials, instructional strategies, etc.) are presented—even if in student-organized seminars. Furthermore, given active student interest, the chance for faculty cooperation in such an effort should not be underestimated. Thirdly, in the course of your field experiences, be on the lookout for the kind of school in which you might be most comfortable and, hence, most effective. Take a look at rural, suburban and urban schools. And don't overlook the nonpublic schools. Independent schools, church-related schools and schools run by governmental agencies (e.g., in institutions for delinquents) provide exciting opportunities for those individuals who are aware of the consistency between the school's assumptions and theirs. Finally, relax a bit. In your first year or two of teaching, you *are* going to be especially concerned with everyday "detailia," i.e., "important trivia." But when you have your classes and other activities running smoothly, and when seniority and effort place you on decision-making committees, the basic issues—the "why" questions—will become increasingly vital. To the degree that it is a profession and not merely a job, education is not a mere "nuts and bolts" affair.

And now to the inservice teacher . . . Let us take a look at possible uses of your growing philosophical sophistication in terms of the various "intentional activities" involved in education. For instance, we can speak of *curricular activities.* Herein you have a magnificent opportunity to help students become aware of the deeper issues—the "why" questions, the basic human concerns—which underlie your curricular area. Art, history, literature—subject after subject—are filled with metaphysical, epistemological, axiological and ideological questions. Literary classics and great historic events are not important simply in themselves. They also illustrate human values, questions of freedom, views of the role of the State and of human nature, and positions on the goals of life and the proper means thereto. As Alfred Hall-Quest notes,

> *Educational content must be related to understanding, imagination, thinking, the recognition of problems, the judgment of values, etc. Attitudes are not less important than skills; valuated interpretation is not less important than information.*[38]

More than ever before in your career, you are now equipped to sense and explicate these questions and thus enrich the learning of your

[38] Alfred L. Hall-Quest, "Design for Philosophy of Education," in *What Is Philosophy of Education?*, ed. Christopher J. Lucas (New York: The Macmillan Company, 1969), p. 233.

students. Although much of philosophical importance can and should be treated in standard courses, there is also some formal elective instruction possible in philosophy, especially at the secondary level. New programs are now underway to ready middle and high school teachers for this task.[39]

In terms of the curriculum, of course, conscious awareness of your own frame of reference at least gives you a better chance to avoid unconsciously indoctrinating students with your own biases. Defuse the problem by being frank about your own assumptions—even to the extent of joking about the limitations of your own viewpoint—and reinforcing students to express and defend their own positions. Even the youngest first graders need to continue becoming involved in the "intellectual weaning process." They will not be helped to enter upon the path of self-actualization by your refusal to play any role other than that of mother surrogate. Finally, let us suppose you are a middle school social studies teacher. Realize that the philosophical assumptions of the other social studies teachers in your school tend to influence their coverage of material. Certain units tend to receive greater emphasis and others less. Use this knowledge to ensure that students in your class are exposed to ideas and approaches they may have missed in other classes.

With regard to *instructional activities*, be especially concerned with materials selected for your courses. Textbooks, programs and hardware tend partially to reflect the frames of reference of those who developed them. Marked dissonance between the assumptions of materials and teacher (and students? and community?) can cause great conflict, wasted effort and lowered achievement. Carefully examine text and accompanying teacher's manual. Delve beneath the surface illustrations and promotional literature, and work out the assumptions on which the materials are based. Compare them with your own. If materials are normally selected by your district's administrative staff for use by all teachers in a given grade and subject, and if these teachers hold markedly different frames of reference, *at least* suggest that a teacher committee be formed to "make recommendations." In a more positive vein, note that some of the assumptions within your personal philosophy of education are firmer than others. Occasionally try out procedures and activities which are seemingly consistent with assumptions *less* firmly held. In doing so,

---

[39] Interested teachers might consult 1) the July 1967 issue of *Educational Theory* (Vol. XVII, No. 3), which is devoted to the topic of "philosophy in the curriculum of the high school"; and 2) Hugo W. Thompson's "Report of a 1968–1971 Feasibility Study in High School Philosophy," which is available from the Center for High School Philosophy, CSCA, 1308–20th Street, Rock Island, Ill. 61201.

you may not only increase your repertoire of activities, but you may firm up additional elements within your frame of reference.

Many of the same points made concerning instruction should also be made with regard to the *organizational activities* of the teacher. Professional educators must give attention to those horizontal and vertical structures[40] which are consistent and inconsistent with their own frames of reference. Team-teaching or the self-contained classroom may well be the very last thing with which you should become involved. Again, if a number of teachers with markedly different frames of reference are involved, decisions should be made cooperatively. In fact, they *will* be made cooperatively—or they *will* be subverted. If an entire district is involved, it may be necessary to allow various schools to be organized according to different structural patterns. Unfortunately, such matters are all too often handled according to the "bandwagon approach." The results can be disastrous. Time after time, schools designed for open, perhaps ungraded, movement have been transformed by their staff. Bookcases, filing cabinets and other furniture have been used to form the separate little cubicles more consistent with the views of the teachers—and even their principals. For many of the same reasons, the professional educator should be highly concerned with the horizontal organizational patterns of the levels above and below his own. Structure influences student attitudes and learning modes. Middle school teachers cannot be unconcerned with the structure of their district's lower schools—unless, that is, they are willing to spend a considerable amount of energy and time reshaping established student habits. And although these remarks have been directed to teachers, the implications for administrative leadership should be reasonably clear.

Perhaps the most important *administrative activity* of the philosophically knowledgeable teacher involves serving as a "communications expediter" in committee and department work. A cross-cultural knowledge of philosophical assumptions allows you to suggest points of disagreement, agreement and potential compromise in the swirling, indecisive discussions which so often characterize such activity. Sometimes a quiet, insightful comment can cut short hours of wrangling. At the very least, the areas for necessary coexistence will become more clear even if the door to active compromise or consensus is temporarily closed. In such matters, Raths's clarifying response technique seems especially useful. Secondly, the philosophically knowledgeable teacher might suggest electives or alternative courses in required areas of study which are consistent with frames of refer-

---

[40] See Chapter 9, footnote 56.

ence held by students with whom he has a friendly and personal relationship.

A final administrative note: sooner or later, you will be asked to serve on a committee charged with formulating a district, school or department "philosophy of education." Unfortunately, such statements seem designed to do little more than fulfill the letter of an accreditation requirement or soothe contentious factions. They are so *nonphilosophical* as to give no direction whatsoever to important professional activities. In no way, for example, do they allow school personnel to take the next step, namely, developing behavioral objectives consistent with the philosophy. Consider two such examples which are quite typical and are drawn from widely separated sections of the country:

> *The Philosophy of This School System Is One Which Believes:*
>
> 1. *That education is tremendously important in this country—in this city.*
> 2. *That every child who enrolls here is entitled to the kind of educational opportunities which a democratic society needs.*
> 3. *That teaching is a real profession and that only people who want to help promote it as a profession should be in it.*
> 4. *That every person on the Board of Education payroll is important and should know it.*
> 5. *That all pupils should be held for respectable work—based on ability.*
> 6. *That good relationships—showing a wholesome respect for authority—are necessary to excellent teaching.*
> 7. *That girls and boys should be taught to understand what it means to be able to live in a country like ours.*
>
> *The Board Charges the Superintendent of Schools, as Its Chief Administrative Officer, with the Responsibility for Executing These Policies.*

> *We the professional staff of the . . . District, committed to the development of a positive sense of self for each individual, guarantee unlimited opportunities for successful learning experiences. We recognize the uniqueness of the individual and emphasize the right of the learner to prescribe, in conjunction with us, personal objectives based on realistic self-appraisal.*

You are now prepared to "philosophize" such statements. Use this text and the "Philosophical Concepts-Assumptions Checklist" as a foundation. Spell out in nontechnical terms those metaphysical, epistemological, axiological and ideological assumptions which are shared by the members of your committee. Work through this first draft with the administration, the full faculty, student groups and the PTA. Note topics of shared agreement; negotiate alternatives for those topics where there is mixed sentiment; and eliminate (for the time being) those topics where agreement is impossible. It is entirely possible in a pluralistic culture to develop a quite adequate document which results in no forced resignations and which provides many guidelines for action.

Profession-building activities provide many opportunities for the development and use of your personal philosophy of education. Respond to what you take to be unfair or inaccurate newspaper criticisms of education. Work for a school environment which functionally respects (that is, rewards) different teaching and learning styles. Seek to revitalize your PTA as an instrument for adding community resources to the decision-making resources provided by administrators, students and teachers. Take social action concerns to your professional organization, whether it be the AFT, NEA or AAUP. Beyond such matters as academic freedom and different financial remuneration plans, for instance, the question of "accountability" is properly one to which professional organizations should address themselves. Of one thing we may be sure: If teachers fail to take a lead in setting accountability standards, they will be imposed on us by those far less experienced than we in understanding the complexities of teaching-learning variables. If we do take the lead, however, it may even be possible to develop accountability standards appropriate to different frames of reference. And in a pluralistic culture this might be entirely proper. Then again, it may be necessary to negotiate political compromises with which most teachers can at least coexist. But let us begin by encouraging teachers of different orientations to propose standards for which *they* feel they should properly be held responsible. Then we may see more clearly what possibilities exist.

As a parting word, let me suggest that a personal philosophy of education as a unique correlation of fact and belief is especially important in that it allows us to pose alternatives to that viewed by others as "common sense." If this is done with humility, with sensitivity to the human condition and with the widest perspective on the potentialities of this land and its peoples, we truly may have hope . . . hope for the growth of rationality . . . hope for ourselves and future generations . . . hope for an exciting and demanding profession.

Suggestions for Further Reading

Resources for Finding Reasons and Generating Possibilities

The literature on locating assumptions is not very promising. Many philosophers appear either to have assumed that common sense would reveal them or, sensing the difficulties inherent in constructing defensible inferences, have turned their attention to other tasks. The following sources, therefore, provide additional resources only for generating possibilities.

BARRY, RUTH, HARVEY HALL, ESTHER LLOYD-JONES, THOMAS SHREWSBERRY, JEAN WELLINGTON and BEVERLY WOLF, eds., *Case Studies in College Student-Staff Relationships*. New York: Bureau of Publications, Teachers College, Columbia University, 1956.

BRACKENBURY, ROBERT L., *Getting Down to Cases: A Problems Approach to Educational Philosophizing*. New York: G. P. Putnam's Sons, 1959.

OZMON, HOWARD, *Dialogue in the Philosophy of Education*. Columbus, Ohio: Charles E. Merrill Publishing Company, A Bell and Howell Company, 1972.

PERRY, GEORGE and PAULINE, *Case-Studies in Teaching*. New York: Pitman Publishing Corp., 1969.

PIGORS, PAUL and FAITH, *Case Method in Human Relations: The Incident Process*. New York: McGraw-Hill Book Company, Inc., 1961.

Procedures for Developing a Personal Philosophy of Education

Again, the literature of philosophy of education is long on theory and short on the types of practical problems held by undergraduates and inservice teachers. The following two references may provide some insights into the problems discussed in Chapter 11.

BUTLER, J. DONALD, *Four Philosophies and Their Practice in Education and Religion*. 2nd ed. New York: Harper & Brothers, Inc., 1957. Chapter XXIV (The third edition does *not* contain this material).

MORRIS, VAN CLEVE, *Philosophy and the American School: An Introduction to the Philosophy of Education*. Boston: Houghton Mifflin Company, 1961. Chapter XVI (Morris's "Inductive Method" appears to have severe weaknesses in light of the transactional model, but his other comments are quite useful).

APPENDICES

Historical Notes on Philosophical and Ideological Systems

Philosophy and Schooling is not a text in the history of ideas. Rather, it focusses directly on the relevance of philosophy to the problems of contemporary American education. Nevertheless, for those of you who do have some background in the history of philosophical ideas and/or the history of education—as well as for those who do not— some attention to the historical dimension seems proper. If you are in the former category, these appendices may allow you better to correlate your knowledge. If you do not have this background, these brief notes will provide some perspective and, hopefully, interest you in more formal study of another vital element in professional decision-making.

The appendices which follow contain historical notes on the six philosophical systems (or schools) and ideologies referred to in this text. Each appendix is subdivided into several sections: 1) a brief sketch of the history of the system; 2) notes on the importance of the system to American education; and 3) a listing of assumptions developed in *Philosophy and Schooling* which are commonly held by the system's adherents.

Appendix A:
Idealism and American Education

1. Idealism: An Historical Sketch

Idealism as a school of thought has the deepest roots in ancient Indo-European culture. Plato (427?–347 B.C.) is generally accorded the title of the "Father of Idealism." By the time of Jesus its influence had permeated the ancient world. Due to this factor and to the compatibility of many of its assumptions with religious dogmas, Idealism was drawn into the Christian movement which vied with Rome for control of man's mind—and allegiance. Indeed, it was St. Augustine (350–430) who provided the epitaph on Rome's fall in his *City of God*. The synthesis, expressed in various accents, dominated Western thought throughout the Middle Ages and into the Renaissance. Only with the coming of the Enlightenment was it seriously challenged.

Revitalized both by the Reformation and the thinking of philosophical giants such as René Descartes (1596–1650), Baruch Spinoza (1632–1677) and Gottfried von Leibnitz (1646–1716), Idealism spread to the New World. Such colonial figures as the Calvinist Jonathan Edwards and the Anglicans Bishop Berkeley and Samuel Johnson did much to guarantee its lasting place in American thought. Meanwhile, its revitalization continued in Europe with the work of such writers as Immanuel Kant (1724–1804), Johann Fichte (1762–1814), Georg Hegel (1770–1831), Samuel Coleridge (1772–1834) and Thomas Carlyle (1795–1881). Its theological overtones softened by the Enlightenment, Idealism absolutely dominated American thought in the nineteenth century—first with the Transcendentalism of Ralph Waldo Emerson, William Channing and Bronson Alcott, and then with the Neo-Hegelianism of Wm. Torrey Harris, Bordon P. Browne and Josiah Royce. A final note must include the names of the Europeans Henri Bergson (1859–1941), Benedetto Croce (1866–1952) and Giovanni Gentile (1875–1944).

2. Idealism: Importance to American Education

Colonial education in New England, which foreshadowed the later American public school pattern, was generally dominated by Idealism. This was true both in those regions given to Calvinism and in those areas where the influence of the Anglican (Episcopal) church was strong. Theologically-centered materials and harsh discipline were only gradually softened by growing familiarity with Enlightenment thought among the intelligentsia. Deism, Transcendentalism and the development of a more humanitarian sentiment and liberal religious expression (e.g., Unitarianism, Universalism) paved the way for the Common School Reform Movement in the 1830s and 1840s. Not only was the notion of universal public education and a dedication to nonsectarian Protestant morality accepted throughout most of the country, but along with them spread the influence of Idealism. Not surprisingly, most of the movement's leaders were sons of New England, for example, Horace Mann in Massachusetts, Henry Barnard in Connecticut and Rhode Island, Calvin Stowe in Ohio and Willard Hall in Delaware. Also influential was the St. Louis superintendent of schools, William Torrey Harris, a prominent Neo-Hegelian and later first United States Commissioner of Education.

In the last quarter of the nineteenth century, Darwin's empirical evidence for the evolutionary hypothesis hit idealists with the force of a sledgehammer. Their accent on the discipline of the mind as the chief instrument for gaining knowledge, on the individual and on orthodox morality was soon under vigorous attack by a new reform effort known as the Progressive Education Movement (see Appendix D.2). Not until the 1930s did they regain any vigor and make some contribution to the attack on educational progressivism under the banner of the so-called "essentialists." Since the turn of the century, however, their influence on the American public school has been informal and exerted chiefly through their religious commitments and their essential ideological conservatism. Their influence on church-related and some independent "college preparatory" schools has been more obvious. In higher education, moreover, a vigorous theoretical battle has continued to be waged in behalf of Idealism under such outstanding philosophers of education as J. Donald Butler, Michael Demiashkevich, Herman H. Horne, Rupert C. Lodge and Robert Ulich.

3. Idealism: Common Assumptions

A. METAPHYSICS

BR:Creative, Purposeful, Spiritual Energy
HN:Inherently Evil
HN:Inherently Good
HN:Inherently Superior or Inferior
FW&D:The Free Self
G&F:The Orthodox God

B. EPISTEMOLOGY

M:Mind-Soul as an Immaterial Entity
I:Archetypes of Existents
EXP:Contact with a Given Reality
OBJ:Alignment with a Given Reality
FofR:Limitation-to-Be-Transcended
K&T:Consistency Theory

C. AXIOLOGY

V/N&L:Property of Objective Reality
VJ/V:Traditional Modes of Knowing
V/C&O:Hierarchy of the Given
MOR:Morality of Seeking and Conforming to Objective Good
OBL&C:Obligation to Follow Conscience toward the Good
E-M-P:Growth toward an Ultimate Goal

Appendix B:
Realism and American Education

1. Realism: An Historical Sketch

Like its classical relative, philosophical Realism is also deeply rooted in ancient times. The thought of Aristotle (384–332 B.C.), who is revered as the "Father of Realism," not only set many of the problems to which adherents of the system have addressed themselves throughout the centuries but is still influential in contemporary Classical Realism. Although submerged in the Idealist-Christian synthesis of the Roman and medieval periods, it was finally reconciled with religious thought by St. Thomas Aquinas (1225?–1274). The medieval, renaissance and reformation periods, however, were not ones of great productivity.

The Enlightenment and the rising tide of science finally awakened Realism from its dormancy. John Amos Comenius (1592–1670); Descartes, Spinoza and Kant (also identified with the history of Idealism); and John Locke (1632–1704) all made contributions to the assumptions discussed in this text. The thinking of Thomas Reid (1710–1796) and his fellow Scottish Common Sense realists was carried to the American middle colonies by Presbyterian ministers, from whence it spread west and south with the Scots-Irish colonists. In Germany, Johann Herbart (1776–1841) made education a field for university study and laid the foundations of the social psychology of education.

The cultural turmoil of late nineteenth and early twentieth century America provided the milieu in which Realism began to assume the dominant position in American culture which (though under attack) it occupies today in alliance with ideological Conservatism. Hand in hand with experimental science, the inquiries of William James (who, though he made some contributions to Realism, is basically identified with Pragmatism), Ralph Barton Perry and the Neo-Realists, and Roy Wood Sellars and the Critical Realists finally established the contemporary realist tradition. In Europe development was also marked under such philosophers as Alfred North Whitehead, Bertrand Russell and George Santayana.

2. Realism: Importance to American Education

Reference has already been made to Scottish Common Sense Realism which came to the American middle colonies in the eighteenth century and whose influence has often been underestimated. In fact, Presbyterian ministers such as Alison formed one of the most learned groups in the colonies. They were instrumental in establishing many academies, some of which grew into institutions such as Princeton University, the University of Delaware and the University of Pennsylvania. Alison, for example, was not only a brilliant scholar, but in the course of his career taught some four governors, eight congressmen and four signers of the Declaration of Independence, as well as many other influential colonial Americans. It was Realism which heavily influenced the McGuffey Readers so popular outside of New England. Professors such as Princeton's James McCosh (1811–1894) kept the realist spirit alive in America during the idealist-dominated nineteenth century—even in the academic circles of New England.

Naturally, with the coming of the twentieth century and the rapid development of experimental science, the realist influence has been felt more heavily. Informally, it has provided much of the philosophical basis for the school testing movement and the development of educational psychology. Examples include the spelling tests of J. M. Rice; the development of intelligence testing by Binet, Terman and Judd; and the measurement of curricular and instructional variables systematically pursued by Edward L. Thorndike and his successors. All were quite in accord with the realist's accent on the scientific method and the development of empirically-tested bodies of knowledge for transmission by the schools. Realists along with idealists were leaders in the essentialist protest against progressive education in the 1930s. Following Sputnik (1957), realists led the successful battle for a strong emphasis on science in school curricula and teacher education programs. Educational philosophers such as Frederick S. Breed, John Wild and Harry Broudy have contributed to the examination of educational policy and practice in light of philosophical theory. Today the pedagogical possibilities suggested by Russell and Whitehead are achieving some attention. The continuing influence of the realistic outlook over an overwhelming segment of American public school education will be treated under Conservatism and education (Appendix C.2).

3. Realism: Common Assumptions

A.   METAPHYSICS

BR:The Orderly, Knowable, Sensible World
HN:Inherently Evil
HN:Inherently Good
HN:Inherently Superior or Inferior
FW&D:The Free Self
FW&D:Basic Determinism
G&F:The Orthodox God
G&F:The Humanistic God
G&F:The Denial of God

B.   EPISTEMOLOGY

M:Function of Bodily Processes
I:Natural Reflections of an External Reality
EXP:Contact with a Given Reality
OBJ:Alignment with a Given Reality
FofR:Limitation-to-Be-Transcended
K&T:Correspondence Theory

C.   AXIOLOGY

Realists hold the widest variety of axiological assumptions, a phenomenon explained in Chapter 6.

Appendix C:
Conservatism and American Education

1. Conservatism: An Historical Sketch

America has rarely lost sight of its deeply-entrenched conservative
tradition.   From the days of Puritan control over the Massachusetts
Bay and Connecticut Valley settlements to the Revolution and the
shaping of the new government along lines suggested by John Locke
and Edmund Burke, Conservatism has never lacked adherents.
Washington, Hamilton, the Adamses, Madison and John Marshall all
made their contributions.   Alexander de Tocqueville, Daniel Webster
and John Calhoun made theirs.   Conservatism, then, was well-established prior to the Civil War.

In fact, from the end of the Civil War until the early years of this
century, conservative assumptions were widely accepted as common
sense.   Taken together, political equilibrium, sectionalism and the

rising power of Big Business assured little governmental interference in social and economic matters. "Classical Liberalism" (as Conservatism was known in the nineteenth century) became identified with the rise of industrial capitalism and political laissex-faire. True, suffrage was extended to the upper middle classes of trade and manufacturing, but not to those without substantial property. The names of prominent conservatives of the period are familiar to us all; e.g., Andrew Carnegie, J. P. Morgan, John D. Rockefeller, Leland Stanford and Cornelius Vanderbilt.

A revolt of the farmers and the rise of organized labor at the end of the century led to a temporary eclipse of Conservatism during the so-called "Progressive Era." Following World War I, however, Americans sickened of our international involvement and the excesses of the political progressives and voted a return to "normalcy" under the administrations of Harding, Coolidge and Hoover. Big Business, aghast at the alternatives, supported "reasonable" antitrust and welfare legislation. A partnership between government and "responsible elements" in the nation controlled the occasional dissent of urban ethnic groups, farmers and blacks. What was good for Big Business was clearly good for the nation. In fact, minimal social needs were not being met, the masses were increasingly unable to play an effective role as consumers and the financial stability of European nations was being impaired by our economic success. Industrial self-regulation failed, and the economic crash of 1929 and the presidential election of 1932 swept the conservatives out of office.

For the first time since the Hoover years, Republicans gained control of the Congress in 1946 and slowed liberal social legislation. Conservatives, however, were frustrated by the moderate and liberal control of the G.O.P. The conservative protest increased with the defeat of Dewey by Truman, the failure of the Eisenhower administrations to institute conservative reforms, the Russian Cold War challenge, Nixon's compromise with moderate Republicans which conservatives felt led to his defeat by Kennedy, the failure of welfare legislation to eliminate social ills, civil rights agitation and the War in Vietnam. Although Goldwater failed to capture the presidency in 1964, he set the stage for conservative control of the Republican party. Under the prodding of conservative theoreticians such as Wm. F. Buckley, Jr. and Russell Kirk, the conservatives elected Richard Nixon in a close race in 1968 and by a landslide in 1972. In spite of Watergate, today's conservatives are trying to recall America to her traditional values and sense of honor. They are instituting programs for law and order, the return of finances to local control and a transformation of the federal "welfare mentality" into a dependence upon individual initiative.

2. Conservatism: Importance to American Education

Much of American education as we know it today represents the legacy of the educators whose contributions have been summarized in Appendices A.2 and B.2. To these conservatives, we might add the names of Mortimer Adler, Wm. Bagley, Arthur Bestor, James Conant, Robert Hutchins, Jacques Maritan and Admiral Rickover. As we have seen, the twentieth century has witnessed their joint struggle against progressive education. The retention of the humanities and some place for religion has occupied idealists, while realists have tended to call for a general modernization of the curriculum, especially as regards science. In both cases, a sharp conservative demand has been heard for distinguishing solid from "frill" subjects and for enforcing vigorous intellectual discipline. Affective, moral and physical activities have some place in the curriculum—as long as they do not interfere with intellectual discipline.

Today, given the disorganization of pedagogical progressives, the conservatives are actually more concerned with the threat of educational radicals (see Appendix F.2). Two alternatives seem to be occupying the attention of conservatives such as Harry Broudy, Max Rafferty, B. F. Skinner and Mortimer Smith: 1) a strict adherence to traditional schools, standards and procedures; and 2) various modifications which still accent the learning of prescribed subject-matter and teacher control of the classroom. Examples of such modifications include individualized learning and ungraded structural plans which vary rate of learning but not content, team teaching which promotes a differentiated approach to the same content, modular scheduling and behavior modification techniques. Given the present conservative mood in the country, it is not surprising that the overwhelming majority of American youth are exposed to these two basic alternatives.

3. Conservatism: Common Assumptions

A.   PHILOSOPHICAL ASSUMPTIONS

See Appendices A.3 and B.3.

B.   IDEOLOGICAL ASSUMPTIONS

S&GW:The Limited State
I&S:The Individual within Tradition
F:Freedom without License
J&E:Just Rewards
COM:Voluntary Association
SP:Competitive Individualism

Appendix D:
Pragmatism and American Education

1. Pragmatism: An Historical Sketch

Pragmatism as a formal school of philosophy is a modern movement which originated in the intellectually and socially turbulent years at the end of the nineteenth and the beginning of the twentieth centuries. Although parallel ideas were presented in England by F. C. S. Schiller and Arthur Balfour and in Germany by Hans Vaihinger, Pragmatism basically represents an American philosophical development. Of course, there are antecedents of pragmatic thought going back as far as the ancient Greek Heraclitus (535?–475? B.C.), who emphasized the constancy of change. Additional progenitors include the Sophists of the fifth century B.C., who denied the possibility of knowing ultimate reality; Quintilian (35–95), a Roman orator who emphasized action rather than deductive reasoning or meditation as the pathway to learning; Francis Bacon (1561–1626), who foreshadowed the scientific cast of pragmatic Epistemology; Kant (1724–1804), who used the word "pragmatic" to distinguish between rules and standards based on experience and those above or beyond experience; and Auguste Comte (1798–1857), whose Positivism included a stress on the social dimension consistent with that of the pragmatists.

In addition to these ancient traces, mention must be made of Pragmatism's modern roots in the peculiarly American moral preoccupation with harmonizing individual and society; the new experimental science, especially Darwinian evolutionism, Newtonian physics and the new psychology; and the rising progressive sentiment in American politics and social philosophy occasioned by social class strife between workers and Big Business.

Kant's distinction was picked up by Charles Sanders Peirce (1839–1914), a Massachusetts-born logician and mathematician, who in 1878 published an article entitled "How to Make Our Ideas Clear" in the *Popular Science Monthly*. It would be twenty years, however, before his ideas received serious attention. Then, William James (1842–1910), a Harvard scientist turned philosopher, created a storm with his lecture entitled "Philosophical Conceptions and Practical Results." Brilliantly interpreted by James, Pragmatism soon caught the attention of a young Vermonter, John Dewey (1859–1952), who developed it to full philosophical maturity over a long and distinguished academic career. Additional contributions to the assumptions detailed in this text have been made by pragmatists such as Boyd Bode, John Childs, H. Gordon Hullfish, Wm. H. Kilpatrick, Ward Madden, E. Verne Sayers and Lawrence G. Thomas.

2. Pragmatism: Importance to American Education

In 1894, John Dewey came to the new University of Chicago as chairman of the combined departments of philosophy, psychology and education. On the basis of his doctoral work at Johns Hopkins and his first professorial assignments at Michigan and Minnesota, he had come to believe that the processes of education provided the proper testing ground for philosophical theory. Within two years he had established the University Laboratory School for such testing and remained intimately associated with it until his departure for Columbia University in 1904. His work at Chicago and books such as *My Pedagogic Creed* (1897), *Schools of To-Morrow* (1915) and *Democracy and Education* (1916) distinguished Dewey. Until his death in 1952, he was clearly the foremost pragmatist in education and also a major leader in the Progressive Education Movement (treated in Appendix E.2 under Liberalism and education).

As we shall see, Pragmatism was not the only contributor to the progressive movement, nor are the two strictly to be identified. In books, articles and speeches, for instance, Dewey railed against those educational progressives of the 1920s who emphasized the individual (rather than individual-social balance which depended upon the cooperation of teacher and student), and stressed activity for activity's sake (rather than *evaluated* activity which led to a reorganization of experience). He was no less gentle with the progressives of the 1930s who demanded that the schools take an actual lead in social and economic reform. Dewey reminded them that the school was only one social institution, that school and social reform had to go hand in hand and that indoctrination was no less deadly because it involved a position with which one happened to agree.

The leadership of pragmatists such as Dewey and Kilpatrick at Teachers College, Columbia, produced more than a generation of educational leaders deeply influenced by pragmatic thought. It heavily influenced teaching at the elementary level, although its influence at the secondary level was much less, and at the collegiate level less still. Many of the textbooks being written today, as well as the ways in which we view professional problems, still bear the marks of pragmatic assumptions. Given philosophical and ideological changes outside institutions of teacher preparation, however, this phenomenon needs careful scrutiny. Compatible with ideological Liberalism, Pragmatism was violently attacked in the 1920s and the later 1930s, as it is being attacked today by more traditional and conservative elements in our culture. Indeed, for contemporary conservatives such as Max Rafferty much that is evil and dangerous in American culture is identified with Dewey, Pragmatism and Liberalism. As with competing positions, this text will give you opportunity to make your own assessment and commitments.

3. Pragmatism: Common Assumptions

A. METAPHYSICS

BR:Experience of Individuals-in-Society
HN:Constructed and Evaluated Transactionally
FW&D:Basic Determinism
G&F:The Humanistic God

B. EPISTEMOLOGY

M:Purposeful, Problem-Solving Behavior
I:Man-Created Plans of Action
EXP:Transactional Doing and Undergoing
OBJ:Intersubjectivity
FofR:Self-in-Becoming
K&T:Transactional Theory

C. AXIOLOGY

V/N&L:Product of Contextual Inquiry
VJ/V:Experimentation
V/C&O:Hierarchy of the Situation
MOR:Morality of Critical Inquiry
OBL&C:Obligation to Be Intelligent
E-M-P:Growth as Its Own End

Appendix E:
Liberalism and American Education

1. Liberalism: An Historical Sketch

The origins of modern Liberalism are found in the American Enlightenment. Transmitted by Jefferson, given a popular base by Jackson and fired by the humanitarian strain deep in American character, Liberalism came to be as much a part of American thinking as Conservatism. Its full force would not be felt in modern America, however, until the turn of the century.

In the waning years of the nineteenth century, small businessmen, farmers and factory workers began to demand a greater share in the products of their labor and a greater voice in the affairs of a nation monopolized by a relative handful of industrial capitalists. They—and, indeed, much of the middle class—began to demand that government cooperate more actively with them in alleviating social ills so complex as to defy individual solution. Reformers in the humanitarian tradition demanded a better lot for the new immigrants being pushed into urban ghettos. Increasing cries were heard for the emancipation of women. In time, increasing agitation and worsening conditions gave rise to what has been called the "Progressive Era."

Progressivism must be seen as an explosive, many-sided reaction to decades of unsolved social problems and frustrated dreams. In fact, the almost sudden and widespread realization that America had entered a new era and faced many new and complex problems which *could* be met by cooperative action unleashed a flood of economic, intellectual and political energy. The result was a liberal transformation of American arts, economic theory, jurisprudence, literature, philosophy, politics, science and—yes—education. The years of Teddy Roosevelt's "Square Deal," of Wilson and even of Taft were exciting, precedent-breaking years indeed.

In reaction to the restraints of World War I, the conservative return to "normalcy" was sketched in Appendix C.1, as was the catastrophic collapse of self-regulation on the part of Big Business. Not surprisingly, the presidential election of 1932 saw liberals returned to office, for all intents and purposes to remain for thirty-six years. Under the New Deal of Franklin Roosevelt, the Fair Deal of Truman, the moderate Republicanism of Eisenhower, the New Frontier of Kennedy and the Great Society of Lyndon Johnson, the federal government was used as a powerful instrument for righting social wrongs. With the support of a broad coalition of labor, ethnic and regional groups, much of the middle class and the intellectuals, major social efforts were mounted in support of the industrial worker and farmer, social security, international cooperation, civil rights, medical care and education. Capitalism was regulated and a serious attack on poverty begun.

Exhausted by three and one-half decades of social and international effort, shaken by the now secure working and middle classes' fear of accelerated demands for minority rights, and haunted by the horrors of a hopeless war in southeast Asia, the liberal coalition was narrowly defeated in the election of 1968 and utterly shattered in 1972. Disorganized, its accent on cooperative rationality unappealing to a fearful and tired America, the liberal in every walk of life faces a severe challenge in the last quarter of the twentieth century.

2. Liberalism: Importance to American Education

For decades, nineteenth century American educators had been traveling and studying in Europe, especially in the German-speaking lands where exciting developments were underway. Based on the legacy of Comenius (1592–1670), Rousseau (1712–1778), Basedow (1724–1790), Pestalozzi (1746–1827), Herbart (1776–1841) and Froebel (1782–1852), the European message was fourfold: 1) a faith that kindness to children was right and pedagogically sound, 2) a belief that a science of education could be built through child study, 3) a belief that educational methods and content could be derived from the study of child development, and 4) a concern for the relation of individual and society.

Combining these themes with the new science, the pervading influence of industrialism and a commitment to popular democracy consistent with philosophical Pragmatism, the Progressive Education Movement was launched in the late part of the century by professional leaders such as Francis Wayland Parker (1837–1902). When Dewey joined Parker in Chicago in 1894, its momentum quickly increased.

Obviously, educational Progressivism was a most heterogeneous movement in which all sorts of disparate elements were caught up in its reformist zeal. Protest against educational practices based on classical and conservative assumptions, a concerted effort to define and meet the social needs of oppressed Americans, and efforts to encompass the goals of scientist and romantic alike gave it massive strength and appeal—and in time led to its disintegration as a cohesive reform movement. Its basic elements included: a focus on the child; attempts to motivate effort by appealing to the actual interests of the child; a cooperatively democratic relationship between teacher and student; knowledge as arising out of cooperative doing, undergoing and evaluating; and an involvement of the school in the present problems of child and society.

Dewey's protests against the excesses of elements within the movement—against the Harold Ruggs and the George Countses—have been traced in Appendix D.2. Basically they were to no avail, and the late 1930s saw a rising tide of conservative protest against a position most of whose emphases its opponents abhorred. With the 1950s came a revival of educational policies and practices consistent with the assumptions of Scientific Realism. The 1960s saw a call for educational radicalism born in part of existentialistic assumptions and in part of American weariness with cooperative effort and the restrictions of over a quarter century of conflict both international and domestic.

Although disorganized by attack and almost disoriented by the eclipse of Liberalism, educational Progressivism has left an indelible mark on American education. Its basic themes still remain as viable alternatives to traditional approaches. As we wind our way into the last quarter of the century, the call for alternatives *within* the public school system—more open schools, schools-without-walls, and cooperation between educator and student to create an academic community—are far from dead.

3. Liberalism: Common Assumptions

A. PHILOSOPHICAL ASSUMPTIONS

See Appendix D.3.
Liberals have also often accepted the assumptions of the free self and of human nature as inherently good.

B. IDEOLOGICAL ASSUMPTIONS

S&GW:The Active State
I&S:The Interdependent Society
F:Freedom as Power
J&E:Egalitarianism
COM:Dynamic Association
SP:Cooperative Individualism

Appendix F:
Existentialism and American Education

1. Existentialism: An Historical Sketch

Although not without ancient and modern antecedents and highly indebted to the Danish philosopher-psychologist-theologian Søren Kierkegaard (1813–1855), contemporary Existentialism has arisen Phoenix-like out of the ashes of a Europe decimated and disillusioned by two great world wars and the failure of science and reason alike. Consciously antisystematic to the point where its very existence as a philosophical "system" is questionable, certain basic themes are nonetheless found among the various emphases of existentialistically-oriented writers: 1) The human situation is one of meaninglessness, alienation, anguish and death. 2) Man has both absolute freedom and absolute responsibility to authenticate himself, make meaning in the world and avoid meaningless, unauthentic life. 3) In so doing, he must have the courage to be, make decisions in the face of despair and realize that truths and values are created by his subjective choice. 4) The Other represents a great danger to self-actualization, but a meaningful relationship with him is probably necessary to the achievement of one's own self.

These themes (developed in detail in the text) have been treated by *atheistic existentialists* such as Martin Heidegger, Friedrich Nietzsche and Jean Paul Sartre. They have received the attention of *theistic existentialists* such as Martin Buber, Nikolai Berdyaev, Karl Jaspers, Søren Kierkegaard, Gabriel Marcel, Reinhold Niebuhr and Paul Tillich. Several *psychotherapists* have been heavily influenced, including Ludwig Binswanger, Igor Caruso, Viktor Frankel, Rollo May and Carl Rogers. And, of course, the world well knows *literary existentialists* such as Albert Camus, Fyodor Dostoevsky, André Gide, Franz Kafka, André Malraux and Rainer Maria Rilke.

Existentialism had very little impact on the American scene until the late 1940s. Since that time, however, its influence as a radical protest against the depersonalization of man in mass society and American optimism with regard to reason and science has been steadily rising.

2. Existentialism: Importance to American Education

Articles by Theodore Brameld, Ralph Harper, Van Cleve Morris and Arthur Wirth in the mid 1950s and the publication of George Kneller's *Existentialism in Education* in 1958 signaled a dawning awareness that existentialistic themes might have significant importance for American education. The publication of A. S. Neill's *Summerhill: A Radical Approach to Child Rearing* in 1960 and the organization of the American Summerhill Society in 1961 sparked a decade of intense excitement and investigation by American educators and other scholars. The formal funeral of the Progressive Education Association in 1955 and a growing dissatisfaction in the late 1950s and throughout the 1960s, with the full consequences of returning education to more traditional paths, created something of a vacuum. For some time, it appeared that Existentialism might well provide the philosophical base for a new movement in educational reform.

Several reasons suggest that this will not be the case, the most powerful being that the radical individualism central to Existentialism does not have an adequate base in American culture. Nor has our societal frustration reached a level where the majority of Americans would countenance the anarchistic revolutionary tendencies contained in ideological Existentialism. Indeed, the "freeing of American culture" among the younger generations is viewed with wide suspicion by older citizens—conservatives and liberals alike—and calls forth increasingly prompt and repressive measures if it goes far beyond the symbolic rebellions permitted the young. Hence, school reforms designed to give students full control over such basic variables as the curriculum, the techniques by which it is to be presented and the rate at which it is to be learned are likely to be about as long-lived and as

widely-accepted as they were in the 1920s. This influence will undoubtedly continue in a very small number of private schools which
enroll a miniscule percentage of American students. Its inclusion as a
viable, long-term alternative in the American public schools seems
most unlikely. Far more likely is the possibility that the writings of
Ivan Illich, Allen Graubard, John Holt, Herbert Kohl, Jonathan Kozol,
Everett Reimer, Sidney Simon and others will serve as a leaven for
new reform efforts still in the making.

3. Existentialism: Common Assumptions

A. METAPHYSICS

BR:Experience of the Solitary Individual
HN:Constructed and Evaluated Individualistically
FW&D:The Free Self
G&F:The Orthodox God
G&F:The Denial of God

B. EPISTEMOLOGY

EXP:Being in the World
OBJ:Intrasubjectivity
FofR:Self-in-Becoming
K&T:Appropriational Theory

C. AXIOLOGY

V/N&L:Creation of Subjective Choice
VJ/V:Authentic Choice
V/C&O:Hierarchy of Individual Decision
MOR:Morality of Authenticity
OBL&C:Obligation of Free Commitment
E-M-P:Growth in Self-Direction

Index of Names

Index of Subjects